WHAT OTHERS ARE SAYING

"We urgently need the excellent antidote to pessimism that Melissaratos and Slabbert offer. They remind us of the power and adventure of human intelligence. Essential reading for everyone who is in any way concerned with public policy or entrepreneurial development."

-- Gilbert F. Decker, Science Advisor to the US Secretary of Defense, Assistant Secretary of the Army, Research, Development & Acquisition (1994-1997); former Chairman, Army Science Board. Mr. Decker has also served as a Member of the National Academy of Sciences' Board of Army Science & Technology, as Trustee of the Association of the US Army, and as Executive Vice President of Engineering & Production, Walt Disney Imagineering.

"This book's motivating, thought-provoking message could not have come at a better time for America and the world. It is a stimulating, readable and valuable overview of technological innovation's role as the creative engine of our civilization."

-- Jacques S. Gansler, Professor and Roger C. Lipitz Chair, Director: Center for Public Policy and Private Enterprise, School of Public Policy, University of Maryland, former United States Under Secretary of Defense for Acquisition, Technology and Logistics.

"There is only one way out of the country's economic, environmental and energy mess and it is described with rare clarity in this book."

-- Richard McCormack, Editor & Publisher, Manufacturing & Technology News.

"Melissaratos and Slabbert excitingly signpost the way out of America's crisis of confidence. All business, government and educational leaders will benefit from this timely, nationally and internationally relevant work, which convincingly shows that industrial and manufacturing ingenuity is an engine of limitless economic growth potential."

-- Emily DeRocco, president of The Manufacturing Institute and the National Center for the American Workforce, Senior Vice President of the National Association of Manufacturers, US Assistant Secretary of Labor 2001-2008.

"This wise and well-written book, inspired by an immigrant's optimism, shows lucidly how and why America must marshal its capacity for innovation and ingenuity in order to compete in the global marketplace of the 21st century."

-- George Vradenburg, Executive Vice President, AOL-Time Warner (retired), and Herb Miller, Chairman, Western Development, Co-Founders of The Chesapeake Crescent Initiative, which works with leading universities, federal agencies, venture capitalists, high-tech firms and state and local governments to develop new innovation models for 21st-century America.

All the Best
Aris

INNOVATION:
The Key To Prosperity

Technology & America's Role In The 21st Century
Global Economy

By
ARIS MELISSARATOS
N.J. SLABBERT

First Edition

Montagu House

INNOVATION: THE KEY TO PROSPERITY

Technology & America's Role in the 21st Century Global Economy

by

Aris Melissaratos
N.J. Slabbert

Montagu House USA
An imprint of Truman Publishing Media Group
Copyright© 2009
ISBN 978-0-9823734-0-8
Library of Congress Control Number: 2009928216

DEDICATION

This book is dedicated to the Hellenic spirit of freedom and discovery that formed the foundation of democracy and Western political and scientific thought, passed down to me and my sister, Stella, by our parents, Panagiotis and Anthippi Melissaratos.

-- Aris Melissaratos

In keeping with the above dedication, may these pages encourage every inventor, scientist, entrepreneur, political leader and educator who works to promote public support and understanding of scientific and technological advance.

-- N.J. Slabbert

The authors

The Hon. Aris Melissaratos, founder of The Aris Institute ᵗᵐ and Senior Advisor for Technology Enterprise Development to the President of Johns Hopkins University, served as Secretary of Business and Economic Development for the State of Maryland from 2003 to 2007. He worked for Westinghouse Electric Corporation for 32 years, retiring as Chief Technology Officer and Vice President for Science and Technology, responsible for research and development. Before that he was Chief Operations Officer for the company's Defense Electronics Group, responsible for $3.2 billion in sales. He also founded Armel Scientifics, LLC, which has invested in over 30 start-up companies in advanced technology

N.J. Slabbert, is an internationally award-winning writer. He is International Editor of Truman Publications, a Brussels-based group focusing on public policy, technology and economic development. His work has appeared in publications including *The Washington Post, Harvard International Review* and *Reader's Digest*, of which he is a former senior editor and staff writer. He is co-author, with Professor Morton White, Professor Emeritus of Intellectual History at the Institute for Advanced Study, in Princeton, N.J., of the forthcoming book *The Intellectual versus the City: Anti-urbanism in America from Jefferson to the 21st Century.*

ANALYTICAL TABLE OF CONTENTS

INTRODUCTION: *THE DREAMS THAT MOVE THE WORLD*

A plea for a massive, government-backed technology initiative. Improving the US's education system and creating a new infrastructure. Creating an effective energy policy, including a widescale adoption of *nuclear technology*. Environmental challenges. Infusing the national technology mission into all levels of government. Making better use of the vast intellectual capital of the US academic world. *An immigrant's story*. A quarter of a century's experience at Westinghouse Defense Electronics. The language of Wall Street. Maryland as a successful example of a *knowledge economy* state. The transfer of knowledge capital from academe to the private sector. America as creative crucible of the world's greatest ideas. America, democracy and the Greek intellectual tradition. America's interests are necessarily global. *The quest for international stability as a battle of ideas*. Experience at Westinghouse, Maryland's government and Johns Hopkins illustrating ideas in action.

CHAPTER ONE: *HOW WE LOST OUR TECHNOLOGICAL NERVE (And Why Our Survival Depends On Getting It Back)*.

How we have failed science and technology. The US enters the 21st century as hostage to interests controlling fuels for obsolete technologies. Instead of funding technological advances *America bails out corporate bureaucracies producing piles of worthless paper*. "Modern" is not necessarily scientifically or technologically advanced. Innovation not an Aladdin's Cave of ready-made wonders. *An obsession with consumer gadgets not necessarily a culture of science and innovation*. American culture agrarian rather than futuristic. The Soviet Union an example of how flawed philosophy can destroy a seemingly powerful society. *The myth of technological inevitability*. The idea that technology innovation "just happens". The obsolescence of conventional rail and air transportation. *America's failure to adopt maglev*. An overview of maglev's energy efficiency, general economic, safety, environmental and other benefits.

CHAPTER TWO: *NANOTECHNOLOGY & THE CRITICISM OF SCIENCE.*

The vision of nanotechnology. *Reasons for optimism.* The 21st century can see an end to poverty, environmental degradation, international conflict over resources. *Nanotechnology arguably the most important field of contemporary science.* Fournier d'Albe's faith in science, technology and the "infra-world". Controversy over what nanotechnology can deliver. The vision of Eric Drexel. If even a fraction of nanotechnology's promise is achieved, human life will be transformed. The field's numerous applications. It challenges us to *stretch our imaginations.* The booming industry of nanotechnology guides and critics. The problem of media professors who develop careers as critics of technology. *The culture of negativity* toward science and technology that holds America back.

CHAPTER THREE: *SCIENTIFIC INNOVATION VERSUS THE CULTURE OF NEGATIVISM.*

America's story as a history of technological achievement and inventive determination. *Democracy itself an experiment* disdained by many thinkers including Plato, Nietzsche, Marx and H.L. Mencken. Some examples of philosophical reaction against science and technology. *Healthy skepticism versus negativism toward science and technology.* Negativism dressed up in language that sounds scientific. Simon Newcomb's reluctance to accept the reality of human flight. *The New York Times "debunks" human flight ... then goes on to "debunk" the possibility of space travel.* Scientific and technological innovation as interdisciplinary. The politics of "fiefdoms" of knowledge. *Social criticism of science* that mimics the interdisciplinary language of scientific innovation. Physicist Alan D. Sokal spotlights the problem of scientific vocabulary and interdisciplinary politics by getting an academic journal to publish a nonsense paper.

CHAPTER FOUR: *THE CAN-DO CULTURE: THE RISE OF MODERN TECHNOLOGY.*

Karl Marx's masterpiece of mythic fiction, *Das Kapital.* Adam Smith's *The Wealth of Nations.* The superstition of technology on tap. The founding of the Royal Society and the writings of Sir Francis Bacon. The British Government's decision to take an active role in sponsoring technological innovation. *The popularization of science* and the advent of a sense of historical change. Britain's Great Exhibition of 1851. Prince Albert's battle against the naysayers. The Exhibition shows that science and technology are not only nationally important but can be fun. *The Exhibition and the Crystal Palace, capture the imagination of Britain and the world. George Stephenson and the birth of the railroads.* Marc Isambard Brunel and his son Isambard Kingdom Brunel exemplify the new breed of determined technological-entrepreneurial visionaries. The Baconian vision unites with imperial Britain's sense of national pride. *Cecil John Rhodes* envisions a continent-spanning British railroad.

CHAPTER FIVE: *THE CHICAGO WORLD'S FAIR: THE EMERGENCE OF AMERICA AS A TECHNOLOGICAL POWER.*

London's Great Exhibition finds a counterpart in America's Columbian Exposition of 1893 (the Chicago World's Fair). Daniel H. Burnham, designer of the Exposition, as a spokesman for technological optimism. The Exposition sums up America's entrepreneurial spirit and determination to unite the nation in a single framework of innovative technologies. The creative technological presences of Thomas Edison, George Westinghouse and Nikola Tesla dominate the Exposition. The US Government entrenches its role as midwife of a national technological effort, ushering America into an age of road, rail, telephones, radio, aviation and television. America struggles to define the relationship between private and public sectors, evidenced in the murky world of Tammany Hall. The bizarre career of Aaron Burr. The "robber barons" and their role in building American industry and national infrastructure. American infrastructure rooted in government-private dealmaking. Thomas Scott and the Pennsylvania Railroad. Jay Gould.

CHAPTER SIX: *THE JANE FONDA SYNDROME.*

A brief history of the physical science that became the center of American scientific and technological leadership in the 20th century. *Ancient Greek philosophers and their intellectual heirs.* The quest for the ultimate constituents of matter. Discovery of the elements. Newton, Dalton and modern atomic theory. Maxwell's unified body of electromagnetic theory. *Chemistry and physics converge in the late 19th century.* Röntgen and X-rays. Becquerel, the Curies and radioactivity. Thomson and the electron. Rutherford and the atom's orbital structure. *Einstein* shows that to understand the relation between matter and energy we must transcend Newton. The new physics triggers a chain of practical effects. Hertz's work leads to *radio and radar research*, making possible vacuum tubes and transistors. Microchips, cell phones and personal computers. The remarkable decline of the public image of nuclear physics. The Jane Fonda Syndrome. *The case of Three Mile Island.* Emotion obstructs access to a vital source of energy.

CHAPTER SEVEN: *THE BIOTECHNOLOGY REVOLUTION.* Humans manipulate the processes of life since ancient times. The mapping of *DNA* brings biotechnology to a new level of sophistication. A brief history of biology's search to understand the supersmall. Van Leeuwenhoek, Hooke and the technology of microscopy. The convergence of studies of the living and non-living microworlds in the work of Delbrück and Schrödinger. *Watson, Pauling, Crick, Franklin and Gosling.* The DNA molecule discovered to be a double helix. Blurred boundaries between physics and molecular biology. The mid-20th-century clash between scientific-technological triumphs and a popular culture that rejected the spirit of those triumphs. The cultural paradox of *2001: A Space Odyssey.* The fallacy of the released genie. Reaction against biotechnology similar to that against nanotechnology, showing *skepticism* of its potential while also *fearing* that potential. The parallel with nuclear technology, biotechnology's intellectual cousin. The Hubble Space Telescope. *Proteomics.* Synthetic biology.

CHAPER EIGHT: *THE COMING TOGETHER OF ALL SCIENCES* Reactions against specific technologies driven by general hostility to science and technology. The positive energies of scientific and technological innovation must be seen as *an integrated enterprise* rather than as a fragmentary collection of projects. Computer science as a new lingua franca among technologies and sciences. The advent of *the digital age.* The slow development of the computer over centuries. The interdisciplinary rise of information theory. Shannon's work combining logic and electronics. *Marvin Minsky,* artificial intelligence and robotics. Digitalization illuminated by parallels with the rise of rocketry and space exploration. Goddard's struggle against naysayers and negativists. *Oberth, Von Braun and the bold vision of space travel.* Russia's philosophical champions of space exploration. Sputnik's galvanizing effect on the US space program. *Apollo.* Space exploration, artificial intelligence and technological motivation

CHAPTER NINE: *THINKING MACHINES, TELETECHNOLOGY AND THE KNOWLEDGE ECONOMY.*

Minsky again. His vision of artificial intelligence as large and transformative as the vision of space exploration. *The problem of funding AI research.* The rise of the *Internet* out of US Government research. Basic AI research funding ended. Minsky's vision of AI closely linked to nanotechnology. An economic counterpart to Minsky's concepts: *the knowledge economy.* Drucker. 12 principles of the knowledge economy: *Civil society transformed,* the broadband knowledge grid, education, telecommunities, revitalization of small towns, reducing road traffic and road pollution, heightened national security through worker dispersal, the US's rise as *the world's foremost knowledge exporter,* a new American commitment to basic research and long-term research, the rise of a new regionalism, diversity of media and the need for newspapers, extending the knowledge grid throughout government. Knowledge economy thought in urban planning. *Virtual Adjacency®.* The Department of Homeland Security.

CHAPTER TEN: *CHOOSING A FUTURE.*

The strange and ancient industry of futurology. *Kurzweil's* vision. Building a culture of scientific and technological innovation. The myth of technological inevitability again. The strangeness of new technologies. *The paradox of science fiction.* Crichton. Technology feared as a threat to the best of the past. Bradbury. The culture of negativism versus healthy skepticism. *Interdisciplinary fluidity.* Differences between technological evolution, technological impact and technological navigation. *Navigation distinct from regulation and management as currently conceived.* Cybernetics. Much popular management literature dislocated from realities of genuine innovation. Roots of the the concept of navigation in the Greek intellectual tradition. Need to build a culture of scientific and technological motivation and an economy of scientific and technological innovation. Britain's Great Exhibition of 1851 and America's Chicago Exposition of 1893 again, as examples.

CHAPTER ELEVEN: *WHAT MUST BE DONE: TEN POINTS TO RETURN AMERICA TO THE TECHNOLOGY STANDARD.*

The US must restore its *world leadership* in innovation and build a renewed global economy. A new era of innovation-based economic partnerships. *Orbach's warning* that "we are now at a perilous moment in the history of funding for science in the United States" and that without more funding "the future of the physical sciences will be in jeopardy. Opportunities will be lost forever: for science, and our country." Empower the US to meet the needs of not just the domestic but *the global marketplace*. Improve US education and public respect for science. Build *a new American infrastructure*, rather than rebuilding the old one. A national smart grid. *Go nuclear* while launching a determined national effort to create a new alternative energy industry. Create a radically new national mass transit system. Create a government-led *national culture of technological innovation*.

INTRODUCTION:

THE DREAMS THAT MOVE THE WORLD

By Aris Melissaratos

This is a book of ideas. I have compiled many of these ideas over the last fifty years as I have dealt with, managed and learned from tens of thousands of people in industry, government and academia, while addressing some of the most sophisticated technological challenges of our time. Combined, the ideas offered here form a vision of how innovation, scientific advance and technology can lead to a new era of unprecedented national and global prosperity.

This is a relatively short book, because a lifetime of communicating with busy people in business and government has taught me that if you want to impress someone with an idea or a set of ideas, you do not give them a gigantic treatise. I assume that you, the reader of this book, are a busy person, and my co-author and I respect your time. This book therefore does not present a detailed recipe for each of its suggestions. It does not offer wording for new legislation. Its premise is that as a prerequisite for effective new policies, we must revisit some of our fundamental attitudes to and about scientific and technological innovation. Only if we renew these attitudes and the ideas that underlie them will we be able effectively to attain prosperity in the 21st century, in the United States and the rest of the world.

A fundamental tenet of this book is that if the U.S. is not prosperous, the rest of the world will have great difficulty in securing a durable prosperity; and, conversely, that the U.S. can not meaningfully pursue prosperity in isolation from the rest of the world. The interests and activities of the global community are now too closely interwoven – economically, technologically, geopolitically and in other ways – to make isolationism a realistic option for any country. We are approaching and must achieve a level of interdependence that assures both economic and political stability. This means global prosperity and peace. To make this book a compact read, however, the authors focus on what the United States needs to do, rather than on what other countries need to do.

Another basic premise of this book is that innovation and technology can solve most of the world's material problems by creating new products to improve the global standard of living and quality of life, and to restore the environmental health of a planet in peril.

Here is a quick summary of the overlapping and interlocking actions that the U.S. must embrace if we are to renew America and the world economically, environmentally and technologically on the basis of this book's comments:

1. Encourage technology to flourish

We must revise our philosophical attitude toward technology, because neither the political Right nor the Left are presently disposed, in their belief-systems, to encourage the conditions needed for technology to flourish as it must if we are to be prosperous. Accordingly, much of this book is about the history of technological growth and of our ideas about technology. We can not revise our ideas properly without considering how they were formed, nor can technology be properly discussed without reference to how it evolved. But with a new historical perspective we will equip ourselves to do what it takes to retain or regain global leadership in innovation.

2. Embark on a massive government - backed technology initiative

We must launch a massive new government-backed technology initiative, comparable in size, scope and energy with the New Deal program of national renewal and reconstruction undertaken by the administration of Franklin Delano Roosevelt, with the Apollo Space Program that put a man on the moon, and with the Manhattan Project that created the atomic bomb. Yet we must also soberly acknowledge the unique features of these historical examples that make them, at best, limited analogies rather than models which we must slavishly follow.[1] Of these three analogies, the Manhattan Project is particularly apt for us now because it was undertaken in a race against time, to win World War II. We need the same sense of urgency and national will to prevail against our current economic and environmental challenges as we needed to prevail against the Axis powers. We also need the same kind of creative cooperation between government and the private sector, and a similarly unprecedented cooperation among government agencies.

3. Encourage relationships between government and entrepreneurs

We need to make technology innovation, research and development a primary priority of the federal government at presidential and cabinet level. This does not mean the government must control and direct all technological innovation: such a step would be disastrous. But the federal government needs to take the leadership initiative and responsibility to encourage innovation in the public interest, especially where it does not necessarily lead to the kind of short-term profits that are conventionally required by private investors. Accepting this concept requires us, again, to look afresh at history, which shows us that contrary to widespread belief, much if not all of our most important technological innovation, at least since the 19th century, has involved relationships between government and entrepreneurs as well as the actions by lone entrepreneurs that form such an important part of American business folklore. As we will see in coming pages, this government-private interaction has not always been officially sanctioned and conducted according to the letter of the law. This has resulted in the rise of entrepreneurial adventurers who have sometimes operated in a gray area between government and the private sector. This important fact has often been obscured by subsequent publicity romanticizing the innovative process as an activity of lone entrepreneurs somehow standing aloof from government and even from society.

4. Improve the U.S. education system

We must drastically improve the U.S. education system, especially in connection with mathematics and science, to fully respond to the National Science Foundation's "Gathering Storm" report. We must emphasize high standards as opposed to "social promotion" to ensure that all our children are intellectually prepared to contribute and thrive in an innovation economy.

5. Transform our infrastructure

We must embark on a concerted national initiative no only to improve but to transform our decaying nation-wide infrastructure, including water and sewage management, energy and transportation. Besides rebuilding the traditional infrastructure, we must add broadband availability to the entire nation and a futuristic smart transmission grid. This will be a national reinvention program fully comparable to FDR's New Deal – but with major new technologies added. This will galvanize the economy, create new jobs throughout America and renew the country's sense of national unity. This program will range from the extension of fiber optic telecommunications technology to all communities to replacing the national highway system, with its now obsolete over-reliance on automobile travel, with an efficient, clean, quiet transcontinental maglev (magnetically levitating) coast-to-coast rail system that will put effective and astonishingly swift transportation at the disposal of everyone. With international co-operation there is no reason why this system should not extend from Halifax to Miami and Alaska to the tip of South America, providing enormous economic benefits to all communities through which it operates, and bringing about a new era of trans-American prosperity and good will. Besides the North/South lines, we need to lay three East/West lines across North America.

6. Create an effective energy policy

We must create an effective energy policy, including such steps a new initiative for the domestic production of shale and the overall management of hydrocarbon drawdown. We must manage the last few decades of hydrocarbon fuel availability by becoming independent of foreign oil. We must show OPEC that we are serious by drilling now on the continental shelves and Alaska, at the same time using every technologically innovative means at our disposal, and the full array of our scientific knowledge, to manage these actions in an environmentally responsible and sensible way: there is no reason why economically effective action should be incompatible with technologically sophisticated environmental sensitivity. Also, we must break ground immediately on the most futuristic oil shale processing facility (which may take decades to complete and design) to prove our full intent on hydrocarbon self sufficiency. We must invest in clean coal technologies such as liquification, gasification, and particulate filtering as well as CO_2 sequestration. Concurrently, we must embark on full-scale wind, solar, geothermal and biofuel development to assess the full scalability and potential of these technologies. Most importantly, we need to embark on a determined drive to take the United States nuclear, manage nuclear waste effectively and create a zero-emission, hydrogen-based economy. Several decades hence, nuclear must be the predominant mode of base electric power generation. Its hydrogen byproduct can drive a national hydrogen distribution system, allowing our cars to be powered by hydrogen fuel cells with zero emissions. Today's hybrids or even the envisioned plug in electrics should become mere bridges to hydrogen fuel cell vehicles. Technologically, there is no reason for Americans to be at the mercy of foreign political interests who like to hold us hostage with fossil fuel prices, or of the natural depletion of such fuels, or of ruthlessly exploitative oil speculators, or, on the other hand, of those who would like America to return to the horse and buggy age for aesthetic reasons.

7. Elevate the national technology mission to the highest levels of government

We must transform all our government institutions appropriately, making them standard-bearers of a new national mission to elevate ourselves technologically, instead of allowing them to be or become bureaucracies interested more in the preservation of political fiefdoms than in the efficiencies that technological innovation can introduce in the public interest.

8. Make better use of our academic research establishments

We must tap the vast intellectual resources of our academic research establishments more effectively. These contain some of our richest intellectual assets, but many of these assets are not being optimally unlocked to the private sector. There is no single cause at which a finger of blame can be pointed in this respect; the cause is a complex interplay of habits and historical momentum which has led us greatly to underestimate the extent to which academia and the private sector can fruitfully cooperate. Companies are not always sufficiently conversant with the procedures of academia, and the gap that this creates between the campus and the marketplace can be much to the detriment of the consumer. Academics, on the other hand, are often over-wary of cooperating with commercial interests, fearing that the intellectual independence of scholarship, and the health of disinterested basic research, may be prejudiced. No self-respecting scientist or scholar wishes to become a corporate servant, the idea of which flies in the face of the dedication to an independent life of the mind which pure researchers embrace as a fundamental career choice. However, speaking from decades of experience in activities in which government, academia and industry intersect, I can attest that there is no essential contradiction or incompatibility between the objectives of the pure researcher and those of the corporate technologist seeking to solve a practical, market-related problem. My years at Westinghouse, my tenure as Secretary for Business and Economic Development and my work to date at Johns Hopkins University have all shown me unequivocally that this is the case. Basic research (that is, research unrelated to any specific practical objective) and applied research (scientific investigation geared to solve a specific problem, generally with a commercial application) are in fact very closely related. They tend to be mutually nurturing and reciprocally reinforcing rather than opposed.

No sane and informed corporate executive looking for new products is going to disdain basic research, since his every commercial instinct must tell him that this is the fountainhead from which comes the greatest number of fertile ideas. The discipline of applied research, on the other hand, with its focus on solving a specific problem or set of problems, can be highly stimulating to the basic researcher, and can, moreover, suggest new areas of basic research which might not otherwise have occurred to a pure scientist without a specific, applied task to complete. The history of science and technology is replete with examples of such fertile relationships between applied tasks and purer forms of investigation. What is abundantly clear, however, is that effective communication and cooperation between the basic researcher and the commercial executive are often bedeviled by differences of language, research timeframe and resource management. In these areas I have found that government has a potent role to play – not as a controller but as a facilitator, encourager, sower of seeds, go-between, translator and honest broker.

In this capacity, government can help instrumentally in furthering the cooperation of those several constituencies on which technological progress must depend, including the academic researcher, the applied researcher and technologist, the private investor, the taxpayer and the consumer. These groups are of course not isolated from each other in the first place. It is not only possible but necessary for both individuals and organizations to belong to more than one such group at the same time, and even to pursue the interests of more than one at the same time. Government can help clarify the confusions that attend this process, and, by striking a wise balance between interference and intelligent facilitation, can make it more fruitful from the point of view of the combined interests of all of these groups. And it is to me very interesting and exciting to note that just as confusions about technological innovation are not limited to either the Left or the Right, so are technological solutions and facilitations capable of being developed and implemented across the broad spectrum of current American politics.

I speak here again from personal experience. In Maryland, I served a Republican Governor effectively and enjoyably even though I was and am a longstanding Democrat. More than once in this book the reader will find an analogy between this book's vision for technological renewal and the Roosevelt New Deal. This comparison should not, I believe, prevent enlightened leaders on any point on the American political continuum from cooperating on bipartisan or even multipartisan lines to advance the ideas that this book recommends. The reason for this goes deeper than party politics, into the very essence of what it means to be American. For I believe, as this book seeks to demonstrate, that science and technology are not merely tools of American life. In a profound sense they are, I believe, what America is all about. Which brings me to perhaps the most personal part of this statement.

The United States is the greatest country in the world. I say this with deep conviction, not least because I belong to a group of people who, I believe, are uniquely qualified to pass judgment on America: immigrants.

In a time when America is focusing so much of its time and energy on screening immigrants and formulating ever more complicated immigration safeguards -- resources which could be used on other things, like jump-starting our sagging economy - I speak as one who is proud to call himself an immigrant. And it is wholly appropriate that my co-author, with whom I share the American values and interests that this book is intended to serve, also happens to be of foreign birth. Out of such a gathering of the best intellectual traditions and assets of all the world is American made.

The United States is a nation of immigrants and of intellectual capital brought to these shores by immigrants. Because America is such a young country it can safely be said that all that is brightest in it came from men and women with roots in other lands. Many of these came to the U.S. with great difficulty and separated themselves from their native countries traumatically. America's War of Independence from Britain was such a trauma. Sometimes immigration has been motivated by the need to escape persecution.

Sometimes it has been a quest for opportunity and self-improvement. But always it has been difficult, except perhaps for a very few whose path to America was eased by wealth.

I was not among that wealthy elite, although I later became wealthy by hard work and by availing myself of the opportunities that America offers. Like that of many immigrants, my journey has been one of work, work, work, and yet not a single day ever seemed like work. It was an experience of learning and cumulative knowledge-building that created a foundation that served me well in all I have tried to do.

My parents brought me to this country when I was thirteen. We settled in Baltimore, which has been home ever since. Although I could not speak a word of English, I immediately went to work six days a week at Ernie's Grocery Store in Greektown and, two days a week, at a bakery that eventually became our family business. This arrangement prevailed through my graduation from Patterson High School. While studying electrical engineering at Johns Hopkins University, my 24/7 employment continued at the family bakery and at a great old machine shop: the Slaysman Company. I revere academic learning and promote it wherever I can, yet I admit that on a deep personal level I value the learning from the work experience more than academic learning. Work experience taught me to interact with the public and how to learn from co-workers much more experienced than I ever hoped to be. This proved invaluable in establishing my leadership style throughout my industrial and government career.

This bit of autobiography is not inserted here as an author's self-indulgence. It is directly relevant to the book you hold in your hands. I ask you to bear with me as I explain this, because if you are to understand the message of this book it is important that you understand why it was written.

Both intellectually and emotionally, these pages are the logical outcome of the more than half century of work that has occupied me since my arrival in America. It is an intellectual outcome because most of my professional life has been concerned with the issues dealt with in this book: science and technology, economic growth, the relationship between government and the private sector, and the effective unlocking and management of America's greatest resource – its intellectual power.

The first twenty-five years of my industrial career were spent at the Westinghouse Defense Electronics Group in Baltimore, which ultimately was acquired by Northrop Grumman Corporation. Prior to the sale, I had been promoted to Westinghouse Electric Corporation's Headquarters in Pittsburg where I eventually became Vice President for Science and Technology and Chief Technology Officer managing the venerable research and development center where the "book was written" on just about everything electrical. All in all, I spent thirty-two years at Westinghouse. Those were enormously exciting decades. They crackled with intellectual energy and the sense of technological change. I had the privilege to work in an environment in which some of the most important scientific and technological work of the 20th century was being done.

Every day at Westinghouse a new piece of our technological history unfolded. At the Baltimore operation, we designed and built just about everything that was featured in Hollywood-slanted technological bestsellers like Tom Clancy's *The Hunt for Red October,* from radar systems and countermeasures to sonar systems and satellite surveillance systems. We built the camera that sent back to millions of people on earth Neil Armstrong's first steps on the moon. I was fortunate to have the opportunity to manage as many as 16 000 people: 9 000 of the most brilliant engineers in the world and 7 000 manufacturing workers who could produce miracles in scheduling and technological achievement. It was there that I learned the power of people and ideas, and how the two are inextricably intertwined. I can honestly say I knew about 80% of my people by first name and I tried to include them all in the corporate strategies and successes of the enterprise. I said before that this is a book of ideas. Well, ideas come from people and it takes special leadership to capture and develop those ideas, to give people appropriate credit, and to achieve successes through management policies that live up to the ideal that the whole is, quite literally, much larger than the sum of its parts.

After Westinghouse, I worked for three years as Vice President of Research for ThermoElectron Corporation managing thirteen defense and research-oriented businesses. I went to ThermoElectron because of my admiration of its founder, George Hatsopoulos, and of its pioneering implementation of the spin-out model of innovation management, where every new product was spun out as a publically traded company. I wanted to learn how Wall Street worked and how valuations were assigned to young publically traded companies. When the ThermoElectron version of the spin-out model began to crumble under pressure of changing times – a condition for which all management ventures must prepare – this, too, taught me extraordinarily valuable lessons in the innovation cycle, since I ended up getting experience in selling most of the businesses I was responsible for. This was a very valuable lesson indeed, for I came to understand that knowing how to wind an enterprise down and dispose of it intelligently is as important as the very different matter of knowing how to launch it and (also very different) knowing how to run it during its years of stability. Following ThermoElectron I retired for two years and became an "angel investor". In those two years I worked in technology-oriented entrepreneurial investing and wrote checks totaling four million dollars of my own money to thirty-one different start-up companies. Even though I broke every rule of venture investing, I am pleased to say that the first deal to achieve a liquidity event returned more than twice my aggregate investment. So this two-year retirement became another integral part of my experience of the interlinked American enterprise landscapes of finance, technology, innovation and management.

I then accepted an invitation to serve as Secretary for Business and Economic Development of the State of Maryland under Governor Robert L. Ehrlich, Jr. I did that job for a full four years until a new administration came in. What an adventure it was! Most importantly, it turned out to be a continuation of the themes of my work at Westinghouse, because Maryland is a state whose economy is driven by the science, technology and knowledge economy industries. Working in every corner of the State of Maryland, we were able to reduce unemployment to 3.3% with nine of our twenty-three jurisdictions being under 3%. In fact, we achieved a full-employment economy during a period when the state was transitioning from a manufacturing-oriented economy to a technology and knowledge-based economy. The crowning achievement of that period was Maryland's successful strategy in the BRAC (Base Realignment And Closure) process – a strategy geared to bring 60 000 technology- oriented jobs to the state and assure Maryland's leadership in the knowledge economy.

On leaving the secretaryship, I was swiftly honored with an offer, which I immediately accepted, to become the senior advisor on enterprise development and technology transfer to the president of one of America's leading technology research institutions, the Johns Hopkins University. My job: to help this venerable center of American scientific and technological learning transfer its technology more effectively from laboratory to marketplace. I quickly found that this assignment, too, was a logical extension of the work I had done at Westinghouse and for the State of Maryland. In the two years or so that it has been my pleasure to do this job from my appointment to the writing of this book, Johns Hopkins technology has been used to create over a dozen companies.

You will see, therefore, why I say that this book, which deals with the urgent relevance of science and technology to our economic well-being in the 21st century, is an intellectual outcome and consummation of my career to date.

But I have also said that this book is also an emotional outcome of my life. In a sense this is, for me, even more important than the intellectual motivation behind these pages. This takes me back to the remarks I made above about being an immigrant, and about America being the greatest country in the world. These statements are closely linked.

You see, there is a unique quality about America as far as immigrants and immigration are concerned. It goes deep into the heart and bone of the country and its history. And it's a kind of paradox.

If an immigrant to any other country proclaims that the adopted land is the greatest in the world, there is always an emotional ache to that statement. It is a kind of renunciation of one's native land. And whatever your native land has done to you, whether it has persecuted you politically, or whether it has forbidden you to express your religious beliefs, or whether it has discriminated against you because of your race or ethnicity, it is still, after all, your country of origin, and it is wrenching to proclaim a different country as its moral superior.

But with America, it is different. America is *made up* of immigrants and is the invention of immigrants. The spirit and ingenuity and ambitions and follies and foibles and genius of all corners of the Earth, and of all peoples, have made their way to it and are in it. It is a wonderwork of not just one ethnicity or tradition, but of the human race itself. *In a very real sense, America belongs to the world.*

For this reason, no immigrant to America is disloyal to the memory of the Old Country, wherever that may be, if he or she says America is the greatest country in the world. Because the immigrants, tide upon tide of them, over generations, have brought the best of the Old Country - all the Old Countries - to America's shores.

It is true that democracy has had many cradles. Tolerance, political enlightenment and free, critical thought have had courageous champions in many cultures throughout history. I myself was born in Romania of wealthy parents of Greek descent. During my first 6 years of life, we lived through the end of World War II running from Russian and German air raids over my birthplace of Galatz. We finally left as refugees to my parents' ancestral Greece, having seen the destruction of war and the totally negative influence of communism. From the ages of six through thirteen I was educated in Greek schools and got a thorough foundation in the heritage of Greece. I am hugely proud of this heritage, which played a pivotal role in the birth of both democracy and rational Western philosophy, as well as in the mathematical and scientific foundations of current Western thought. Moreover, it is in America, uniquely, that democracy took shape in its full and modern form, bringing into potent combination such elements as political and religious freedom, a healthy separation of Church and State, checks and balances on concentrations of power, an independent judiciary, a free press, an overriding respect for human rights and individualities, a philosophy of self-reliance and opportunity, a belief in free critical thought, and a climate of free trade conducive to entrepreneurial creativity. So there is a direct and ancient connection that links the greatest accomplishments of the Old World to the deepest values of America.

This uniqueness of America, in representing the full potential and democratic expression of the best that the human race can achieve, is at the heart of the emotional reason for my role in this book. This reason is an urgent concern not just for the well-being of the United States but for the prosperity and even the survival of the world.

The dangers to the world that this book is modestly designed to help address, and the solutions that I believe are available, are discussed in the pages to come. But in explaining the personal commitment that underlies what you are about to read, it is important for me to repeat and emphasize my earlier remark that the interests of the United States and the interests of the rest of the world in the 21st century are inextricably interwoven.

This does not mean I think that what is convenient for the United States will necessarily be good for the rest of the world. On the contrary: I fully expect the ideas that this book offers, as contributors to global prosperity in this century, to be initially quite uncomfortable for many Americans. Embracing these ideas will require Americans to change customary habits of thought, which is always difficult. It will also require money, since if my long and successful career in business has taught me anything, it's that you don't achieve anything without investment. And everything this book outlines will require an immense effort of work, public education and persuasion, research and development, and sheer determination.

I am not daunted by these challenges, because they are all already built into the fiber of American society. I believe that to pursue the aims of this book, the overriding requirement is inspiration. I hope this book will help provide it.

You may well ask: if the commitment to technological innovation that this book champions is going to be so hard for America to achieve, assuming that it is (as I firmly believe it is) achievable, why should America put itself out so much for the rest of the world? Is America the world's keeper?

Well, shocking as this may be to many people, both outside and inside America, the answer is YES, at least, in some critically important senses.

I have already indicated one such sense, in my statement that America uniquely represents the spirit of democracy in its fullest and most modern form. I believe this utterly. I also think many Americans believe it, whether they have thought about it consciously or whether it has just permeated their minds by their daily absorption of American culture, lifestyles, assumptions, political institutions, manners and ideals.

The millions of immigrants who have streamed into America from all quarters of the globe, and who continue to contrive to do so in such numbers, both legally and illegally, that a wall has now been conceived to keep the illegal ones out (a great mistake, in the opinion of both authors of this book), is a glaring testimony to America's enduring status as the world's beacon of freedom and opportunity. Foreign protesters may posture against this and that aspect of American culture, but the immigration stream tells the deeper story. The world wants to be in America and to be like America, no matter what rhetoric implies the opposite.

America's record of international relations has not been perfect, and its salesmanship of its own values and accomplishments has in recent times been appalling. How could the country that virtually invented modern marketing have failed so abysmally to market its own best qualities around the world? But the real point is not that America has failed to market itself, but that there is so much to market -- not just in quantity, but in quality. American ideals and values still remain the best in the world.

This places a vast moral responsibility on America's national shoulders. Like it or not, the United States has created a society which, in its best features, is an example to the world. This statement should not be confused with the imperialist doctrine that asserts that Americans have a duty to rule the world because they have amassed the military and economic might to do so. What I am talking about is rather the belief that if circumstances of history have put you in a position to serve as a role model for others, you have a duty not to shun the spotlight.

Professor Joseph Nye has spoken of the need for America to

learn to distinguish between hard power (military force or the threat of it) and soft power, the power of persuasion. To this useful classification my co-author and I believe it is necessary to add a third category: demonstrative power. This is simply the power of example. It does not set out to persuade or coerce in any way. It just demonstrates a model for behavior which is so compellingly effective that people will want to copy it. A form of demonstrative power can be seen at work in the marketplace when a company comes up with a commercial innovation that works so well that other companies must have it, and if they cannot license it they may copy it, sometimes leading to lawsuits in which the originator of the model may seek legal action to prevent it from being stolen. In the political version that this book offers, however, there will be no desire to prevent others from copying the model.

The political strategy that this entails therefore does not require the United States to go out and try to talk other countries into adopting American democratic procedures. The best way to influence other countries, we argue, is to conduct our society so obviously well, with so many benefits arising from our policies, that other countries will be eager to copy us. This is, in fact, just a restatement of a very old precept: that the best way to teach is by example. And America's role in bringing democracy to its most fully realized modern form places upon it a powerful responsibility to teach internationally in this way. For anyone who truly believes, as I do, that democracy must be spread throughout the world if the human race is to survive the 21st century, this responsibility is paramount.

But this consideration, important though it is, is not the only reason why the United States must ensure that it takes a leading global role in coming decades. Another reason is that environmentally, economically and militarily, it is in the interest of American well-being to do so. Anyone who has an informed grasp of the current state of the world surely cannot fail to see that whatever validity there may have been in the past for isolationism – the belief that a country such as the United States can ignore what happens elsewhere in the world as none of its business – no longer applies. For better or worse, the world has shrunk, and if it is not quite the global village that philosopher Marshall McLuhan once forecast, it is certainly home to what is now a global civilization. It is undeniably and at times perhaps even uncomfortably diverse, but it is unquestionably *one* in the sense that the fates of all countries are now inextricably intertwined.

Environmentally, the overwhelming consensus of scientific

opinion and fact now recognizes that global climate change caused by human activity is a reality that the world needs urgently to address with maximum cooperation if the conditions of human life on earth are not to become so threatened that our continued viability as a species will be called into question. Economically, the economies of the countries of the world, especially the developed countries, are so interlinked as to make it abundantly clear that no country can prosper or even survive economically without policies that provide for rational and realistically unrestricted trade with other countries. Attempts to seal America off from the rest of the world by artificial restraints on global trade are doomed to fail as surely as the Prohibition laws of the early twentieth century, in which American politicians naively tried to legislate the United States into an era of abstention from the use of alcohol; all they succeeded in doing was to create a massive wave of gangsterism, and eventually Prohibition had to be repealed. Similarly, attempts to legislate America into a fictional political realm, somehow divorced from the economic interests and activities of the rest of the world, are doomed to fail.

Increasingly throughout the 20th century, interactions between the economies of different countries have been welded together ever more closely through complex systems of international compacts and treaties, such as the Bretton Woods agreements that followed World War II and provided a framework for global monetary management. These treaties have evolved so massively that in sum they today form what is arguably the largest and most complex single artifact that humanity has created. Even the Internet, which many people mistakenly think is just a system of hardware connections and structures, is in fact governed and made possibly by an enormous set of interlocking international agreements. These agreements – not just texts but expressions of international trust and good faith that codify the very basis of what we understand by orderly civil society – have been given vast substance and material force in recent decades by the increasing sophistication of Internet technologies. The technologies have a reciprocal relationship with the treaties in that they are made possible by the treaties while at the same time giving the treaties greater reality and influence with every technological advance that is made. For all these reasons, the only way to create American jobs and prosperity is to make the United States once again the world's leading center of technological and commercial innovation, doing so within a realistic global framework.

In addition to the pursuit of environmental security and economic security, the third reason for America to engage its global role, in the manner suggested in this book, has to do with national security, in the sense of safeguarding the country from military and terrorist aggression. That the United States was traumatized by the cowardly and heinous attacks of September 11, 2001 is a fact. That America must do all that is reasonably achievable to ensure that such atrocities do not recur is another fact. But it is equally a fact that America's prolonged war in Iraq is not the way to accomplish these essential objectives. While the nature of human history is such that the use of military power is from time to time unavoidable, it should not and cannot be realistically regarded as a means to ensure peace. Peace must be waged on its own terms and with its own strategies, which are different than the terms and strategies of war.

The communist leader Mao Zedong said, "Power grows from the barrel of a gun." Well, it does not, and that is one of the reasons communism has failed. Power grows from ideas. Behind every war with guns there is a greater war of ideas, and that is the war that must be fought and won if peace is to be real and lasting, and not just a lull between battles. Undeniably, there is a war of ideas under way in the world today, as there has been throughout history. Each epoch has its own war of ideas, and ours in the 21st century is a war to convince all peoples in the community of nations that democracy, incorporating freedom of the individual, tolerance, the separation of Church and State and a commitment to human rights, is the surest path to universal prosperity and the fulfillment of the human spirit.

The best way to fight and win this war of ideas is to show the world that America is a continuing success story, capable of using democracy as an engine of technological capability to address environmental, economic and other challenges on a continuously innovative basis, sharing the techniques of this success with the entire world. Because my co-author and I believe in the truth of this proposition, this book is addressed to Americans even though what it contains is no less important and relevant to the interests of readers around the world.

When I speak about the practical effects of ideas, I do not speak idly or in the abstract. I have seen the power of ideas at work throughout my career. To me, ideas do not represent empty words. They are realities, big and difficult and hard to manage and filled with potency. They are often dangerous but are the source of all that is good in human life. In my years at Westinghouse I witnessed daily the capacity of ideas to remake the world, generate wealth and solve problems. In my tenure as Secretary for Business and Economic Development of the State of Maryland, I saw how the technology industries, academic institutions, and federal agencies based in Maryland formed an engine of economic growth in which the ability to innovate was central to the success of private companies and the state alike. At the Johns Hopkins University I am concerned with the effective transferral of leading-edge research outputs to the private sector. No job could conceivably offer more convincing and inspiring evidence of the fact that America's richest assets lie in its commitment to create new knowledge. So please bear with me as I tell you a little about Johns Hopkins, because this information is relevant to much that this book is going to tell you.

Johns Hopkins receives more dollars in federal research grants than any other university in the United States. It is one of the United States' and the world's leading centers of scientific, medical, and technological research, and was the first academic institution in the U.S. to emphasize research as a key university activity distinct from teaching.

According to the National Science Foundation ranking, Johns Hopkins scientists and technologists performed $1.49 billion in science, medical and engineering research in 2006, making it the leading US academic institution in total Research and Development spending for the 28th year in a row. The university also ranked first on the National Science Foundation's separate list of federally funded Research and Development, spending $1.3 billion in Fiscal Year 2006 on research supported by such agencies as the National Institutes of Health, NASA, the National Science Foundation and the Department of Defense. In FY 2002, Johns Hopkins became the first university to cross the $1 billion threshold on either list, recording $1.14 billion in total research and $1.023 billion in federally sponsored research that year.

Hopkins research spans the biological and natural sciences, biomedical engineering, economics, international studies, medicine, genetics, neuroscience, nursing, public health and public policy. The institution is home to, among others:

* The Johns Hopkins School of Medicine, widely regarded as one of the best medical schools and biomedical research institutes in the world, operating in affiliation with Johns Hopkins Hospital, which is widely regarded as one of the world's greatest hospitals and has topped *U.S News and World Report's* ranking of American hospitals for 17 consecutive years. For medical research, *U.S. News* ranked the Hopkins School of Medicine second nationally and the School of Public Health first nationally for 2007.

* The Bloomberg School of Public Health (first and largest public health school in the world).

* The Whiting School of Engineering, the Krieger School of Arts and Sciences, the Carey Business School, the Peabody Institute, the School of Nursing, and the School of Advanced International Studies.

* The Applied Physics Laboratory, which specializes in research for the U.S. Department of Defense, NASA and other Government agencies.

* The Space Telescope Science Institute, which controls, analyzes, and collects data from the Hubble Space Telescope.

* A great number of exciting inter-disciplinary institutes and centers which are accelerating innovations across disciplines, including the Institute for Basic Biological Sciences, the Institute for Computational Medicine, the Institute for Biomedical Innovation and Design, the Institute for Nanobiotechnology, the Brain Sciences Institute, and many others too numerous to mention here but all involved in leading-edge breakthroughs in scientific advance and/or technological innovation.

The 2007 Academic Ranking of World Universities, produced by Shanghai Jiao Tong University's Institute of Higher Education, ranked Johns Hopkins 19th among universities globally in award-winning scientific research, while *The Times Higher Education Supplement* of Great Britain, using a ranking system based on peer review by scholars, placed Hopkins 10th nationally and 15th worldwide.

The above information is not included here as a commercial for Johns Hopkins. If anything, it should confirm that this august institution needs no commercial from me. (And I should point out that this book is not a Johns Hopkins publication. All that you will read in it reflects the personal and private opinions of myself and my co-author.) I have related these facts about Johns Hopkins to make two points clear. First, that when I speak about the practical power of ideas in action, I do not speak from wishful thinking. I know what I am talking about. I know, from my years of professional experiences at the interface between academia, government and business, what marvels research can introduce into the world for our benefit. Secondly, the above is a kind of honest disclosure statement, in that I would like you to know before you read any further that when it comes to the effectiveness of ideas as instruments to change the world, I am not unbiased. I believe completely in the power of ideas to transform both the physical world and our society for the better, and it is because my co-author and I share this belief, and wish to share it with others who can profit from all that it implies, that this book has been written.

Finally, I want to explain that this book is not intended to be or resemble an academic treatise. It is partly a personal discussion and partly a personal plea to the reader to think about the ideas and issues that are discussed here, even if you do not agree with what the authors have to say about them. Because we wanted this to be an informal conversation rather than a treatise, we've been relaxed about footnotes and citations, limiting these to what we considered to be bare necessities. Dates of birth and death of people referenced are included where we thought it useful and omitted where we felt it would clutter the narrative. Since this book is intended to be the basis of a conversation with readers, we will welcome feedback and promise to take all reader comments into account in bringing out another edition if we decide to do so. Meanwhile I sincerely hope you will enjoy reading even those pages with which you disagree. I believe you will, because this is not just a book about ideas in the abstract. It is rather about the ideas that have motivated and continue to motivate and drive the people, societies, decisions, institutions and technologies of our greatest periods of history as well as of our present day. And more: it is about our ability to dream great dreams, the dreams that move the world. May these pages stimulate you to participate as fully as you can in the great work that awaits us all.

Aris Melissaratos
Baltimore, Maryland
2009

NOTES

1: The New Deal sought a massive extension of existing infrastructural technology rather than to introduce a major wave of new technology, the Apollo Space Program was essentially a short-term tactic in the Cold War, with political rather than long-term scientific aims, and the Manhattan Project was conducted in secrecy rather than in the public eye, as part of an open technological enterprise. Thus, all three examples contain both positive lessons for the 21st century and examples of what we should avoid. See Slabbert, N.J., *The New Deal, The Bomb, The Man On The Moon: Three Mixed Intellectual Blessings for 21st-Century Policymakers,* THE TRUMAN LIBRARY (2008).

CHAPTER 1

HOW WE LOST OUR TECHNOLOGICAL NERVE

(And Why Our Survival Depends On Getting It Back)

It's a truism that much technological progress has taken place over the past century or so. There is indeed a record of accomplishments to be proud of. But the last few generations can also be regarded as a time of immense technological failures.

We have failed to replace the pollution-producing transportation and industrial technologies of the late 19th and early 20th-centuries with environmentally clean technologies like solar and wind power. As a result, severe damage has been done to the Earth's ecological systems.

We tapped an astonishing source of energy in the form of nuclear power and unleashed it for military purposes in the forms of bombs and submarine propulsion, but neglected to harness anything near its full potential for peaceful use.

Amazingly, the greatest organization of economic and technological resources in the history of the world, the United States, closed the 20th century as a hostage to foreign government and commercial cartels controlling fossil fuels which should by then have passed into technological history.

We failed to cure cancer, AIDS or even the common cold.

We've devoted astronomical sums to military exploits and bailouts for private companies run by inept managers, including corporate bureaucracies whose main output has been piles of worthless financial paper.

America went to the Moon, not really for the sake of science but as a one-time political stunt, then we largely lost interest in the space exploration program, which has had to fight tooth and nail for its budget every year.

Despite the enormous power delivered into our hands by the engines of technology and scientific advance, poor education, poverty and hunger continue. Moreover, much of our mass media industry has persistently and methodically waged a propaganda war against science and technology, merchandising an image of them as villainous and sinister. This campaign has been aided by environmentalists and nostalgic pastoralists preaching a message of enlightenment through a retreat from technology.

The Wall Street bailouts, energy crisis and overall state of the economy have a common theme: America's desperate need to launch a new technological era. If the U.S. can find billions to rescue companies that have produced piles of unproductive paper, we should spend at least a comparable amount on massive new technological innovation that will create jobs and genuine prosperity instead of financial bubbles. For too many decades America has been making do with obsolete technology, confusing Wall Street's houses of cards with the genuine prosperity that only new inventions can bring.

A national initiative to reverse this trend, led by the White House, is needed to drive the U.S. into a technological era in all fields of endeavor, not only a few arenas that happen to be fashionable or in the current political spotlight.

If you think it's unrealistic to wish for a president who's passionate about new technology, think again. Such a chief magistrate was Abraham Lincoln. Though his legacy is dominated by his role in saving the Union, future historians may praise him equally for his resolve to unite America not only politically but via its first great national technological infrastructure: the transcontinental railroad, which in those days was as new-fangled an idea as you could get.

Lincoln was a railroad lawyer, representing and supporting the leaders of technological change. Putting a railroad advocate in the mid-19th century White House was like electing an ardent magnetic levitation, artificial intelligence, nanotechnology or Mars colonization proponent today. Historian Stephen E. Ambrose calls Abe "one of the great railroad lawyers in the West" and "the driving force" of a railroad system that was the century's greatest building project.[1]

Our society is very different from Lincoln's, and we can't replicate the leadership of an historical icon. But we can learn from Lincoln's sense of national purpose and determination to develop the most advanced technological infrastructure that's possible. Lincoln didn't think government could solve all problems. But he realized that so vast and urgent an undertaking as a new technological infrastructure for the Republic wouldn't happen soon enough if left to unaided private initiative alone, with its time-limited investment horizon. He understood that government had a responsibility to midwife long-term national projects. As a result, the world's greatest national railroad system was born.

In sensing the link between government and technological innovation, Lincoln intuited the dynamic of history. In 1660, encouraged by the writings of Francis Bacon, science became a national enterprise with the creation of the Royal Society of Science under British Crown patronage. This introduced the development of scientific knowledge with government authority and resources no individual researcher could match. Contrary to myths shared across the political spectrum, technological innovation doesn't just "happen" if you leave bright people alone in a room to brainstorm over sandwiches and coffee. Like any great undertaking, it needs leadership. Much of our central technology today stems from the Baconian vision of public-private partnership.

But we've managed this inheritance erratically. A federal technology impetus on a scale comparable to America's national railroad didn't reappear in the U.S. until World War II's Manhattan Project to create the atom bomb, and the Apollo Program to put a man on the moon. And both of these undertakings were reactive products, undertaken by government grudgingly, rather than proactive initiatives. After the U.S. beat Russia to the Moon, space research became, for many in Congress, a burdensome drain on pork funding rather than an exciting national mission.

Sadly, America today has an atrophied sense of the adventure and value of the risk of technological innovation, and little reverence for the hard-won knowledge that's needed to achieve it.

It's claimed by some critics of science and technology that these enterprises have let us down, by creating artifacts that have despoiled the Earth and placing undeserved power in the hands of fallible mortals. But this is not true. It is we who have let science and technology down. We have become a civilization that likes to fantasize about state-of-the art technology but that in fact shies away from imaginative scientific initiatives and from the will, commitment, sense of purpose, hard work and high educational accomplishments that these demand.

We have betrayed the promise of science and technology by failing to act on the astonishing scientific and technological potential that we showed in the first half of the 20th century. As a result, we have entered the 21st century in economic, infrastructural and environmental crisis.

This disconnect from science and technology is reflected in the nation's ebbing standard of science and technology education. In 2007 the Swiss-based World Economic Forum ranked the U.S. an embarrassing seventh in worldwide production of new technologies able to influence the development of nations.² Popular television and movie space operas, which are really westerns in disguise rather than celebrations of technology and scientific discovery, strut their ignorant distaste for real science in howlers like interplanetary ships that make dramatic noises in space where no noise is possible. And the *Harvard International Review* has reported a grave warning by Admiral William Owens, former vice chairman of the Joint Chiefs of Staff, about the security and economic risks of America's waning technological competitiveness.³

The White House needs to create a Cabinet post entrusted with the task of revitalizing America's sense of the wonder of scientific discovery, and of making the U.S. a 21ˢᵗ-century beacon of the world's technological genius, with the full weight and prestige of the presidency behind this mission.

America: Land of Retro-Techno

In June 2006 *Discover* magazine assigned former Oxford University lecturer David Bodanis, author of *E=mc2: A Biography of the World's Most Famous Equation*, to investigate "the pace of innovation these days in America." Bodanis filed his findings in a series of letters which began with this statement: "I just finished my research trip for you, hanging out with software developers and venture capitalists in Silicon Valley, and, boy, am I confused. Everyone here believes that technology is being introduced faster than ever. But in their private lives, hardly anything has changed in years. The plane I flew in on, for example, was a Boeing 747. It's a great jet, but it was designed more than 30 years ago. There are more movies to watch on board than there used to be, but the basic idea—a metal tube attached to jet engines that burn modified petroleum, carrying a lot of people at around 600 mph—is much the same as it has been for all planes since then."

When he landed, Bodanis reported, he rented a car with his credit card – a financial technology almost half a century old. His rental procedure used computers that were faster than in the past but relied on a basic technology that was decades old. "The rental car itself was a lot like a car from two decades ago: It got similar mileage, had a similar internal combustion engine, and gave me a familiar driving experience. Clicking a few buttons on the dashboard led me to Motown tunes of 40 years ago. The process was a bit less efficient than putting in a tape, but not too much worse. The news of the day was about plans for the next launch of the space shuttle, which at first glance seems a mark of high-tech modernity. But the shuttle was designed in the 1970s, using a great deal of 1960s technology. Its design was locked in around the time Ford introduced the Pinto. It goes on and on. Oil rigs and nuclear missiles and microwave ovens and the New York Stock Exchange and international phone calls—all work more efficiently than in decades past, but they still feel much the same as they did many, many years ago... The cars and fridges and bikes and almost everything else could easily have come from a movie set in 2006."

Bodanis typed his report to *Discover* on an Apple iMac which, though new, featured a graphic interface (icons representing folders on a simulated desktop) developed at Xerox PARC in the 1970s. "The computer mouse was developed by Douglas Engelbart around the same time, as a modification of the control systems he used while operating 1940s-era radar oscilloscope screens."

Bodanis's editor asked him why innovation should be slow when high technology enjoyed such a high profile. He replied: "America is changing so slowly compared with many countries in East Asia precisely because we have so much invested in our success this far. When a technology is central to our life, who's going to shut it down for uncertain, aiming-in-the-dark upgrades? Air traffic computers and software are often decades old: It's dangerous to bring in entirely fresh ones. The situation is much the same with PC software. Computer clock speed keeps increasing, but hardly anyone wants to accept the downtime that would result from having to learn fundamentally new programs. Browsers are similar to what they were a decade ago; spreadsheets are similar to those of two decades ago. It gets worse, because the organizations that have been the most successful at developing new technologies aren't going to let go of their success easily. Microsoft CEO Steve Ballmer is an energetic guy, but if I work for him and have an idea for a stunningly new product that will undercut something the company is already selling, I will learn that his energy extends to protecting his home turf. My brilliant idea is not going to get approved."

Bodanis saw a tendency for American corporations to hire the brightest people from around the world, then ensure "that they never again contribute anything fundamentally new." He also faulted U.S. patent laws, which were supposed to foster innovation but had evolved into tools for companies whose interests lay in preserving old technologies. "The problem is especially bad in medical research. Many common procedures, like certain tests central to breast cancer research, have recently been patented, even though a previous generation of researchers would have considered that outrageous. A good many smaller labs, where some of the most innovative ideas traditionally arise, can't afford to stay in the research game." Then there was liability litigation: "Even as undoubtedly useful a drug as penicillin probably wouldn't be approved today, because of the (albeit low) frequency of toxic side effects."

Nor, Bodanis suggested, could universities any longer be counted on to promote innovation as they had once done. "I was tangentially involved with astrophysics research at the University of Chicago back in the mid-1970s," he wrote, "and I remember using a simple e-mail system then. It linked several main universities and took a mere 20 years to spread to the general public." And science was hard and relatively poorly paid, so that "fewer and fewer Americans get degrees in the hard sciences even as the economy keeps growing", while visa restrictions and terrorism anxieties were curtailing the exchange of foreign students. "At the same time, a lot of top Ph.D.'s are finding that their home countries are ever more attractive to return to after a stint in the United States." [4]

America has entered the 21st century not as the world's leader of technological innovation but as a land of retro-techno.[5] It is at least symbolically appropriate, if not symptomatic of the U.S.'s technological malaise, that two of its presidents in recent decades built their careers in industries which have vigorously protected the continued use of obsolete fossil fuel technology; that one of these presidents has wound down his presidency by extending federal protection to save a technologically obsolete automobile industry from extinction; that another U.S. president of the 20th century's last quarter represented a motion picture industry rooted in technology from the first quarter of the century; and that recent president came from a generation of baby boomers that, at least in its youth, belonged to a mood swing in American cultural history that contributed mightily to the identification of high technology with evil corporations and militarists. The flower power generation was not notable for its devotion to the expansion of technology. Truth to tell, America has been technologically coasting for decades on the brilliance of previous generations, especially that of the first half of the 20th century. It is a society ruled by the technological choices of its grandfathers.

We must embrace science and technology now

We cannot afford to allow America slip further technologically and scientifically.

As the world advances into the 21st century, we are beset by problems greater than any that have previously been encountered in history. Whether they are more complicated than those that our ancestors knew is debatable. The ancient philosophers of

Greece, China and other cradles of humanity's possessed powerful intelligences that engaged great philosophical problems in forms that continue to frame our thinking today. Civilizations that have passed from the Earth endured political, economic, technological and other upheavals that were no doubt no less taxing to their greatest minds than our problems are for us today. We flatter ourselves if we exaggerate the uniqueness of the modern situation. But we certainly face enormous problems that are specific to our time, with a scope and magnitude that seems to dwarf others that historians have recorded.

Since the invention of atomic weapons we have lived with the prospect of nuclear annihilation. For decades this seemed to be linked to war between nations large enough to wield a certain critical mass of economic, technological and military resources. We now know that quite small states, and even terrorist groups that operate statelessly, may threaten the peace with nuclear and other sophisticated weapons of mass destruction.

It is now widely recognized that we face serious changes in the physical constitution of the Earth itself.

Moreover, the industrial and economic systems that have long formed the mainstay of the world's developed societies have shown us that they do not rest on the bedrock that they formerly seemed to. We have realized that the natural resources that are required by these systems, and which once appeared inexhaustible, are in fact finite. The very methodologies and underlying assumptions of these systems have even become suspect. Great American corporations, which once seemed invulnerable bulwarks of the capitalist system, have crumbled or have had to be subjected to government rescue actions in ways which not too long ago would have been unthinkable. From all this it seems difficult not to draw a conclusion that the world is in a state of momentous transition.

Historians might argue that we are always in a state of transition, because change is never-ending, and seemingly quiet periods of history are often ones in which the greatest changes are occurring; they are just are taking place so incrementally that no one notices them. This may be so. It doesn't detract from the fact that certain moments in history are visibly ones at which civilizations stand at the crossroads. We are such a crossroads now. The world in the 21st century faces a technological crisis that is arguably greater than any crisis humanity has known in its history. And the biggest choice that confronts us is whether or not to become a genuinely scientific civilization.

To speak of such a choice will shock many. It will be countered that the global civilization that is more or less shared by the leading industrial and political powers of the world in the early 21st century, especially that part of it which is democratic, is and has long been scientific – certainly in its industries and technological infrastructures, and to at least some extent in its vision of the universe.

But this belief is a myth. Neither "modern" nor "democratic" are necessarily synonyms for scientific, and the truth is that modern civilization, in the sense that we've just indicated, is not a scientific civilization at all. It is at best partly scientific in its techniques and its attitudes. In important respects it is decidedly unscientific or even anti-scientific. In the late 19th century and the began to form a scientific civilization. But, to use a sporting metaphor, we fumbled the ball. We lost our scientific nerve. To survive the challenges of the 21st century, it is essential that we recover it.

We have much to gain by doing so. And the good news is that we can meet this challenge and solve the problems it presents if we put our minds to it. Our intelligences and resources are equal to the task. In fact, we have it in our power not only to surmount the crisis but to build a prosperous and peaceful global civilization based on liberty, tolerance, learning, creative activity, freedom from poverty and better health for all.

Although these accomplishments are well within our reach, however, they will not just fall into our laps. We will have to work very hard to secure them, changing some of our most comfortable attitudes and habits.

We must begin by facing unpleasant facts. Environmental science has provided us with overwhelming evidence that human activity has impacted the climatic processes of the earth severely – so much so that unless we do something about it very quickly, we are in grave danger. We face a future, not too far off, in which the Earth will become a less and less hospitable place for us to live, with changes in weather that will reduce our supply of food and drinkable water, change sea levels and thus coastlines, and, by causing political emergencies throughout the world, dangerously destabilize relations between nations, thereby creating civil unrest and increased risks of war as countries compete for vital resources.

In March 2007 – the same month in which the United Nations Security Council held its first briefing on global climate change -- the U.S. Army War College funded a two-day conference on the national security implications of global climate change.[6] The following month a group of 11 retired senior U.S. generals issued a report asserting that global warming presents significant national security challenges to the U.S. via destabilization risks in Africa and

Asia, hurting water and food availability and driving refugees to richer countries. The generals said the U.S. must address this or face serious consequences.[7]

Apart from their geopolitical security and military implications, these environmental problems are very clearly linked to fuel and energy issues of enormous economic importance. It is accurate to say that both the world economy, as an increasingly interlinked whole, and the separate economies of individual nations, are functions of our ability to manage our relationship with the physical environment. Recent decades and especially the past several years have seen steady confirmation of the pivotal role played in our economy by energy availability and prices, and the types of fuel on which we allow ourselves to become dependent.

Since our relationships with our physical environment and our fuel sources are, in our civilization, essentially technological relationships, it is clear that the crisis we face is a technological one. The technologies that have seen us into the 21st century are clearly no longer appropriate to our circumstances. The major questions we must now urgently confront are how quickly we can replace them and how to go about this.

We have the technological potential to triumph spectacularly

Having made a case above for the technological failure and complacency of our civilization, it's necessary now to make the point that our technological potential is gigantic. Far, greater, indeed, than we can conceive. It may seem that we contradict ourselves by taking this opposite tack, but this is not so. It is rather that our technological failure is reprehensible precisely because we are capable of so much *if we will only exert ourselves technologically.*

Although in recent decades we have not come anywhere near the extent of the technological possibilities available to us, our modest achievements already give us a glimmering of what we are capable of.

Consider the extent to which medical technology has extended human life. Consider the number of ways in which the quality of human life has been improved over the past century by a vast array of technological innovations which have enabled the average inhabitants of industrially developed countries to take for granted amenities which were beyond the reach of kings in previous times.

Science and technology have enriched and empowered us all to an extent, and in ways, that were once limited to the dreams of fiction-writers. Everything we have learned about ourselves as a species in the past few generations tells us that whatever our failings, we are not lacking in technological ingenuity, nor in imagination. What we lack is technological will, commitment and purpose. Like all other positive opportunities in human life, however, our ability to innovate technologically comes with a price tag. As a civilization (meaning for this purpose the present community of nations, led technologically by the more industrially developed countries), it is highly questionable whether we have ever really understood this fact fully. Those nuances of it that we have grasped from time to time over the past century or so have not lingered in the collective public mind but have been quickly forgotten.

It is a seriously significant feature of our technological society that we have taken science and technology and their products for granted. We have become so used to a constant stream of lifestyle-improving, economy-stimulating technological innovations that we have failed to ask ourselves whether we have been doing what is necessary to create the conditions required for such innovation to occur. We have adopted, to our great detriment, an attitude of naïve entitlement toward technology, assuming that it is like Aladdin's Cave of ancient fable – a treasure-house inexhaustibly filled with readily available wonders to which, once you know the magic password, you can return again and again to stuff your pockets.

Well, modern scientific technology isn't like that at all. It's more like a rare flower growing on a remote mountaintop, which can be visited only after a long and perilous journey filled with hardship and sacrifice, and which, once found, cannot simply be brought home to grow abundantly by itself but, on the contrary, can exist only in unusual soil under conditions which must be carefully maintained and respected if the flower is to survive, let alone flourish. It must be nurtured with immense care, awareness and sensitivity. Why else would it be a phenomenon that did not appear in full force until so very recently in human history?

As a society we have failed to appreciate the rarity of the outpouring of technological progress that has characterized much of the past two centuries or more. This failure is especially striking, and nationally embarrassing, in the case of the United States, which throughout the greater part of the 20th century has prided itself on being the world's engine of leading-edge technological innovation – the very fountainhead of scientific and technical progress. U.S. global technological leadership can no longer be regarded as a given. The U.S. has slipped badly in science and technology. Its educational system is demonstrably outperformed in these fields by the systems of other countries and its international ranking as a technological innovator has plummeted.

How could this happen to the world's technological superpower? Because the processes that make technological growth possible have never really been widely understood and fully embraced in the U.S. to begin with. This proposition will be unpalatable to many people; it may even seem a shockingly un-American statement. But it is profoundly pro-American to anyone who realizes that caring about the future of America entails delivering a good dose of truth from time to time, even when the truth is bitter. Painful as it sounds, the U.S. has liked to think of itself as being drenched in technology, but a preoccupation with the consumption of gadgetry doesn't make a society pro-technology. As eminent historian of ideas Professor Morton White has shown, while America has liked to think of itself a sophisticated urban society, having a few densely-populated American cities with impressively tall skylines doesn't make a pro-urban country, and American culture has been shaped by powerful anti-urban intellectual influences.[8] Analogously, American culture has liked to see itself as futuristic, yet it has historically been strongly attracted to agrarian frontier philosophies in which rugged individualism has been seen as antithetical to a vigorous high technology and the kind of self-conscious intellectualism that both defenders and critics of cities tend to associate with urban life.

The above observations mean that much of America's national image has for a long time been quite seriously distorted. If it seems hard to believe that an entire society can rest on a set of basically flawed presuppositions, think about the Soviet Union. Because the USSR was so closed a society, there is no reliable way to judge what the mass of Soviet citizens thought about anything, but it is sobering to remember that for decades a substantial community of Soviet leaders, at any rate, evidently saw their society as the vanguard of the world's future, with endless expansion as their birthright. But today the Soviet Union is no more.

Some would say: yes, but the Soviet Union was totalitarian, as was Hitler's Third Reich, which saw itself as heir to a thousand-year reign. The United States is not a totalitarian society but is as open a society as human political ability has yet been able to develop. Surely this makes a great difference. It does, and these statements are true. But what about Victorian Britain? That was not a fully democratic society in the sense that we would now find acceptable, but it can be strongly argued that Victoria's Empire was, from many points of view, the most humane, open and enlightened society the world had by that time experienced – certainly a far cry from the Soviet Union and Nazi Germany. And it, too, believed that it rested on a sure self-understanding and set of historical premises that guaranteed that the sun would never set on it. The same expectations of permanence, and of faith in the solidity of its sense of national identity, can be found in civilizations throughout history. It can be compelling asserted that America is indeed unique, in many vital respects. But is it wise, and in the country's best interests, to assume that this uniqueness is so broad and all-encompassing that it protects the country against all forms of grave national error? Our answer to this question is No.

As powerful as the awesome forces are that created the United States and have given it continued cohesion from its founding to the present day, the country is not exempt from the errors of national self-knowledge and failure of purpose that have afflicted societies through all the recorded centuries. And this affliction has, we contend, struck America in the form of a national alienation from the roots of that spirit of technological progress which has long been regarded by so many, both within the U.S. and around the world, as a defining element of America's national character.

The myth of technological inevitability

Interestingly, the affliction is associated with neither side of the political spectrum. It is evident on both the Left and the Right.

Leftist intellectuals have a solid tradition of portraying technology as a sinister presence which gives undue power to elites, especially to those who are unscrupulous about despoiling the environment in order to fatten their purses. These groups like, further, to depict technology as dehumanizing, and conducive to a dumbed-down mass society in which individuality is sacrificed to the emergence of a gray, faceless mass of cynically exploited consumers.

Conservatives, on the other hand, have an equally cold attitude toward technology but for different reasons. One reason for this is implicit in the very name of their ideological position. To conserve means to resist change, and technology is an agent of change. It changes not only the physical landscapes and structures of a society but also the behaviors of its citizens.

Despite what many leftist intellectuals maintain, technology innovation is indeed unsettling. It does not favor anciently established power structures but can help to create new alignments of economic, media distribution and political power, breaking up old coteries and bringing new players on to the field.

However, although all of these considerations have helped retard the progress of technology innovation, the most obstructive attitude to technology is one that is common to both the Right and the Left sections of the ideological spectrum. This is the assumption that technology innovation does not really have to be nurtured by the careful creation of the right conditions but that it just, well, *happens*. This belief is a central superstition of our time, and like a virus which does not care who its host is, it moves with a blissful lack of discrimination up and down the political spectrum with no respect for the political party of the opinions it inhabits and shapes. Because of this ubiquity, and its pervasiveness in one form or another in all corners of American cultural life, a good name for it could be called America's Soviet Superstition. It is the American counterpart to the former Soviet Union leadership's belief that the Soviet Union was a favorite child of history.

The American version is *the myth of technological inevitability*. Fortunately, because of its open society and mechanisms for free thought, self-criticism and social change, the United States, unlike the former Soviet union, has opportunity to correct this flaw in its national perceptions. It also has some time in which to do so before its technological crisis becomes, for all the practical purposes that are important to us today, unfixable. Some time. But not much.

Many of the points made above – the mistakes we have made, the exciting potential that exists to put ourselves on a new and better path, the cultural implications of technology innovation, the time pressures – can be usefully illustrated by the story of a technology that we have shockingly failed to exploit and which almost certainly represents a significant part of our future: the maglev train.

By the third quarter of the 20th century it was growing increasingly clear that we needed a new generation of overland transportation technology. Financially, logistically and environmentally, the automobile-and-highway system needed replacing. Highways were becoming more and more congested, gasoline prices were rising alarmingly (although they were still far from today's prices, the trend was there for all to see) and environmental researchers were amassing disturbing evidence that automobile emissions were environmentally problematical. The only alternatives to highway travel were a railroad system that was geared to replace highways (the automobile had in fact originally replaced the railroad as the country's dominant mass transit technology) and the airlines, which, like automobiles, were vulnerable to rising fuel prices.

In the last several decades all these challenges have grown steadily worse, with oil prices reaching crippling proportions, environmental impact being recognized as a national and international crisis, and many airlines battling to survive financially, not all of them succeeding. A June 2008 report announced that Amtrak, "America's struggling passenger railroad", had reported record passenger demand for the sixth consecutive year, with an eleven percent increase over its previous fiscal year's total of 26 million passengers riding its 21 000 miles of track. The company attributed about half the increase to commuter gas prices. Amtrak President Alex Kummant said the railroad was "up against capacity limits." Reuters reported that Amtrak, a for-profit federal corporation "that has bled red ink since its 1971 creation", faced a White House threat to veto a multi-billion-dollar House of Representatives package aimed at funding Amtrak to improve passenger service – "an arrangement Kummant says is crucial for any expansion." According to the company's president, "We are in a different world than even just three or four years ago with gas prices at these levels, with the congestion we face on the highways and with the difficulty in air travel."

But, astonishingly, the United States is a world laggard in rail development. Japan's high-speed railroad system carries about 18 percent of the country's total annual passenger travel miles, while Britain, France and Germany have railroad networks that carry six to eight percent. Amtrak bears less than one percent of America's.

The Reuters report noted that Amtrak is criticized for being "woefully slow and inefficient", adding that Amtrak's premier service averaged 82 miles an hour (132 kilometers per hour) although it could reach 150 mph (241 kph) in parts of Rhode Island and Connecticut. Japan, France and Germany, on the other hand, had national rail services capable of 150 mph (241 kph) to 185 mph (297 kph) on dedicated tracks with sophisticated signaling systems designed for high-speed trains. Japan introduced high-speed rail in 1964 and France in 1981. Amtrak's Acela Express began running between Washington, D.C., and Boston only in 2000.

The U.S., in short, has substantial problems with the service capacity of its current railroad system. Air transport, meanwhile, is not without problems of its own. Britain's Guardian newspaper reported in May 2008: "The list of bankrupt airlines is growing by the week, but the biggest casualty of the oil squeeze in the airline industry could be the cheap fare and the holiday plans of a generation weaned on affordable air travel."[10] The newspaper quoted the investment bank Credit Suisse as commenting that without fuel hedging and mitigating action by management teams "we do not believe that any airline can be profitable in the medium term", and Willie Walsh, chief executive of British Airways, as stating that the era of cheap flights was coming to an end. According to the Guardian, "BA and carriers around the world are facing extinction due to

soaring fuel costs."
Which brings us to the maglev train.

The promise of maglev

The essence of this astounding technology's exciting promise is well captured by an article written by Peter Hall for the U.S. magazine *Metropolis* in 2004: "It's eight o'clock on a crisp morning in New York. You settle into a large reclining seat inside a spacious cabin resembling an aircraft interior. The cabin makes a slight shudder to indicate that it has assumed a traveling position a fraction of an inch above a steel guideway, then begins a rapid acceleration, easing into a comfortable glide at 270 mph. An hour later you pull into Union Station in Washington. By noon you are walking through downtown Atlanta, 870 miles away—and your feet haven't left the ground." [11]

This imagined scenario, Hall points out, isn't science fiction. Magnetic levitation, or 'maglev', trains have been in development in countries such as Germany, Japan and China for some time. Hall notes that maglev offers America an era in which a newly implemented (but already available) technology will "stitch together the country, when journey times between cities shrink dramatically and travel becomes calm, even fun, again. No lurking paranoia of a terrorist hijacking; commuting will be an effortless transition between city centers, all achieved without burning fossil fuels mid-air." He quotes New York architect Alex Washburn as observing: "It's a spectacular form of transportation. There are no pollutants, and it's low maintenance because there are few moving parts. In terms of post-9/11 concerns, it's safer as it cannot become a missile." Washburn adds: "Once you ride it you understand that it's the next form of transportation."

It's important to understand that maglev differs from conventional rail, including high-speed systems like Japan's Bullet Train, by being wheel-less. (The maglev system also requires its own elevated path that doesn't intersect automotive roads and highways.) But as far as the interests and lifestyles of Americans in the 21st century are concerned, the real story about maglev isn't how exciting and amazing the technology is – this information has been around a long time—but rather, the even more amazing fact of America's sad failure to adopt it with all possible haste as its national transit technology. The title of Hall's article is telling: *The maglev train is the future of twenty-first-century transit. Why won't we see it in the U.S. anytime soon?*

Hall's piece recounts maglev's history, which is depressingly familiar to its American advocates. In 1968, scientists at New York's Brookhaven National Laboratory worked out how to propel a train electromagnetically to achieve speeds unavailable to vehicles that ran on friction-inhibited wheels. They interested the government and a test track was built in Colorado. Then interest fizzled out and nothing further was done in the U.S. for the next twenty years or so. However, other countries moved to continue the research, especially Germany and Japan, both of which developed working maglev systems.

Japan's maglev trains reach over 350 mph. Japan and Germany have each poured billions of dollars into maglev development, compared to the few million dollars spent in the U.S.. In 1998 the U.S. Congress approved up to $950 million to develop a maglev track, but the award of the money was put on hold indefinitely. According to Suhair Alkhatib, a U.S. Department of Transportation engineer, "It comes down to how many supporters you have in Congress. You need more than just two senators and a few congressmen for a project of this magnitude to happen."

One of the political challenges to maglev is that unlike highways and conventional railroad tracks, which can snake and zigzag around existing properties and other features of the landscape, maglev trains need straight tracks to achieve their great speed. This means not only expense but a lot of local politics and negotiation with property owners whose real estate may lie in the path of the proposed maglev route. Maglev project groups in places including Washington D.C., Maryland, Pennsylvania, California, Nevada, Georgia, Tennessee, Florida and Louisiana have been trying to get to grips with these and related problems so as to try to jump-start the flow of federal funding, but it's clear that what is really needed, at least to implement maglev on a national scale in the U.S., is not the fragmented interest of various regional advocacy groups but a concentrated maglev leadership initiative from within the federal government, driven by the White House.

As Hall correctly puts it, "until America believes in it, maglev cannot be built." To achieve this belief, it is necessary for maglev to be adopted by the federal government as a major national priority, with the same enthusiasm and sense of national purpose that characterized the campaign to put a man on the moon.

Some of the far-reaching implications of maglev for the U.S. are usefully summarized in a 2005 report titled *The Urgency of Reclaiming the United States Lead in Magnetic Levitation (Maglev) Transportation: How U.S. Maglev Technology Can Help Sustain Continued Economic Development After Global Oil Production Peaks,* by Gordon

Danby, James Jordan and James Powell.[12] The three are partners in a commercial venture, the Interstate Maglev Project (IMP), formed to create a national maglev network in North America based on innovations developed by Danby and Powell. According to the report, Danby holds a Ph.D. in nuclear physics from Canada's McGill University, is a fellow of the American Physical Society, and a recipient of the New York Academy of Sciences' Boris Pregel Award for Applied Science and Technology. Jordan is cited as a former energy research director for the U.S. Navy and as a graduate of the Industrial College of the Armed Forces. Powell is cited as holding a doctorate in nuclear engineering from the Massachusetts Institute of Technology and as being a co-recipient with Danby of the 2000 Benjamin Franklin Medal in Engineering for their work on maglev technology, especially that part of it which uses the scientific phenomenon called superconductivity to create enormously powerful magnets. (Franklin Medal recipients have included inventor Thomas Edison and physicists Albert Einstein and Stephen Hawking.)

Their report says: "Maglev will soon become a major mode of transport in the world, as important as autos, railroads, and airplanes are today. Maglev does not burn oil, is much faster and simpler to operate than present modes of transport, free from congestion and weather delays, and very energy efficient." According to Danby, Powell and Jordan, the U.S. faces a transportation crisis in the next 10 to 20 years – a " 'perfect storm' of declining World oil production, rising fuel prices, increased roadway congestion and accidents, more global warming from vehicle emissions, and dirtier air." They cite a U.S. Federal Department of Transportation forecast that under currently available technology, the mileage travelled by automobiles and freight trucks will probably almost double over the next two decades.

To meet this vast transportation demand and deal with the strain that it will clearly place on already inadequate facilities, the authors say the U.S. has the capability to implement a maglev system that is superior to both the German and Japanese systems, even though these countries are presently ahead of the U.S. in maglev development. Japan, they comment, "has clearly demonstrated that superconducting technology works safely and stably and is very reliable in all operating conditions. Their passenger Maglev vehicles hold the Maglev World speed record at 350 mph." (This applies to travel in the open air, which provides resistance that mitigates speed. The authors estimate that in specially-constructed tunnels from atmosphere has been removed, a maglev train could reach thousands of miles an hour.)

Government must be the midwife

The report proposes that the U.S. adopt a maglev system using superconducting magnets that will allow transportation of inter-city freight and passengers at 300 mph in all weather. The construction cost of their proposed design, the authors say, will be half that of the German and Japanese systems. Moreover, they forecast that initial investment in the system will be recouped "in only a few years." However, to attract private investment in the system it will be necessary to launch it with government funding, as has been done in Germany and Japan.

According to the authors' 2005 estimates, federal funding of about $80 million a year for six years will establish a maglev network that will set a new international maglev standard. They forecast that the superiority of the U.S. system will be significant enough to create an international demand for export of the U.S. technology around the world, thereby bringing American private investors a substantial new entrepreneurial opportunity that will benefit the U.S. economy over and above the domestic benefits of the U.S. implementation.

The development of a U.S. Maglev industry, the report argues, is thus of great economic importance to sustaining the U.S.'s global economic leadership: "It will help reduce dependence on foreign oil, improve our trade balance by the reduction of oil imports and the export of high value U.S. Maglev systems, make our industries more efficient and competitive, and save time and money for U.S. workers and consumers. China and India are rapidly industrializing. Their vast populations will soon require efficient and cheap transport. For the U.S. to leave the field to Germany and Japan for Maglev sales, which will be very great in the years to come, would be an economic tragedy."

Using 2005 data, Danby, Powell and Jordan note that the U.S. uses a quarter of the world's oil production although it has only four percent of the global population. It is obvious that as previously non-industrialized countries like India and China build increasingly sophisticated infrastructures and economies, the U.S. cannot count on a continuation of this situation -- quite apart from the problems created by rising oil prices and the fact that commercially exploitable oil deposits will eventually run out.

"For every 10 barrels consumed, only 4 new barrels are being discovered. One need not be a rocket scientist to realize something has got to give." Since transportation is at the heart of the U.S.'s economic system, the authors warn, a failure to take quick action to implement a new mass transportation technology will result in "catastrophic and permanent" results, including wars over ever-dwindling energy resources and shrinking food supplies, not to mention the increasing environmental degradation caused by existing transportation modes.

They cite U.S. Department of Energy projections that under prevailing technologies, U.S. transportation oil demand will rise almost eighty percent from twelve million barrels a day in 2000 to 21 million barrels per day in 2025, with world demand by 2025 totaling more than 120 million barrels a day. But there isn't this much known or expected oil on the planet, at least in accessible form. "Known oil resources," say Danby, Powell and Jordan, "are a bit more than one trillion barrels. Optimists believe that another trillion barrels will be discovered, pessimists that new discoveries will be small and scattered, and not substantially increase the pool of oil ... At 120 million barrels per day, all of the world's known oil would be gone in only 25 years." Moreover, they warn, at current rates of consumption, almost all oil reserves outside the Middle East will be gone within only 15 years, putting the entire world at the mercy of suppliers in this region. "If hostile forces take over Saudi Arabia and other countries in the region, and deny oil to the West, America and many other countries would face economic collapse. Major wars, potentially nuclear, could result."

Danby, Powell and Jordan outline three potential paths for the U.S. to deal with this situation:

1. Develop alternative fuels for our automobiles, trucks and aircraft.

2. Reduce the amount of transportation we need by concentrating America's population into dense urban areas serviced by urban mass transit systems.

3. Implement a national maglev network.

Regarding the alternative fuel option, the authors say that natural gas reserves are larger than oil reserves, but are insufficient to replace oil, while also being essential to fertilizer production industries that would be undermined if gas were diverted in large quantities for transportation. Known coal reserves, on the other hand, are so extensive that there is little chance of our using them up for centuries. Moreover, technology exists to convert coal into liquid and gas fuels. The pollution impacts of increased coal use, however, would be "catastrophic". The authors also reject hydrogen-based systems, maintaining that the storage of hydrogen is so dangerous and logistically difficult as to make this option impracticable: "The vision of daily commuting to work, dodging burning mini-

Hindenburgs on the roadway, is a daunting one." To this is added the challenge of sourcing hydrogen in environmentally acceptable ways. The report also rules out electrically driven cars as a mass substitute for existing technologies, owing to their limited range and performance.

Regarding the option to concentrate the U.S. population into new, very dense, walkable urban areas served by local mass transit systems – so-called "re-urbanization" – Danby, Powell and Jordan see this as unworkable, not least because of the cost of such an immense relocation of nationwide population, particularly in the present economy (which has worsened considerably since the authors published their report), not to mention the political difficulty of persuading millions of people to embrace an urban existence that may be unacceptable to them. A totalitarian society might be able to consider such wholesale reconstruction of people's lives, but this would hardly be possible for a democracy like the U.S..

Danby and his colleagues therefore conclude that the only feasibly path forward for the U.S. is to implement a national maglev system. Maglev, they predict, will be as fundamental to the 21st century as mechanized road transport, airplanes, railroads and shipping were to the 20th.

A maglev overview

The maglev advantages of maglev, based on the Danby-Powell-Jordan report, can be summarized as follows:

· Independence from oil (it runs electrically).

· Environmental cleanliness.

. The incidental of use of maglev technology to store bulk amounts of electric energy at low cost without damaging the environment, something that is not currently possible. This would eliminate the need for gas and oil-fired plants to provide energy at peak consumption periods and would increase the widespread usability of highly variable energy sources like wind and solar power facilities.

· Greater energy efficiency than alternative transportation modes.

· Greater safety (than, for example, travel by road).

· Lower expense in terms of travel cost.

· Independence from weather.

· Much faster travel than alternative surface transportation.

· Immunity from traffic delays.

· Much lower maintenance than alternative technologies.

· Much longer service life than alternative systems.

· Because of the affordability and speed of maglev, it will be possible for people to live much farther from their workplaces than highway commuting presently makes possible. The average worker 100 miles from his or her workplace will be able to make the journey in much less than an hour. This will open up new employment opportunities and work patterns, a benefit which can be substantially enlarged by the development of telecommunications-driven workforces, or telecommunities (which Danby and his colleagues do not even take into account, but about which we'll have more to say later).

· It will become feasible to build new housing developments far from urban centers, thereby making affordable housing much more widely available, and at the same time opening up a new real estate boom.

Danby and his associates concede that maglev cannot meet all transportation needs and that the construction of a national maglev system will not mean we won't still use other the older forms. Their argument is rather that by instituting a national maglev network we will significantly reduce our dependence on the older forms and open up a wider range of transportation options for everyone.

In evaluating their report, it is natural to take into account the fact that their enterprise is commercial and that they presumably hope to reap financial reward if the U.S. adopts this technology on a widescale basis – via patents, consulting fees, entrepreneurial shareholdings flowing from their expertise, or other means. These circumstances do not in themselves call into question the validity of any of their assertions, since the development of most if not all of the major technologies that have defined the American economy (and the economies of all industrialized nations) has involved the efforts of entrepreneurs seeking financial reward.

There are, however, some immediate critical impression created by the Danby-Powell-Jordan report. One is the readiness with which the authors dismiss alternative systems such as hydrogen-based fuels and electrical systems. While these are beset by problems it seems reasonable to surmise that if they could benefit from a government-led development initiative as politically (and perhaps financially) as massive as that required to launch a national maglev system, solutions to these problems can and will be found.

Moreover, in view of the deep entrenchment in our economic system of the conventional transportation technologies, it seems unlikely that these will go away quickly, but will rather undergo various forms of technological transformation which will similarly be driven by considerable inventive ingenuity as economic and environmental pressures mount – especially if programs to refurbish existing technologies are given the benefit of government finance, leadership and the kind of sense of national urgency that the authors are pleading for on behalf of maglev. Thus, the authors' seemingly somewhat grudging admission, about the future holding a mix of conventional systems with maglev technology, is probably likelier than their role as maglev advocates would lead them to prefer.

At the same time, several key points are greatly to the authors' credit:

First, the scientific credentials of the authors is extraordinarily impressive.

Secondly, an overwhelming mass of evidence is now available from both within and outside the U.S. showing the viability of maglev as a transportation infrastructure suitable for national implementation in the U.S..

Thirdly, the sense of urgency that the authors' report conveys has no appearance of being spurious; if anything, their deliberate, staid approach has probably greatly underestimated the seriousness of the U.S.'s national need to focus its attention on maglev technology at the highest level of government.

Fourth, in their desire to focus narrowly on the most quantitatively supportable arguments to sustain their case, the authors have omitted from their report two of the greatest possible reasons that arise for the U.S. to focus national attention on maglev. These are (a) the fact that the construction of a new national infrastructure of this kind will be a boost to the U.S. economy of virtually incalculable proportions, and (b) the fact that it can reasonably be expected to trigger an even greater stimulus to America's national psyche. Demoralized by economic woes and the long and wearying experience in Iraq, with its divisiveness and national fatigue at home and a demoralizing erosion of the U.S.'s standing around the world (as confirmed by independent polls), the American national consciousness is sorely in need of a new national beginning that will be capable of restoring faith in the country's historical self-perception as a world leader in innovation. There could hardly be a better way to achieve this than by making a national commitment to become the world's showcase for a state-of-the-art transportation technology that will be economically more effective than anything available anywhere else, technologically cutting-edge and environmentally clean -- all features that will define America anew as the technological driver of the 21st century.

For this to happen, and if maglev is to deliver the national benefits of which it is capable, it must become a national system, just as the railroads, highways and airline services were developed. Danby, Powell and Jordan call for a maglev network that connects all U.S. metropolitan areas, "including the urban cores and the surrounding suburbs, into a seamless whole." They propose a 16 000-mile network built on the rights of way along the existing 43 000-mile Interstate Highway System, also using existing railroad routes. The estimated construction cost, including stations: some $300 billion. To put this into perspective, they argue, it should be borne in mind that at present the U.S. spends around $1400 billion a year on automobile, truck, airplane and railroad travel, a figure that comes to $28 trillion ($28 000 billion) -- without adjusting for inflation, increased transport demand and rising oil prices; by this reckoning, a national maglev system will cost only 0.6 percent of currently projected transport expenditures.

As Danby, Powell and Jordan envisage it, everyone in the U.S. will eventually live within a few miles of a maglev station, for long-distance as well as urban use. A two-way maglev track (or "guideway") built on a right-of-way narrower than 50 feet will, they say, be able to transport more than 100,000 people per day - more than a six-lane highway – "with virtually no environmental pollution and noise, and minimal impact on the land."

Danby and his colleagues point out that because maglev is electrically driven, it will encourage the use of clean energy sources like wind, solar systems and nuclear power. (One of the implications of maglev will, in fact, be that the U.S. will have to generate more electricity, and it is one of the theses of the present book that in tandem with maglev implementation the U.S. should adopt a wide use of nuclear power -- see our later chapter on this.) According to the Danby group, a U.S. maglev system will cut carbon dioxide emissions by billions of tons a year, since the hydrocarbons, nitrogen oxides and ozone currently emitted by automobiles, trucks and aircraft will be drastically reduced. Additionally, pollution caused by oil spills and by the mining and processing of billions of tons of coal will be eradicated.

What's holding things up?

If even a significant part of the Danby-Powell group's arguments are valid, the question arises: why aren't the federal government and Wall Street rushing to join forces in implementing a national maglev system? Danby and company offer three answers:

1. To think maglev, you have to think long-term. But politicians (and therefore the government agencies they control) think only as far as the next election, while Wall Street thinks as far as the next quarter's earnings report.

2. Maglev is perceived as unaffordable. Both federal and state agencies have huge deficits, the economy is in the doldrums and there isn't enough private investment capital available to fund such a major infrastructural initiative.

3 .Moves to introduce a major change in our existing national transportation systems are powerfully resisted by the vested interests who control those systems and do not want to see their spheres of influence diminished.

Let's look at these three theories.

As far as the short-term visions of politicians and private investors are concerned, the group has a good point, in that both politicians and investors do have planning horizons that favor fairly quick returns rather than long-term projects that require persistence and patience over the long term. Politicians want to report tangible results to their voters by the time their next campaign comes around, while private investment fund managers are under pressure to show their principals early and ongoing proof that their investment is earning healthy returns. With regard to the latter, though, the Danby group overstates the case somewhat by saying that investors tend to look not much beyond the next quarter, because many investors are in fact comfortable to look at a profit horizon of a few years. Since the group has stated that private investment in maglev should be recoverable "within a few years", a realistically marketable five-year financial plan shouldn't be that hard to formulate.

Regarding the unaffordability of maglev, it is true that the U.S. economy is today, and has been for some time, under considerable financial pressure – perhaps the most dangerous combination of pressures since the Crash of 1929. But just as there were ways to pull the U.S. out of the great depression that followed the Crash, so there are ways to pull us out of the country's present economic condition. A national maglev initiative is, in fact, one of these ways. According to the Danby group's figures, maglev will save the country money in numerous ways and generally be economically more effective than any of our presently struggling transportation technologies. So it will be a fiscally remedial step for the U.S. just on those grounds alone. But perhaps more importantly, it can realistically be expected to be a wealth generator, for all the reasons already mentioned. Not least among these is the psychological effect it will have in restoring national (including investor) morale.

With respect to the obstruction of maglev efforts by vested interested with a stake in existing technologies which they do not want to see replaced, there is no reason to suppose that this is not an important factor retarding maglev introduction. But this is nothing new. Controllers of older technologies have always done what they could to preserve the longevity of their fiefdoms as much as possible. It is in the nature of economies, and of basic human psychology, for this to happen. But new technologies have come about anyway, because nobody, not even the most powerful corporate group, can indefinitely block a technology whose time has come, especially if the general public is in favor of change. They can at best postpone it, or influence the determination of the country that is first to implement it or which exerts the most power over its uses and standard forms.

Thus, while all the factors identified by the Danby group no doubt have roles in the circumstances of maglev's slow progress in the U.S., the real problem, which the group seems to have missed, isn't financial, or even political in the narrow sense, as much as it is imaginative. Making a five or even ten-year financial bet isn't unheard of for investors, even if common sense tells us that investors would obviously like to start making a profit as soon as possible. What puts investors off, however, is investing in something that's not just an interesting innovation on existing technology but represents a quantum leap into a new technological world. Americans like to think of themselves as future-oriented people, but whether or not they really are is highly debatable. Loving gadgets which incrementally enhance our convenience in a myriad of small ways isn't the same thing as hungering for large-scale change. America may have been born in revolution, but for all that it's in many ways an inherently conservative country whose culture is geared to incremental small improvements rather than sudden sweeping changes.

The main problem with maglev, then, is that it is *strange*. It represents a vast change in national direction and long-accustomed habits which is an unknown quantity to most Americans. The existing technologies may be creaking, they may have for practical purposes broken down, they may be fiscally ruinous, they may be environmentally catastrophic, they may be obstructing American progress and prosperity and hurting the lifestyles and well-being of millions upon millions of Americans, but they are at least familiar. They have been around a long time and, such as they are, and with all their faults, represent the devil we all know. Generations of Americans have grown up with automobiles, trucks, and the rest of the established infrastructure. They are part of our culture, our folklore, of the fabric of our society, of (in a literal as well as metaphorical sense) the very air we breathe.

How have the proponents of maglev responded to these facts? The answer can be quickly seen by anyone who takes the time to look over the array of currently available books and articles on the subject. They tend to fall into two groups. One consists of technical papers in which technicians appear to be writing for other technicians. The other consists of popular communications in which maglev is presented as akin to science fiction, or as something which is so science-fictionish in concept that the writer must make a special point of explaining that it is not fiction but a real and currently available technology (as in the *Metropolis* magazine article cited above).

The imaginative and psychological barrier

This pervasive science-fiction flavor, which somehow permeates the writings of even enthusiastic maglev advocates, stamps maglev as something on the edge of reality rather than as a serious and urgent national policy option. It is an imaginative and psychological obstacle which lies at the heart of the U.S.'s slowness in engaging the technology. For example, a 1991 book called *Supertrains*, by Joseph Vranich, about various types of high-speed rail technology including maglev, carries an introduction by thriller writer Tom Clancy and a blurb on the back cover by science fiction writer Ray Bradbury. These may have been good choices on the publisher's part from the standpoint of marketing the book, but identifying maglev with creators of fantasy doesn't help sell the technology to the public as a realistic policy option. Similarly, a 2007 article in the magazine *Popular Mechanics*, headlined *Super Trains: Plans to Fix U.S. Rail Could End Road & Sky Gridlock*, by John Quain,[13] describes a maglev test track developed in Torrey Pines, Southern California, as being reminiscent of the guideway to the monorail at Walt Disney World. "As I climb aboard the chassis," Quain writes, "a researcher waves enthusiastically from a nearby control room like a parent sending his child on a first roller coaster ride." The article is favorable to maglev, affirming that "the technology used on this modest test track may power a new generation of ground transportation in the United States." But it still projects the atmosphere of a visit to a kind of fun fair, or a novelty sideshow like the Ripley's Believe It Or Not exhibitions – even though Quain, like Hall in *Metropolis*, dutifully points out to his readers that "commercial high-speed train travel is no mere fantasy", a disclaimer that once again acknowledges the temptation to see it as such.

Nor does it help that the company that built the installation that Quain visited is called General Atomics, a name that sounds like something from an old *Buck Rogers* or *Flash Gordon* comic strip, apart from unfortunately conveying the false impression that maglev is nuclear-powered (in fact, its electricity can come from any power source).

These circumstances don't warrant criticisms of any of these media products, whose authors are simply telling the story as best as they can. Maybe, for instance, the California site *does* suggest the Walt Disney World monorail, in which case a journalist who notices this can hardly be faulted for mentioning it. But the fact remains that maglev *as a concept*, apart from its cost and logistics, political or otherwise, has not yet been effectively sold to the American public or to the social and cultural leaderships who influence public perception, and this is why maglev development has been moving so painfully slowly. The problem isn't technological (even though maglev certainly needs ongoing research to refine it, something that will have to be built into any implementation program), or financial, or a lack of compelling evidence in favor of maglev, or even political in the sense that sinister groups are conspiring to block the new technology. Opponents of maglev don't have to resort to conspiracy because there is no major maglev movement to conspire against. The reason for this is a public education and awareness gap – a challenge of informing the public and igniting its imagination. Quain attests: "As a proof of concept, the General Atomics maglev is impressive, but to fully grasp the potential of high-speed trains in this country, you still have to use your imagination." He adds: "A few hours after my ride on the experimental maglev track, I find myself back in the real world behind the wheel of a rental car, baking in bumper-to-bumper traffic on Interstate 5. As I fret about getting to the airport on time, I wonder how many other drivers around me are wishing there was a more efficient way to travel. There may be a better way – I just tried it."

The challenge is to reach out to the U.S. public and convince it that maglev isn't something beyond "the real world", but very much of the here and now. The speed and vigor with which we engage and adopt maglev will go a long way toward shaping the condition of our real world for much of this century.

But maglev is just the beginning...

NOTES

1. Ambrose, Stephen E., *Nothing Like It in the World: The Men Who Built the Transcontinental Railroad, 1863-1869* (2000), P.4

2. http://arstechnica.com/business/news/2007/04/world-economic-forum-releases-annual-it-rankings-us-slides.ars

3. Slabbert, N.J., *The Technologies of Peace*, HARVARD INTERNATIONAL REVIEW (May 2, 2007), http://www.harvardir.org/index.php?page=article&id=1336&p=

4. Bodanis, David, *Slow Forward: Is The Speed Of Technological Change An Illusion?*, DISCOVER(June 19, 2006), http://discovermagazine.com/2006/jun/feature-one

5. Slabbert, N.J., *Retro-Techno Nation* (May, 2007), TRUMAN LIBRARY REPORTS

6. Eilperin, Juliet, *Military Sharpens Focus on Climate Change:A Decline in Resources Is Projected to Cause Increasing Instability Overseas*, WASHINGTON POST (April 15, 2007), http://www.washingtonpost.com/wp dyn/content/article/2007/04/14/AR2007041401209.html

7. BBC NEWS, *U.S. generals urge climate action* (April 15, 2007), http://news.bbc.co.uk/go/pr/fr/-/2/hi/americas/6557803.stm

8. Slabbert, N.J., *Morton and Lucia White: The Anatomy of Antiurbanism*, URBAN LAND (July 2007)

9. Szep, Jason, *As Oil Rises, Americans Rediscover The Railroad*, REUTERS (June 12, 2008), http://www.reuters.com/article/inDepthNews/idUSN0428607520080612

10. Milmo, Dan, *The End Of The Budget Airline?*, GUARDIAN (May 23, 2008), http://www.guardian.co.uk/business/2008/may/23/theairlineindustry.ryanair/print

11. Hall, Peter, *The Maglev Train Is The Future Of Twenty-First-Century Transit. Why Won't We See It In The U.S. Anytime Soon?*, January 1, 2004 METROPOLISMAG.COM, http://www.metropolismag.com/story/20040101/speed

12. Danby, Gordon; Jordan, James; Powell, James, *The Urgency of Reclaiming the United States Lead in Magnetic Levitation (Maglev) Transportation: How U.S. Maglev Technology Can Help Sustain Continued Economic Development After Global Oil Production Peaks (2005)*, http://magneticglide.com/reclaim.pdf

13. Quain, John, *Super Trains: Plans to Fix U.S. Rail Could End Road & Sky Gridlock*, POPULAR MECHANICS (Dec 2007), http://www.popularmechanics.com/technology/transportation/4232548.html?nav=hpPrint&do=print

CHAPTER 2

NANOTECHNOLOGY AND THE SOCIAL CRITICISM OF SCIENCE

Despite economic crises, war, energy challenges, terrorist threats, climate change, AIDS and the evolution of new strains of bacteria that increasingly resist known antibiotics, there's much to be optimistic about.

Despite our technological lag, if we manage our intellectual assets properly we can use science and technology to develop a global civilization of peace, progress, dignity and greatness of spirit in the 21st century.

Not paradise, though. Differences between cultures will continue to create tension. Freedom means risk. As long as we pit our limited minds against the awesome complexity of nature, we'll make mistakes: failing is how we learn. As long as we dare to invent, there will be unintended consequences of our inventions. We'll never foresee the implications of every innovation.

But all the above leaves an immense amount for us to accomplish. The 21st century can end poverty, environmental degradation and the squabbling over resources that has been a major cause of war. It can bring a new era in which global scientific cooperation becomes the basis of a new international civil society -- a great stabilizing force in which the knowledge-sharing becomes as geopolitically important as military and economic alliances were in the past. And while it's unlikely we'll ever be safe from disease, we have the potential to end the chief diseases that have up to now afflicted millions. New medical tools are within reach to equip us better than ever to safeguard human health and promote human physical and mental well-being.

But this will require new attitudes. We must resolve to bring about a new scientific and technological era. This will require a bigger role for government than we've become used to. Many people will dislike this because (a) they don't like expanding government intervention, and (b) they believe technology is the private sector's job alone.

But consider this. If we had an Abe Lincoln representing the entrepreneurs of the maglev industry, it would do the maglev advocacy movement some good, don't you think? As we've mentioned, Lincoln was actively promoting an emerging technological infrastructure which he helped develop – the railroads.

Historian Stephen E. Ambrose calls Lincoln "one of the great railroad lawyers in the West" and acknowledges that he played a key role in inaugurating "the greatest building project of the nineteenth century" – America's transcontinental railroad. Lincoln's role in creating his country's national railroad system was pivotal; Ambrose calls him "the driving force". Lincoln's contribution was motivational, organizational and financial. He wanted the country bound together physically and socially. This sense of national purpose was swiftly translated into financial support for railroad entrepreneurs. According to Ambrose, "Government aid, which began with Lincoln, took many forms."

We today have much to learn from the excitement, commitment, national drive, vision and practical support that Lincoln brought to developing the railroads. He didn't think government could solve all problems: he encouraged entrepreneurs. At the same time he understood that as vast and urgent an undertaking as a nationwide rail system wouldn't come about soon if left to private initiative alone, with its time-limited investor responsibilities. He saw that government must spearhead the national development of a vital new technological infrastructure.

Lincoln also understood that technological innovation is bigger than politics. This connects well with our current technological experience, since no U.S. administration of recent decades couldn't and shouldn't have done much more to promote new technology. But more to the point is what we can and should do now, together. In this regard, it seems plausible that if Lincoln were alive today, maglev wouldn't be the only technology he'd promote with all his might. Another would very probably be nanotechnology.

The technology of the micro-world

Nanotechnology is about developing appliances and other products so small they can't be seen by the naked eye, by manipulating molecules and atoms. The name of the discipline is derived from *nanos* -- Greek for *dwarf*.

Nanotechnology is arguably the most important area of current technological advance, yet, like all science, it has ancient roots.

It was foreshadowed by numerous earlier philosophical and scientific thinkers who speculated about terrains beyond the visible.
Ideas of worlds within worlds absorbed great scientific figures like
French philosopher-mathematician Blaise Pascal (1623–1662), Italian
physician Marcello Malpighi (1628-1694), who pioneered microscopic anatomy, and Dutch mathematician Nicolaas Hartsoeker (1656-
1725), who theorized about little men – "homunculi" – existing in
semen. American science fiction writer Ray Cummings (1887-1957)
wrote of the micro-world in his novel *The Girl in the Golden Atom*
(1922). British scientist, philosopher, polymath and science popularizer Edmund E. Fournier d'Albe (1868-1933), in his 1907 non-fiction
book *Two New Worlds*, forecast the conquest of both the worlds of
the atomically small (the "infra-world") and the astronomically vast
(the "supra-World), consisting of planets and galaxies.

Fournier believed humans would create marvels of technological transformation, reaching into the finest structure of matter as
well as to the stars. He wrote of the "chemistry and biology of
the infraworld", and of humanity's destiny "to pierce into the in-
nermost recesses of nature, to mould natural forces to our will, to
make life happy and glorious for ourselves and our kind, to assert
our supremacy over disease and death, to conquer and rule the
universe in virtue of the infinite power within us – such is our task
here and now."

Man, he wrote, governs the earth. "It is changing its face for
him. Other beings are flourishing or disappearing at his pleasure.
Soon he will govern the more powerful elements, the sea and the
wind, and the heat of the sun ... By-and-by, also, the earth will show
signs of becoming uninhabitable. He will readjust it, and bring it
nearer to the sun or further away. More likely, perhaps, he will discover that Jupiter offers superior inducements to colonists, or he
will come to some understanding with the inhabitants of Jupiter,
if such there be, with regard to future co-operation. It is pretty
certain that nothing will bar the conquering march of human intelligence, except a similar intelligence. Either man will come upon a
civilization resembling his own or he will not. In the former case
he will, after a trial of strength, perhaps, ally himself with that
other race. In the latter alternative he will mould all matter to his
will. He will control the sun with a switch like an electric lamp.
His physical acts will require a minimum expenditure of energy;
but they will let loose or guide all the huge forces of the universe.
In proceeding to greater conquests, man simply draws upon the al-
mighty power within him. He is not alone in either world, material
or mental. He has infinite reserves in both. His physical organism is

specially adapted to the conquest of the earth. When he proceeds to greater spheres it may change; but the change, we may anticipate, will not be as great as his change of power."

The extension of human scientific and technological power outlined in Fournier's treatise *Two New Worlds* was so startling for its time that it was erroneously described as science fiction by distinguished French-American mathematician Benoit B. Mandelbrot, (1924-), in his 1983 book *The Fractal Geometry of Nature*, an error repeated in a 2003 paper by P. V. Grujic, of the Institute of Physics in Belgrade, Serbia.[1]

The term "nanotechnology" has been credited to Japanese engineer Norio Taniguchi, of Tokyo Science University, but was widely circulated by an American, *K. Eric Drexler*, notably in his 1986 book *Engines of Creation: The Coming Era of Nanotechnology*. Until fairly recently nanotechnology has been relatively remote from the awareness of the general public while being controversial among specialists, although it has now begun to appear in popular culture. The imaginative vistas and philosophical choices arising from it are at the heart of our landscape of scientific research and speculation, as evolution was a central reference-point of discourse in the late 19th century (and still is, to some extent). It's also similar to the imagination-stretching researches and theoretical constructions of physicists in the early 20th century, in areas like relativity and quantum mechanics -- work that unfolded in a small community of experts before percolating into general public awareness.

Nanotechnology is important for three reasons -- practical, conceptual and cultural. Practically, it's the likely source of tools we'll use in future to achieve vast physical changes in areas of human life ranging from medicine and manufacturing through food production to computerization and energy efficiency.

Machines of creation

A key premise of nanotechnology theory is based on the fact that deoxyribonucleic acid (DNA, the molecule that carries the genetic programming of life as we know it), functions like a computer, storing and transmitting coded information that allows molecular "engineering" to occur in the deepest organic processes. Nanotechnology postulates that if DNA can successfully "program" the creation of such complex molecular arrangements as the enormous variety of living things, including human beings, we should be able to duplicate and extend it to create substances we need, in the forms we need.

In principle, the results could range from new building materials, with properties specifically designed to suit our purposes, to microscopic medical robots and machines the size of molecules which will automatically develop molecular "seeds" into whatever we want, from a leg of lamb to an automobile. Drexler has described the emergence of an engine from a nanotechnological broth. In theory, nanotechnology holds out the promise of micromachines -- "assemblers" -- that will protect human cells from illness and ageing, rid our air and water of pollutants, create new energy sources and miracle materials, and generate all the food we could ever need.

This conception recalls futurist Arthur C. Clarke's dictum that a sufficiently advanced technology is indistinguishable from magic. It seriously envisages a situation similar to the "replicators" of the *Star Trek* television franchise -- devices converting energy into patterns that create, seemingly out of thin air, a range of items like clothing and foodstuffs. Nanotechnology tantalizingly holds out the prospect of something which, though not identical with the fictional replicator, is very like it.

According to a report by the Project on Emerging Nanotechnologies, a group that promotes nanotechnology, three to four nanotechnology products were coming on the market every week by April 2008 – a list of hundreds of products including food, clothing, cosmetics, packaging, paints and household appliance applications. However, many products marketed as nanotechnology may not really deserve this label, bearing it purely to benefit from its leading-edge connotation. So the real era of nanotechnology lies ahead of us. Its possibilities, though, are genuine and far-reaching. In his afterword to the 1996 edition of *Engines of Creation*, Drexel observed that two years after the 1986 edition's publication, William DeGrado at the DuPont Company reported the first substantial progress in "de novo protein design". Drexel wrote: "There is now a journal titled *Protein Engineering*, and a growing stream of results. What is more, additional paths to the same goal have emerged, based on different molecules and methods. The 1988 Nobel Prize in Chemistry was awarded to Cram, Pedersen, and Lehn for their work in building large molecular structures from self-assembling parts. The 1995 Feynman Prize in Nanotechnology was awarded to Nadrian Seeman of New York University for the design and synthesis of DNA structures joined to form a cubical framework. Chemists have started to speak of doing 'nanochemistry.' In recent years, molecular self-assembly has emerged as a field in its own right."

In his foreword to the 1996 edition of Drexel's book, Professor Marvin Minsky, of the Massachusetts Institute of Technology (and widely recognized as one of the world's most distinguished scientists), confirmed that "Drexler has built on the soundest areas of present-day technical knowledge." And he noted: "*Engines of Creation* begins with the insight that what we can do depends on what we can build. This leads to a careful analysis of possible ways to stack atoms. Then Drexler asks, 'What could we build with those atom-stacking mechanisms?' For one thing, we could manufacture assembly machines much smaller even than living cells, and make materials stronger and lighter than any available today. Hence, better spacecraft. Hence, tiny devices that can travel along capillaries to enter and repair living cells. Hence, the ability to heal disease, reverse the ravages of age, or make our bodies speedier or stronger than before. And we could make machines down to the size of viruses, machines that would work at speeds which none of us can yet appreciate. And then, once we learned how to do it, we would have the option of assembling these myriads of tiny parts into intelligent machines, perhaps based on the use of trillions of nanoscopic parallel-processing devices which make descriptions, compare them to recorded patterns, and then exploit the memories of all their previous experiments. Thus those new technologies could change not merely the materials and means we use to shape our physical environment, but also the activities we would then be able to pursue inside whichever kind of world we make." Minsky suggested that nanotechnology promises to change our world more meaningfully than television, radio and airplanes, the next fifty years bringing "more change than all that had come about since near-medieval times", with even greater effect on our material existence than the harnessing of electricity. He has compared prospective developments in artificial intelligence technology, which some think nanotechnology will facilitate, with the advent of language and writing.

Technology theorist Ray Kurzweil, meanwhile, has forecast that nanobots – very tiny robots – will extend human lifespans. The *Forbes/Wolfe Nanotech Report* has declared that "None of the global warming discussions mention the word 'nanotechnology'. Yet nanotechnology will eliminate the need for fossil fuels within 20 years." (This cites the potential of nanotechnology to greatly increase the energy-efficiency and cost-efficiency of solar-power capturing materials.) Writing in the 2007 edition of Drexler's book, Kurzweil has said: "Some seminal works stand out like beacons in the history of science. Newton's 'Philosophiae Naturalis Principia Mathematica' and Watson and Crick's 'A Structure for Deoxyribose Nucleic Acid' come quickly to mind. In recent decades we can add Eric Drexler's

'Engines of Creation,' which established the revolutionary new field of nanotechnology. In the twenty years since this seminal work was published, its premises and analyses have been confirmed and we are starting to apply precise molecular assembly to a wide variety of early applications from blood cell sized devices that can target cancer cells to a new generation of efficient solar panels. We can now see clearly the roadmap over the next couple of decades to the full realization of Drexler's concept of the inexpensive assembly of macro objects constructed at the nanoscale controlled by massively parallel information processes, the fulfillment of which will enable us to solve problems -- energy, environmental degradation, poverty, and disease to name a few -- that have plagued humankind for eons."

The Nanotechnology Wars

Nanotechnology has attracted opponents. Some don't believe its potential is real (at least in the forms and timelines described by its advocates). Others fear that it is indeed real and might unleash a dangerous new set of uncontrollable technologies. Interestingly, these two sets of concerns *seem to coexist side by side* in the minds of at least some critics. Such is the intensity of some of those who profess skepticism toward nanotechnology's realism that it's hard to believe anyone would devote so much energy to demolishing something they really believe is nonsense. What comes across more convincingly is fear – not that nanotechnology *won't* deliver on its promises but that it *will*. Although widely circulated books and articles have been written about it, both to promote it and to criticize its claims as a mirage, it remains strangely on the edges of public awareness. But within a substantial and rapidly growing circle of technology policy debate and science journalism, it has struck a nerve.

What seems clear is that if even a fraction of nanotechnology's promise comes true in the next few decades, the implications for the world are immense. So great is this potential that it is, in a way, nanotechnology's own worst enemy, because like the potential benefits of maglev technology we mentioned earlier, much nanotechnology forecasting sounds too much like science fiction for its own good. However, a sober review of the history of science and technology shows that it's dangerous to dismiss technological possibilities just because they sound like science fiction.

Moreover, when minds as bright and as scientifically informed as Minsky's express technological opinions, we should listen. This is in part why the National Science Foundation's 2008 budget included $390 million for nanotechnology research and development, aimed at increasing basic knowledge of the subatomic, atomic and molecular structure of materials, and of seeking ways to build micro-machines of previously unimagined size and capabilities.

One of the most compelling arguments for developing nanotechnology is that much if not all of it appears to continue or logically extend previous scientific work, especially the mapping of the atom and the molecule that took place in the late 19th and early 20th centuries. That work led to molecular biology and the discovery of the gene. Along a separate but related route the same developments led to the computer microchip. In its full-blown, most technologically ambitious form, nanotechnology is a convergence of the invention-and-discovery trajectories of atomic physics, molecular biology, genetic engineering, medicine and computer science (the micro-storage and manipulation of information). Appreciating this convergence is a key to appreciating the potential of technological innovation, because it shows us that while invention and discovery can't be predicted, there's a direction of tenable extrapolation that makes certain expectations reasonable.

We mentioned that nanotechnology is important practically, conceptually and culturally. We've indicated some practical considerations. The *conceptual* reason is that nanotechnology powerfully illustrates the unity of scientific endeavor and the interdisciplinary nature of scientific research and technological innovation. (The terms "interdisciplinary" and "cross-disciplinary" have different nuances but as these aren't critical to this book we're going to use them more or less interchangeably.)

These interdisciplinary linkages aren't just historically interesting: they're also important for practical policymaking purposes because they show *scientific advance as a whole whose parts are closely interwoven.* This can be seen by examining the cross-disciplinary interests of many pioneers of scientific and technological development. There comes a point where scientific and technological innovations benefit from the organizational power of intensive specialization, but the imaginative driving force of innovation needs conceptual room. Its state of mind has a sprawling character and a somewhat untidy excitement, irreverent toward disciplinary boundaries, that's uncomfortable to many administrators and lovers of narrow academic specialization. We ignore this state of mind at our peril, for it's where much of the energy and originality of science comes from. *Nanotechnology is presently permeated with this state of mind.* It spills into many disciplines.

Thirdly, the *cultural* importance of nanotechnology is that it represents many of the most vexing challenges that science and technology pose for our culture. Nanotechnology forces us to re-think our long-established distinction between pure science and the applied science we call technology. This traditional distinction conveniently helps us divide the scientific community neatly into (a) those who perform the theoretical labors of scientific specula-tion and research, in the dignity of academic environments, and (b) those who apply scientific knowledge in the rough-and-tumble of business and government. In the 17th and 18th centuries, Isaac New-ton held down a civil service job as head of Britain's mint, but this bread-and-butter role was separate from his intellectual pursuits. In the 19th century, no one would have thought of Charles Darwin as anything but a scholar removed from the hurly-burly of practi-cal affairs. Nor, in the first half the 20th century, did Albert Einstein form a company to commercialize his theories.

But times changed within Einstein's lifetime. He did find him-self increasingly drawn into political matters, and by mid-century physicists such as Robert Oppenheimer found themselves immersed heavily in the practical political implications of nuclear science.

The ethics of the ethicists

In subsequent decades, the emergence of computer technolo-gies and genetic engineering blurred the distinction between sci-ence and business, as technological entrepreneurs ventured into business to exploit their intellectual products for financial gain. As science became increasingly positioned as a source of marketable assets, its products became subject to the same regulatory interest that politicians applied to any commercial commodities. The ethics of scientific activity and of the regulation of technological products became a quasi-profession. And interesting questions arise here about *the ethics of ethicists*. When does the prudent scrutiny of scientific products become an obstruction to the healthy develop-ment of science? At what point does social criticism of science morph into a love of political power over science and technology, or into a desire to market career-enhancing critiques of science and technology in the forms of books, professorships, consulting con-tracts, board memberships and television appearances? Are some environmental organizations concerned less with the fate of the environment than with publicity and power? Since nanotechnology promises to generate even more critical discussion than nuclear technology, these cultural questions are important to our under-standing of it.

Nanotechnology is also culturally significant because of the extent to which it requires us to stretch our imaginations. When Einstein revised our notions of space and time, numerous popularizations of his ideas were produced. But the ideas remained theoretical. No one marketed a working time machine or a portal to other dimensions. However, if even some of the potential that nanotechnology's champions claim for it is achievable, it portends so remarkable a leap in humanity's power over both the physical and biological worlds as to herald the dawn of a new kind of human existence.

Nanotechnology's demands on our attention are bolstered by the fact that the U.S. Government's 2009 budget allocated $1.5 billion to support nanotechnology research and development in thirteen federal agencies, including Defense , Energy, National Institutes of Health, National Aeronautics and Space Administration, Environmental Protection Agency, Agriculture, Homeland Security and Transportation. The funding fell under the 21st Century Nanotechnology Research and Development Act of 2003. In announcing its promulgation, the White House said:[2]

"Nanotechnology offers the promise of breakthroughs that will revolutionize the way we detect and treat disease, monitor and protect the environment, produce and store energy, and build complex structures as small as an electronic circuit or as large as an airplane. Nanotechnology is expected to have a broad and fundamental impact on many sectors of the economy, leading to new products, new businesses, new jobs, and even new industries.

"Nanotechnology is the ability to work at the atomic and molecular levels, corresponding to lengths of approximately 1 -- 100 nanometers, or 1/100,000th the diameter of a human hair. Nanotechnology is not merely the study of small things; it is the research and development of materials, devices, and systems that exhibit physical, chemical, and biological properties that are different from those found at larger scales...

"Nanotechnology promises to be both evolutionary and revolutionary--improving and creating entirely new products and processes in areas from electronics to health care. Carbon nanotubes are essentially sheets of graphite rolled into extremely narrow tubes -- a few nanometers in diameter. Because of their nanoscale size and excellent conductivity, carbon nanotubes are being studied as the possible building blocks of future electronic devices. Nanotechnology may one day enable the detection of disease on the cellular level and the targeting of treatment only to tissues where it is needed in a patient's body, potentially alleviating many unpleasant and sometimes harmful side effects. Nano-manufacturing of parts and materials 'from the bottom up'--by assembling them on an atom-by-atom basis--may one day be used to reduce waste and pollution in the manufacturing process.

"Nanosensors already are being developed to allow fast, reliable, real-time monitoring for everything from chemical attack to environmental leaks. Nanotechnology can help provide clean energy. For example, carbon nanotubes are a form of nanomaterial with many potential applications. Woven into a cable, carbon nanotubes could provide electricity transmission lines with substantially improved performance over current power lines. Certain nanomaterials show promise for use in making more efficient solar cells and the next-generation catalysts and membranes that will be used in hydrogen-powered fuel cells."

Yet controversiality persists. In one sense this is healthy; in another it is potentially disturbing when one considers that the advance of applied nuclear technology was significantly retarded by public campaigning. And that was technology that was already in successful use. Nanotechnology still needs a sustained research effort before it can deliver. The nanotechnology industry itself is divided about the future direction of the field. Some want it to stay with short-term deliverables; others are more interested in its larger potential. Exchanges can be lively. In 2004 the president of the NanoBusiness Alliance, F. Mark Modzelewski, contrasted the "grave and serious" issues facing the nanotechnology industry with the "comic relief of the writings of Eric Drexler".[3] Nobel Prizewinning chemist Richard E. Smalley has called Drexler's vision "just a dream".[4]

The new industry of nanotechnology guides

In 2005 a book came out with the title *Nano-Hype: the Truth Behind the Nanotechnology Buzz*, by David M. Berube. It contrasted nanotechnology's more ambitious claims and its trivial deliverables to date, which, rather than changing the world, seemed limited to mundane things like stain-resistant trousers and scratch-resistant paint. One of its reviewers was Dr. James Lewis.[5] Its theme, Lewis wrote, was "the extensive misinformation that has accumulated as a result of hyperbole on the part of both those who advocate for and those who warn against" nanotechnology. "The many and complex debates and discussions that have accompanied the emergence of nanotechnology from the realm of theorists, futurists, and experimental scientists into the arenas of government, business, and public perceptions are clearly described, explored, and referenced," according to Lewis, but "the effort to distinguish hype from reality is less successful... Berube makes an excellent start in framing the arguments and the participation by consumers, citizens, and commentators in guiding nanotechnology development, but he provides limited guidance to making sense of the issues. Useful insights are presented, but it usually remains unclear whether a given example represents hype or not.

"A brief introduction to the agencies through which the US federal government supports science and technology development-makes clear that the government's decision to adopt an initiative to encourage nanotechnology (NNI, the National Nanotechnology Initiative, which was institutionalized in 2003 via the 21st Century Nanotechnology Research and Development Act) was exceptional. Prof Berube establishes his contention that the success of the NNI is jeopardized by the potential of a public backlash fueled by unrealistic perceptions about nanotechnology. He then proceeds to analyze current discussions by describing in detail the individuals, organizations, initiatives, and controversies that have defined public discussion."

In Lewis's view, "Berube seems to agree with several other quoted sources that simply denying the feasibility of molecular manufacturing is not an adequate response to Drexler's vision. A better course is to show that the consequences of molecular manufacturing are manageable and still distant." The problem he detected in the book was that "Exactly where the hype is in all of this remains unclear." Berube, he wrote, "succeeds in describing how nanotechnology has been communicated to diverse audiences. However, the effort to distinguish hype from reality is less successful. Potential exaggerations from various sources are flagged and most debates are described in some detail, but no clean guidelines are presented for identifying whether a statement is indeed hype, or merely sounds fantastic because reality will bring radical change."

The issues Berube raised were very important, Lewis observed, "but what is realistic and what is hype, how do we identify the real problems, and how do we develop wise policy to deal with them?"

This book and Lewis's review are particularly interesting for two reasons. One is that both demonstrate that nanotechnology has "arrived". A sign that a subject has acquired a significant place in public discourse is the demand it creates for popular guidebooks. Although Berube's book title, designed to hook the eye from an advertising and bookselling point of view, suggests the revelation of unsuspected truths, it's in fact a summary and exegesis of published materials. The mount and diversity of these materials (which creates the market for a guidebook) shows that even if nanotechnology hasn't yet come anywhere near fulfilling its product potential, it's certainly spawned a substantial media industry catering to a large subculture, of both of which Berube is and his book are part. This is further indicated by the forum in which Lewis's review appeared: a publication of the Foresight Nanotech Institute, a nonprofit organization based in Palo Alto, California. The institute was co-founded in 1986 by Drexler and his former spouse, Christine Peterson, under the name Foresight Institute. (Drexler has left the institute.)

Foresight is one of a multitude of nanotechnology interest groups, consulting entities, academic entities, projects and publishing ventures related to nanotechnology. A Google search for "nanotechnology" on December 10 2008 turned up 10 500 000 items in 0.08 seconds. An Amazon Books search turned up 12 064 results for "nanotechnology", with titles such as *Nanotechnology For Dummies; Understanding Nanotechnology; Nanotechnology: A Gentle Introduction to the Next Big Idea; Nanotechnology: Science, Innovation, and Opportunity; Soft Machines: Nanotechnology and Life; Nanotechnology Demystified; Nanofuture: What's Next For Nanotechnology; Nanophysics and Nanotechnology: An Introduction to Modern Concepts in Nanoscience; Nanotechnology: Understanding Small Systems; Introduction to Nanotechnology; Nanotechnology: Basic Science and Emerging Technologies; Nanotechnology 101; Nanotechnology: Health and Environmental Risks; An Introduction to Nanosciences and Nanotechnology; Investing in Nanotechnology: Think Small. Win Big; Introduction to Nanoscale Science and Technology; Nanotechnology in Biology and Medicine: Methods, Devices, and Applications; Introduction to Nanoelectronics: Science, Nanotechnology, Engineering, and Applications; Our Molecular Future: How Nanotechnology, Robotics, Genetics and Artificial Intelligence Will Transform Our World;* and so on.

The second interesting thing about Lewis's review leads directly off the above facts. It's the frustration Lewis expresses in finding no substantive guidance from Berube in evaluating nanotechnology. The purported "truth behind the hype" really boils down to the advice that, well, we mustn't rush too hastily into decisions about nanotechnology. This position is related to a popular approach to scientific and technological advance which amounts to a kind of professional fence-sitting about technological initiatives that might best called "science as mediation".[6] A brief examination of this concept will help us orientate ourselves better to nanotechnology and other areas of scientific and technological innovation.

The idea of science as mediation is illustrated by the impressive renown Berube has achieved as a commentator on nanotechnology. According to the website of The Lifeboat Foundation, he serves on the foundation's nanotechnology advisory board. The foundation describes itself as "a nonprofit nongovernmental organization dedicated to encouraging scientific advancements while helping humanity survive existential risks and possible misuse of increasingly powerful technologies, including genetic engineering, nanotechnology, and robotics/AI, as we move towards a technological singularity." (The latter term describes a postulated enormous spurt in technological innovation, such as the development of machines with self-replicating ability and/or intelligence greater than that of humans, or some other technological transformation that changes the nature of human life fundamentally.)

The foundation's site says Berube's works include testimony before the Committee to Review the National Nanotechnology Initiative, Assess the Responsible Development of Nanotechnology, and Determine the Technical Feasibility of Molecular Self Assembly, National Materials Advisory Board, National Academy of Sciences, Washington, DC, February 9-11, 2005, as well as *Claims of Techno-Visionaries: An Analysis of Nanotechnology through the Rhetoric of K. Eric Drexler and the Foresight Institute*, a paper presented at the Communication in High Risk Technologies: Global and Local Ethical Concerns Seminar, Speech Communication Association Convention, Atlanta, 31 October 1991. He is, we're told, on the advisory committees of the U.S. Environmental Protection Agency, Office of Pollution Prevention and Toxics, and the International Council on Nanotechnology, and is author of the blog *NanoHype: Nanotechnology Implications and Interactions*. When this blog was accessed on December 13 2008, a panel proclaimed that Berube has been a Principal Investigator or Co-Principal Investigator on five National Science Foundation grants totaling about $5 million.

Who has more hype? The nanotechnologists or their critics?

Out of this chain of credentials, a point arises that should provoke thought in anyone concerned about how U.S. attitudes and policies on technological innovation. This is that although Berube has been building an impressive career as a critic and interpreter of nanotechnology, he himself isn't a nanotechnologist. What, then, is his background? He is or has been, it transpires, a professor of communication studies and rhetoric teaching in the speech division of the Department of English at the University of North Carolina, having also taught film, popular culture and science fiction and been an Equity actor. In a university document published in 2000, advertising for prospective student assistants for a master's degree program in speech communication in the Department Of Theatre, Speech and Dance, Berube identified himself as associate professor of speech communication in the Department of Speech and Theater. A North Carolina State University web site called NANO@ NC STATE, describing itself as "a gateway to the dynamic world of nanotechnology" at the university, which is referenced as "an emerging leader in the field of nanotechnology", located Berube in the Communication Department of the College of Humanities & Social Sciences. It said he was "actively researching both (sic) intuitive nanotoxicology under a NIRT grant to explain how the public unpacks and understands technical human toxicological information and risks under conditions of high uncertainty." (A NIRT grant is a National Science Foundation Nanoscale: Interdisciplinary Research Teams grant.) The site added that Berube's 2008 articles include *Intuitive Toxicology: The Public Perception of Nanoscience*, in *Nanoethics: Emerging Debates* , *Future of Nano*, in *Nano-Predictions: Big Thinkers on the Smallest Technology, Stakeholder Participation* in *Nanotechnology Policy Debates*, in *Nanotechnology: Ethics and Society, Nanoscience, Water and Society*, in *Nanotechnology Applications: Solutions for Improving Water Quality, Public Acceptance of Nanomedicine: A Personal Perspective*, in *Nanomedicine*, and *A nanotale of opportunities, uncertainties and risks*, with Paul Born, in *Nano Today*.

Now, the concept of guidance being given to the U.S. in cutting-edge technological research in fields such as toxicology, technology policy, water science and policy and medicine, by a specialist in theater, speech and dance, is thought-provoking, to say the least. What is most interesting about it has less to do with Berube, who is evidently an admirable asset to his university, than with what it tells us about our attitudes to scientific and technological innovation. These attitudes are usefully illuminated by comparing Berube with two other writers on science and technology who are so eminent in our intellectual pantheon that no one can be disrespected by being compared with them. These are Marshall McLuhan and John Dewey.

This comparison isn't meant to suggest that Berube must be measured by these two writers' accomplishments. McLuhan and Dewey possessed rare originality. Dewey (1859–1952) commanded a stature in his lifetime that few writers on ideas achieve: his position in the pantheon of great American intellectuals is unique. But both McLuhan and Dewey represented the idea of *science as mediation* in ways that help us understand the media marketplace in which Berube and similar commentators function. McLuhan (1911-

1980), a Canadian, was, like Berube, a media professor. In such inventively publicized books as *The Gutenberg Galaxy: The Making of Typographic Man* (1962), *Understanding Media: The Extensions of Man* (1964), *The Medium is the Massage: An Inventory of Effects* (1967) and *War and Peace in the Global Village* (1968) he ingeniously marketed a clever, imaginative vision of the effects on society of the evolution of communications media.

Although McLuhan's formulations have dated surprisingly quickly, he anticipated some impacts of computerization and raised questions of genuine interest about the social implications of technology. The relevance of McLuhan to a discussion of nanotechnology commentators, though, is that McLuhan managed to position himself successfully as a technology "guru" (*Wired* magazine, a periodical devoted to computer artifacts and subculture, named him its "patron saint") without having any electronic or technological expertise. He probably hadn't the faintest idea about the workings of many of the technologies about which he wrote so authoritatively and with such glittering literary success. He was a literary scholar, a professor of literature, a student of advertisements and comic strips, and (like Berube) a student of rhetoric. McLuhan understood publicity very well. He referenced the techniques of the advertising industry in his work and incorporated them into his writing, with startling effects that helped very successfully to market his writings.

In short, McLuhan was a very effective self-promoter. This isn't a negative reflection on him. He believed his ideas were worth the widest possible circulation and he possessed sophisticated skills to seek this objective. If it seems bizarre for a literary academic to secure prominence as a commentator on technology, as McLuhan did, it's also not all that surprising, because in any competition in public communication between a technologist and an advertising expert, the odds favor the advertising man. Advertising and the professional study of rhetoric are, after all, about making a communications impact. By contrast, science and technology are generally (and sadly) dry fields not noted for their eloquence.

Now, the American public happens to be very fond of advertising specialists and experts on rhetoric. This goes back to at least the days of the great showman P.T. Barnum. America likes these figures not only because they are accessible and entertaining but because, as the popularity of today's television and radio pundits illustrate, America loves convenient packages of interpretation that explain current events and what we should make of them. McLuhan's success was in part an ability to persuade a large public that he was the one to mediate thoughtfully, and with wisdom and gravitas, between the public and the changes that were occurring in communications technology. McLuhan himself was part of the media industry about which he wrote. He was a skilled entertainer in the popular intellectual marketplace, and this rhetorical skill, more than any truth he possessed, made him an effective communications presence.

The conundrum of science and society

We turn now to John Dewey. He was arguably the most highly regarded American philosopher of the first half of the 20th century. His books include *The School and Society* (1900), *How We Think* (1910), *Reconstruction in Philosophy* (1919), *Experience and Nature* (1925), *The Public and its Problems* (1927), *The Quest for Certainty* (1929), *Philosophy and Civilization* (1931), and *Logic: The Theory of Inquiry* (1938). Where McLuhan was an imaginative showman of words, ideas and images, Dewey was a dull, wooden, plodding writer. But this style was appropriate to Dewey's milieu and to the public image he sought, which was that of a judicially impartial evaluator and mediator of points of view in philosophy and public policy. An appearance of magisterial objectivity was basic to his persona. Dewey presented himself as a professional writer about the pursuit of truth, the growth of knowledge, and the relation of these to the public interest. He identified himself strongly with science, projecting himself as an interpreter of scientific method, and in the public eye he was so perceived – although, like McLuhan, Dewey was neither scientist nor technologist. He was interested in the psychology, methodology and history of science from a philosopher's point of view.

In addition to emphasizing science in his philosophical commentaries, Dewey emphasized democracy. In his imagination the sense of orderly, participatory community life was of the highest importance. If ever a thinker believed human beings attain their highest wisdom through democratic discussion, it was Dewey. The sincerity of this belief gave his works an awe-inspiring tone of moral authority. Even when you don't agree with Dewey's views, it's hard not to be moved by his faith in the ability of democracy to guide the human mind to truth. To him, an open-minded social forum, facilitated by a reasonable, fair-minded moderator (like himself) is the very seat of human rationality. Here science and democratic join hands.

The problem with this is that scientific progress isn't a matter of consensus alone. People can vote on many things, but truths, like scientific discoveries and the implications of the laws of nature on which technology depends, aren't among them. We can resolve human conflicts by mediation, if we're skilled enough, but mediation by itself can't produce new scientific discoveries or technological innovations. British philosopher, logician and mathematician Bertrand Russell (1872–1970) put it thus: "Dr. Dewey's world, it seems to me, is one in which human beings occupy the imagination; the cosmos of astronomy, though it is of course acknowledged to exist, is at most times ignored. His philosophy is a power philosophy, though not, like Nietzsche's a philosophy of individual power; it is the power of the community that is felt to be valuable." (*A History of Western Philosophy*, 1967 edition, pp 826, 827.)

Russell didn't mean there's no social dimension to science and technology. He believed, on the contrary, that there were extremely important social aspects to them, and that they could scarcely be understood without attention to these aspects. Consistently with his view, it's our argument in this book that scientific and technological innovation depend heavily on social and cultural support for innovation, and that a major reason for our scientific and technological lag is our inattention to these requirements. But there's also another reason for scientific and technological retardation, namely the confusion of social criticism of science, by people who may be distinguished but aren't scientists, with scientific and technological work itself. This confusion is part of a culture of negativity toward science and technology in America. This culture has damaged our interests, and is holding us back.

NOTES

1. Grujic, P.V., *The Concept Of A Hierarchical Cosmos*, Institute of Physics, Belgrade, Serbia, PUBL. ASTRON. OBS. BELGRADE No. 75 (2003), 257 - 262 http://www.aob.bg.ac.yu/paob/75/pdf/257-262.pdf

2. Office of the Press Secretary, White House, *President Bush Signs Nanotechnology Research and Development Act* (Dec 3, 2003) http://georgewbush-whitehouse.archives.gov/news/releases/2003/12/20031203-7.html

3. Reynolds, Glenn Harlan, *Keeping Up "The Weird Fight"*, TECH CENTRAL STATION DAILY (Feb 11 2004), http://www.tcsdaily.com/printArticle.aspx?ID=021104A

4. Smalley, R.E., *Nanotechnology: Drexler and Smalley make the case for and against 'molecular assemblers'*, CHEMICAL AND ENGINEERING NEWS(Dec 1, 2003) Vol 81, No.48, 37-42, http://pubs.acs.org/cen/coverstory/8148/8148counterpoint.html

5. Lewis, James, *Nano-Hype: The Truth Behind the Nanotechnology Buzz by David M. Berube*, FORESIGHT NANOTECH UPDATE (No.56, Summer 2006)

6. Slabbert, N.J., *Is Science Mediation? Scientific Method As Parliamentary Procedure* (June, 2003),TRUMAN LIBRARY REPORTS

CHAPTER 3

SCIENTIFIC INNOVATION VERSUS THE CULTURE OF NEGATIVISM

In early America, much excitement came from the sense of the unknown. America's culture is filled with images of brave pioneers blazing trails in the wilderness. This sense of adventure and discovery wasn't limited to explorers of forests, deserts, plains and mountains. It applied equally to builders of towns and commercial enterprises.

Part of America's history of innovative resourcefulness and determination was thus social, revolving around a belief that in the New World, a new kind of community life could be invented and made to work. Democracy in its American form was (and still is) a bold experiment contending against skepticism. The idea that ordinary people can join together to run a complex society is daring and even radical against the background of much of the world's philosophical thought.

Various religious movements have disliked the secular nature of democracy. Aristocrats have disliked its openness to reform and the curtailment of elitist privileges. The great Greek philosopher Plato, who lived in the fifth and fourth centuries before Christ, criticized democracy as a gateway to government by an irrational mob. French writer François-Marie Arouet, who published as Voltaire (1694–1778), viewed the general public as fools who should be governed by an elite of brilliant people like himself. German philosopher Friedrich Nietzsche (1844–1900) faulted the "herd mentality" of democracy. German philosopher Karl Marx (1818–1883) saw democracy as a tool of a capitalistic class structure. American journalist-critic Henry L. Mencken (1880–1956) mocked democracy as a breeding-ground for mediocrity. Yet America has persisted with the great experiment of democracy.

But political inventiveness is only one side of America's story. Another is innovation in science and technology. A founding father who helped form America's national spirit, Benjamin Franklin (1706 –1790), was an inventor and scientist. The urinary catheter and bifocal spectacles were among his inventions and he introduced the terms negative and positive into studies of electricity. To honor his research Oxford University bestowed an honorary doctorate on him and Britain's national scientific organization, the Royal Society, awarded him a medal and made him one of its Fellows. Franklin launched the American Philosophical Society to promote science. Thomas Jefferson (1743–1826), third President of the United States and chief author of its Declaration of Independence, enthusiastically promoted science and pursued studies at a high intellectual level in sciences including mathematics, astronomy, physics, engineering, botany and paleontology.

Inventive progress in science and technology played a major role in building America's industry and infrastructure into one of the wonders of the world. And like the political side of American inventiveness, the technological side has contended with negativism.

Technological negativism, is sometimes called Luddism, after Ned Ludd, who is supposed to have lived in late 18th-century Britain and to have destroyed a textile-manufacturing device in protest against the perceived threat that this new technology posed to traditional working methods. Whether he really existed is unknown, but his name was taken by early 19th-century British textile workers protesting against a loom enabling employers to produce more products with fewer people and less training than older looms. "Luddite" workers destroyed mills, and troops were deployed to restore peace. The name Luddite stuck, coming to mean a technophobe. But this historical baggage can be misleading, because technological negativism can take more forms than the connotations of Luddism suggest.

Technological negativism may include aesthetic dislike of technological artifacts and lifestyles, objection to the political or economic systems associated with the highly organized institutions that high technology requires, religious objections, the belief that technology has a strangling effect on the human spirit, a fear that technology threatens the environment, or an association of technology with militarism. Technological negativists may oppose technology (usually advanced rather than simple technology) by campaigning against it directly, by producing art forms that portray it as evil or by opposing it legislatively with regulations. They may also undermine it philosophically by teaching that the only reality knowable to human beings is social reality, so that it's a mistake to think that non-social or non-human, objective truths exist. This philosophical attack assails the belief in non-human reality and non-human truth on which science and technology depend.

Some examples of philosophical reaction against science and technology

An example of philosophical unease about technology is American writer Henry Adams (1838-1918), whose book *The Education of Henry Adams* is a landmark of technological anxiety. It won a Pulitzer Prize and rankings of the best nonfiction books of the 20th century, one by the editors of the Modern Library series of books (in 1998) and the other by the Intercollegiate Studies Institute (1999), have placed it in number one position.

The Education of Henry Adams was issued by a publisher n 1918 but it had been circulating privately since 1905 or so. On the surface it's a personal memoir of a wealthy Bostonian's intellectual development, but it's really an essay on how the 20th century was introducing a new society drastically different from that of the 19th. Adams explained how his 19th-century literary learning gave him no preparation to deal with a world shaped by new discoveries in the sciences and by new inventions of far-reaching impact. He saw that these innovations were only the beginning, and that new philosophical attitudes were needed to integrate the new science and technology with the tradition ideas underlying American culture.

Adams' reactions aren't really as negative or pessimistic as some have interpreted them to be. In part, his sentiments even reflect excitement about science and technology. He speculated about applying scientific principles to the study of history, a prospect he found fascinating. But his response to scientific and technological innovations was colored by misgivings. He sensed that these advances weren't superficial but required America to examine deep philosophical habits. Adams' awareness was given extra importance by the fact that he belonged to a family in which political sensitivity to social change formed a long-established tradition. (John Quincy Adams (1767-1848), the U.S.'s sixth president., was his grandfather; John Adams (1735-1826)), the second, was his great-grandfather.)

Adams' ambivalence toward technology, veering between unease and a sense of both new requirements and possibilities, differed greatly from the anti-technological spirit of philosopher Herbert Marcuse (1898-1979), a German immigrant who acquired American citizenship in 1940. Marcuse was immersed in the ideas of philosophers G.W.F. Hegel and Karl Marx, who both pictured the universe as being made up of social processes driven by obscure metaphysical forces. There's little understanding of technology or science in Marcuse's thought. The closest his work comes to discussing anything even vaguely scientific is his interest in psychologist Sigmund Freud. Even there, Marcuse was drawn to the least scientific aspects of Freud – those elements closest in tone to 19th-century German metaphysical philosophy.

Yet, Marcuse set up shop as a critic of technological society, obtaining teaching positions at Columbia, Harvard, Brandeis and the University of California at San Diego. In books like *Reason and Revolution: Hegel and the Rise of Social Theory* (1941), *One-Dimensional Man* (1964) and *Eros and Civilization* (1955) Marcuse merged Marxism, Hegelian cosmology and Freudian jargon into a polemical metaphysics that attacked American culture as a wicked amalgam of technology, capitalism and political repression. Marcuse urged a revolution against this "Establishment". His woolly utterances were marketed as a creed for the spirit of reform and rebellion that was popular among students in the 1960s.

How much influence Marcuse really had is uncertain, but his work connected powerfully with the protest climate of the 1960s. Marcuse saw science and technology as parts of an evil social and political structure from which we need to be "liberated". This was and remains a highly destructive philosophy.

Another important figure in the anti-technology movement was French philosopher Jacques Ellul (1912–1994). He represents several anti-technology impulses that aren't always combined in a single viewpoint. Some of these, like antipathy toward capitalism and religious opposition to perceptions of dehumanizing effects of technology (Ellul was also a theologian), seem to be opposed to each other as much as they are to technology. But in his book *The Technological Society* (1964) Ellul combined them into a picture of technology as a force that artificially and rigidly subjected human beings to a search for cold efficiency, the erosion of human values and the manipulation of mass opinion by media technologies.

Adams, Marcuse and Ellul represent three different but related forms of negativism toward science and technology. In Adams, science and technology are sources of unease which we might be able to deal with if we absorb them into more familiar kinds of intellectual activity, like the philosophy of history. In Marcuse, rejecting science and technology is part of a political mission of rebellion and social revolution. In Ellul, opposing science and technology becomes a quasi-religious crusade to protect our basic humanity from being undermined. All these anti-technological voices are reminiscent of the fierce reaction evoked by the great biological work *On the Origin of Species by Means of Natural Selection, or the Preservation* of *Favoured Races in the Struggle for Life* (1859), by English biologist Charles Darwin (1809–1882). Anti-Darwinism, which continues today in the dispute over intelligent design, stemmed from a moral repugnance toward Darwin's ideas. A similar moral repugnance runs through the fabric of reaction against science and technology.

Negativism toward cities

Although there's fairly wide awareness of anti-Darwinism, some people may find it hard to accept that there is a similar reaction against science and technology in the U.S. These seem so integrated into America that it appears preposterous to claim otherwise. But this impression is mistaken. To grasp this, it's helpful to consider America's attitude toward cities.

The concept of the city is closely related to concepts of advanced technology. Cities are concentrations of highly organized people, institutions and resources. They form the milieu that is required to advance complex, large-scale technology. Airliners, automobiles, computers, spacecraft, telecommunications infrastructures like cell phones and cable television, and cutting-edge medical developments aren't products of agrarian communities. They are creations of urban societies.

Now, Americans like to think of themselves as an urban people, just as they like to see themselves as a high-technology society. Magazines, television programs and films feed America's desire to think of itself as sophisticated and given to the efficiency, pace of living and grit that our media portray as elements of city life and culture. But this imagined urbanism is significantly a veneer covering a rural mentality, or at least a rural mythology. Rural life may no longer be dominant in America, but its powerful imaginative associations are older and deeper than the mythology of the city. It's also highly suspicious of urban life.

Intellectual historians Morton and Lucia White documented in their study *The Intellectual Versus the City, from Thomas Jefferson to Frank Lloyd Wright* (1962) how the history of American thought is shot through with antipathy to urbanization. The "antiurban roar", they wrote, was a tradition extending from the birth of the Republic through writers like Ralph Waldo Emerson, Herman Melville and Theodore Dreiser to philosophers William James, George Santayana, John Dewey – and Henry Adams.

Even as the U.S. grew increasingly urban in the 19th century, the Whites have shown, denigration of the city became shriller; the city "became the bête noire of our most distinguished intellectuals." The Whites' summary of mid-20th-century American attitudes to the city sounds familiar to us in the 21st century. "The decay of the American city is now one of the most pressing concerns of the nation. Every day we hear of a continuing flight from the central city; of explosions into the suburbs and more distant places; of sprawling supercities; of automobiles crawling through and around the city on roads that strangle it; of a city-based culture that is allegedly destroying our spiritual life; and of lonely crowds of organization men."

The 20th century's most influential representative of this reaction against cities was probably American writer Lewis Mumford (1895-1990). Significantly, he was also a critic of technology, for whom criticism of cities and of technology went hand in hand. Mumford's perspectives are so ingrained in today's urban discourse that many urban professionals are his intellectual heirs even if they've never read him. Understanding Mumford is arguably essential to understand contemporary and recent American attitudes to both the city and technology.

Mumford started out with an open mind toward the beneficial possibilities of technology. But as the 20th century passed he lived through two world wars waged by technology-wielding, monolithic states, growing degradation of the physical environment and a dread of annihilation through nuclear technology. His early faith in the transformative powers of human ingenuity was overshadowed by alarm at human destructiveness and by a suspicion of huge, dehumanizing structures. He came to associate these with advanced technology and cityscapes alike. He opposed what he called *Megalopolis*, which for him meant not only a gigantic city dwarfing the natural scale of its human inhabitants, but also the whole complex of advanced industrial technologies that we identify with modern cities.

Mumford targeted the city and "big technology" together as an amalgam of some of America's worst political, moral, social and aesthetic errors. His intellectual authority as an enemy of these perceived errors was formidable. He was for many years a columnist for the magazine *The New Yorker* and wrote influential books like *Technics and Civilization* (1934), *The Culture of Cities* (1938) and *The City in History* (1967). His deep suspicion of technology, and his linkage of it with an inhumanity represented by large-scale urbanization, entered American culture on many levels. An example of this worldview appears in American writer Leigh Brackett's 1955 novel *The Long Tomorrow*, which imagines a post-apocalyptic rural America in which advanced technology is taboo and the Constitution has been amended to ban cities. The book describes the city as "megalopolis, drowned in its own sewage, choked with its own waste gases, smothered and crushed by its own population."

This dark vision of cities has become part of American culture films, television, prose fiction, video games and comic books. The 1982 film *Blade Runner*, based on a story by famous science fiction writer Philip K. Dick, portrayed the city of the future as an overpopulated, collapsing nightmare of pollution and commercial exploitation. Gotham City in the popular Batman franchise is a cesspool of corrupt politicians and cynical businesspeople.

In the 1960s, reaction against technology fused with resentment of the perceived materialism associated with commerce, industry and big government. Charles A. Reich's best-seller *The Greening of America* (1970) reflected a yearning for a lifestyle free of technological contrivances. Tranquil rural imagery was common in the songs of the time. Reich cited with approval Marcuse's writing, which characterized science and technology as repressive tools of military and commercial interests. This sentiment persists today in books of popular philosophy like Morris Berman's *The Twilight of American Culture* (2000) and is by no means confined to the political Left. Many conservatives see science and technology as threats to time-tested human values, regarding technology as an instrument of a pernicious urban culture conflicting with the wholesome rural heartland. Critics from both Right and Left associate urban technology with big government. The former fear it as a tool of secular collectivism, the latter as a tool of quasi-fascist government aligned with unscrupulous corporate interests.

Skepticism versus negativism

This brings us to the nature of skepticism.

It's important to perceive the difference between healthy skepticism, which enables science to progress, and negativism toward the possibilities and aims of science and technology.

Healthy skepticism is a cornerstone of science's rational quest to develop testable and falsifiable theories, based on evidence rather than unsubstantiated assertion. Healthy scientific skepticism is informed by a democratic spirit because it links the growth of knowledge to constructive, free exchanges of ideas. It's not negative but positive. It's balanced by affirmative principles: that knowledge is valuable in itself, that the universe has an order which intelligence can reasonably hope to fathom, that there are such things as objective truths which aren't human inventions.

Negativism toward science and technology, on the other hand, may superficially resemble scientific skepticism but is quite different from it. It has little to do with the growth of knowledge and is rather derived from a desire to further social objectives, like the retention of a lifestyle which is deemed to be aesthetically, theologically or for other reasons threatened by scientific and technological innovation.

Negativism toward science and technology may be driven by convictions which are diametrically opposed to those on which the science and technology depend. These may include the idea that knowledge has no value in itself but is worth while only to serve a religious dogma or political agenda, that the universe either has no order or that it has one which is beyond human fathoming, and that there are no such things as objective truths which aren't human inventions.

Because negativism is often dressed up in scientific-sounding language, it can be hard to distinguish between genuine scientific skepticism and negativism that seeks to obstruct scientific and technological development. Negativism may even purport to favor scientific and technological development while in practice seeking to stall it in a science-policy equivalent of what politicians call filibustering: that is, by insisting that a scientific of technological program is subjected to so much bureaucratic (rather than purely scientific) review that in practice such work is indefinitely obstructed.

Then there's negativism within science itself, when scientists oppose new theories or technological advances not for scientific reasons but because they threaten theoretical positions or established technologies on which careers rely.

Some useful comments on negativism toward science and technology have been provided by an American expert on the bibliographic organization and citation of scientific knowledge, Eugene Garfield (1925 -), founding editor of the magazine *The Scientist*. In a 1977 article[1] Garfield wrote: "The history of negative science has long fascinated me. There are always theoreticians around who can 'prove' that almost anything can't be done."

Garfield cited the dismissal by Canadian-born mathematician and astronomer Simon Newcomb (1835–1909) of the prospect of building a flying machine. He noted that Newcomb was a distinguished professor of mathematics and astronomy at Johns Hopkins University, founding president of the American Astronomical Society, vice-president of the National Academy of Sciences and director of the American Nautical Almanac Office, a navigational science entity. Newcomb even apparently had a creditable role in early science fiction: in 1898 he wrote about "hyper-space", and before that, British science fiction pioneer H.G. Wells (1866–1946) connected the idea of a fourth dimension with a "Professor Simon Newcomb" in his 1895 novel *The Time Machine.*

Yet, Newcomb has gone into history as a scientific negativist. Here's how:

In 1903, an unsuccessful attempt to launch a heavier-than-air flying device was supervised by American inventor Samuel Pierpont Langley (1834-1906). The aircraft came apart and fell into the Potomac River along with its pilot, Charles Manly.

Langley's career included positions as professor of mathematics at the U.S. Naval Academy and professor of astronomy at the Western University of Pennsylvania, and he founded the Smithsonian Astrophysical Observatory. Late in life he began making prototype models of flying machines. In 1898 he secured grants from the U.S. War Department and the Smithsonian Institution to develop a piloted aircraft. But when his 1903 test failed, his funding was halted, he was mocked in the press and he came under risk of being investigated by Congress.

Newcomb commented[2] on this: "We may look on the bird as a sort of flying machine complete in itself, of which a brain and nervous system are fundamentally necessary parts. No such machine can navigate the air unless guided by something having life. Apart from this, it could be of little use to us unless it carried human beings on its wings. We thus meet with a difficulty at the first step—we cannot give a brain and nervous system to our machine...

"We cannot have muscles or nerves for our flying machine. We have to replace them by such crude and clumsy adjuncts as steam engines and electric batteries. It may certainly seem singular if man is never to discover any combination of substances which, under the influence of some such agency as an electric current, shall expand and contract like a muscle. But, if he is ever to do so, the time is still in the future. We do not see the dawn of the age in which such a result will be brought forth...

"There are many problems which have fascinated mankind ever since civilization began which we have made little or no advance in solving. The only satisfaction we can feel in our treatment of the great geometrical problems of antiquity is that we have shown their solution to be impossible. The mathematician of to-day admits that he can neither square the circle, duplicate the cube or trisect the angle. May not our mechanicians, in like manner, be ultimately forced to admit that aerial flight is one of that great class of problems with which man can never cope, and give up all attempts to grapple with it?

"... To judge it sanely, let us bear in mind the difficulties which are encountered in any flying machine."

Newcomb presented, in extremely authoritative-sounding language, the mathematical and physical arguments against heavier-than-air flight, adding: "The difficulties which I have pointed out are only preliminary ones, patent on the surface. A more fundamental one still, which the writer feels may prove insurmountable, is based on a law of nature which we are bound to accept. It is that when we increase the size of such a machine without changing its model we increase the weight in proportion to the cube of the linear dimensions, while the effectiveness of the supporting power of the air increases only as the square of those dimensions. Quite likely the most effective flying machine would be one carried by a vast number of little birds...a sufficient number of humming birds, if we could combine their forces, would carry an aerial excursion party of human beings through the air."

However, nine days after Langley's failure -- on December 17, 1903 -- the first heavier-than-air, powered and controlled human flight was made at Kitty Hawk, North Carolina, by American aviation pioneers Orville Wright (1871–1948) and Wilbur Wright (1867–1912).

Garfield notes that amazingly, "almost five years went by before it was generally accepted that the Wright brothers had flown in their machine. After all, who were the Wright brothers to make such a claim when the most learned professors--

including Professor Simon Newcomb--had 'proved' that powered flight was impossible?"

A newspaper, the *Dayton Journal,* was given the story but didn't publish it. When it was eventually printed, little excitement arose. So solid was skepticism about human flight that the first eyewitness account of the Wright brothers' triumph wasn't published in a leading scientific journal or major newspaper but in a periodical called *Gleanings in Bee Culture,* whose editor, A.I. Root, had attended the event. This report appeared only in 1905.

Three years after the Wrights' success, Newcomb remained adamant that humans wouldn't fly. In 1906 he wrote: "The demonstration that no possible combination of known substances, known forms of machinery, and known forms of force can be united in a practicable machine by which men shall fly long distances through the air, seems to the writer as complete as it is possible for the demonstration of any physical fact to be."

Supporting Newcomb's opinions, *The New York Times* said in an editorial: "We hope that Professor Langley will not put his substantial greatness as a scientist in further peril by continuing to waste his time, and the money involved, in further airship experiments. Life is short, and he is capable of services to humanity incomparably greater than can be expected to result from trying to fly . . . . For students and investigators of the Langley type there are more useful employments, with fewer disappointments and mortifications than have been the portion of aerial navigators since the days of Icarus."

The political correctness of negativity toward human flight was thus a well-established intellectual tradition. Garfield has noted that in 1888, American geology professor Joseph Le Conte (1823-1901) declared: "A pure flying-machine is impossible."[3] Another famous "debunker" of human flight was British physicist and engineer Lord Kelvin (1824-1907), who declared in 1896: "I have not the smallest molecule of faith in aerial navigation other than ballooning or of expectation of good results from any of the trials we hear of," and in 1902: "No balloon and no aeroplane will ever be practically successful." Kelvin represented what is perhaps the most destructive form of negativism in the learned community: the belief that the present generation of experts owns a definitive, final perspective. In 1900 he wrote: "There is nothing new to be discovered in physics now. All that remains is more and more precise measurement."

A similar view had been expressed by American physicist Albert A. Michelson (1852-1931), co-discoverer of the speed of light, who wrote in 1894: "The more important fundamental laws and facts of physical science have all been discovered, and these are now so firmly established that the possibility of their ever being supplanted in consequence of new discoveries is exceedingly remote... Our future discoveries must be looked for in the sixth place of decimals."

Such statements aren't scientific. They are philosophical pronouncements derived from the desire of experts to reinforce their authority. (It's noteworthy that Morley gave his non-scientific, dogmatic proclamation the appearance of science by making it sound mathematical.)

The culture of negativity toward aviation technology was so deeply rooted that as Garfield noted, "even after the Wright brothers' 1903 success, some commentators hedged their bets, conceding that a heavier-than-air machine just might possibly fly, but certainly never would carry passengers, be used commercially, etc." These debunkers included noted American astronomer William Henry Pickering (1858-1938), who wrote: "The popular mind often pictures gigantic flying machines speeding across the Atlantic carrying innumerable passengers. It seems safe to say that such ideas must be wholly visionary. Even if a machine could get across with one or two passengers, it would be prohibitive to any but the capitalist who could own his own yacht." He also pooh-poohed the "popular fantasy" that aircraft could be used to drop explosives during war.

Garfield pointed out that even as the 20th century advanced and air travel became common, "the naysayers were in abundant supply. Now their attention was focused on rocketry, paralleling and repeating the embarrassing mistakes of their predecessors. Since these later pessimists were probably familiar with the ridicule directed at the airplane, which had resulted in embarrassment for those who said it couldn't be done, perhaps we should admire the blind perseverance of those who continued to insist that the next step--space travel--remained impossible."

Even as commercial airmail services flourished, Garfield observed, *The New York Times*, not content with having editorialized against aircraft, now opposed space travel. In 1920 it disdained the research of American rocket pioneer Robert H. Goddard (1882–1945), suggesting that Goddard lacked the basic knowledge of physics that was "ladled out daily in high schools." Many press items ridiculed Goddard, whose work formed the foundation of U.S. space and missile technology. Garfield also noted the declaration in 1935 by American astronomer Forest Ray Moulton (1872–1952) that "In all fairness to those who by training are not prepared to evaluate the fundamental difficulties of going from one planet to another, or even from the Earth to the Moon, it must be stated that there is not the slightest possibility of such journeys," and a 1948 editorial in the London *Daily Mirror* saying: "In our candid opinion is that all talk of going to the Moon . . .is sheer balderdash."

Garfield concluded: "How the openmindedness of a Benjamin Franklin and the closed-mindedness of a Simon Newcomb can be compared is a subject inadequately treated by philosophers and historians of science. Even the formal training of most Ph.D.'s today would not enable them to deal with the persuasiveness of a Simon Newcomb. I wonder how many of the readers of the reprint could write the appropriate rebuttal--even though all of them take flying for granted! In fact, for lack of a proper citation index, I can not determine whether anyone ever did publish a paper showing that Newcomb was wrong. The important point to be made here applies equally well to the flying machine, the computer, the laser, nuclear fusion, and every other important invention ever produced ... Those phenomena and discoveries which do not fit into the present paradigms of science are not merely discredited, but are sometimes flippantly ridiculed. Negative scientists can avoid future embarrassment by helping their antagonists design experiments that might prove or disprove the disputed scientific wisdom."

Negativism and the non-social reality of science and technology

The difference between healthy scientific skepticism and obstructive negativism isn't just one of degree. The two viewpoints represent qualitatively different attitudes. Healthy scientific skepticism says: "Here's a vision of what we might accomplish if we're determined to do so, so let's commit our energies and ingenuity to making this work in whatever way we can devise to cooperate with the laws of the non-human universe."

Negativism says: "These alleged possibilities are rubbish, because we know what we can do and what we can't do, and what we can know and can't know, and we know in advance that we can't do these things. End of story, and anyone who believes otherwise should be laughed into obscurity."

History hasn't been kind to the second attitude. Yet it remains strongly embedded in our society.

A fundamental difference between the two attitudes is the concept that science and technology depend on non-social reality. This takes us back to the idea of science as mediation. Negativists may dismiss a new line of scientific or technological development on the grounds that it offends the laws of nature, but closer examination often shows they really dislike it because they would prefer to preserve the professional authority of an older body of knowledge. Signs of this kind of motivation include arguments for new research not to be undertaken, or for research to be discontinued or filibustered. Yet research, coupled with a determination to solve problems, is the only way to develop our technological cooperation with the laws of nature.

Science and technology require constant collective review, but what is scientifically and technologically feasible can't be decided by vote. Only research can determine this, and even then it's necessary for research to be conducted with high motivation so adequate resources can be brought to bear. This means accepting that science and technology are rooted in a non-social reality as well as in a social reality. Let's look at some of the ways in which scientific and technological development is non-social:

Substantial capacity to operate independently of society

In principle, scientific and technological work can be conducted secretly, by small groups operating independently of the broader mass of society. In wartime, scientific and technological advances can be accomplished separately from the larger processes of government, from the mass media and even from a global scientific community. Such secret scientific and technological endeavor runs counter to our rightly cherished beliefs about democratic openness and the publicly participative community of science, but its history is a fact. Significant scientific and technological work can also be done by individuals, thinking quite apart from their peers.

American engineer Adrian Bejan (1948-) has argued that science in fact proceeds most effectively when it recognizes the role of solitary researchers who produce fertile ideas on their own, away from collectives. "The history of scientific achievement is marked by solitary investigators, from Archimedes to Newton to Darwin," he notes. "Solitary thinkers have flourished throughout history because it is natural ... Even though the trend is toward the creation of large research groups, the individual will always flourish." [4]

Of course, even solitary researchers are social beings, relying on accumulated knowledge transmitted by books and other cultural products, plus social support systems for their subsistence. Still, meaningful scientific work can be done by individuals operating independently of social institutions. This doesn't negate the need for the social support of science, which is today more essential than ever; it just shows that science is not *merely* a social construct.

Falsifiability and unpredictability

Empirical science is built on propositions which are falsified when they conflict with factual evidence. This idea comes from British-Austrian philosopher Karl Popper (1902–1994), whose view of science is often contrasted with that of American scholar Thomas Kuhn (1922–1996). For Kuhn, science was a group enterprise in which individuals were overshadowed by communal thinking. To Popper, science was more akin to democracy, where free critical thought enabled individuals to challenge conventional wisdom. Kuhn emphasized scientific collectives and orthodoxies; Popper stressed the role of mavericks with contrarian ideas. [5]

Renewed attention to Popper's concept of the limitations of socially shaped knowledge is a badly-needed corrective to the idea of science as a wholly social phenomenon (as opposed to a phenomenon entailing non-human truths that social organization helps us discover). Popper's view is illustrated by his criticism of Karl Marx and others who purported to be able to predict history. Popper pointed out that since the growth of knowledge is unpredictable, and societies are shaped by knowledge, historical prediction is impossible. This powerful observation means knowledge can't be socially determined, although it can be encouraged by the right social conditions.

A feature of Popper's thought setting him apart from both Dewey and Kuhn is his emphasis on the objective testing of scientific claims by recourse to evidence which might conflict with a claim and thus render it untenable. It can be argued that this doesn't rescue science from being hostage to social consensus, since evidence must be sanctioned by a parliament of scientific peers. But this isn't so. Prior to Popper, a fashionable theory of science was that of verification. This is a much more socially disposed theory, since it regards claims as scientific if they can be verified, creating a picture of science as a socially endorsed treasury of established claims. To Popper, there are no verified claims in this sense, only ones which haven't so far been demonstrated to be false. Our supposed bedrock of amassed scientific knowledge is in fact an assemblage of individual conjectures. For Popper, truth exists independently of human wants, needs, convenience or decisions, and while we can never hope to attain it fully, we can approximate it increasingly through critical thought and the testing of hypotheses against the bar of falsification. This is a far-reaching step away from the idea that science is a human invention rather than an accommodation to non-human truths.

Interdisciplinary fluidity

One of the most politically charged areas in thinking about science and technology is the tendency of innovation to be interdisciplinary. Scientific discovery and technological invention don't respect the neat parcels, boundaries and intellectual jurisdictions into which experts like to divide knowledge and its management. There's nothing new about this. Since the earliest times researchers have been aware of the interconnectedness of seemingly separate natural processes. Great scientists throughout history have had encyclopedic interests. And this phenomenon doesn't belong only to science's past: the pioneers of contemporary nuclear science, genetics, molecular biology, computer science, chaos theory and certain branches of economics are conspicuously interdisciplinary. Thus, there's a substantial tradition of interdisciplinary research and speculation in science and technology. What's new is not this but rather the relatively recent tradition of specialization that's emerged over the past century or so. Nature is seamless, but budgets and organizational hierarchies require specialization. Hence the creation of spheres of professional authority with clear-cut boundaries and jurisdictions -- social constructs with which the interdisciplinary nature of the non-human universe doesn't always fit well conveniently.

Interdisciplinary politics

The interdisciplinary character of much cutting-edge science and technology often politically inconveniences experts whose prestige is based on the authority of a particular discipline. The professionalization of knowledge, based on the existence of cadres of certified experts who jealously protect their turf, is an engine of career-building. It's not only an economic mechanism but a political one that places power in the hands of well-organized groups of experts. It can be irksome when discoveries and inventions appear without deference to where such experts would prefer them to appear in the landscape of disciplines and funding.

An amusing example of this connection between experts' fields of authority and the way scientific knowledge is packaged concerns a review in the magazine *Science*, by biologist-environmentalist Barry Commoner, of science writer Isaac Asimov's *Intelligent Man's Guide to Science* (1960). According to Asimov, his editor had inserted into his book a statement that advances in science had "all but wiped out the distinction between life and nonlife." In Commoner's review, Asimov reported, "he attacked the book in a totally overreactive way" and "his most stupid remark was to ask what would happen to biology as a science if the distinction between life and nonlife was wiped out. I wrote a brief and reasoned response (which *Science* dutifully printed) in which I pointed out that Copernicus, over four centuries ago, had wiped out the distinction between Earth and the other planets – and what had happened to geology as a result? Nothing." [6]

Another illustration of this jurisdictional territoriality was provided by a co-founder of nuclear science, New Zealand-born physicist Ernest Rutherford (1871–1937). He is said to have declared that in science, everything other than physics was just stamp collecting. (There's controversy over his exact wording, but this seems to capture the spirit of it.[7]) Rutherford of all people should have known better, because although his great work on the atom was primarily part of physics, the Nobel Prize judges rewarded him with a prize in chemistry. The point is that the disciplinary landscape of science is fluid. New disciplines arise when the experiences of disciplines overlap and combine into a new field, or part of a discipline branches off on its own, establishing its independence from the parent profession, with its own journals, organizational fiefdoms and competing budgets.

Sociobiology is an example. Also *bioinformatics*, which fuses computer science with molecular biology, the latter itself being the product of a convergence of physics, chemistry and biology. As knowledge ebbs and flows in this way it redraws the political (and budgetary) maps between disciplines, as when physics detached itself from its roots in a more inclusive Natural Philosophy. A substantial political realignment of disciplines took place when the sciences in general established themselves in the late 19th and early 20th centuries as intellectual domains equal in importance to traditional fields of literary scholarship. British physicist-novelist C.P. Snow (1905–1980) recalled[8]: "I remember G. H. Hardy once remarking to me in mild puzzlement, some time in the 1930s, Have you noticed how the word 'intellectual' is used nowadays? There seems to be a new definition which certainly doesn't include Rutherford or Eddington or Dirac or Adrian or me? It does seem rather odd, don't y'know." (Hardy was an eminent mathematician; Rutherford, Arthur Eddington and Paul Dirac were physicists; Edgar Adrian an electrophysiologist.)

Some die-hard adherents of the supremacy of social reality over the non-human world might argue that all this political sensitivity shows that science is after all a social construct. But the claim rings hollow. Experts understandably try their best to take maximum career advantage of opportunities that disciplinary shifts open up, but the shifts themselves (at least in the physical sciences) result from unpredictable developments including new theories, conclusions, vocabularies, speculations, experiments and technologies. These can vex experts who have a career interest in preserving older protocols.

As science and technology grow, such political impacts will multiply, requiring us to accept that the nurturing of new knowledge must be tailored to what scientific and technological innovations make necessary rather than to what committees find convenient. This point was reflected in a 2004 article in the *Los Angeles Times*[9], which noted the history of political obstacles encountered by interdisciplinary researchers. It also reported a new wave of interest at universities in encouraging interdisciplinary studies. Computerization was cited as a force encouraging interdisciplinary work.

According to the article, California's leading research universities, including Stanford, the University of California (Caltech) and the University of California system "are among the pace-setters" freeing researchers to "energize hybrid fields with offbeat names such as neuroeconomics, computational biology, geobiology, and brain-based humanities. The trend has been especially dramatic in engineering and the sciences, particularly biology-related fields." Schools were "turning adventurous scholars loose to pierce the barriers between fields of knowledge and to search for discoveries at the intersections of traditional academic disciplines. They are teaming psychologists and anthropologists with economists, laboratory biologists with computer-modeling experts, and scientists who study the brain with humanities professors who explore music and art."

The article cited a study by the RAND Corporation as showing that "federal funding for interdisciplinary research and development at US universities climbed to $675 million in 2002, more than double the $330 million in 1997. Other analysts contend that the spending is higher. In addition, the National Institutes of Health, the biggest federal patron of academic research, a year ago announced a 'roadmap' for the future that stressed interdisciplinary initiatives. It budgeted $2.1 billion over five years for the effort." New interdisciplinary units were being developed "to cut through customary academic rivalries."

The *Times* quoted Caltech president David Baltimore, a Nobel-prizewinning biologist, as describing the mapping of the human genome as both a product and an encourager of interdisciplinary research, since biologists alone couldn't deal with all the issues and needed help from experts including computer scientists, mathematicians, engineers, chemists and physicists. Roberto Peccei, UCLA's vice chancellor for research, was quoted as stating: "For any problem that has some importance today, you find that, really, it doesn't fit neatly into biology or into chemistry or into law. It tends to have many ramifications. If you think of universities as trying to address problems, then it's natural that they should be engaged in broad, multidisciplinary research."

As an example the article described Caltech neuroscientist Richard Andersen's research on "a futuristic way to help people with paralyzed limbs", so they would be able to move a mechanical arm by thought alone. The project required a roboticist, electrical engineers, a physicist and a neurosurgeon.

The *Times* acknowledged that such teamwork "was once a rarity at the nation's most prestigious universities. But only in recent years has the university world – often slow to change because of entrenched bureaucracies and academic turf fights – warmed to that idea." It quoted Veronica Boix Mansilla, a Harvard University researcher, as commenting that interdisciplinary research at universities remained "a risky route for young researchers to take." According to the article, Duncan Watts, associate professor of sociology at Columbia University, reported that when he submitted his doctoral dissertation to a publisher, the editor sought opinions from a mathematician and a sociologist, because the thesis combined both these disciplines. But the mathematician didn't see the work as mathematics and the sociologist didn't recognize it as sociology, so it was rejected. (It was eventually accepted by another publisher.) "Even so," the article added, "Watts says he and other interdisciplinary researchers often face similar objections."

Tension between interdisciplinary scientific-technological research and the social business of science management is both unavoidable and healthy. Organized scientific and technological research has many social impacts, so scientists and technologists must engage social establishments effectively. However, where this engagement impedes scientific advance, or foments public negativity toward science and its products, this helps neither science nor society.

As we've seen, then, social criticism of science comes from two different sources. One is the scientific community itself. Specialists in a discipline may criticize a body of scientific work not on scientific grounds but socio-politically, as in the case of the mathematician referenced above who didn't like a mathematical dissertation because it contained sociology. Confusion arises because although this opposition is socio-political, not scientific, coming from a scientist makes it look scientific.

The other source of social criticism of science and technology is from non-scientists in positions of influence who criticize science for social reasons, often with claims that the social critic has a superior ability to judge what is scientifically valuable. A classic example is the Church's opposition to Galileo, which was motivated at least partly by social reasons (the Church saw Galileo's work as a threat to its political power) and was justified intellectually by the Church's claim that its cultural insights gave it a perception of the universe that was superior to Galileo's. Science was thus confused with social decision. Another example, possibly apocryphal but no less useful, is the tale of King Canute, an eleventh-century monarch of England and Scandinavia who is said to have commanded the tide to turn back. Interestingly, Canute's motivation may have been the opposite of that of Galileo's critics: it's been speculated that Canute didn't really expect the tide to obey him but that he rather wanted to demonstrate the weak power of society (including kingly power) compared to the greatness of the non-human universe.

Nevertheless, the confusion of science with social decision-making is alive and well in our time, and some opposition to interdisciplinary science is an example of it.

Negativity masquerading as interdisciplinary science

We now come to a curious feature of the social criticism of science: its tendency to mimic the interdisciplinary nature of much creative science even while criticizing science. This phenomenon, which creates a tangled web of cross-disciplinary feuds and political sensitivities in the sciences and humanities, is important to our understanding of the culture of negativity toward science and technology.

We've noted that social criticism of science comes from within and without science. These two streams of criticism aren't necessarily allies. They can be bitter enemies, with the pots sometimes calling the kettles black. The *Times* article cited above quotes Howard Gardner, "a Harvard Graduate School of Education professor studying interdisciplinary trends", as commenting that in certain cases in the humanities and social sciences, "interdisciplinary work simply provides a home for misfits, malcontents, those who are anti-disciplines without being pro-anything." The article says Gardner "expressed skepticism about the quality of scholarship in 'soft' fields lacking assessment standards, which he said included such areas as women's studies, Latino studies and media studies." (Note that McLuhan was a media scholar, as is Berube.) Gardner (1943-) himself has distinguished credentials in interdisciplinary science, including as Professor of Cognition and Education at Harvard University's Graduate School of Education and author of the book *Frames of Mind: The Theory of Multiple Intelligences* (1983).

Generally, antipathy of this kind toward "soft" fields of expertise comes from experts who see themselves as "hard" (or real) scientists as opposed to "soft" scholars who are armed with opinions and political agendas rather than research-based facts, and who give their work the appearance of hard science by assuming impressive interdisciplinary vocabularies peppered with scientific-sounding terms. For example, ethicists interested in nanotechnology might call themselves *nanoethicists,* which makes them sound rather more scientific than if they were called just ethicists. Similarly, there is *roboethics* and *bioethics.* By the same token, it seems to make sense to call ethicists who are interested in murder *homicidoethicists,* or in murder by gunshot *ballistoethicists,* or in the moral principles governing the installation of electrical wires *electroethicists.*

A famous example of this controversy was a hoax perpetrated by American physicist Alan D. Sokal (1955-). He wrote a pompous paper concocted from fictitious expertise and dressed up in the language of a pretentious, invented, pseudo-scientific scholarship, and he submitted it to an academic journal for writers on cultural studies. (*Transgressing the Boundaries: Towards a Transformative Hermeneutics of Quantum Gravity*, in *Social Text*, spring/summer 1996 Duke University Press.) Sokal later co-authored a related book with Jean Bricmont, *Fashionable Nonsense*, (1997), criticizing nonscientists who adopt and distort scientific terminology in order to criticize science socially. Sokal's hoax triggered a wave of discussion in which he commented that his article had spotlighted "the silliest things about mathematics and physics (and the philosophy of mathematics and physics) said by the most prominent academics", and that "unfortunately the authors quoted are among the most prominent in the field. For example, nearly all of the most prominent French poststructuralists (Deleuze, Guattari, Derrida, Lacan, Lyotard, Serres, Irigaray, Virilio) are exhibited in my article spewing forth utter nonsense about mathematics and physics (all the while pretending to be knowledgeable)."

Sokal added that the hoax had spoken "volumes about the cultural authority of scientists, which is accepted (when it suits their political and polemical goals) even by those who claim to be most skeptical of it."[10] On one side of the debate were those who saw themselves as defending science as a seeker and custodian of hard facts independent of social decisions. On the other hand were social critics of science and technology arguing that the purported objective truths and non-human realities of science were social inventions, often masking political agendas. These academic disputes about the politics of science have come to be known as the Science Wars.

The literature of this discourse includes books like *Higher Superstition: The Academic Left and Its Quarrels With Science*, (1994), by Paul R. Gross, a biologist, and Norman J. Levitt, a mathematician. Sokal has said he got the idea for his hoax after reading this work, which distinguished between the recognition of science as a social enterprise and the argument that science is a social construct. Gross and Levitt linked certain ideological agendas with scientifically inept nonsense posing as criticism of science. They argued that the educational system was being debased by this trend: "We encounter increasing numbers of students, graduate as well as undergraduate, whose primary contact with science has been through the work of feminist or cultural constructivist critics, and who are convinced, moreover, that they have imbibed doctrines that are wise (as well as stylish)."

All this takes us into deep political waters. But it's not necessary to venture far into them to see that non-scientific critics of science undoubtedly like to mimic scientific terminology in interdisciplinary ways, thereby seeming to be part of the cutting-edge world of science when in fact they're not. There's clearly a political agenda in an enormous amount of this criticism. It complicates things further when the antipathy toward science that comes from nonscientific critics unfolds alongside the suspicion felt by some scientists toward any erosion of the borders of their own fields of expertise, whether by nonscientists or scientists. This means scientists and technologists engaged in interdisciplinary work face opposition from two directions. For example, Buckminster Fuller (1895–1983), a passionate advocate for aggressive and imaginative technological expansion who believed in the ability of technology and science to abolish poverty within his lifetime, had heavy odds against him. He represented the American techno-industrial system which political critics of science and technology dislike, and he also offended conventional scientific protocol by possessing a maverick mind with little respect for conventional disciplinary boundaries. This potent political crossfire makes for a culture of negativity toward scientific and technological innovation that is a serious problem for our society's well-being and future.

NOTES

1. Garfield, Eugene, Negative Science and "The Outlook for the Flying Machine" (1977), http://garfield.library.upenn.edu/essays/v3p155y1977-78.pdf

2. Newcomb, Simon, The Outlook for the Flying Machine, THE INDEPENDENT: A WEEKLY MAGAZINE (Oct 22, 1903) http://www.garfield.library.upenn.edu/essays/v3p167y1977-78.pdf

3. Le Conte, Joseph, The problem of a flying-machine, POPULAR SCIENCE MONTHLY (Nov. 1888)

4. Bejan, Adrian, Constructal Self-organization Of Research: Empire Building Versus The Individual Investigator, INTERNATIONAL JOURNAL OF DESIGN & NATURE AND ECODYNAMICS (Vol.3, Issue 3, Dec. 2008)

5. Popper, Karl R., CONJECTURES AND REFUTATIONS: THE GROWTH OF SCIENTIFIC KNOWLEDGE (1963; Kuhn, Thomas S., THE STRUCTURE OF SCIENTIFIC REVOLUTIONS (1962)

6. Asimov, Isaac, I, ASIMOV: A MEMOIR (1994)

7. Birks, J.B., RUTHERFORD AT MANCHESTER (1962)

8. Snow, C.P., THE TWO CULTURES AND THE SCIENTIFIC REVOLUTION (1959)

9. Silverstein, Stuart, Teamwork, Not Rivalry, Marks New Era In Research, LOS ANGELES TIMES (Nov.3,2004), http://articles.latimes.com/2004/nov/03/local/me-hybrid3

10. Sokal, Alan D., The Sokal Hoax: The Sham that Shook the Academy, LINGUA FRANCA (2000)

CHAPTER 4

THE CAN-DO CULTURE: THE RISE OF MODERN TECHNOLOGY

In 1867 one of the world's greatest works of mythic fiction saw print in London. Like many imaginative creations, it was produced by a poor, struggling author who had toiled on it for years, dreaming up a passionately felt mental landscape that he yearned to bring before the public. It achieved a rare success: it was read internationally and, like the output of 19th-century novelist Charles Dickens, and later fantasy franchises like television's Star Trek, J.R.R. Tolkien's Lord of the Rings and J.K. Rowling's Harry Potter series, it provided millions with a captivating visionary world to explore. But this one was neither a novel nor a theatrical entertainment. It was the first volume of a densely written nonfiction book called Das Kapital. The fertile brain behind it was that of Karl Marx.

It's no insult to Marx to compare his work to the spectacularly successful mass entertainments mentioned above. Although most people think of him only as the intellectual father of modern communism, he was a highly imaginative writer. Edmund Wilson, perhaps America's most eminent literary critic of the past hundred years, acknowledged Marx as a gifted artist and dreamer. Had he been born in Britain rather than Germany, Marx might have channeled his fondness for complex creative narrative into writing long novels of the sort that were then popular. Instead he contrived an ingenious nonfiction saga as intriguing as any popular melodrama. It was richly charged with proletarian heroes and capitalist villains, and finely woven with sub-plots including tantalizing indications of a final episode to come in which History would reward all the favored characters. Best of all for readers wanting not just a story but an imaginative world to live in, Marx presented all this not as something that was happening in some alternative universe spun out by a fiction factory like Hollywood, but as reality.

That's what makes it myth. Fiction is a made-up tale intended to entertain, and is generally recognized as such by sane, reasonably educated people. Lies are narratives made up to deceive. But myths are stories that, while not literally true, answer emotional needs for many people who believe they contain truths that apply to the real world.

The problem lies in disentangling the fiction from the wisdom. If we can't, we're left with not a powerful, enriching story but a superstition. Now, not all superstition is dangerous: an inclination to be especially wary on Friday the thirteenth may be silly but it's harmless unless it becomes obsessive. But some superstitions can be dangerous. And Marx's mythology contains at least one very destructive superstition: its view of technology.

Marx's work contributed significantly to a vigorous campaign against technology that began with the critics of the Industrial Revolution and extends through the 20th century to the present. One of its most harmful aspects is the myth of inevitable technological progress. This forms a central part of Marx's system and is tremendously important for us in the 21st century. This myth continues to handicap the thinking of people who wouldn't dream of calling themselves Marxists. It undermines our ability to deal with issues ranging from the ecological degradation to problems of medical services, energy independence, productivity and unemployment. It threatens the prosperity of not just the United States but the world.

How can a myth propagated by Karl Marx possibly threaten the U.S. in the 21st century – or, indeed, the rest of the world, given that the Soviet Union, a state founded on Marxist principles, no longer exists? And given also that communism in other countries has undergone dramatic changes (with China, for example, though still a nominally quasi-Marxist state, today maintaining an economy increasingly similar to the economies of non-communist countries)?

The answer is that while the myth of inevitable technological progress was incorporated into the overall Marxist mythology with vast dramatic effect, it's also present, with perhaps even more durable force, in the literature of capitalism.

To anyone who embraces capitalist economic customs, this proposition may be shocking – even a kind of heresy against beliefs that are so deeply held they seem ingrained in the fabric of common sense. Yet, a close examination of Marx's doctrine, and of the teachings that have shaped modern capitalist theory, shows that however these two traditions of thought differ, they have remarkably similar conceptions of technological progress.

Capitalism of course differs from Marxist thought on important issues like private property, control of the means of production, the role of government and relationships among various elements of society. But regarding innovation there's a substantial overlap. This can be seen in a book that's widely viewed as a formative work of modern capitalism, The Wealth of Nations (1776), by Adam Smith.

The doctrine of technology on tap

Smith (1723–1790) was a Scottish philosopher. Before pursuing economics he taught and wrote moral philosophy. He came to economics with a moral conception of the world that shaped his subsequent opinions. His The Theory of Moral Sentiments (1759), which he revised through six editions, was more important to him than The Wealth of Nations. The moral philosophy extends greatly into Wealth, with Smith's economic views growing out of his moral vision. Both books expound profound faith in the spontaneous creative potential of people left to associate freely, exercising reasonable self-interest in an orderly civil framework of mutual respect.

Both books contain the same telling metaphor – a striking image that sums up much of Smith's vision. This is the idea of a benign "invisible hand" which, in a reasonable social climate, makes everything happen for the best.

As a rhetorical device to help promote a free society, this image is effective and inspiring. It captures the optimism of the early American republic. It seems symbolically significant that Smith published Wealth in 1776, the year of America's revolutionary war that led to the establishment of the United States as a sovereign country. The U.S., perhaps more than any other country, based its culture on Smith's precepts.

Unfortunately, there's a problem with Smith's image. Like Marx's mythology, it assumes that innovation in answer to our needs happens spontaneously, as a by-product of orderly society and trade. This is a doctrine of innovation on tap.[1] It suggests innovation is already somehow there, like the water in our pipes, and all we need do to get it is turn a faucet. This implies that our only worry is how to use it as it comes out of the pipe. But history shows us otherwise.

While free trade and other features of non-authoritarian societies are good for innovation, freedom by itself doesn't automatically produce innovation. History has seen civilizations with varying degrees of liberty, many encouraging trade and initiative with an enthusiasm comparing favorably with modern industrial democracies (and with less red tape). While many produced innovations, we don't associate them with the outpouring of new technologies that characterizes the past two hundred years or so.

Whatever the conditions are that enable science and technology to flow vigorously, they are clearly more than freedom alone. Yet, the two most influential modern economic belief-systems – capitalism and the communist and socialist theories of which Marx's teachings form part – both assume or imply that technology "just happens", and that the major challenge facing our societies isn't innovation but rather managing the products of innovation. The emphasis hasn't been on how to bake the pie but on how to govern and share it (or sell it). Thus, though it may surprise and even outrage many, the boardrooms of American corporations share with the Marxists a superstition about innovation which is today the single greatest obstacle not only to our prosperity and progress but to our survival.

To appreciate how the Marx-Smith doctrine of inevitable technological progress relates to us in the 21st century, we must again look back into history, this time even further than the era of Adam Smith and the American revolution. In 1660, the Royal Society of Science was established under patronage of the British Crown. With that act, scientific research in the modern sense was institutionalized with the full authority and dignity of the state. Previously, science had been conducted by private individuals. Now a statutory organization, protected and encouraged by Parliament and the monarch, was charged with advancing the public welfare by amassing scientific knowledge and innovation with government backing and collective resources no individual researcher could match.

Momentous as this step was, its full effects worked their way through British society slowly. For example, Isaac Newton, possibly the greatest scientific mind in history, was still a teenager when the Royal Society was formed, but despite the incalculable value of his scientific work even grew up to earn his living in ways unrelated to science, such as by working as a justice of the peace and as head of the government mint. (When Newton was knighted, it was for this service -- not for his astounding achievements as a scientist.)

A major impetus to form the Royal Society came from the writings of Sir Francis Bacon (1561–1626), a pioneering thinker about the nature of science and the role played in its progress by experimentation and the proactive search for new information and techniques. Bacon, who penned the saying *Knowledge is power*, saw science in a highly practical light, whereas most previous thinkers had seen it largely bookish. Bacon was a lawyer and a shrewd intriguer at the royal court, a brilliant theoretician yet deeply practical. His approach to science was governed by the questions: *How does this work? How can I control it? What can it do for me?* Paradoxically, this down-to-earth realism was coupled with a feature of his mind that many people might easily mistake for otherworldliness: an ability to lift his gaze from his immediate surroundings and look ahead.

The sense of change

Bacon understood the importance of patience and long-term vision. This is relevant when we hear people today urge that we must fund only research and development that can deliver products quickly to the marketplace. Bacon would have recognized this as a short-sighted strategic mistake. Before Bacon, the transmission of information from generation to generation in an institutionalized way had been the monopoly of priesthoods. Bacon introduced the notion that such highly organized knowledge management could transform science and human power over the physical world.

An early example of the far-reaching effects of the British Government's decision to take an active role in sponsoring innovation is the development of the marine chronometer, a device enabling ship captains to determine their position at sea. For a nation whose imperial ambitions depended on its fleet, this was a top priority for the government, which offered to pay a successful inventor 20 000 British pounds – the equivalent of millions of U.S. dollars in the 21st century.[2]

The realization that science and technology were keys to national prosperity didn't come overnight. It grew slowly, helped by several developments during the 1700s.

One was *publicity*. There was a widespread dissemination throughout Europe of information about science and the role of public criticism in promoting rational thought. Popular writers like Voltaire played a vital role in this changing conception of the sources of knowledge. The public prestige of organized science rose so steadily that in 1799 a group of the most prominent British scientists launched the Royal Institution, another government-sanctioned body focusing specifically on promoting invention and technological innovation.

Additionally, a sense of historical *change* took hold among the informed public and in government. This awareness of long-accepted intellectual structures being swept away by new insights was a highly Baconian development, with its exciting suggestion of new vistas awaiting discovery. Part of it involved the emergence of new political orders. The American Republic was born, as was the United Kingdom of Great Britain. France enacted the Declaration of the Rights of Man.

This sense of change manifested itself in the first industrial revolution, an early version of the 19th-century one, when new methods of organizing knowledge began to change Britain's social and physical landscapes.

The time all this took is important. Some historians have even questioned whether such a thing as "the" industrial revolution" ever happened – that is, a single, all-defining season of change. We tend to think of revolutions as sudden events, but what we generally call the industrial revolution was really a series of incremental developments. Acknowledging that what at first looked like a sudden event was really more gradual often helps us understand that it may also have been much more complicated than we first supposed.

In considering the transformation of society by innovation, a longer and larger view helps us see that many more players were involved than we first thought. We can also see that events that seem to stand alone may in fact have been building up for a long time. We can today see that while the 19th century was blessed with many remarkable individuals of enormous drive, ability and vision, its technological boom wasn't the product of their skills and motivation alone.

This doesn't undermine their great achievements. It rather helps us appreciate them. By admitting the political complexity of their world, and the many social and political factors they had to contend with, over and above purely technical problems, we can see their tasks as even more remarkable than would have been the case in simpler situations.

This relates to our situation in the 21st century because it shows the importance of public motivation and high-level political leadership if we're to achieve a new technological era. An example of the public motivation and political support that characterized the 19th century in this respect is the Great Exhibition of 1851.

***

The Great Exhibition, an international display of industrial products and design staged for five and a half months in London's Hyde Park, wasn't the first major show of manufactures, crafts and technologies. Others had been held in Europe and America. But this massive event set a new standard and in an important sense set the tone for the second half of the 19th century in Britain and all nations influenced by British culture. However, it continued a process of cultural reorientation toward technology that had been taking place since Bacon. It also demonstrated Britain's conscious adoption of a national sense of purpose as a world leader in new technologies.

The Exhibition was an iconic convergence of innovative know-how, private-sector initiative and political management. Its aim was to show that Britain was second to none in leading-edge discovery and industrial design. The government's role in this was paramount, and it stemmed from the center of British political life, power and national identity: the monarchy.

National determination versus the naysayers

The individual who drove the Great Exhibition was Queen Victoria's German husband, Prince Albert. At Bonn University, he had studied political economy and philosophy. As Victoria's consort, he was determined to play a part in public life despite the non-political stance the British monarchy was expected to maintain. He thus became, for instance, President of the Society for the Extinction of Slavery. But his whole-hearted dedication to the Great Exhibition stands as arguably his greatest legacy.

Albert's work on this project was influenced by his keen interest in promoting science to the public. He was proud of a term he served as president of the British Association for the Advancement of Science. This institution was formed in 1831 to promote science as an essential area of national life; it followed publication of an 1830 essay titled *Reflections on the Decline of Science in England*, by Professor Charles Babbage, a Cambridge University mathematician and engineer who pioneered the idea of a computer in the modern sense. The association's founding proposal called for the new body to "give a stronger impulse and more systematic direction to scientific inquiry, to obtain a greater degree of national attention to the objects of science, and a removal of those disadvantages which impede its progress, and to promote the intercourse of the cultivators of science with one another".

Prince Albert identified himself with this movement, putting the monarchy's prestige behind it. His actions in support of science included instituting the Natural Science Tripos study program at Cambridge University while he was Chancellor there, and founding the Royal College of Science which would become Imperial College in London, the first British University dedicated to scientific research. Albert also promoted the modernization of Britain's military.

His espousal of science didn't win him friends in religious circles or among conservative politicians who viewed innovation dimly. This contributed to the failure of his effort to reward Charles

Darwin with a knighthood in recognition of the great biologist's work on evolution.

But Albert's success in promoting the Great Exhibition gave science , discovery and thoughtful invention "mass appeal", turning them from perceived activities of elite scholars into a popular area of public support and fascination. It brought them from the cloistered shadows of the study into the public spotlight for the combined entertainment and edification of the masses. It was the grandparent of the Discovery Channel and science popularizers like Carl Sagan, Isaac Asimov, Arthur C. Clarke, Bill Nye the Science Guy. It made science and technology *fun*. (The exhibits included the world's first dinosaur display, which was restored in 2002.)

And it demonstrated that science and technology could be profitable. The Exhibition not only showcased British technological artifacts that were commercially successful (or whose promoters hoped they would be): it was a successful exercise in commercial showmanship. The profits earned by admission tickets were used to buy land for what would become the Victoria and Albert Museum, and to create London's Science Museum and Natural History Museum, all of which still operate.

The Exhibition didn't happen easily. It attracted a flood of political opposition which Prince Albert had to battle every inch of the way. The objections formed a gallery of the reasons that anti-science-and-technology interests advance to this day. The Exhibition, it was said, would be an eyesore. It would create a mess. It would drain the public purse. It would attract foreigners into England to steal the ideas of British entrepreneurs. (In fact, the 14 000 – plus exhibitors came from many countries, and instead of prejudicing domestic British interests, putting up the Exhibition building alone created work for 5 000 British laborers. So much glass had to be produced that Britain couldn't meet the demand and extra workers had to be recruited from France.)

There were fears it would attract terrorists and revolutionaries, and that it would undermine religion. (As a counterbalance, Karl Marx condemned it as an evil embodiment of capitalism.) Prince Albert got hate mail. His motives were called into question. Some protesters noted the apparently sinister fact that he himself was an immigrant.

But Albert persisted, not only in the monumental tasks of overcoming political opposition to the Exhibition and putting into place the extensive management structures that such a vast undertaking needed, but also in the conception and construction of a special building in London's Hyde Park to house the event. This was an astonishing accomplishment in its own right. The structure, the Crystal Palace, was designed by Joseph Paxton (who received a knighthood as a reward), assisted by Charles Fox and supervised by a group including Isambard Kingdom Brunel (about whom we'll say more later). Inspired by Paxton's work as a greenhouse designer -- he was a professional gardener -- it was composed of iron frameworks and glass, and was, essentially, an enormous greenhouse. But its scale (1848 feet x 454, providing some 990 000 square feet of exhibition space) achieved a cathedral-like sense of awe and majesty. It was a thing of beauty. Both serene and dynamic, it combined technology and art with a splendid dignity that few would expect in an exhibition of industrial technology. It was a breathtaking marvel in its own right, as impressive a statement of technological ingenuity than anything in it.

A society energized by technological possibilities

Paxton's design enabled the Exhibition organizers to put up, very quickly, a huge, strong building that could eventually be dismantled. Because its designer was a gardener, the building was what we'd today call environmentally friendly. There were mature elm trees on the site, so the design provided for the walls to be put up around them, including them in the building. In its visual grandeur, the glass-and-iron Palace had something of the wonder a spacecraft might have for us today. Its curiosity value alone was a major reason why six million visitors thronged through it in the five and a half months of the Exhibition's duration. Our sense of numbers today is somewhat jaded by the sizes of audiences that flock annually to entertainment venues like Disney World, but the Exhibition's success comes into perspective if we remember that the whole population of Britain at that time totaled around eighteen million, so it was proportionately equal to 100 million or so people attending an event in the contemporary U.S. By contrast, Disney World, in Florida, described as the world's most visited resort, drew an estimated attendance of a little under 47 million people at its combined theme parks and other attractions throughout 2007.

So successful was the Crystal Palace as a structure that when the Exhibition ended, it was relocated to an upscale part of London (again in the face of political opposition), where it was gradually extended. In World War I it became a training facility for the British Navy. After the war it took on new life as the Imperial War Museum. Appropriately to its technological history, its subsequent use included experiments by Scottish inventor John Logie Baird (1888–1946) during his development of television. It remained part of London's landscape until a fire put an end to its use in 1936. The area in which it stood is still called Crystal Palace.

It's difficult for us today to imagine the Exhibition's effect on visitors, and even on those who just heard about it. The Crystal Palace was like a great glass-and-iron door into Tomorrow. Despite our favorable comparison above of its attendance figures with Disney World's, this comparison doesn't convey all. While the Exhibition entertained, it wasn't just an entertainment. It was intended to reflect reality, immediate and potential -- a new world of science and technology bursting into view. One of its exhibitors, for example, was Frederick Collier Bakewell, an English scientist who demonstrated his "image telegraph", transmitting pictures electrically -a precursor of the fax machine. (It was based on an earlier version devised by a Scot, Alexander Bain, who invented the electric clock and a telegraph system that competed with, and incurred the litigious wrath of, Samuel Morse.)

Another exhibitor was a plumber and engineer, George Jennings, who earned the gratitude of millions with his exhibit: hygienic (relatively, by 19th-century standards) public pay latrines, where for a Victorian penny you got not only a clean toilet seat but also a comb and use of a towel. And your shoes were polished. There were musical instruments, scientific apparatus, weapons, diving suits, industrial appliances and tools, construction materials and designs, and household goods of mesmerizing variety.

More important than any single exhibit, however, was Exhibition's spirit of modernity, progress, optimism, national (and international) excitement, faith in human capability, cooperation, and an intimation that science and technology offered virtually incalculable power to improve the quality of human life in ways scarcely yet dreamed of. And a remarkable feature of the Exhibition, especially to our specialized 21st-century minds, was its multidisciplinary character: lifestyle artifacts, works of artistic design and technological innovations were amalgamated in a panorama of creativity.

An eyewitness impression has been left us by English author Charlotte Brontë (1816-1855), whose works include the classic novel *Jane Eyre*. She wrote:[3] "Yesterday I went for the second time to the Crystal Palace. We remained in it about three hours, and I must say I was more struck with it on this occasion than at my first visit. It is a wonderful place - vast, strange, new and impossible to describe. Its grandeur does not consist in one thing, but in the unique assemblage of all things. Whatever human industry has created you find there, from the great compartments filled with railway engines and boilers, with mill machinery in full work, with splendid carriages of all kinds, with harness of every description, to the glass-covered and velvet-spread stands loaded with the most gorgeous work of the goldsmith and silversmith, and the carefully guarded caskets full of real diamonds and pearls worth hundreds of thousands of pounds. It may be called a bazaar or a fair, but it is such a bazaar or fair as Eastern genii might have created. It seems as if only magic could have gathered this mass of wealth from all the ends of the earth – as if none but supernatural hands could have arranged it this, with such a blaze and contrast of colors and marvelous power of effect. The multitude filling the great aisles seems ruled and subdued by some invisible influence. Amongst the thirty thousand souls that peopled it the day I was there not one loud noise was to be heard, not one irregular movement seen; the living tide rolls on quietly, with a deep hum like the sea heard from the distance."

Not just consumer goods, but ideas

A reaction to the Crystal Palace very different from Brontë's, though no less eloquent, appeared in the 1864 novel *Notes from Underground* by Russian novelist Fyodor Dostoevsky (1821–1881). The ethos of the Great Exhibition and that of Dostoevsky's writing starkly contrast two streams of thought which continue to shape our culture today. Discussing suffering, Dostoevsky wrote[4] that "in the 'Palace of Crystal' it is unthinkable; suffering means doubt, negation, and what would be the good of a 'Palace of Crystal' if there could be any doubt about it? And yet I think man will never renounce real suffering, that is, destruction and chaos. Why, suffering is the sole origin of consciousness."

The Exhibition's mood was directly opposed to the idea that consciousness meant suffering. It was confident, optimistic, full of faith in technology, progress and human potential. The mood of Dostoevsky's book emphasized irrationality and the kind of psychology that measures profundity by the amount of gloom generated. The history of the 20th century is a struggle between these frameworks of thought and feeling. Scientific and technological progress is bound up with the mindset of the Crystal Palace. The great wars of the age are bound up with philosophies that stress and even embrace irrationality.

The Exhibition wasn't just about physical goods: it was about ideas. Not just the technical ideas that went into designing and manufacturing the exhibits, but also larger ideas about innovation. The Exhibition was followed by an innovation boom. Invention after invention followed for a century or more, in Britain and America, whose culture was closely interwoven with Britain's by continuing immigration and cooperation.

The forces behind this golden age of innovation were too complex to be reduced to a simple formula. But we can see the commanding role played by a sense of national purpose, the importance of optimistic public excitement about the possibilities of technological change, and the role of government in leading the campaign for technological progress within a context of democratic tolerance, encouragement of entrepreneurial competitiveness and political idealism.

In these senses, the Exhibition can trace its origins to the dawn of modern science in 1662 when Britain's King Charles II (1630–1685) chartered the Royal Society to come into being, to promote science, encourage scientists to share research, and make innovation a public pursuit. We can trace a direct line from this event to the Great Exhibition of 1851. Like the Exhibition, the Society brought science to the people. It initiated an age of well-attended, popular public lectures on science. Government championed a connection between the public and the scientific community. In the 19th century, Prince Albert and his projects and campaigns together formed a defining symbol of this role.

This brings us to the great technological infrastructures of the 19th and 20th century – those immense constructions whose evolved forms are with us still today, and which we must now try to update with an energy worthy of their pioneers.

An exhaustive survey of technological evolution over the past century and a half or so is beyond our scope, but we'll outline the careers of a handful of representative figures. All were remarkable. Not least of their extraordinary features were the ways in which they resolutely met the frustrations involved in crafting relationships between the private sector and government. We also see in their lives the powerful effects of social continuities. Though highly individual, they built intelligently on what had preceded them.

George Stephenson: Optimism, pride and wonder

George Stephenson (1781 – 1848) made his first foray into invention with a safety lamp for miners, but is better known today as the father of a technology that changed the world -- railroads.

Emerging from obscurity with no scientific training, Stephenson began his career with a mining lamp design that competed with a similar one produced by well-known scientist Sir Humphry Davy. The Royal Society awarded a cash prize of 2 000 pounds sterling to Davy, and Stephenson was investigated by a committee on suspicion of having stolen Davy's idea. Stephenson was cleared, the committee finding that he'd come up with his design independently, and he received a prize of 1 000 pounds. Davy persisted in maintaining that the untrained Stephenson couldn't have designed such an artifact, and the matter was referred to parliament. This is equivalent to a congressional committee in today's U.S. concerning itself with a dispute between two inventors. The parliamentary investigators upheld the finding that Stephenson had developed his lamp independently.

Stephenson's ordeal with the miners' lamp was only the beginning of an illustrious career that mirrored the spirit of his age. The first steam locomotive was built by Richard Trevithick (1771–1833), but, in a chain of events illustrating the new era's rapid flow of interwoven modifications of ideas, Stephenson evolved the first commercially workable locomotive and railroad combination. After he successfully demonstrated several prototypes, Britain passed a law in 1821 authorizing the construction of 25 miles of railroad in a coal mining region. Property owners who didn't want this new technology in their back yards delayed developments, but eventually a locomotive called the Rocket, largely co-designed by Stephenson's son Robert, was unveiled to the public in 1830 in the presence of the Prime Minister.

The public was captivated by national pride and excitement. The mood of triumphant celebration even survived the fact that during the Rocket's demonstration it ran into and killed a Member of Parliament, William Huskisson. Despite this, Stephenson was hailed as a hero. Imagine the campaign against him and his new technology that would take place today. In 1847 he became first president of Britain's Institution of Mechanical Engineers, helping to professionalize his field of expertise.

Stephenson's career illustrates the extent to which public optimism and enthusiasm, actively supported by government, fueled the inventions of the modern era. There was in the air a sense of limitless possibility. It was an atmosphere compared to which the late 20th and early 21st centuries seem jaded and timid.

The phenomenal success of 19th-century French novelist Jules Verne (1828–1905) was due not to his image as a writer of fantastic fiction but rather to the belief that his stories were anticipatory journalism, describing technologies which were not too far in the future. (Many technologies imagined in Verne's tales, like submarines and helicopters, have in fact come to be.) And while empires and nationalism are now politically unfashionable, the cultural climates of empire and nationalism powerfully drove the inventive impulse. Victorian Britain, at least in its dominant institutions, was permeated by a spirit of national identity that made it logical for government to support scientists and technologists.

It's hard to overestimate the importance of this national sense of purpose in Britain's technological boom. Empire saw in technology a way of fulfilling national destiny. To technology, empire was a fortuitous source of government support and public endorsement of projects that promoted new technologies.

This triggered chain reactions of mutual support between different lines of technological development. The railways required better means to mass-produce iron and to mine and use masonry for railway stations, and better techniques to build not just locomotives but also stations and bridges. British rail became no less crucial to the empire than the British fleet. In immense dominions like India and South Africa, rail became an instrument of economic management, government administration and military presence, giving London the ability to deploy personnel in far-flung lands. The railroads took manufactured goods to distant markets, increasing demand and further spurring productive ingenuity. Rail itself produced a spin-off technology in the form of the London underground (subway) system, boosting the metropolis's economy. This complex weave of technology-on-technology inspiration, support, government-private sector cooperation, political-economic facilitation, and public as well as individual motivation, powered a chain reaction of technological progress. Its processes are illustrated by the amazing career of engineer Isambard Kingdom Brunel.

The Brunels: Determination, vision and the rise of the technological era

Brunel's relatively short life 1806-1859) dramatically links the birth of the railroads with the rise of other technological infrastructures that have shaped today's world. It shows how rail facilitated new shipping technology, global telecommunications and the large-scale engineering projects of the modern era. Brunel also typifies the rugged individualist's underlying dependence on others, including trail-blazing precursors.

Brunel's most important precursor was his father, Sir Marc Isambard Brunel (1769–1849), whose engineering talents so impressed the British Government that it took the extraordinary step of agreeing to pay his private debts. His famous son's career is so intertwined with his that the two form one continuous epic. Born on his family's farm in Normandy, Brunel Senior joined the French Navy as a trainee on a frigate. He hadn't served for long when the French Revolution broke out in 1789. Brunel's pro-aristocracy views became hazardous, so he took ship for New York, where he became a U.S. citizen. To show his mettle as an engineering visionary, he put forward a plan for the Capitol in Washington (it was rejected but attracted attention) and participated in an enterprise to build a canal between Lake Champlain and the Hudson River.

He then secured an appointment as New York's City Engineer. In 1798, not yet thirty, Brunel heard that the Royal Navy was having trouble supplying its ships with enough hand-made pulley blocks. Here was an opportunity to use his talents to land a government contract: he seized it. Coming up with a blueprint to mass-produce blocks, he booked passage to England, where he finagled appointments with high British officials as well as to network with associates who could help him with his tender. (He was also reunited with an English governess he had met in France, Sophie Kingdom, whom he married.)

Well before the end of the 19th century's first decade, Brunel was mass-producing blocks for the Royal Navy. But instead of bringing him prosperity, it foreshadowed the problems that would arise in later interplays between government and private initiative. Brunel learned what others would as the 19th and 20th centuries unfolded -- that in managing relationships with government you don't need less skill than in the private sector, but more. You need not only the talents of an entrepreneur but also the administrative deftness, tact, patience and human insight that characterizes the best diplomacy. In subsequent years the ability to meet these challenges would enable some rare groups and individuals to bring about some of the most momentous technical transformations in history, while in other cases, the difficulty of such balancing acts of negotiation would obstruct progress.

Brunel Senior had engineering skills, technological vision and a shrewd sensitivity to the opportunities created by the imperial government's needs. But he wasn't a natural businessman. It was hard for him to summon up the craftiness needed to negotiate head-to-head with the Crown. Brunel sunk his own cash into the venture even as the government stalled its payments. The back-and-forth of continuous negotiation with officials made for an enduring struggle.

However, he not only persisted in his government work but expanded it, even designing mechanical systems to automate the manufacture of boots for the British Army. However, although he received the honor of being made a Fellow of the Royal Society, his difficulty in managing finances, and his willingness to overextend his personal assets while he waited for government contracts to pay, brought financial ruin. In 1821 he was jailed in a prison for debtors. Months went by. Then, in an episode anticipating the technological competitiveness between nations in the 20th century's hot wars and cold war, Brunel wrote, with majestic audacity, to Czar Alexander of Russia. His offer: to cross over and put his talents to work for Russia if only the Czar would pay Brunel's debts and get him out of prison.

It seems bizarre that a person with expertise important to the military should be jailed for debt alone, and even more grotesque that he should then manage to correspond with a foreign emperor to arrange what we today would call defection. But all this happened. And it did the trick. The fact that Brunel was marketing his talents to Russia got out and alarmed people in high places, including Napoleon's nemesis, the Duke of Wellington.

The Duke was keenly attuned to technological innovation. (He pioneered the use of rockets designed by Sir William Congreve in 1804, as well as shrapnel-distributing missiles.) As a result of the stir, the government offered to pay Brunel's debts in exchange for his promise not to go over to Russia. He agreed and was freed. Determined to rebuild his fortunes, he now attached himself to a grand new project, again demonstrating the small-world interconnectedness of apparently separate technological innovations. The new enterprise had originated with the participation of none other than Richard Trevithick, the inventor of the first locomotive, which Stephenson refined and took into production.

A company had been formed to build a tunnel under the Thames River, and Trevithick was hired as project engineer. Part of the tunnel was built, but technical difficulties proved so massive that the task was given up. Brunel, however, had envisioned an under-the-river tunnel for Russia. Now that he had no plan to move there, it seemed a heaven-sent opportunity for him to put one under the Thames. He was convinced he could succeed.

His idea was to abandon the strategy of digging a tunnel in a single continuous process, since this exposed the diggers to cave-ins. Instead, he envisaged an incremental technique of creating small digging areas, each protected separately while work on the next space proceeded. Armed with this technology, which he patented, Brunel campaigned to form a new company. He drummed up private financial backing and won government permission to proceed. In early 1825 excavation began. At Brunel's side was his 18-year-old son, Isambard. Because both Brunel Senior and his professional aide were periodically sick, much responsibility was delegated to the young man -- a magnificent education for a teenager who had inherited his father's mechanical aptitude.

Illness wasn't the only challenge. The chairman of the company was constantly at loggerheads with Brunel Senior, carping over costs. As with Brunel's government work, this large private enterprise faced human and management problems that dwarfed the technical ones. Eventually the many technical issues that Brunel hadn't foreseen, together with the hostile criticisms of the chairman, obstructed the additional funds needed to continue. Work ceased in 1828 and Brunel went on to earn his keep from other engineering assignments. But the company wasn't dissolved and in 1832 a new chairman replaced the one who'd made Brunel's efforts so difficult.

In the intervening years the British Government had had time to absorb the implications of such a visionary project. Now the government again came to Brunel's support, just as it had, albeit after delay, when he languished in prison. In 1834 a huge government loan was approved so the tunneling work could be resumed, this time with substantial improvements Brunel had devised, based on ideas which the former chairman had disliked. But it was far from a smooth ride. It was a gigantic undertaking for any era. The ingenuity of Brunel and his staff was tested to the limit. Problems persisted, including the illness of workers due to the pollution of the stinking, refuse-bearing water that poured into the excavation compartments.

In 1841, with the work still under way, Brunel received a knighthood. (Queen Victoria's consort Prince Albert, who as we've seen was the prime mover behind The Great Exhibition of 1851, was responsible for this.) In 1842 Brunel survived a stroke. On March 25, 1843, the tunnel was officially opened. It had immense public impact. It had cost a fortune and men had died in the accidents bedeviling its construction (in one, Brunel Junior had almost been killed). But the fact that human skill had reached beneath a mighty force of nature, the ancient River Thames, and had constructed a walkway enabling people to move safely from bank to bank while the waters continued to flow over their heads, was a stupendous concept to Victorian minds, as it must still be in the 21st century, even with our more advanced technology.

This is especially so when you consider that this tunnel was later incorporated into the London subway system and remains in use today. (It was closed in December 2007 for work to integrate it into the London overground rail system and its public use is scheduled to be resumed in 2010.) It's likely that few Londoners and visitors who pass through it realize that they are moving through the same tunnel that Brunel and his son worked on, or that they know it was constructed with techniques, introduced by Brunel, which are still used in similar projects around the world. Brunel died in 1849: he'd had a second stroke but lived long enough to see his real legacy launched – the career of his son, Isambard Kingdom Brunel, to which Brunel Senior's was a prelude. Isambard's story eclipses his father's achievements and affords us one of our most valuable windows into the social and psychological forces that made the 19th century a golden age of technological accomplishment.

Isambard had been formally educated at a school in Paris, the Lycée Henri-Quatre, and at the University of Caen in Normandy. But his real education was his years of arduous, often dangerous work for his father on the Thames tunnel. The publicity he received from his involvement in his father's renowned work identified him publicly with technological innovation and opened doors for him. Despite this promotional advantage, it's an extraordinary testimony to his technical ability that in 1833 he was made chief engineer of the Great Western Railway, an enterprise enjoying no less publicity than the Thames tunnel. This railroad initially went from London to Bristol; it was subsequently extended to Exeter. Since it was a substantial project aimed at transforming public transportation, the company formed to drive the project had to be chartered by Parliament, which was done in 1835. It's characteristic of Isambard's bold conceptualization of his projects, and his sense of tackling not just an isolated engineering project but the first step in a transatlantic transportation revolution, that his aim was for travelers to be able to board a train in London and travel straight through to New York on a single ticket.

The interconnectedness of technology, with innovations in one field feeding another, was evident in Isambard's bold decision to draw on mining-car rail design for the gauge (length between the rails) of his tracks, choosing to depart from the measure that had become conventional in railroads in favor of a broader gauge, in the interests of greater carrying capacity, speed and passenger comfort. He came to be perceived as a spectacular epitome of technological change and futuristic visions of the landscape of tomorrow, groping toward new possibilities even when his intuitions proved flawed, like his pneumatic or "atmospheric" railroad. This was another instance of his commitment to an innovation he hadn't originated; he rather moved energetically, in a way that became a hallmark of the age, to refine and put into practice the concepts of others. In this case, of Samuel Clegg and Jacob Samuda, who had designed and implemented in Ireland a prototype rail system which did away with locomotives, instead propelling carriages with air pressure.

The version used by Isambard included an airtight tube within which a piston was driven by steam engines fixed to the ground along the route. Unfortunately the system provided for openings sealed with leather coated in tallow; this proved appetizing to rats, which chewed the seals. Problems plagued the pneumatic concept. After a long-drawn out series of trials, errors and failures, attended by much public spectacle and commotion, the system was abandoned at a tremendous financial loss. But so monumental was the reputation Isambard gained as an innovative genius that this disaster, which would have been fatal to many other entrepreneurs, was a temporary setback for him. His diversification into an extraordinary range of activities proceeded. Seeking to capitalize on his fame as a successful applier of steam power in the public interest, he secured backing to build the world's biggest steamship. With an astute eye to public relations, he gave it the name of his railroad: the Great Western.

This 236-foot, paddlewheel-driven wooden ship supplemented with sails, carrying passengers between Britain and New York City, was followed by his 322-foot exclusively screw-driven, ironclad ship Great Britain, heralding a new era for international shipping. Isambard thus used steam and rail technology as stepping-stones to propeller design, for which he came an ardent advocate. As his father had done, he became associated with the Royal Navy, his work proving that propellers rather than paddlewheels represented the future.

In the 1850s, the decade launched by the Great Exhibition, Isambard embarked on his biggest ship yet: the Great Eastern. Five times bigger than its largest predecessor, it measured 692 feet, setting records for length and tonnage that stood until the turn of the century. As with his other projects, Isambard battled budget shortfalls, delays, criticism, skepticism and technical problems during its construction. He became very ill. But in 1859 the Great Eastern was launched. Isambard died days later. But his story didn't end there. When an American group decided to lay a telegraph cable across the Atlantic, the Great Eastern's size made it ideal for the task. This began a new chapter in the ship's life, and it was used for similar assignments around the world. So Isambard's work helped initiate the era of global electrical communication.

A towering creative personality as well as a celebrity, Isambard presaged modern times in several ways. A hands-on man, he did his own math for his projects, personally surveying routes for railroad tracks and personally designing London's Paddington Station and others. He worked incessantly, lived in the media spotlight, smoked constantly, got by with a few hours of sleep a night. It's unsurprising that he collapsed with a fatal stroke at 53. Like Thomas Edison later in America, he seemed to his enthralled society to be entrepreneur, prophet, public leader-benefactor and unlocker of the powers of technological innovation, all in one.

It's hard to appreciate Isambard's achievement from the distance of the 21st century, since so much has intervened and we tend, mistakenly, to take technological innovation for granted. It would be wrong, for example, to see his Great Eastern ship as being significant merely because of its size. Even more important was the extent to which its fittings, general design, use of materials and overall conception signaled to Victorians that here, produced by one of their own, was a physical embodiment of the best that human ingenuity could contrive.

To imagine its counterpart in our own time we'd have to think of not just a gigantic ship but a space station, in which the future is made real and humanity is presented with a bridge to a wholly new level of experience. Fittingly, one of Isambard's company directors said of him: "He'll have us going to the moon yet." It's appropriate that the Great Eastern's launch and Isambard's death both occurred in 1859, since this was also the year in which Darwin published his great book on evolution, which, for many, came to symbolize progress and the dawn of a new intellectual milieu.

The need for technological visionaries

What can we in the 21st century learn from Isambard's life? For one thing, that we need forceful visionaries and risk-takers who will commit themselves utterly to tasks too daunting for others. For another, that for such creative personalities to come into their own, we must furnish them with appropriate settings.

Isambard is considered by some to be the greatest engineer of his time. Even if this isn't true, his abilities were astonishing. He wasn't only an engineer of extraordinary gifts but an inspiring leader, manager and motivator. But he didn't exist in a vacuum. He came of age in a Britain in which what we think of as the Industrial Revolution had been developing for some time, and in which a tradition of government encouragement of technological visionaries and entrepreneurs was conspicuous. Brunel Senior derived significant benefit from his cultivation of people in high places. In Britain then, this encompassed a social spectrum without parallel in the U.S. or even in modern, democratized Britain. Aristocratic influence in Victorian Britain included a hugely important political space between government and what we would now call the private sector. The Brunels were, for example, close to the Spencers, an aristocratic dynasty of whom Princess Diana was a descendent.

When we view the conjoined careers of the two Brunels against the backgrounds of the Baconian tradition and the Great Exhibition, we see not an innovation wasteland into which a handful of entrepreneurs emerged to "fix the world" on their own, but a landscape in which dynamic individuals were actively encouraged by government and the public to improve the technological amenities of their society. It's difficult to disentangle this cluster of motivations from the sense of national purpose that was reflected (rather embarrassingly to us today) in Britain's concept of empire, which had a transatlantic counterpart, to some extent, in America's notion of Manifest Destiny.

An intriguing symbol of the union of technological-infrastructural, economic and political interests in Britain's psychology of empire was financier Cecil John Rhodes (1853–1902), who dreamed of laying down a continent-spanning British railroad from Cape Town, at Africa's southern tip, all the way to Cairo, Egypt. He didn't achieve this goal, but for many it summed up the charisma and will of the British Empire. Rhodes founded the De Beers diamond corporation and a country (Rhodesia, now Zimbabwe), and shaped South Africa's development. He was gripped by a Baconian sense of the future, being concerned not just with the next five or ten years but with coming generations. He believed, sincerely if in our eyes narrowly, that Britain represented the best among nations. He wanted to see it lead the world, even to the point of regaining control of the United States.

To Rhodes, education, science and technology were instruments to improve the world for all humankind. For this belief he created the Rhodes Scholarships, which endure to this day. They were intended to produce world leaders by enabling bright students from many nations to attend England's Oxford University. Rhodes Scholars to date include President Bill Clinton, astronomer Edwin Hubble, discoverer of the existence of other galaxies, former U.S. Secretary of State Dean Rusk, and pharmacologist Lord Howard Florey, who shared a Nobel Prize with Alexander Fleming and Ernst Chain for discovering penicillin.

What should we make of Rhodes? From one perspective he seems mad. He wished he could annex other planets for the British Empire, and to some he was an embodiment of the worst features of British imperialism and colonial exploitation, an archetype of the multinational magnate using money and political pull to impose a grandiose vision on the lives of millions. From another point of view he was a dreamer as well as a doer, a man of action who was also a patriot, idealist and far-sighted strategic thinker who knew the value of thinking big and planning for the long term. From a third perspective he was a product of his time, illustrating the fusion of imperial, economic and technological excitement that characterized Victorian Britain. (Interestingly, Rhodes and the Indian leader Mohandas Gandhi, whose missions appear so different, were both inspired by the same Victorian thinker, John Ruskin, whose aim was to create a better society.)

From an American standpoint, perhaps the most interesting thing about this very British man is that he strikingly represents qualities of the United States of his time. There are thought-provoking similarities between his British imperial spirit and the mood of expansionism that prevailed in 19th-century America.

These often uncomfortable similarities, and the interplay between the historical forces that drove innovation on both sides of the Atlantic, sheds useful light on America's technological boom in the 20th century -- and helps us understand how to try and create another in the 21st century.

Nobody fully understands why the new industrial age dawned in Britain rather than anywhere else. France, for example, was then richer than Britain and seems to have had a more sophisticated scientific community. Historians continue to debate it, but it seems clear that public mood, national motivation and government support played vital roles. With these thoughts we now turn to the United States, where the technological era found its fullest expression – and where the battle to launch a new age of technological innovation in the 21st century must be waged.

NOTES

1.Slabbert, N.J., *Innovation On Tap: A Philosophical Myth* (May 2005), TRUMAN LIBRARY REPORTS

2.Sobel, Dava, *Longitude: The True Story Of A Lone Genius Who Solved The Greatest Scientific Problem Of His Time* (1996)

3. Brontë, Charlotte, *To Revd Patrick Brontë, June 7 1851*, in *Selected Letters of Charlotte Brontë* (2007, P.190

4.Dostoevsky, Fyodor, *Notes From The Underground* (1864) P.62, http://books.google.com/books?id=7fvb86orPHgC&printsec=frontcover&dq=notes+from+underground#PPA62,M1

CHAPTER 5

THE CHICAGO WORLD'S FAIR: THE EMERGENCE OF AMERICA AS A TECHNOLOGICAL POWER

If London's Great Exhibition of 1851 demonstrated that Britain was oriented toward the future, America's Columbian Exposition of 1893, also known as the Chicago World's Fair, showed that the U.S. had already started living in the next century. This extraordinary event brought together not only the forces that launched a new technological era in late 19th-century and early 20th-century America but also many of the principles necessary to build a new age of innovation in the 21st century

The Exposition was a multimedia cultural phenomenon of gigantic impact. The public thronged to it in tens of millions. A roll call of celebrities provided visitors with a continuous pageant of national icons. It was like a 21st-century Oscar Night, presidential inauguration, rock concert and theme park in one.

It symbolized the U.S.'s transition from an agrarian country to a technological superpower and we still live today in the shadow of its repercussions.[1] While history never repeats itself exactly, or offers us simplistic formulae, the Exposition holds invaluable lessons for us as we seek to create and sustain prosperity in the 21st century.

The Exposition was an enormously complex event, involving the creative efforts of a vast number of remarkable people. But to the extent that it bore the stamp of any single mind, it was that of American architect and urban planner Daniel H. Burnham (1846–1912). He remains today a towering presence in his field. At the time of writing this book, hundreds of events were being planned to mark the centenary of one of his major accomplishments, his 1909 plan for the city of Chicago.[2]

In the closing years of the 19th century, when Burnham was in his fifties, he was what today would be called a superstar. To many he was America's leading architect of the day, but his vision transcended his profession. He saw himself as a creative force destined to help shape 20th-century America. Burnham's appointment as the Exposition's director of works was a unique opportunity. Few urban designers ever secured a chance to mold an undertaking of comparable importance.

The Exposition, named after Christopher Columbus, came at a moment of great American cultural ferment. It enabled the country to reveal, to itself as much as to the world, its priorities, direction and national aspirations. Just as London's Great Exhibition had helped Britons project themselves into a new age of scientific marvels, the Chicago World's Fair made innovation a conscious American theme as a new century approached. It was the biggest U.S. media event of its age, outside wars and presidential politics. It divided the long aftermath of the Civil War from the onrush of an era of automobiles, mass production, modern advertising, aircraft and motion pictures.

The Exposition's physical form was spectacular. It was a city within a city, exceeding 600 acres and incorporating waterways and 150 to 200 new buildings (depending on how you define a building), most of them temporary but looking remarkably finished and boasting the skills of celebrated architects. Its hub was called "The White City" because of its ample street lighting and use of white stucco: the name came to denote the entire fair.

To understand the event's sweeping impact, it's necessary to look beyond architectural trappings. It summed up the country's entrepreneurial spirit and technological optimism, brimming with confident intimations of the beckoning wonders of 20th-century innovation. To visit it was to glimpse tomorrow. From the instant that U.S. President Grover Cleveland pressed the button that turned on the fair's 100 000 electric lights, the public was treated to an extravaganza of amazing novelties: numerous new products that were to become household names, including ones that endure today; the first modern amusement park, with the first Ferris wheel; the U.S. Post Office's first commemorative stamps.

The fair was a national stage on which was played out the drama of the new technology. The contest over who was to preside over its electrification involved the lasting adversity between inventors Thomas Edison (1847–1931) and Nikola Tesla (1856–1943), and between two corporations whose impact would loom large in the new century, General Electric and Westinghouse.

There was something in this Exposition for everyone. Edison had invented the light bulb which he thought would give him an edge in illuminating the exposition. However, Edison lost the bid to power the exposition because George Westinghouse, using Nicola Tesla's alternating current system, was much more efficient and delivered at one-half the price. An angry Edison tried to prevent the use of his light bulbs in Tesla's work but Westinghouse quickly designed a double stopper light bulb which was different from Edison's patents and quite capable of lighting the fair. As we will discuss later, Edison and General Electric had a major role here by demonstrating the electric railways. After the success at the Chicago Exposition, Westinghouse built major research laboratories in Pittsburgh's Forest Hills and Churchill and major electric manufacturing plants in East Pittsburgh's Turtle Hill Valley and Lester, in South Philadelphia. These were followed later with many production facilities around the country that produced hardware for the generation, transmission, and distribution of electrical products, and always in competition with General Electric.

As with Britain's Exhibition, designing and building the Chicago Exposition was a study in large-scale urban management. Like a general directing a great military campaign, Burnham contended with crisis after crisis, including seemingly impossible deadline pressures, logistical issues, financial emergencies, and the oversight of an army of professionals who included some of America's most creative (and difficult) personalities.

A cavalcade of new technologies to unite the nation

To appreciate the Exposition's relation to the 20th century and our options in the 21st, one must look at its role in a technology that came to be closely identified with American technical ingenuity: the gasoline-driven automobile. The first American automobile manufacturing business was established in the year of the Exposition by Charles and Frank Duryea. The automobile wasn't an American invention, but European. It's distinctively American quality came from what Americans did with it, in answer to the U.S.'s will to create a national transit system.

This will was clear at the Exposition. Despite the display of gasoline-driven, steam-driven and electrical automobiles, these were dwarfed by railroad exhibits, including electrically-driven trams for urban transit. Linked imageries of rail and electricity dominated the Exposition. Both evoked a determination to unite America progressively in a national technological grid. The display of streetcars and other short-distance mass transportation technologies included not only electrical trams but also cable-powered, horse-powered, compressed air, elevated and underground vehicles (subways). The German Daimler engine, exhibited at the Exposition, became the basis of a Daimler company that began producing autos in New York in 1895. Interestingly, it was soon sold: its financier, piano tycoon William Steinway, was more interested in mass transit than in individually owned vehicles. Historian Peter J. Ling has suggested[3] Steinway's real interest in gasoline engines lay in their possibilities for public streetcars. (Steinway ran a horse-drawn trolley system in New York City and became a member of the city's transit commission, which devised the plan for the city's first subway.)

Ling has argued that while the automobile was later built up by advertising into a symbol of the freedom of the American individual, it was really developed as part of the national political movement for mass public transit. Indeed, it was at the Exposition that the federal government made public its decision to set up a national Office of Road Inquiry. Ling notes that even automobile magnate Henry Ford's original aim wasn't to supply individuals with a new technology of independent transportation, but rather to develop a trucking system for conveying farm produce.

The Exposition's connection of mass electrification with the call for public transit is illustrated by the background of the General Electric Corporation, which won the contract to provide the Exposition with an elevated electric railroad. GE had been formed by uniting the Thomas-Houston company with Edison General Electric, two firms which each held patents in electric streetcar technology. GE won the contract in a contest with Westinghouse, gaining a publicity coup that helped GE get hired to electrify Chicago's elevated railway, the nation's first electrified el-train system.

Edison's rival in pioneering American electrification, George Westinghouse Jr. (1846–1914), was himself a railroad man (he invented the railroad air brake). The Westinghouse Air Brake Company had been set up to manufacture the massive quantitites of air brakes required to supply the needs of the expanding railroad network. Given this convergence between electrification and the widespread interest in mass transit, it's unsurprising that the first major investment channeled into automobile technology was finance for the Electric Vehicle Company, which planned to secure a monopoly on electric taxicabs in all America's biggest cities. This venture was formed in 1897 by a group of companies manufacturing battery-powered automobiles. After 1900 it had to contend with competition from gasoline engines as well as legal challenges to its monopoly scheme.

The origins of the automobile industry thus lay in the movement toward *mass transit* that was showcased at the Columbian Exposition. But even if mass transit gave the auto industry its formative push, you may wonder: didn't Ford's production techniques put the automobile on the map as a quintessentially American form of *individualized* transport? In a sense, yes. *But highly systematized and mechanized production techniques didn't arise with automobiles.* They were used in manufacturing bicycles as well as, believe it or not, wooden horse-drawn carriages. Examples of both were on prominent display at the Exposition. Some pioneers of the auto industry were already prominent in the wagon business.

The manufacturing practice of interchangeable parts and highly planned, sequential production, later incorporated with formidable success into the auto industry as the basis of assembly-line mass production, was first an integral part of American *bicycle* production. And bicycle manufacturer Albert Pope was founder of the national cycling organization that had pressed the federal government to form its Road Inquiry Office to look into building a nationwide network of roads. Pope also invested in Boston's electric street trolley system.

In addition to state-of-the-art bicycle manufacture, the Exposition put on public display an array of horse-drawn carriages which, far from being representatives of antiquated technology, were products of a sophisticated production system. The progress that carriage manufacture had made since the Civil War is indicated by the fact that in 1865 six workers were typically assigned to make a carriage, a ponderous, highly labor-intensive process; but in 1894 the job had been broken down into a highly regimented sequence of mechanized steps completed by 116 workers in a fraction of the time.

Big carriage producers who were later to go into automobile manufacture (like Studebaker) also introduced *national dealerships* for their wooden products – a phenomenon that would later become one of the most visible aspects of the auto industry. It's easy to see how these lessons were learned and used by auto manufacturers like Ford. One of the most successful of these wooden-carriage manufacturers, William Durant, went on to apply the principles of his wagon business in the horseless carriage field by founding General Motors in 1908.

Government as the midwife of new technology

We can thus see the Columbian Exposition as the prelude to the age of the automobile, but not so much because of the steam-powered, electrical and gasoline automobiles exhibited there. An arguably more important factor was the government-supported industrial momentum, public sentiment, national demand for mass transit, industry-to-industry technological "fertilization" and progress-oriented political will that the Exposition spectacularly brought together.

These social and cultural elements heralded the rise of not only the automobile industry, the national highway system and the related oil business, but also the airline industry and the national telecommunications grid that spread throughout the U.S. over the first half of the 20th century. The latter included nationally unifying telephone, radio and television systems. The result was the world's most advanced infrastructure for advertising, marketing, product distribution, political unification and cultural integration.

Innovation was the focus of numerous social forces driving the country forward with a national purpose that mirrored the British sensibility that had been showcased in London's Great Exhibition. By the 1920s, says technology historian Carroll Pursell, "The thread of technology ran throughout social relations." Pursell adds that "industry was seen as the link between science and the consumer, but during the decades after the close of World War I the federal government played an increasingly active role in the relationship. The power and resources of the state were mobilized to stimulate the production of science, facilitate its transfer to industrial control and embodiment, and create social mechanisms and facilities for maximizing public consumption of these technologies."[4]

Pursell notes that in a 1934 study of *The Growth of the Federal Government*, scholar C.H. Woody estimated that between 1915 and 1930 federal science and research spending increased 323 percent against a general government spending increase of 237.2 percent. In 1915 the Bureau of Standards' expenditures stood at $661,100; by 1930 it was $2,759,200. The budget of the federal agency promoting aviation, the National Advisory Committee for Aeronautics, (which coordinated federally financed civilian aircraft research with military aviation interests and the development of a private sector air transportation industry) rose from just $3,900 in 1915 to $979,700 by 1930. In his study, Woody remarked in particular on the support that aviation and the development of the radio industry received from the federal government during this period.

In addition to spending money on research and other activities to develop aviation, the federal government endorsed the concept of a national aviation infrastructure by establishing a government air mail service between Washington D.C. and New York in 1918, run by the U.S. Army. A U.S. Post Office air mail service between Cleveland, Ohio, and New York was launched in 1918, with air mail service to other centers following in the early twenties. While transatlantic flight was massively publicized (and associated with the romance of the pioneering individual) by the genuinely heroic 1927 non-stop flight of a private aviator, Charles A. Lindbergh (1902–1974), the first transatlantic flight was in fact accomplished by the U.S. Government in 1919. Albert C. Read (1887- 1967) commanded a U.S. Navy aircraft that flew from Rockaway, New York, to Plymouth, England, making various stops along the way.

By 1958 the National Advisory Committee for Aeronautics was superseded by the National Aeronautics and Space Administration (NASA). In 1940, looking to a decade that would form the bridge between early and mid 20th-century technological infrastructures, the federal government's National Resources Committee proclaimed that "the government today assumes responsibility for scientific studies which deal with many general problems, such as the improvement of agriculture, the conservation of natural resources, and the development and maintenance of physical standards."

The Government's purpose, the committee stated, included "supplying the people with important scientific findings which they need for their private purposes." Interestingly, the dramatic expansion of overt federal government involvement in innovation included the administration of Herbert Hoover (1874–1964),who tends to be popularly remembered as a president who minimized government's active role in the nation's economic well-being. It's significant to recall that Hoover's professional background was technological (he was an engineer).

It's thus understandable that Pursell concludes: "Between the wars, the government accepted a responsibility not only to help foster basic science but also to guide it to industrial acceptance and finally create both the rules and the playing field for public acceptance. The burgeoning of radio use and air travel, automobiles and home appliances, would have been impossible without the regulatory activities and engineering infrastructure provided by governments at all levels, from local to national."

A flood of innovations issued from this government-supported technological momentum. No aspect of American culture was untouched. Ripples from each emerging infrastructure spun off into other areas of life. The need to enable ordinary people to afford automobiles, for example, resulted in the birth of installment-plan purchasing.

The critical seeds of this chain reaction of innovation appeared in the Columbian Exposition. America's space program and the In-

ternet eventually occurred within the same framework of government impetus that nurtured the railroads and the automobile.[5]

The Exposition shows that while the sense of non-human scientific reality and experiment is essential to innovation, as we
discussed in earlier pages, innovation is profoundly human. The
genius of the individual is needed, and also the determination of
society. Government has a central role in providing both length and
breadth of vision.

The Exposition embodied six key aspects of this political aspect:
(a) interdisciplinary enthusiasm; (b) a determined commitment to
innovation as a cornerstone of progress; (c) a sense of social continuity between the nation's past and its future; (d) a willingness
to think on a large, even sweeping scale; (e) effective mass communication to bring the public into the innovation process, and
(f) the role of government and public policy as partner of private
invention.

These points provide windows on how America's technological infrastructures have evolved over the past century or more, as
foundations of the nation's prosperity. They also offer guidelines
to help us pursue a new era of technological prosperity in the 21st
century. Let's look at each in turn.

(a) interdisciplinary enthusiasm

The Exposition was permeated by a sense of innovative excitement bubbling across conventional boundaries between different
areas of expertise. The importance of this for the flowering of technology in the first half of the 20th century, and for us today in the
21st, can scarcely be underestimated. In describing Britain's Great Exhibition and the industrial climate that led up to it and surrounded
it, we remarked on a tendency toward cross-disciplinary fertilization: innovation in one area industry triggered innovation in another. In America this interdisciplinary tendency took many forms. It
crystallized, for example, into modern management theory, which
evolved in turn into a cluster of scholarship and applied management practices called knowledge management.

Combined with the information processing systems made
available by computerization and telecommunications, this management approach created what we now call the knowledge economy. A feature of this is the long-established but increasing convergence of disciplines, and the emergence of new technologies
at the boundaries between disciplines. For example, our cumulative knowledge of the physics and chemistry of the microfabric of
matter is connecting fruitfully with our growing knowledge of the

genetic micromechanisms of life. This requires a pooling of the resources, interests and vocabularies of life scientists and physical scientists. Computerization in turn is increasingly merging with the research domains of both physicist and life scientist, resulting in new directions for nanotechnology. Such engineering and information processing on a microscopic scale promises astonishing new capabilities to create a world physically healthier than anything our parents and grandparents thought was within human grasp.

The 21st century has yet to embrace fully the exciting possibilities of interdisciplinary knowledge management. To do that we must appreciate the interdisciplinary scope of the innovations that the knowledge economy offers us, and we must learn to navigate the intricacies of interdisciplinary politics.

(b) A determined commitment to innovation as a cornerstone of progress

The Columbian Exposition vigorously embraced innovation as a key to human progress. It was an enormously positive, optimistic event, drenched in confidence about the potential of the American spirit. Part of this feeling was related to the political idea of Manifest Destiny. This term was popularized after Democratic politicians introduced it in the 1840s. It originally signified a belief in the rightness of incorporating all Western lands into the Union. But by the time of the Exposition, this narrow meaning had given way to a certitude that America was an unstoppable avalanche of increasing economic power, cultural integration, creative development and vitality. While the very poor and the marginalized can hardly be expected to have shared this enthusiasm, many Americans felt very good about themselves and the prospects of their country.

It would be a mistake to see this as merely crude, unthinking patriotism. No doubt it contained an element of this, but there was more to it. There was in the air an almost religious sense of general human progress that was certainly connected with, but also transcended, a narrow nationalism. One of the most influential public intellectuals of the time, for example, was the British philosopher Herbert Spencer (1820–1903). His writings were eagerly studied by many Americans. Spencer didn't preach Manifest Destiny but a philosophy of inevitable progress that borrowed some nuances from Darwin's concept of evolution. He built these into a metaphysic in which the universe was believed to be constantly struggling to bring forth its finest beings. It was a small leap of imagination for Americans to see their country and its styles of life and enterprise as the cutting edge of this process of evolutionary development.

American ways were thus seen as expressing not just nationalism but the growth of the human race. Industrial expansion and ceaseless innovation were seen as visible manifestations of this growth. In this philosophy, the creation of ever new products of American ingenuity, supported to the fullest possible extent by the coordinative and facilitative powers of political leaders and government agencies, wasn't just a social good. It was, in a very serious sense, a cosmic responsibility.

We in the 21st century like to think of ourselves as more sophisticated than our forebears, yet it's rash to look askance at whatever sources gave them their buoyant dynamism, for it was vastly fertile in steering America into the 20th century as a young technological giant. By contrast with the mood of that time, that of recent decades has been tepid at best.

We have not rushed forward to innovate with anything like the fervor that pervaded the Columbian Exposition. Instead, we have clung in recent decades to technologies dating largely from that earlier day, like the gasoline-driven automobile, reliance on fossil fuel, and the railroad. We've failed to take advantage of the promise of maglev transportation. We've shied away from nuclear power, leaving ourselves hostage to the economic and political vicissitudes of dwindling oil reserves. We've failed to adapt adequately to the environmental impacts of older technologies. We have failed so far to take optimal advantage of computerization and telecommunications in streamlining our society's government and other structures. We launched a national space program in the mid-20th century in a spirit of national competitiveness rather than innovative exuberance, only to follow it up with decades of half-hearted budgeting.

To build the marvels of which we're capable, we must change our attitude, learning to embrace fully a culture of innovation and trust anew in our intelligence.

(c) A sense of social continuity between past and future

Having just spoken about the need to embrace innovation, aren't we contradicting ourselves by admiring the Columbian Exposition's sense of social continuity with the past? This question is decisive. Technological innovation is at the heart of some of the most burning political debates in contemporary America. To address them it's essential to emphasize the human dimension of technology. This in turn means showing that innovation needn't reject the past. It can connect it to the future.

This connection can be called the *Janus Law of Technology*. In

Greek myth, Janus is the god of portals, and of beginnings and endings (doorways being crossed when you end a journey as well as when you start one). The Janus Law of Technology reflects an aspect of technology which can be stated thus: *The more advanced a technology, the more opportunities it offers its users to engage the best of their past, and connect it to the possibilities of the future.*[6]

To an extent perhaps unique among nations, America combines a powerful sense of the future with an equally strong attachment to the national past. Americans have possessed this attribute even when they've chosen not to act on it. This feature of the national psyche was palpable at the Columbian Exposition, which was the last word in the futurism of its period, while successfully (and passionately, on the part of its designers) projecting reverence for the past. Its design, especially its many specially-constructed buildings, took inspiration from neoclassical American architecture rather than making a strained effort to "look" futuristic. Architect Louis Sullivan (1856–1924), a pioneer of modern skyscraper design, bitterly criticized this, claiming it had set the cause of progressive American architecture back decades.

With input by famed landscape planner Frederick Law Olmsted (1822–1903), the Exposition took shape as a showpiece of what designers call the Beaux Arts style. This aesthetic, espoused by Paris's École des Beaux Arts, was already influential in the U.S., but its enshrinement in the Chicago fair gave it a massive impetus that helped it pervade American design over the first quarter of the 20th century. Beaux Arts looked to Europe's heritage for its models: classical Rome, Greece, motifs of the Baroque, Renaissance and Gothic periods. More eclectic than the Greek revival that had been popular among American architects in the early 19th century, it treated Europe's architectural heritage as an inventory for modern designers. But no U.S. architect had so far applied Beaux Arts principles on so monumental a scale as that of the Columbian Exposition.

However, it's a mistake to single out individual buildings from the complex whole that the Exposition formed. Burnham viewed the fair as a vehicle for new technology and a forward-looking ethos to define the new America. But he saw it as vital that there should be convincing bridges between the familiar and the innovative. He regarded retrospective architecture as an instrument of continuity in a rapidly changing urban landscape. For Burnham, the metropolis that Americans would inhabit in the 20th century and beyond would have to be designed to provide cultural bridges between yesterday and tomorrow.

Sullivan's criticism therefore missed Burnham's wish to show that a technologically cutting-edge America needn't turn its back on its past. Some nations had renewed themselves by abandoning much that was best in their past, replacing it with disorder, while others clung to their past so intensely it obstructed their passage into the future. Burnham wished to present an America that, Janus-like, looked both forward and back, creating a workable synthesis. The streets and parks through which visitors to the fair strolled evoked not an abrasive tomorrow but an idealized vision of 19th-century communities. It foreshadowed Walt Disney's fusion of the futuristic Epcot Center with affectionate tributes to a romanticized history of American values in recreations of America's small towns and folk heroes. (Disney's father, Elias, was employed on the construction team that built the Exposition.)

But whereas Disney conceived commercial amusement and nostalgia centers, the Exposition was aimed at articulating the national purpose. It's significant that it provided the occasion for historian Frederick Jackson Turner (1861–1932) to deliver his landmark paper about the defining impact on America of the frontier experience. The fair was American innovation's answer to the end of the physical frontier: in future, America would continue as a frontier nation, but its frontier would be that of human knowledge, capability and innovation that included both new physical products and inventive new synergies between government and the private sector.

(d) A fearless willingness to think on a vast and sweeping scale

The Exposition powerfully expressed American readiness, indeed eagerness, to develop innovative private and public projects of monumental scale. More than any other people, Americans would bring to such undertakings a predisposition to think big. This mustn't be confused with the centralized "command economy" approach of socialist states.[7] It did not represent a generalized state control but a complicated, project-driven set of alliances between entrepreneurs and public policy visionaries, on a scale unprecedented in other societies.

"Make no little plans; they have no magic to stir men's blood," is a quote often attributed to Burnham. But its full context better conveys Burnham's philosophy: "Make no little plans; they have no magic to stir men's blood and probably themselves will not be realized. Make big plans; aim high in hope and work, remembering that a noble, logical diagram once recorded will never die, but long after we are gone will be a living thing, asserting itself with ever-growing insistency. Remember that our sons and grandsons are going to do things that would stagger us. Let your watchword be order and your beacon beauty."

Even though these lines have been sourced by no less an authority than the Library of Congress, there's room for dispute as to whether even they are exactly what Burnham said. They were evidently spoken in London in 1910, but have been handed down to us not by Burnham but his partner Willis Polk, who included them in a Christmas card he sent out after Burnham died.

However, there can be little doubt that the quote reflects Burnham's vision. A point that isn't captured by the more popular version is that he believed it wasn't essential for ambitious undertakings to be *implemented* to succeed – at least not in the short term. More important was launching big ideas that would inspire future generations. The vision of the Exposition was such a big idea, as was the Chicago Plan, Burnham's prototype of the new American city. This same big-idea thinking later carried over into the Apollo Space Program, in which America successfully committed itself to putting a man on the Moon. Because of the size of the challenges confronting us in the 21st century, we badly need to return to this big-picture / big-project thinking now.

(e) Use of mass communication to bring the public into the innovation process

The Exposition was a spectacularly effective case study in mass communication. It brought together into a single event a set of images, moods, ideas, physical displays and institutional cooperations that captured America's attention as forcefully as London's Great Exhibition had gripped the British national imagination in 1851, if not more so. It rendered into concrete and human form the idea of national progress through innovation fueled by determined private-sector and public action. It made people eager to know more about new technologies in development, creating a sense of national expectation about these as pregnant as the suspense of an audience before the curtain rises on a much anticipated drama.

But its overriding mood wasn't one of passive public spectatorship. It's doubtful whether it could have had its massive effect if the millions who marveled at its exhibitions had seen themselves as merely buying an excursion to an amusement. The Exposition was a successful mass communication because of its convincing note of history-in-the-making. It reflected what the public believed would be a new, technologically empowered America of which they were part and whose shaping was a participative national project.

America needs a similar sense of public participation in the great work of national renewal today. We are, of course, in a different era. No reasonable person would suggest we can renew America simply by holding another national fair. But there's no need to. We possess mass communication tools of unprecedented power. What we need is the determination to use these to create a new national sense of the opportunities of innovation. A properly implemented commitment by the federal government to make national technological innovation a top Cabinet-level priority can achieve a sense of public technological mission similar to the Columbian Exposition's. Another way to build such a sense of national mission is through the most important mass communication system America has: its schools.

These opportunities offer extraordinary potential to equip America to lead world innovation and problem-solving in the 21st century, steering a community of free nations into a new era of global peace and prosperity.

But all these lessons of the Chicago Exposition revolve around yet another principle of crucial importance, and which may be of one the most difficult for Americans to engage. This is the role of government in innovation. Accepting that government must endorse this new public mission isn't enough. We must also subtly revise our conception of the leadership role of government in innovation.

(f) The role of government and public policy as partner of private invention

We've seen how a vigorous government commitment to science and technology in Britain helped usher in a new age of progress. This philosophy spilled over to the U.S., where one of its greatest impacts was America's creation of a transcontinental transportation and communications system the like of which had never been seen. This system came to encompass a railroad infrastructure that brought together the far-flung territories of the U.S., economically, politically and culturally, as well as an automobile-and-highway system and powerful network of airlines.

As with all major national transformations, however, the development of the U.S.'s gigantic technological infrastructures have been obscured by folklore. Because of America's historical commitment to frontier individualism and entrepreneurism, its technological story has been dominated, in popular perception, by the idea of rugged individuals coming out of nowhere, armed with just determination, a dream and an instinct for what will work.

Of course the history of America has been rich such dynamic personalities. But it's a mistake to lose sight of the complex roles played by creative partnerships between the private sector, political leaders, government facilitators, the public mood, and the sense of national purpose. A better appreciation of this political and social aspect will help unlock the enormous promise of innovation in the 21st century.

19th-century American experience teaches us that much technological infrastructure arose because of a combination of national purpose, political will, democratic institutions, free trade ... plus government facilitation and official support. America's story in the late 19th and early 20th centuries is substantively a narrative of numerous public-private sector cooperations. To gain a sense of this background story, and of how America's experience differed from Britain's, we must consider the profound cultural differences that had emerged between the two countries by the 19th century. These gave the U.S. its own distinctive approach to enterprise.

Britain was a highly centralized, imperial power structure. Political influence flowed from London through the symbolic presence of the monarchy and a civil service answerable to Parliament. The U.S., by contrast, was much more politically fragmented. Its system of government combined federal authority with extensively localized political power, the effects of which were greatly magnified by the country's size. Much U.S. history of the 19th and 20th centuries is a tale of the constant tension between federal and local powers, and of a characteristically American brand of improvised entrepreneurialism that emerged of this tension. This didn't involve only business ventures in the sense of private risk-taking, but a subtle blend of business and political dealmaking, both in the public eye and behind closed doors.

This dealmaking was repeatedly done by entrepreneurial individuals operating on the borderline between government and the private sector as commonly conceived. Many such individuals were perceived as rule-breakers, scoundrels, or, at the very least, colorful characters. They didn't function in the private sector "proper" but in a kind of no-man's-land between government and business. They gave 19th-century and early 20th-century America a political tone we find nowhere else.

It's important for us to understand them, not because we should try to emulate them today – apart from any other consideration, times have changed too much – but because they show that the relationship between government and private sector in America was far from settled in their era, as it remains far from settled today, as is shown by recent government intervention to save great private sector concerns from collapse. American commercial philosophy is a work in progress. The U.S.'s ability to create a new era of technological progress in the 21st century requires an acceptance of the creative and evolving nature of partnerships between government, the private sector and other institutions like universities.

Looking back at the birth of American technology shouldn't be regarded as a search for 19th-century role models, but rather for better appreciation of the fact that redefining the relationship between government and the private sector isn't un-American. It's something America has been doing all along.

Of course, cooperations between businesspeople and politicians existed in Britain, as elsewhere throughout history. But in the U.S. such cooperations matured into an art form. Where local political fiefdoms arose, entrepreneurs saw these as opportunities to form strategically useful alliances. This often led to mutually supportive deals being struck between politicians and businesspeople in ways that would today strike us as improper and shockingly incestuous. This was the world of those phenomenally successful entrepreneurs who came to be called "robber barons": business leaders who incurred both envy and animosity by acquiring gigantic fortunes through the launch of national empires of infrastructure in the oil, railroad, financial and other industries, often by murky means.

Even in those days such private-public associations drew accusations of corruption which eventually grew so loud that as the 19th century gave way to 20th-century mores and media structures, a new kind of sensationalistic investigative journalist – the so-called muckrakers – emerged to specialize in exposing this gray area between business, politics and government. Yet, this media phenomenon flourished as a novelty precisely because there was such a well-established tendency among the press, authorities and general public to turn a blind eye to such dealings as part of the natural way of the world.

Uncomfortable though it may be to some who prefer a purer separation of government and business, this exploration of the complex nuances of informal as well as formal private-public relationships is a characteristically American feature of the history of U.S. commerce and government. Recognizing it is important to understand American technological and infrastructural development, which is in fact a multi-generational process of experimentation to find pragmatically successful styles of private-public association.

One of the best-documented examples of such private sector/public sector entanglement was the political world of New York's Tammany Hall. In seeking to understand the complex of government – private sector relationships out of which American technology arose, it's worthwhile briefly to visit this thought-provoking chapter in American history for its illustrative value. Tammany Hall was the name given to a Democratic Party political organization that wielded a sweeping power over New York City politics from the end of the 18th century right into the mid-20th. (In 1928 New York's Tammany-backed Governor, Al Smith, became the Democratic presidential candidate.)

The strange story of Tammany Hall

The name "Tammany" came from a club that was its power base and from the New York City building in which the club was housed. The watchword of this milieu was patronage: if you agreed to support a politician with votes, either directly or by voters you could sway, you were rewarded with a political favor – a job, a government contract, passage of a much desired piece of legislation. While Tammany Hall's political manipulators happened to be associated with the political group known in those days as the Democratic Party, the businesspeople who ingratiated themselves with this political machine weren't limited to any particular political faction.

Many business figures who were associated with the Hall supported, in other contexts, the Republican Party, or identified themselves with doctrines that were then, or are now, thought of as Republican. (Thomas Jefferson and James Madison formed the Democratic-Republican Party in the late 18th century. It became the dominant political party until the 1820s, when it split into competing factions, one of which became the modern-day Democratic Party. The Republican Party was formed in 1854. Before that, the Whigs were the chief alternative to the Democrats.)

Thus, for either Democrats or Republicans to complain that their political rivals were responsible for private sector/public sector "collusion" in America's history is like the pot calling the kettle black. It's a shared piece of political baggage, an awareness of which helps us see that a government role in enterprise in America is anything but new.

The history of Tammany gives us an interesting window on America's long (and still ongoing) struggle with the nature and best use of cooperations between government and the private sector. Although Tammany was a local New York City phenomenon, it's in fact a doorway into a bigger national tale involving one of the most colorful figures in U.S. history: Aaron Burr.

The Tammany Society, named after a native American chieftain, was formed in 1789. A great interest was taken in it by Burr (1756-

1836), who came to be U.S. vice president in the administration of Thomas Jefferson.

Burr's life, and especially the vision of government-business relations that surrounded his Tammany activities, is significant for anyone wishing to understand the interplay between government and business in America. Burr represents, in a sense, a landmark in this interplay. He was as remarkable a character as any later industrial magnate. We pause here to look at only a snippet of his life, which was full of enough extraordinary events to dominate newspapers, television programs and radio talk shows for years if he'd lived in our day. His place in history has been overshadowed by his fatal shooting of Alexander Hamilton (1757-1804), the first U.S. Secretary of the treasury (you can see Hamilton's picture on today's ten-dollar bill) in a duel in New Jersey in 1804, following remarks which Hamilton had made about Burr and refused to retract. Burr was indicted for murder but never stood trial.

The Hamilton-Burr feud isn't just a dramatic incident. It illuminates the story of government interaction with the private sector in America. Hamilton's demise derailed the Federalist Party, sending the U.S. in a political direction which has repercussions to this day. Hamilton stood for an overtly strong federal government role in American national development. Jefferson stood for a minimization of federal authority and the devolution of as much government involvement as possible to the local level.

Burr sat between Jefferson and Hamilton on this issue. He was more of a practical politician. To him, it was inevitable that government and industry would form alliances out of the exigencies of the moment. His instincts turned out to be more in tune with the America of his time than either of his rivals: his vision is in fact how American industrial history unfolded over the 19th and 20th centuries.

Born in Newark, New Jersey, Burr earned a theology degree at Princeton University and served with great distinction as a soldier in the Revolutionary War, including a stint under George Washington. He fought under such awful conditions that he had a stroke, although he recovered sufficiently to continue his career. The events of his military service included the crushing of a mutiny and the enforcement of martial law in a region where both civil and military discipline had broken down. Such leadership experiences required pragmatic, thinking-on-your-feet decisions in circumstances where the exigencies of the moment determined how to interpret the written rules. It's understandable how they would encourage a philosophy of government that saw politics and business as two sides of the same coin.

On leaving the military, Burr completed the law studies that his army service had interrupted and became a successful trial lawyer in New York City. He became New York State Attorney General and served in the State Assembly and the U.S. Senate. As a politician, Burr seems to have avoided limiting himself with clear party allegiances, choosing instead to forge alliances with individuals irrespective of their ideological labels. In this spirit he helped build the Tammany Society into a political organization. He did this with an eye to the presidential election of 1800. By then two major political parties were emerging: the Federalists, who favored centralized national authority, and the Democratic-Republicans, who favored localization. Burr's manipulations in New York, through his Tammany influence, helped win the election for the Democratic-Republicans. But Jefferson and Burr had equal support for the presidency, so the House of Representatives had to make a decision and awarded the presidency to Jefferson.

This choice was accomplished with Hamilton's political support, since he didn't want either of them as president but regarded Jefferson as the lesser of two evils. Jefferson duly cut both military spending and the national debt. But while Jefferson thus sought to reduce the formal scope of the national government's activities, Burr effectively sought to increase the informal role of government at the local level. A skilled businessman, he quickly learned the mutually reinforcing advantages of alliances between government and business. An example is the bank he created as the election of 1800 approached.

The bank that Burr built

As the election of 1800 approached, New York's banking was wholly in the hands of Hamilton and other political foes of Jefferson and Burr.

Since there was little chance of a new bank being authorized in the teeth of Federalist political influence, Burr came up with an ingenious plan which showed his gift for intrigue. Instead of applying for authorization to establish a bank, he petitioned to set up an entity to be called the Manhattan Company, whose business would be to deliver clean water to a city threatened by yellow fever. The water would come from the Bronx River. Neither city nor state legislatures could find fault with such a petition. But Burr cleverly structured the complicated paperwork to allow the company to use its financial resources for purposes wider than those required just to run a water utility. Effectively he obtained a bank charter by stealth. When his opponents realized what they had approved there was nothing they could do about it. The entity that came into being, the Manhattan Company, was able to assume banking functions swiftly by an increase in capitalization, and it became a successful financial institution that later grew into the Chase Manhattan Bank (subsequently JPMorgan Chase).

The political effect of the new bank's sudden emergence was momentous. Members of the electorate who were unhappy with the challenged power of the existing bankers were delighted with Burr's coup, which offered them a welcome and long-hoped-for new source of financial services, assuring a decisive strengthening of his political faction's popularity at the polls. It was both a practical and symbolic event of immense importance for the shaping of America: practical because it helped bring about Jefferson's presidency, symbolic because it illustrated that in the very act of causing the retreat of Hamilton's Federalist philosophy of a nationally activist government, Burr's political manipulation of the city and state political systems established a pattern for the intertwining of political and private-sector interests at the local level, in contexts relevant to national affairs.

Burr's entire life was enmeshed with such minglings of politics, business and the gray areas of the law. Eventually, seemingly not content to have shot and killed a founding father of the United States, thereby altering the course of American history, he got himself into a series of events with which the best of today's thriller writers would be hard pressed to complete. He was accused of treason by conspiring with politicians, military officers and farmers to establish a new sovereign country which would include areas of North America and Mexico, splitting the U.S. and fomenting war with Spain. It was claimed that this grandiose international plot had been hatched by Burr to enable himself to enrich himself in various ways. He was arrested, indicted and brought to trial in Richmond, Virginia, where the court acquitted him.

In retrospect, Burr seems to have possessed a bizarre talent for engaging in acts that raised uncomfortable questions about the nature and limitations of government and its relations with private activities. For example, Jefferson, who was by then strongly alienated from Burr and had ordered his arrest, was subpoenaed on behalf of the defense, but invoked executive privilege to refuse to provide the information that was demanded. Jefferson argued that his position as president exempted him from the court's authority. This was the first time executive privilege had been invoked in the U.S. It opened up lines of argument that still bedevil legal scholars.

The clash between Burr and Hamilton symbolized a basic uncertainty in American thought and culture about the role of government, and how government can best interact with private enterprise, particularly regarding innovation. This ambiguity permeated the rise of American business and the development of the U.S.'s national infrastructures throughout the 19th and 20th centuries and persists into the 21st. It is seemingly built into the fabric of American society. It contradicts the misleading perception that the relationship between government and the private sector is a largely settled issue, and that it is somehow unpatriotic to seek to clarify or redefine it. Moreover, it displays not a tension between government intervention and non-intervention, but rather between degrees of government intervention.

Burr represented this ambiguity. He stood for a highly improvised kind of informal, back-room dealings between businesspeople and politicians that ranged from transparent lobbying to shady maneuverings and secret understandings. As things turned out, this style of government-private sector interaction became a feature of American economic life. Its dark side evolved into a peculiarly American culture of organized crime that reached its peak of visibility with the emergence of the swaggering gangsterism of the 1920s and 1930s, when criminal leaders like Al Capone boasted of the numbers of politicians they had in their pockets. Its more productive (although some critics would say no less dark) manifestation was the rise of great infrastructures that characterized the development of America into a technological giant, like the railroads.

These massive infrastructural landscapes weren't sponsored by central government leadership of the kind that drove Britain's entry into the technological era, and still less did they represent the heavy-handed government intervention that we associate with totalitarian states. But they occurred with extensive government involvement nonetheless. It's a myth that they were brought about by super-individuals contending without government support, or even consistently against government. The rise of the railroads illustrates how America's great national infrastructures came into being.

The robber barons as industrial phenomena

The railroads in America were significantly developed by the so-called robber barons, exemplified by figures like Jay Gould (1836–1892). These magnates built and controlled enormous transportation empires in ways that would have been impossible without the close cooperation of powerful friends in government, at both state and federal levels. In fact, while it can hardly be doubted that many of these men possessed organizational and financial abilities that were extraordinary by any standard, it seems equally safe to say that their political abilities, especially their talents to intertwine their own interests with those of the public, were even greater.

Though we loosely speak of "the railroads" when we mean mechanized rail transport, this is a really a misnomer, because rail transportation without mechanized locomotives goes back at least as far as ancient Greece. Mechanized railroad technology was launched in Britain. Other countries were quick to see its potential. A pioneering public railroad in America, grew out of a system that was begun with horse-drawn carriages. This was the Granite Railway, chartered in Massachusetts in 1826. It's telling that this was not originated for commercial purposes but to help implement a project motivated by national pride: the Bunker Hill Monument, an obelisk in Charlestown, Massachusetts, which commemorates the 1775 Battle of Bunker Hill in America's revolutionary war against Britain.

This piece of American railroad history provides an excellent illustration of private - public cooperation in the interests of beneficial infrastructure-building and technological innovation. A non-commercial project of civic value, it was regarded as sufficiently important to the public interest to justify the invocation of eminent domain to obtain the railroad's right of way through private property. Yet the railroad operation itself was a commercial enterprise. American engineer and inventor Gridley Bryant (1789–1867) used the project to introduce several important technological innovations, such as railway points, by which trains switch tracks. Interestingly, Bryant chose not to patent his inventions but wished them to be used for the public good.

Another pioneer in the introduction of public railroads in America was the Baltimore and Ohio Railroad, which at first ran from Baltimore, Maryland, to the Ohio River. Its initiators, Philip E. Thomas and George Brown, joined other prominent citizens to study the rail technology being introduced in Britain and concluded that the implementation of a railroad in Maryland would provide a major boost to the state's economy. At their urging, a consortium of private interests came together in 1827 to secure a charter from the governments of Maryland and Virginia. The government of Maryland contributed to the finance in return for a quarter of the gross passenger income from part of the system. To help make the business viable, the state also agreed not to allow any other railroad to compete for business between the cities of Baltimore and

Washington. In consideration of this public-private partnership, a dozen of the company's thirty directors were chosen by the private shareholders, with the rest being named by the Baltimore municipal government or by the state.

The state of Virginia's Chesterfield Railroad, started in Chesterfield County in 1831, didn't use steam locomotives at all – the cars were pulled by mules and horses uphill and slid downhill. The initial investigations were financed with help from the Virginia state government. The company made money from the start and ran profitably (the shareholders earned back their investment by 1844) under 1850, when the infrastructure that it had put into place was taken over by a system using steam locomotives. The Philadelphia and Columbia Railroad was created in 1834 by the government of Pennsylvania, which owned it until the Pennsylvania Railroad bought it in 1857.

As instructive as these early projects are in illuminating the private-public beginnings of America's infrastructures, it's in the building of America's vast transcontinental railroad system that the real role of private-public partnerships comes most fully into view. It is unsurprising that such partnerships would have been created. It could hardly have escaped the realization of intelligent people that the establishment of such a national grid would bring the country tremendous economic benefits, knitting the great expanses of the U.S. together, making possible an immense amount of interstate and inter-territory commerce, enabling the effective and efficient use of resources from all parts of the country, and creating an enormous number of jobs just by the existence and maintenance of the railroads alone.

As we noted in earlier pages, one of the keenest perceptions of the railroad's importance in binding the country together, and in taking the national social and economic interest to a new level, was formed by Abraham Lincoln. He advocated a transfer by the U.S. government of over two and a half million acres of land to the state of Illinois, in order that these holdings could be given to the Illinois Central Railroad Company, owned by a consortium of Eastern capitalists with founding finance of $27 million obtained in the main from Dutch and British investors. Historian Stephen E. Ambrose points out in regard to the Central Pacific railroad route: "Government aid, which began with Lincoln, took many forms. Without it, the line could not have been built, quite possibly would not have been started."

Because of the unprecedented size of railroad operations, which dwarfed most other commercial operations, conventional investment structures weren't appropriate. The capitalization and conduct of the railroads required the creation of new kinds of business entities and a close interplay between business and government. The pivotal role of such interaction wasn't diminished by the fact it was not always formal and transparent.

Among the narratives that illustrate this history is that of Thomas Scott (1823-1881). The fourth president of the Pennsylvania Railroad, which grew into the world's biggest corporation, Scott was widely recognized as one of the most politically powerful men in Pennsylvania. His career so vividly illustrates the intertwining of government and the private sector in American economic history that it makes it hard to believe how anyone can seriously conceive this saga as a story of private initiative in the simplistic sense that seems so popular on both sides of the political spectrum. (That is, among Leftists who like to see the history of private enterprise as a negative tale of robber barons unrestrained by government, as well as among more fundamentalist conservatives who prefer the myth that all America's major accomplishments have been produced by individuals acting on their own, with government only getting in their way, as though the separation of politics and business is somehow analogous in a democracy to the separation of church and state.)

Careers like Scott's show that building such enormous infrastructures as the railroads have required government resources and purposes to be extensively interwoven with private initiative. When the Civil War began, it was instantly apparent that the railroads would profoundly affect the course of the conflict. This gave the industry's leaders, like Scott, a commanding opportunity to reinforce their political influence in ways that would last long after the war. Scott's knowledge of the railroads was a great strategic asset, and Lincoln appointed him Assistant Secretary of War. (Scott was at that time Vice President of the Pennsylvania Railroad; he became president in 1874.) After the war, the destroyed railroad lines and facilities had to be rebuilt, and Scott came up with a scheme to work with politicians of the defeated South in getting Congress to approve government funding for projects that Scott advocated. This political activity of Scott's had a far-reaching influence on the development of the U.S., helping to build momentum in Congress for the so-called Compromise of 1877, by which federal troops were eventually withdrawn from the South.

One of the best-known railroad magnates, Jay Gould, was born in Roxbury, New York. Gould grew up on his parents' farm and went to work for his father in the hardware trade at 16. He studied mathematics and surveying in his spare time and did freelance bookkeeping and professional surveying and mapmaking. At age 20 he published a book which showed his keen interest in politics, *A History of Delaware County and the Border Wars of New York, containing a Sketch of the Early Settlements in the County, and A History of the Late Anti-Rent Difficulties in Delaware.*

After working in the lumber and tanning industries and in banking, he bought two struggling railroads and turned them around by astute management. This led him to become a New York City stockbroker specializing in the railroad business. He and "Diamond Jim" Fisk then became locked in a battle with Cornelius Vanderbilt for control of the Erie rail system. The story of this battle, and especially of the part played in it by New York's political machineries, is a tale of America's early struggle to define the role of government in the growth of industry and technology.

After Gould and Fisk secured control over the Erie Railway, Gould got himself appointed president. He alienated the company's British shareholders and was compelled to relinquish this post, but not before he and his partner Fisk concluded a pact with Tammany Hall politician William "Boss" Tweed. Tweed, who had become a U.S. Congressman in 1852 and a New York State Senator in 1867, was made a director of the Erie Railroad and orchestrated the legislation that Gould and Fisk desired.

When Gould sought to manipulate the gold market in ways that would affect commodity prices and create a flood of new business for the railroad, he even tried to influence the actions of the President of the United States, Ulysses S. Grant, via Grant's' brother-in-law. Though not all his machinations were successful, Gould was acutely sensitive to the strategic connections between business and government, and was eventually the master of a huge proportion of the U.S.'s entire railroad system as well as holder of a controlling interest in the Western Union Telegraph Company.

To Gould and Fisk, bribing politicians was simply part and parcel of the pragmatic way of doing business in the U.S. at that time – an extension of Gould's belief that business skill required one to be able to identify, and cleverly take advantage of, every opportunity that the social structure allowed. For Gould, forming alliances with politicians was no worse than finding and exploiting an unforeseen loophole in a contract (which he was very good at doing), or filing bankruptcy to outwit one's business opponents (a device of which he was one of the earliest exponents).

Gould was one of numerous ambitious, energetic and crafty magnates who, skillfully navigating the gray areas between business and government, amassed tremendous wealth and power in the development of America's railroad infrastructure. Historian Jill Jonnes references the amazement of a British police officer, James Bryce, at the power of U.S. railroad tycoons. She cites his 1888 comment thus: "These railway kings are among the greatest men, perhaps I may say are the greatest men, in America...They have power, more power—that is, more opportunity of making their personal will prevail—than perhaps any one in political life, except the President and the Speaker."[8]

The technopartnership pioneers

Given the momentous importance that the 19th-century railroads had for the economic, social and administrative future of the country, we can understand why politicians were so ready to cooperate with private developers to make it happen. However, public criticism of tycoons of this kind emerged as crusading journalists turned a spotlight on their business practices. Countering this view, some scholars of the development of American business have rather interpreted the manipulations of such entrepreneurs of the past as products of their age. Allan Nevins (1890-1971), for instance, saw such capitalists as pivotal shapers of the U.S.'s economic landscape and as key contributors to its globally unparalleled accomplishments.[9]

Whatever one thinks of these individuals and of their methods which now seem so alien to our time, it's hard not to see their characters as in a sense dwarfed by the very infrastructures on which they worked, the birth of which made strange demands on both entrepreneur and politician. In 1869 the rail line Abraham Lincoln had helped develop -- the Transcontinental Railroad, backed by U.S. Government bonds – provided America with the first rail link between the country's east and west coasts. It was a phenomenal moment in American history, and it's reasonable to surmise that Lincoln cannot have been alone in understanding what it would mean for the unity and economic growth of the United States, over and above whatever profits it brought to immediate financial participants. It was a triumph of technological construction made possible by convergent and mutually supportive, government and private purposes.

But the successful completion of the 1869 line was only the beginning. The full development of the national rail system continued over the rest of the 19th century and deep into the 20th in a complex interplay between government facilitation and private initiative, between politicians and entrepreneurs. This narrative often combined vision and intrigue in equal proportions. The separate histories of the many individual railroad systems that went to make up the whole network constitute individual sagas on their own. For example, the Pennsylvania Railroad at one point had a budget bigger than the U.S. Government's. In World War I, the running of America's railroads actually became a federal government operation.

If the development of the railroads illuminates the private-public nature of America's technological growth, the coming of the automobile-and-highway system is no less so. The highways were originally an adjunct to the railroads, then a parallel infrastructure. Finally they supplanted the rails. Great as was the impact of the trains on America's culture, the remaking of America in the image of automobile and highway was an even greater social transformation.

It involved not just one but three main interlinked streams of industry: automobile manufacture, road construction and the oil business. The role of government loomed large in each one. It will probably surprise many people to know that long before the New Deal, a proposal was introduced in Congress to launch a $500 million public works program funded by a government bond issue, to provide employment. Aimed at countering the economic slump of 1893 – 1896, this immense plan contained a heavy element of national road improvement. It was defeated in Congress, but is interesting to us here for the national attention it drew to the benefits of a systematically and nationally pursued road improvement program.

The political impetus for such a national initiative came from several sources. The more obvious ones were the automobile manufacturing sector, the many business interests whose expansion depended on an ability to send representatives by automobile into all corners of the nation, and of course companies involved in road construction and maintenance. A less obvious but potent one was the engineering profession, which wished to see a widespread role for its technological expertise established inside the federal government. A leading figure in this mission was geologist-engineer Logan Waller Page (1870-1918). In 1905 he was appointed head of the Federal government's Office of Public Roads and in 1911 he became founding president of the American Association for Highway Improvement.

Page was instrumental in winning recognition for a strong federal leadership role in shaping national highway policy. While he promoted government's administrative involvement he was wary of the political controversiality of federal funding for highway improvement. With a strong federal leadership role having been established for national road policy, however, the financial involvement of the government could not be prevented. When it came, it was through the U.S. Post Office, whose 1913 budget earmarked $500 000 (approaching some $11 million in 2009 money) to improve rural roads used by the mail service, on the basis that every federal dollar was matched with two in state funds. An appropriation of $25 000 more (the equivalent of over $540 000 today) was set aside for a study of possible further federal support for roads. This step opened the way for Page to sponsor a larger federal road finance package -- $75 million, or about $1,4 billion today -- which Congress approved in 1916.

The age of major federal road funding was thereby begun. Moreover, its emergence wasn't the product of the automobile alone, but rather of a complicated mesh of sociopolitical and socioeconomic forces in and outside government. These revolved around America's changing sense of national identity. Historian Peter Ling writes: "The motor car, Ford or not, did not automatically produce a national auto highway system. Rather, the impulse to acquire a car prior to 1920 served to identify those individuals who already favored improved links with the world beyond their own community."

Ling has shown that in the late 19th and early 20th centuries the U.S. was home to a widespread political desire to abolish distance in the interests of a more stable and prosperous society, with technology being seen as an instrument of this progressive social movement. The suburbs formed one outcome of this movement. A steady push to develop a state-of-the-art national highway system, along with the technologies and industries that supported it, was another.

In short, America's development of its impressive national technology infrastructure in the 20th century was as much a phenomenon of national philosophy, social purpose and political will as it was of individual ability and inventive genius, vital as the latter two factors were.

Moreover, the spirit of inventive purpose that informed the birth of the American technological era wasn't an isolated phenomenon. It had clear lines of continuity with the scientific and technological momentum that had begun in Britain and Europe. Its success in the first half of the 20th century attested to America's ability to absorb the Old World's innovative momentum and extend and continue it with increasing force and passion in the new. It flourished dynamically in the first decades of the 20th century, then encountered two massive obstacles: scientific complacency and the philosophies of the technological negativists.

NOTES

1. A connection can even be traced between the Exposition and the authors of this book: one spent over three decades working on scientific and technological development in the Westinghouse Corporation founded by George Westinghouse, who contended at the Exposition with his rival Thomas Edison; the other is co-author of a book on Burnham.

2. Two distinguished architects, Zaha Hadid, of London, and Ben van Berkel, based in Amsterdam, were retained to design temporary Burnham celebration pavilions in Chicago's Millennium Park. Participants in the festivity planning included the American Planning Association (APA), which runs a Daniel Burnham Conference Center in the city and confers an annual Burnham Award for excellence in comprehensive community planning. Burnham has also been re-introduced into popular culture by a bestselling non-fiction book about a series of murders at the Columbian Exposition, *The Devil in the White City: Murder, Magic and Madness at the Fair that Changed America*, by Erik Larsen (Random House, 2003), film rights to which were acquired by Paramount Pictures, having been previously bought by actor–producer Tom Cruise.

3. Ling, Peter J, *America and the Automobile: Technology, Reform and Social Change* (1990). We are indebted to Ling for much factual reference in this chapter.

4. Pursell, Carroll, *The Machine in America: A Social History of Technology*(2007). We are indebted to Pursell for much factual reference in this chapter.

5. Slabbert, N.J., *The Big Bang Theory of Technology* (Oct. 2004), TRUMAN LIBRARY REPORTS

6. Slabbert, N.J., *The Janus Principle and the Idea of a Scientific Tradition* (Mar.2005), TRUMAN LIBRARY REPORTS

7. not the command economy approach

8. Jonnes, Jill, *Conquering Gotham* (2007)

9. Nevins, Allan, with Frank Ernest Hill, Ford (1954-1963), John D. Rockefeller: The Heroic Age of American Enterprise.(1940), Study In Power: John D. Rockefeller, Industrialist and Philanthropist (1953)

CHAPTER 6

THE JANE FONDA SYNDROME

Nuclear technology has attracted deep misgivings about the power science puts into our hands, yet this power, wisely used, can not only improve our society in far-reaching ways but is also a door to knowledge. The corollary of Bacon's statement *knowledge is power* is that technological power can open vast new paths to our understanding of the universe. To appreciate the close, mutually reinforcing links between the growth of scientific knowledge and the growth of technological power, it's helpful to consider the story of scientific and technological development. There are few better places to start than with the story of nuclear science, which is central to much of our other contemporary science and technology.

While nuclear science is forbiddingly technical, its key concepts are so fascinating, and many of historical figures so dramatic, that they make for exciting explanation. The great physicist Albert Einstein himself concerned himself eagerly with the popularizing of physics, even though he is associated with its most abstruse aspects.

Our ideas about the building-blocks of matter form a riveting detective story that stretched far back to antiquity. It seems reasonable to suppose that in the very earliest times, and in all cultures, imaginative men, women and children wondered what the universe is made of, and whether an eye, a bone, a stone and a star share common constituents. Ancient Indian philosophers speculated about the ultimate particles of matter. Am ancient Greek philosopher, Thales (about 624 BC– 546 BC), maintained that water was the basic stuff of the universe. Another, Empedocles (around 492 BC–432), introduced patterns into the explanation of matter: he saw the world as made up of basic elements -- water, earth, fire, air -- in different combinations. Yet another Greek, Democritus, nicknamed *The Laughing Philosopher* (about 460 BC to 370 BC), theorized that there must be bits of matter so small they couldn't be cut up, and he described these particles, which he considered indestructible, with the Greek word *atomos*, which means "that which can't be divided further".

The twin ideas of elements and atoms became enduring themes of subsequent thought. The influential writings of the Greek thinker Aristotle (about 384 BC-322 BC), which persisted through the Roman Empire, the Dark Ages, Middle Ages and Renaissance into modern times, incorporated a theory of elements similar to that of Empedocles.

Persian philosopher Ab   al-Ghaz l (about 1058-1111) explored an atomic vision of nature as part of Islamic theology. Then, in 1667, things took a different turn. German professor of medicine Johann J. Becher (1635-1682), came up with the idea that matter contained something it released when it burned or rusted (which is a form of burning). His student Georg E. Stahl (1660-1734) gave this something a name: *phlogiston*, derived from *phlogisô*, an ancient Greek word meaning *burn*. The phlogiston theory occupies a pivotal place in intellectual history: it marks a time when scientific methods were becoming better understood, and science was moving from metaphysical speculation into the age of modern research. In one sense, phlogiston belonged to the pre-scientific era; in another it helped create modern chemistry, because it lent itself to experimentation which quickly made the phlogiston theory obsolete.

One of the experimenters was Antoine-Laurent Lavoisier (1743-1794), a French lawyer interested in chemistry (one of his government assignments was to manage the military production of gunpowder in Paris). Lavoisier pointed out that when an object burned, its ash weighed more than the original material. So how could something have been released? It seemed, instead, that something was added - presumably from the surrounding air. He compared notes with Joseph Priestley (1733-1804), an English clergyman who conducted pioneering scientific investigations in several fields. Priestley concluded that combustion involved a fundamental gas, which he called "dephlogisticated air". Lavoisier gave this gas (more or less) the name we still use today: "the oxygine principle". And it was realized that matter consisted of a variety of basic elements that interacted with each other in different patterns which could be investigated in a laboratory.

Out of these fumbling beginnings the modern science of chemistry was born. It was given a momentous impetus by English schoolmaster John Dalton (1766-1844). His countryman, Sir Isaac Newton (1643-1727), who systematized the laws of motion and gravity with enormous precision in his book *Philosophiæ Naturalis Principia Mathematica* (1687), had used an atomic theory of matter as a mathematical convenience to calculate the behavior of gases. Newton had said, in effect: "Let's think of a gas as being made up of a gigantic number of tiny balls that keep colliding with each other."

Dalton gave this fertile concept a much wider application, and it's with him that modern atomic theory really began. He wrote: "The ultimate particles of all simple bodies are atoms incapable of further division. These atoms are all spheres, and are each of them possessed of particular weights, which may be denoted by numbers." Dalton further concluded that while atoms of an element were identical, they differed from those of other elements by their weights, and that atoms of different elements could combine to make compounds.

By 1850 about sixty elements had been isolated. (By 2008, 117 elements were known, 92 of which occur naturally.) Chemistry then made huge strides forward as, over the second half of the 19th century, the molecule (the smallest unit of a compound or element) began to yield its secrets. A pioneering insight into the way in which atoms joined together was contributed by English chemist Sir Edward Frankland (1825-1899), who developed the concept of *valence*, which recognized that each atom or set of atoms has a specific capability to bond with other atoms or sets of atoms. Each atom or set could thus be described as having a specific number of bonding points. German chemist Friedrich August Kekule von Stradonitz (1829-1896), gave this growing perception of chemical structure a powerful representation by depicting the benzene molecule as a ring of atoms. This visual aid fruitfully fleshed out our imaginative picture of how atoms and molecules relate to each other spatially.

A different but tremendously fertile approach to unraveling the mysteries of matter was taken by English physicist Michael Faraday (1791-1867) and Scottish physicist James Clerk Maxwell (1831-1879). Faraday studied magnetism and found it to be connected with electricity and light. Maxwell surveyed everything that was known or had been theorized about light, electricity and magnetism, then pulled it all together into a unified body of electromagnetic theory whose brilliant, insightful coherence and explanatory power rivaled Newton's systematization of the laws of motion and gravity.

Maxwell produced a set of equations that showed light, magnetism and electrical currents as sharing a common *electromagnetic* nature based on the propagation of waves. Additionally, following up on Newton's work on gases and on the research of German physicist Rudolf J. Clausius (1822–1888), he formulated a mathematical method to explain the kinetic theory of gases, i.e. how energy and matter interact in a gas. This work played a large part in helping scientists accept that atoms and molecules *weren't just useful fictions but real physical objects*. Maxwell's achievements form a critical link between 19th-century and 20th-century physics.

All this came together dramatically at the turn of the 19th century, when the progress of chemistry converged with that of physics. This convergence is illustrated by several Nobel Prizes that heralded the new scientific era. The first ever Nobel Prize in Physics went in 1901 to German physicist Wilhelm C. Röntgen (1845–1923) for his studies of X-rays, a form of radiation released by atoms of certain materials under a barrage of electricity. In 1903, French researcher Antoine H. Becquerel (1852–1908) shared a Nobel Prize for physics with husband-and-wife team Marie Sklodowska Curie (1867–1934) and Pierre Curie (1859–1906) for their work on naturally occurring radioactivity. (Marie Curie also won the Nobel Prize for chemistry, in 1911.) In 1906, British physicist Sir Joseph J. Thomson (1856–1940) received a Nobel Prize for work including the discovery of the electron, one of the atom's constituents. In 1908 New Zealand scientist Sir Ernest Rutherford (1871–1937) received a Nobel Prize for his work on the orbital structure of the atom. He visualized the atomic nucleus being circled by electrons as a sun is circled by planets.

This convergence of chemistry and physics is illustrated by the fact that although Rutherford was a physicist, his Nobel Prize was for his contribution to chemistry. This didn't prevent Rutherford from becoming known as "the father of nuclear physics". It was now seen that far from being the ultimate building-block of matter, the atom had an internal structure that involved *a complicated interplay between matter and energy*. Understanding this interplay proved to require the biggest revolution in our general ideas about matter since Newton. Much of its conceptual framework was provided by a German-born physicist who wasn't an experimenter, like Röntgen, Becquerel, the Curies, Thomson and Rutherford, but a theoretician, Albert Einstein (1879–1955).

In 1905, Einstein published papers on four subjects. One was on Brownian motion (this term is used to refer to the random behavior of particles floating in a gas or liquid; it's named for Scottish botanist Robert Brown (1773–1858), who first described it after observing spores and pollen in water and noting that they moved about with a curious agitation: Einstein explained this movement in a way that confirmed that molecules and atoms weren't just useful fictions but real physical things. Another of Einstein's papers, about the photoelectric effect, contributed to the idea that light could sometimes be interpreted as a particle and sometimes a wave of radiation. This insight later became a cornerstone of the field known as quantum mechanics.

Einstein's two other papers demonstrated that the emerging new conception of the universe affected not only our ideas about the smallest constituents of matter and the relationship between matter and energy, but also our vision of the relationships between time and space. In one paper, he showed that mass and energy weren't only related but could be *translated into each other*, as indicated in the famous formula $e=mc$ .In this momentous equation lay the seeds of nuclear power. The fourth paper, presenting the theory of special relativity, argued for a new concept of the simultaneity of events, which meant a revision of our idea of time.

Einstein continued his work on relativity theory through the first two decades of the 20th century, but although its brilliance was increasingly recognized, his revision of some of the most basic philosophical underpinnings of our ideas about the universe took much getting used to – so much so that when he was awarded the Nobel Prize for physics, in 1921, it wasn't given to him for his relativity work but for his general services to theoretical physics, with special mention of his work on the photoelectric effect. But the convergence between physics and chemistry was by then quite clear, as was the fact that our probings of the interior of the atom implied not only a new understanding of the universe but also the development of immensely powerful new tools.

How nuclear science has helped us so far

To many people, any talk of the practical applications of nuclear science immediately suggests nuclear weapons and safety issues in nuclear facilities. But this is a very limited and limiting perception. To begin with, while the uses of any technology must be separated from its origins, the spirit and purpose of those origins are not irrelevant in evaluating the technology. It's important to understand that the scientific revolution that led to our understanding of the power locked within the atom was wholly benign. None of the scientists who pioneered nuclear science wanted to use it to build weapons or enrich unscrupulous industrialists. They were a remarkably public-spirited community.

For example, neither the Curies nor Röntgen patented their work. They wanted scientists everywhere to use their discoveries freely. Röntgen gave his Nobel Prize cash award to his university.

If the good intentions of its developers don't make a technology inherently good, the opposite is also true. If a technology comes to be used for harmful or irresponsible purposes, these don't make the technology evil. But it's only human for our perceptions of a technology to be influenced by its uses, and unsurprisingly, our perceptions of nuclear science have been influenced by the development of nuclear weapons the historical and potential horrors associated with it. To balance this set of emotional associations, it's useful to bear in mind not only the positive intent of nuclear pioneers but also the many positive nuclear products that exist.

One beneficial area of nuclear technology application is medicine – for example, the use of X-rays, pioneered by British physician Major John Hall-Edwards (1858-1926). Before Röntgen announced the existence of X-rays in December 1895, Hall-Edwards had experimented with the surgical uses of electricity. On learning about X-rays he quickly began working to develop it as a medical tool. In early 1896 he took an X-ray photograph to guide an operation on a patient. His research was so intensive that within just three years of the discovery of X-rays, Hall-Edwards' left hand was so damaged by radiation that it had to be amputated. It is still displayed today at the Chamberlain Museum of Pathology in Birmingham, England. It reminds us of the dangers of nuclear materials but also of the heroism and idealism permeating much technological and scientific advance.

X-ray technology has become such a central part of what we think of as modern medicine that most of us take it for granted. It would be hard to conceive of medical practice without it. Its usefulness isn't confined to the straightforward "X-ray picture" with which most people are familiar, but includes fluoroscopy (not just photographing the interior of the body but studying internal parts while they're in action) and computed tomography, also called CAT scanning, in which computers create three-dimensional images. Then there's nuclear medicine, in which radioactivity is used to diagnose or treat illnesses. Cancer may be treated with focused radiation or by admitting radiation into the body in controlled amounts, in the form of pellets or radiopharmaceuticals (radioactive drugs).

Another highly beneficial offshoot of atomic science is the development of two enormously powerful types of microscope: the X-ray microscope, which uses X-rays instead of visible light to achieve image magnification great enough that we can see inside bacteria, and the electron microscope, which uses electrons to enlarge images to the order of as much as two million. At the opposite end of the scale, astronomers use X-rays to study distant parts of the universe – not by bombarding the skies with X-rays but by examining the X-rays that emanate from celestial entities like stars and black holes. The development of X-ray astronomy has vastly extended our power to acquire knowledge of the cosmos beyond the Earth.

A further medical use of our knowledge of radiation is the laser. This word is derived from the phrase *Light Amplification by Stimulated Emission of Radiation*. Laser beams have a wide range of medical applications, including surgery. Then we come to the non-medical uses of laser technology. These can be found in all corners of modern life, from bar codes in supermarkets to DVDs and compact discs. In fact, the fundamentals of laser technology enable us to see that atomic science has shaped our entire modern civilization in so many ways it's easy to understand why so many people are unaware of its impact. Laser technology exists because of what we've learned about microwaves, which are a category of the electromagnetic radiation studied by Faraday and Maxwell.

Building on Maxwell's work, German physicist Heinrich R. Hertz (1857–1894) built the first device that generated and registered radio waves, thereby opening the door to radio technology, as well as to radar (from *RAdio Detection And Ranging*). Westinghouse Electric Corporation commercialized radar technology at its Chicopee Falls, Massachusetts and Baltimore, Wilkins Avenue plants, all of which were consolidated in the mid 1950s at the Baltimore airport site which became the Air Arm Division then the Defense Electronics Business Unit. It was here that the Pulse Doppler Radar was patented by Harry Smith, David Mooney and others. Out of radar and radio research came the *vacuum tube*, used to amplify and manage electronic signals, and its successor the *transistor*. The transistor, developed around 1947 by British – American physicist William B. Shockley (1910–1989) and American physicists Walter H. Brattain (1902–1987) and John Bardeen (1908–1991), rapidly became the basis of modern electronic technologies. It incorporated *semiconductor* materials, such as silicon, which are so called because their ability to conduct electricity is flexible and can be cheaply and easily managed.

The advantages of transistors over vacuum tubes included their small size: they made it possible for electronic devices to be *miniaturized*, a process that presently continues. This shrinkage in turn enabled increasing numbers of transistors, and components supporting them, to be *joined together* with electrical circuits in a tiny device called an *integrated circuit, or microchip*. The concept of the integrated circuit was pioneered by British radar researcher Geoffrey W. Dummer (1909–2002) and developed as a commercial technology by Americans Jack S. Kilby (1923-2005) and Robert N. Noyce (1927-1990). The advent of microchips ushered in what we now loosely call the *information era*. One of the various meanings of this term is that microchips enable us to store, transmit and manage great amounts of information in physical media that are getting smaller and smaller, such as a DVD, cell phone or personal computer.

Another meaning of "information era" is that we've extended our information-processing methods from *analog to digital*. Analog technology assists human calculation, or transmits information, via devices that attempt to directly reflect or mimic (i.e. to create an analogy of) a variable real-life situation in the technology. An example is a vinyl record in which the sound of a human voice has been etched into the surface, so a needle traveling along that same surface will reproduce the same information (i.e., whatever the original voice said or sang). Another is an analog clock, which replicates the passage of time in a twelve-hour period and, by the addition of mechanical parts (the hands), enable us to know the time without having to perform an act of calculation or memory. Still another example is any computer that uses mechanical parts to replicate a phenomenon about which we wish to make calculations.

Digital technology, by contrast, doesn't try to mimic the original form of its subject-matter but translates the pattern of the original into a set of numbers. These can be stored or transmitted to another digital device which reassembles them into the shape or sound of the original. Because integrated circuits can compress a great amount of this kind of information into a very small space, it enables us to store huge volumes of communication product very conveniently, as when we watch a movie on a DVD instead of on old-fashioned film, which might have taken up several comparatively bulky reels. We can also store, alongside the information, complicated sets of instructions about how to manipulate it for us.

All the above developments have proceeded, in one way or another, from our investigation of the atom. They may seem like many different developments, since they occurred in different places and times and involved different people with different backgrounds, aims and interests. But these differences are like those of a dispersed family. The factors that unite these different technological accomplishments are strong, and we can trace their lines of intellectual origin in all their stories. They're all part of the story of atomic research.

It's important to give atomic research credit for this vital role when we consider what it can do for us in the 21st century.

The atom as a source of power

We all know today how not only America but the world is facing an energy crisis. The fuel we've been using for decades, and still mainly use, pollutes the Earth to an extent that threatens the future stability and well-being of all nations, and perhaps even human survival. America also faces severe economic and strategic challenges because it relies heavily on technologies that need petroleum, a fossil fuel whose reserves are rapidly dwindling, with remaining supplies being controlled by countries and interests whose politics and objectives can be problematical.

Historically, two companies – General Electric and Westinghouse Electric Corporation – have been at the forefront of commercial nuclear power development. The technological foundations for both companies were developed at their respective research laboratories in Schenectady, New York and Pittsburgh, Pennsylvania. The commercial developments follow closely the progress that both companies made in contributing to military - more specifically naval - nuclear power development, headed by Admiral Rickover, who's program gave us the superbly efficient and accident free surface vessel and submarine nuclear propulsion systems. Much of this development and testing took place at the Westinghouse managed Bettis Atomic Power Laboratory, in Pittsburgh, Pennsylvania. Both of these companies designed and built many of the world's existing nuclear power systems and both designed evolutionary and revolutionary, from a safety perspective, nuclear power plants in the post-Chernobyl and Three Mile Island. General Electric and Westinghouse, and their successor and partner companies, such as Toshiba, Hitachi, Mitsubishi, and Areva NP, are capable and ready to start construction on a safe and cost effective and environmentally friendly generation of nuclear power plants that may be the most effective solution to global climate change and the world's power needs. Coincidentally, nuclear power generation produces, as a byproduct, the hydrogen that is needed to power fuel cell vehicles that further help reduce global CO_2 emissions.

Against this background, on July 29, 2003, the Massachusetts Institute of Technology (MIT) publicly released the results of an interdisciplinary study conducted by researchers at MIT and Harvard University. The study was jointly chaired by Professor John Deutch, Institute Professor of Chemistry at MIT, and physicist Professor Ernest J. Moniz, Director of Energy Studies at MIT's Laboratory for Energy and the Environment. Prof. Deutch called their undertaking "the most comprehensive, interdisciplinary study ever conducted on the future of nuclear energy."

The report[1] stated that "Over the next 50 years, unless patterns change dramatically, energy production and use will contribute to global warming through large-scale greenhouse gas emissions — hundreds of billions of tonnes of carbon in the form of carbon dioxide. Nuclear power could be one option for reducing carbon emissions. At present, however, this is unlikely: nuclear power faces stagnation and decline." It added: "Our survey results show that the public does not yet see nuclear power as a way to address global warming, suggesting that further public education may be necessary."

According to the MIT group, a large, successful expansion of nuclear power required solutions to four critical problems:

* *Cost.* "In deregulated markets, nuclear power is not now cost competitive with coal and natural gas. However, plausible reductions by industry in capital cost, operation and maintenance costs, and construction time could reduce the gap. Carbon emission credits, if enacted by government, can give nuclear power a cost advantage."

* *Safety.* "Modern reactor designs can achieve a very low risk of serious accidents, but 'best practices' in construction and operation are essential. We know little about the safety of the overall fuel cycle, beyond reactor operation."

* *Waste.* "Geological disposal is technically feasible but execution is yet to be demonstrated or certain. A convincing case has not been made that the long-term waste management benefits of advanced, closed fuel cycles involving reprocessing of spent fuel are outweighed by the short-term risks and costs. Improvement in the open, once-through fuel cycle may offer waste management benefits as large as those claimed for the more expensive closed fuel cycles."

* *Proliferation.* "The current international safeguards regime is inadequate to meet the security challenges of the expanded nuclear deployment contemplated in the global growth scenario. The reprocessing system

now used in Europe, Japan, and Russia that involves separation and recycling of plutonium presents unwarranted proliferation risks. We conclude that, over at least the next 50 years, the best choice to meet these challenges is the open, once-through fuel cycle. We judge that there are adequate uranium resources available at reasonable cost to support this choice under a global growth scenario. Public acceptance will also be critical to expansion of nuclear power."

By "once-through", the report refers to the practice (supported by the U.S., Canada, Sweden, Finland, South Africa and Spain) of sending nuclear fuel into storage without additional processing or use after it's been used once. This contrasts with the reprocessing methods that the report rejects on the basis of cost and safety risk; in these, fuel is recycled after initial use.

The group recommended:

* Support for the U.S. Department of Energy 2010 initiative to reduce costs through new design certification, site banking, and combined construction and operation licenses.

* That "safety-enhancing evolutionary reactor design" receive a production tax credit contributing to the plant's construction cost, in order to "challenge the industry to demonstrate the cost reductions claimed for new reactor construction, with industry assuming the risks and benefits beyond first-mover costs."

* That federal or state portfolio standards should include incremental nuclear power capacity as a carbon-free source.

* That the Department of Energy should broaden its long-term waste research and development program, "to include improved engineered barriers, investigation of alternative geological environments, and deep bore hole disposal", and development of "A system of central facilities to store spent fuel for many decades prior to geologic disposal" as an integral part of the waste management strategy. The US should also, the group recommended, "encourage greater harmonization of international standards and regulations for waste transportation, storage, and disposal."

* That the International Atomic Energy Agency should have authority to inspect all suspect facilities and develop a worldwide system for materials protection, control and accountability "that goes beyond accounting,

reporting, and periodic inspections", and that "the US should monitor and influence developments in a broad range of enrichment technologies."

* That the Department of Energy research and development program should focus on the once-through fuel cycle. It should also "conduct an international uranium resource assessment;

establish a large nuclear system analysis, modeling, and simu-lation project, including collection of engineering data, to as-sess alternative nuclear fuel cycle deployments relative to the four critical challenges; and halt development and demonstra-tion of advanced fuel cycles or reactors until the results of the nuclear system analysis project are available."

When the report was released, Prof. Deutch said: "Fossil fu-el-based electricity is projected to account for more than 40% of global greenhouse gas emissions by 2020. In the U.S. 90% of the carbon emissions from electricity generation come from coal-fired generation, even though this accounts for only 52% of the electric-ity produced. Taking nuclear power off the table as a viable alterna-tive will prevent the global community from achieving long-term gains in the control of carbon dioxide emissions."

According to the group's report, "The nuclear option should be retained precisely because it is an important carbon-free source of power."

The group urged the U.S. Government to establish a Nuclear System Modeling project to collect the engineering data for analy-sis to evaluate alternative reactor concepts and fuel cycles, using the criteria of cost, safety, waste, and proliferation resistance. It urged delaying expensive development projects pending the out-come of this multi-year effort. The group emphasized that nuclear power isn't the only non-carbon option and believed it should be pursued as a long-term option along with other options such as the use of renewable energy sources, increased efficiency, and carbon sequestration.

The group said it considered that nuclear technology, "despite the challenges it faces, is an important option for the United States and the world to meet future energy needs without emitting car-bon dioxide (CO_2) and other atmospheric pollutants. Other options include increased efficiency, renewables, and sequestration. We be-lieve that all options should be preserved as nations develop strate-gies that provide energy while meeting important environmental challenges. The nuclear power option will only be exercised, how-ever, if the technology demonstrates better economics, improved safety, successful waste management, and low proliferation risk, and if public policies place a significant value on electricity produc-tion that does not produce CO_2."

The Weapons of Mass Destruction dogma

What should we make of this study? It's clearly the considered, thoughtful product of serious and scholarly minds, and deserves great respect. At the same time, we know from history, including quite recent history, that thoughtful, serious, scholarly minds can make errors of judgment as large as those made by far less thoughtful and apparently less informed minds. They can lead vast corporations into catastrophic decisions that impact the lives and well-being of enormous numbers of people. They can steer national economies into disaster and lead countries into ill-considered and unnecessary wars.

It's perhaps a symbolically useful reminder of this fallibility of judgment that the group's co-chair, Prof. Deutch, isn't only a professor of chemistry but a former Director of the U.S. Central Intelligence Agency, a government agency whose work is of great importance but whose conclusions can't be said to be above errors of judgment. Prof. Deutch, who served as CIA Director in the Clinton Administration, from May 1995 to December 1996, made at least one very serious error of judgment when, after he left the CIA, it came to light that his private computer, or computers, improperly contained classified information. This led to a formal investigation after which he was stripped of his security clearance; and possibility of prosecution was staved off by his being pardoned by President Clinton. The only bearing that this has on his thinking about nuclear power is that it illustrates in a general sense the important point high intelligence and admirable learning are in themselves no guarantees against questionable vision.

And there is questionable vision in the MIT report. Its vision is narrow in relation to the crisis to which it's supposed to respond, and this narrowness flaws it badly. Interestingly, this criticism applies whether you're for nuclear power or against it.

For example, a criticism of the report was published by Amory B. Lovins, Chief Executive Officer of the Rocky Mountain Institute (RMI) in Snowmass, Colorado. RMI opposes the expansion of nuclear power, advising instead that we address our environmental and energy problems by developing alternative sources of energy like wind and solar power. RMI's credo on energy is that "The inefficient use of energy causes many economic and security problems, and most environmental ones. Simply using energy in a way that saves money would avoid most of these problems. RMI therefore works to speed the free-market adoption of a 'Soft Energy Path' — a profitable blending of efficient energy use with safe, sustainable sources to provide the same or better services while saving money, abating pollution and climate change, reducing the threat of nuclear proliferation, and increasing global security."

RMI says nuclear power is too expensive and financially risky;

that it consumes money that could be better invested in alternative energy efficiency measures; and that it poses significant problems of radioactive waste disposal and the proliferation of potential nuclear weapons material.

In his comment on the MIT report, Lovins points out that in regard to non-nuclear energy options, "the study 'did not analyze' any of them – its simplistic projections of electricity demand didn't even mention efficient use, let alone model its competition with supply – so it reached no conclusion about their competitiveness or capabilities. It nonetheless emphatically asserted that 'it is likely we shall need all' these technologies, and 'In our judgment, it would be a mistake to exclude any...at this time,' so nuclear power merits increased subsidies."[2]

Readers might be forgiven, he says, "for supposing that somewhere, the 170-page report provides an analytic basis for that striking claim. It doesn't. The alleged need for all options, including nuclear power, is purely the authors' personal opinion wrapped in a big study of other questions. Also unanalyzed and unmentioned, therefore, is the key policy issue of opportunity cost – how the expanded nuclear subsidies they urge would divert resources from its competitors and thus slow their adoption. The study recommends useful policy shifts on reprocessing and nonproliferation. Yet, disappointingly, its very capable authors spent so long examining uneconomic traditional energy technologies that they had no time left to consider the successful, less centralized options that, despite an unfavorably tilted playing-field, are rapidly displacing them. Global windpower (which could more than power the world), for example, grew in 2002 from 24 to 31 GW—over twice nuclear power's average 1990s annual addition."

Now, this comment by Lovins is clearly *against* the promotion of nuclear power. He's irked by what he sees as the flawed vision of the group because he believes this vision has omitted vital information about non-nuclear technologies, and that if these are not taken into account, what the group has to say about nuclear technologies is weak.

But you don't have to be either anti-nuclear or pro-nuclear to discern the flaws. Boiled down, what the report means is that nuclear power is interesting, but let's wait and see what new information about it comes to light in coming decades, and let's base our decisions on that, and if we can encourage the private sector to do some more research on it while we wait, so much the better.

This may be a somewhat uncharitable paraphrase, but it sums up the spirit of the report. It wouldn't be misleading to call it a bureaucratic report, using this adjective in its meaning of "character-ized by excessive red tape and routine". There's little if any sense of urgency in it. It uses as its framework of discussion a 2050 scenario that assumes dramatically increased worldwide nuclear capacity, but seems to offer little guidance on what we can do to jump-start nuclear implementation immediately. While it makes some recom-mendations, they can scarcely be called proactive, or such as to inspire leadership, or vigorous movement in any direction.

This lethargic mood is particularly striking when it's compared with the statements made in favor of expanded nuclear technol-ogy by Patrick Moore, a Canadian biologist, environmental consul-tant and former president of the Canadian arm of Greenpeace as well an ex-director of Greenpeace International. In the article *Going Nuclear: A Green Makes the Case*, in *The Washington Post* of April 16, 2006[3], Moore reported: "In the early 1970s when I helped found Greenpeace, I believed that nuclear energy was synonymous with nuclear holocaust, as did most of my compatriots. Thirty years on, my views have changed, and the rest of the environmental move-ment needs to update its views, too, because nuclear energy may just be the energy source that can save our planet from another possible disaster: catastrophic climate change."

Declaring that over 600 coal-fired electric plants produced 36 percent of U.S. emissions, and almost a tenth of global emissions, of carbon dioxide, the main greenhouse gas contributing to cli-mate change, Moore called nuclear energy "the only large-scale, cost-effective energy source that can reduce these emissions while continuing to satisfy a growing demand for power." Here are his views on some of the issues raised by opponents of nuclear power:

Cost: "It is in fact one of the least expensive energy sources. In 2004, the average cost of producing nuclear energy in the United States was less than two cents per kilowatt-hour, com-parable with coal and hydroelectric. Advances in technology will bring the cost down further in the future."

Nuclear waste: "Within 40 years, used fuel has less than one-thousandth of the radioactivity it had when it was removed from the reactor. And it is incorrect to call it waste, because 95 percent of the potential energy is still contained in the used fuel after the first cycle. Now that the United States has removed the ban on recycling used fuel, it will be possible to use that energy and to greatly reduce the amount of waste that needs treatment and disposal. Last month, Japan joined France, Britain and Russia in the nuclear-fuel-recycling business. The United States will not be far behind."

The danger of nuclear plants being seized by terrorists: "The six-feet-thick reinforced concrete containment vessel protects the contents from the outside as well as the inside. And even if a jumbo jet did crash into a reactor and breach the containment, the reactor would not explode. There are many types of facilities that are far more vulnerable, including liquid natural gas plants, chemical plants and numerous political targets."

General safety: "Today, there are 103 nuclear reactors quietly delivering just 20 percent of America's electricity. Eighty percent of the people living within 10 miles of these plants approve of them (that's not including the nuclear workers). Although I don't live near a nuclear plant, I am now squarely in their camp... No one has died of a radiation-related accident in the history of the U.S. civilian nuclear reactor program. (And although hundreds of uranium mine workers did die from radiation exposure underground in the early years of that industry, that problem was long ago corrected.)"

The risk that nuclear fuel might be used to make nuclear weapons: "This is the most serious issue associated with nuclear energy and the most difficult to address... but just because nuclear technology can be put to evil purposes is not an argument to ban its use."

Moore put his finger on the most emotional element of the nuclear energy debate: its association with nuclear weapons. This association is so powerful that it's negatively affected the public perception of not only nuclear power stations but nuclear science itself. And yet, it's a very thinly based association, because there is scant evidence that the construction of nuclear power stations can in any meaningful way enable anyone, anywhere, to acquire nuclear weapons more easily than they would otherwise be able to do. There's also scant evidence that nuclear power stations are inherently unsafe.

The association with unsafety and weapons that the opponents of nuclear technology have foisted on nuclear power is similar to the allegations of weapons of mass destruction that launched America into a long and costly war against Iraq. No weapons of mass destruction were found in Iraq because the intelligence that suggested that they were there was poor. The same applies to the dogmas that have been used by negativists to deprive America of nuclear power. They represent   intelligence of poor quality. Yet they've damaged both America's nuclear energy resources and, extraordinarily, even the discipline of nuclear physics to which our present scientific knowledge owes so much.

The public image of nuclear physics

The story of nuclear physics is one of the most remarkable public relations disasters in history. In the space of a few decades, the publicly perceived promise of the atom to serve humanity, and the international admiration that surrounded the many brilliant people who pioneered the unraveling of the mysteries of matter, collapsed. In recent years, some physicists have felt compelled to band together for what is, in effect, a public relations damage control exercise for their discipline.

In 1988 Spencer R. Weart (currently Director of the Center for History of Physics of the American Institute of Physics) published a book aimed at countering this public relations problem: *Nuclear Fear: A History of Images*. It surveyed many symbols in mass culture and folklore which appeared to have influenced negative public perceptions of nuclear physics and nuclear energy, often in ways unsupported or even contradicted by evidence.

Despite Weart's hope that a more enlightened grasp of nuclear issues would, the prestige of nuclear science continued to decline. Theatrical films, television dramas, comic books, novels and other forms of public discourse persisted in promoting a stereotypical image of nuclear science as a dangerous tool of sinister interests. These were often evil or at least irresponsible scientists, corrupt politicians and cynical industrialists, out to impose nuclear technologies of various types on the world for their own reckless purposes.

The threats posed by such nuclear alliances have been presented as including the destruction of civilization by nuclear war, catastrophic malfunctions of power stations, the hijacking and calamitous use of nuclear devices by terrorists and rogue states, and massive contaminations by unsuccessfully stored or transported nuclear waste, with horrific consequences for human and environmental health. By 1998 this media tradition of profound suspicion toward nuclear technologies and its enablers was so great that a group of nuclear physicists launched a European organization to promote a better-informed public understanding of nuclear science. It was named Public Awareness of Nuclear Science (PANS).

One of PANS' founders, Professor Raymond S Mackintosh, of the Department of Physics and Astronomy at Britain's Open University, acknowledged[4]: "Nuclear physics has a particular public relations problem with deep historical roots." One of the steps undertaken by PANS was the writing and publication of a popular book on nuclear physics, *Nucleus: A Trip into the Heart of Matter* (2001), by Mackintosh and three other scientists, J. Al-Khalili, B. Jonson and T. Peña. Mackintosh later recalled[5]:

"In the spring of 1998, a meeting was called by Jules Deutsch, Adriaan van der Woude, and Alan Shotter at Louvain la Neuve to discuss what measures might be taken to improve the image of nuclear physics. This was the beginning of PANS, Public Awareness of Nuclear Science. We quickly recognized that there were three distinct groups to educate: the general public, policymakers, and scientists outside the nuclear field. Of the three, I think we were most concerned with educating the general public, for a number of reasons: (i) it is the most challenging task; (ii) the general public in a democracy have real power, especially when it comes to spending taxpayers' money; (iii) the next generation of nuclear physicists, upon which the continuation of our subject depends, are the younger part of the general public; (iv) the problem is deep—many examples were discussed of the irrationality infecting modern life, and the particular fears roused by the very word 'nuclear', as discussed at length in the book *Nuclear Fear* by Spencer Weart."

It emerged, according to Mackintosh, that there were "clear national differences" as to the nature of the problem, but a few collaborative actions were agreed on, including a popular book. Mackintosh noted that despite a British boom in the publication of popular scientific books, "among all the books on space and time, Schrödinger's kittens, the quark explosion, trilobites, and transistors, there was nothing on nuclear physics."

This astonishing recession of the public image of nuclear science – a field at the heart of the transformation of the modern world – is a grave threat to our future scientific progress. We need to repair it urgently. To do so, we must move on from the negative emotional images that we've associated with nuclear power since the atomic bomb arrived. The intellectual paralysis that these images have caused is evident when you stand back and survey the quality of nuclear debate that's occurred over recent decades. It has a disturbing sameness to it. The extent to which we seem to remain unable to move forward on this intellectually or emotionally is indicated in the very title of a 2007 book, *Nuclear Waste Stalemate: Political and Scientific Controversies*, by Robert and Susanne Vandenbosch, which opens:

"Nineteen years have passed since 1987 when the US Congress selected Yucca Mountain, Nevada, as the only site to studied further as the final resting place for spent fuel produced in civilian reactors. Since then, many new developments have taken place, both in the United States and abroad." But we then learn that these "new developments" have, at least in the US, in fact amounted to a quagmire of political obstruction and endless red tape. "In the United States, which has the largest amount of spent fuel, the secretary of energy recommended and the president approved Yucca Mountain as a geological repository. The State of Nevada vetoed this decision, but its veto was overridden by both the House and the Senate, and the proposal was signed into law by the president in 2002. Subsequently, the Yucca Mountain project has suffered delays in preparing a license application and encountered another roadblock in 2004 when a Federal Court of Appeals upheld a challenge by the State of Nevada and ruled that the 10,000-year compliance period for the isolation of radioactive waste was too short. At this point, the repository has not been licensed, and the possibility exists that it may never accept spent fuel from nuclear reactors."

The Vandenbosches note that "not only does the United States not have a permanent spent fuel storage site operating, it has not even approved of an interim storage facility... This problem is not unique to the United States. No other country in the world has opened a permanent spent fuel waste repository at this point. Some countries, including France, Japan, and the United Kingdom, reprocess spent fuel. Reprocessing still leaves large amounts of highly radioactive waste for ultimate disposal. Accidents at reprocessing facilities have led the United Kingdom to reexamine this approach. Germany and Sweden are investigating geologic disposal. Both of these countries, because of popular movements, plan to discontinue the use of nuclear power... However, many observers feel that nuclear power will have to play a significant role in responding to global warming."

The Vandenbosches' description of the nuclear waste debate as a "stalemate", and their commencement of their book with a reference to the two decades that politicians have taken to discuss a single project – the proposed Yucca Mountain disposal site – eloquently illustrates the psychological and cultural block that impedes nuclear progress. While there's clearly been progress on some levels, such as the gathering of further information (which has changed the minds of some, like Patrick Moore), and while the mere fact that politicians continue to talk about nuclear power provides some ground for hope, the larger truth is that the nuclear enterprise is sadly mired in the emotional prejudices and mindsets of the past. (In February 2009 it was announced that President Obama had ended the government's efforts to store nuclear waste in Yucca Mountain and will seek other options.)

A further illustration of this unchanging set of attitudes can be found in *The High Road* (1981), a book by Ben Bova, currently president emeritus of the National Space Society. A chapter titled *Nuclear Power: The Bad News* paints a picture of political opposition to nuclear technology in 1981 which is disquietingly similar, if not identical, to the political climate prevailing in the early 21st century. Amory Lovins, whom we referenced above, is already there with the repetitive arguments that we continue to hear today. "The Luddites," Bova wrote, "are on the attack and they smell blood. Critics such as Amory Lovins insist that nuclear power stations are too risky, too expensive, too little, and too late to help us solve our energy problems." (What energy independence we might now be enjoying if not for that opposition of the 1970s and 1980s?) Bova noted that the attack on nuclear power was "extremely emotional", and that warned, all too presciently, that "Jane Fonda's anti-nuclear speeches get more attention from the media than the pro-nuclear utterances of Nobel Laureates such as Hans Bethe or Glenn Seaborg."

The Jane Fonda Syndrome

Fonda (1937-) is a film celebrity and political activist; Bethe (1906-2005) a German-American physicist known for, among other things, his work on the nuclear reactions that occur in stars; Seaborg (1912-1999) a Swedish chemist whose achievements include discovering plutonium and other transuranium elements (chemical elements whose atomic numbers are larger than that of uranium). Fonda's odd role in the history of nuclear technology relates to a heavily publicized event in 1979 near Harrisburg, Pennsylvania.

The Three Mile Island nuclear power plant experienced a malfunction called a partial core meltdown. Radioactivity was discharged into the environment. No one died, was hurt or, so far as is known, became ill as a result. But from the point of view of the public image of nuclear technology, the incident could hardly have happened at a worse time. Less than two weeks earlier, a movie, *The China Syndrome*, featuring Fonda and actors Jack Lemmon and Michael Douglas, had come out with a story line that happened to be about a meltdown at a nuclear power plant. The movie portrayed nuclear plant managers as sinister, irresponsible figures who recklessly endangered the public and sought to cover up their actions through skullduggery. To the public it seemed that life was horrifyingly imitating art, and the movie and the real-life incident seemed reciprocally to fuel each other's headlines – happily in the case of the movie, which enjoyed excellent box office, and disastrously in the case of the nuclear industry, which saw its stock plummet in the public estimation.

In addition to the combined negative publicity of the incident and the movie, Fonda began lobbying against nuclear power. The personal celebrity she brought to this campaign (the daughter of movie icon Henry Fonda, she had also attracted attention in protests against the Vietnam War and nuclear weapons) captured enough press attention that prominent nuclear physicist Edward Teller (1908–2003) felt it appropriate to stage a counter-campaign to assure the public of the safety of nuclear power. Teller suffered a heart attack which he attributed to the rigors of his campaign, so an ad to support his media effort was headed *I was the only victim of Three-Mile Island.*[6]

"On May 7, a few weeks after the accident at Three-Mile Island, I was in Washington," Teller said in his ad. "I was there to refute some of that propaganda that Ralph Nader, Jane Fonda and their kind are spewing to the news media in their attempt to frighten people away from nuclear power. I am 71 years old, and I was working 20 hours a day. The strain was too much. The next day, I suffered a heart attack. You might say that I was the only one whose health was affected by that reactor near Harrisburg. No, that would be wrong. It was not the reactor. It was Jane Fonda. Reactors are not dangerous ... If you sat next to a nuclear power plant for a whole year, you would be exposed to less radiation than you would receive during a round-trip flight in a 747 from New York to Los Angeles.

"Let me put it another way: The allowable radiation from a nuclear plant is five mrems per year. In Dallas, people get about 80 mrems per year from the natural background of buildings, rocks, etc. In Colorado, people get as much as 130 mrems per year from the natural background. Therefore, just by moving from Dallas to Boulder you would receive ten times more radiation per year than the person gets who lives next to a nuclear power plant." (A rem is a unit of radiation, and a millirem, or mrem, is a thousandth of a rem.)

In public communications terms, however, Teller was no match for Fonda. He'd been a key figure in the Manhattan Project to develop the atom bomb and was widely known as "the father of the hydrogen bomb". These associations made him the worst possible defender of nuclear power.

There's no reliable way of knowing how much public opinion and public policy have really been influenced by Fonda, by political activist Ralph Nader (1934-), by any other campaigner against nuclear power, or by media products like *The China Syndrome* movie. But what's clear is that the waves of media attention that swirled around Three-Mile Island, and the communications associated with them, strongly reflected certain attitudes toward nuclear power that had been discernible for some time. So strongly did these anti-nuclear cultural artifacts symbolize anti-nuclear public feelings that decades later they continue to haunt nuclear discussion. In an article on "The Jane Fonda Effect" in *The New York Times Magazine* (Sept. 16, 2007),[7] Stephen J. Dubner and Steven D. Levitt wrote: "If you were asked to name the biggest global-warming villains of the past 30 years, here's one name that probably wouldn't spring to mind: Jane Fonda. But should it?"

The article reported that while the Three-Mile Island incident caused no deaths, injuries or significant damage except to the plant itself, "What it did produce, stoked by 'The China Syndrome,' was a widespread panic. The nuclear industry, already foundering as a result of economic, regulatory and public pressures, halted plans for further expansion. And so, instead of becoming a nation with clean and cheap nuclear energy, as once seemed inevitable, the United States kept building power plants that burned coal and other fossil fuels. Today such plants account for 40 percent of the country's energy-related carbon-dioxide emissions. Anyone hunting for a global-warming villain can't help blaming those power plants — and can't help wondering too about the unintended consequences of Jane Fonda."

Dubner and Levitt went on: "Could it be that nuclear energy, risks and all, is now seen as preferable to the uncertainties of global warming? France, which generates nearly 80 percent of its electricity by nuclear power, seems to think so. So do Belgium (56 percent), Sweden (47 percent) and more than a dozen other countries that generate at least one-fourth of their electricity by nuclear power."

In his article quoted above, Moore, the ex-director of Greenpeace, declared: "In 1979, Jane Fonda and Jack Lemmon produced a frisson of fear with their starring roles in 'The China Syndrome,' a fictional evocation of nuclear disaster in which a reactor meltdown threatens a city's survival. Less than two weeks after the blockbuster film opened, a reactor core meltdown at Pennsylvania's Three Mile Island nuclear power plant sent shivers of very real anguish throughout the country. What nobody noticed at the time, though, was that Three Mile Island was in fact a success story: The concrete containment structure did just what it was designed to do -- prevent radiation from escaping into the environment. And although the reactor itself was crippled, there was no injury or death among nuclear workers or nearby residents. Three Mile Island was the only serious accident in the history of nuclear energy generation in the United States, but it was enough to scare us away from further developing the technology: There hasn't been a nuclear plant ordered up since then."

"Wind and solar power have their place," Moore commented, "but because they are intermittent and unpredictable they simply can't replace big baseload plants such as coal, nuclear and hydroelectric. Natural gas, a fossil fuel, is too expensive already, and its price is too volatile to risk building big baseload plants. Given that hydroelectric resources are built pretty much to capacity, nuclear is, by elimination, the only viable substitute for coal. It's that simple." And he made this interesting point: "Over the past 20 years, one of the simplest tools -- the machete -- has been used to kill more than a million people in Africa, far more than were killed in the Hiroshima and Nagasaki nuclear bombings combined. What are car bombs made of? Diesel oil, fertilizer and cars. If we banned everything that can be used to kill people, we would never have harnessed fire."

A similar point was made by Dubner and Levitt in their 2007 piece: "In the United States, an average of 33 coal miners are killed each year. In China, more than 4,700 coal miners were killed last year alone — a statistic that the Chinese government has trumpeted as a vast improvement." And back in 1981, the same note was struck by one of the most distinguished minds of our time, computer scientist John McCarthy (1927-), who is credited with introducing the term "Artificial Intelligence". In his article *Defending and Extending the Freedom to Innovate* (in the book *The Survival of Freedom*, 1981, edited by Jerry Pournelle and John F. Carr), McCarthy wrote: "The most important example of applying differing standards applied to old and new ways of doing things is nuclear energy. A few days after the Three-Mile Island accident, which injured no one, *The New York Times* reported eleven coal miners killed in an accident. Another story somewhat later reported four killed by a wood stove that caught fire. It has recently turned out that well-insulated houses accumulated carbon monoxide, formaldehyde and radon, the latter to levels sometimes illegal in uranium mines, and yet the government continues its campaign for superinsulation. The current evidence is that it is safer to produce the energy than to superinsulate houses." McCarthy concluded that most of the opposition to nuclear energy "involves applying different standards to it and other sources of energy."

Dragging our feet for decades

Where this chain of debate ultimately takes us is to the fact that for decades we've dragged our feet dangerously in developing nuclear power. We've allowed emotion to retard our access to a source of energy that's vital to the interests of the world (to combat climate change and global warming), including the specific interests of the U.S. (whose population and national security are severely prejudiced by being held hostage to cartels that control the now economically as well as technologically obsolete oil industry).

Although there are ideological nuances in the nuclear debate that tie various aspects of it to specific historical events and movements, like the anti-nuclear protestors who made political capital of Three-Mile Island, this technological slothfulness isn't really a party-political issue. There's blame enough to be shared across the political spectrum. While the Right has favored well-entrenched older technologies too much and has relied to a superstitious degree on the dogma that market forces can be left to provide us on their own with what we need, the Left has irrationally demonized the nuclear industry by harping incessantly on only the destructive capacities of nuclear energy.

This perpetual identification of nuclear energy with military applications is further illustrated by a sequel to the MIT report we referenced above. On May 9, 2005, *ScienceDaily* ran a story headlined *MIT Profs, Colleagues Propose Plan For Nuclear Energy*. It stated: "MIT faculty members and colleagues, all former senior energy or security advisors in Democratic and Republican administrations from Carter to Clinton, have proposed a pragmatic plan that would allow the world to develop nuclear power without increased risk of weapons proliferation."

ScienceDaily noted that the new plan – called the Assured Nuclear Fuel Services Initiative (ANSFI) -- drew on the earlier MIT report. This was unsurprising, since the new plan's four co-authors included the two co-chairs of the earlier report: Prof. Deutch and MIT Physics Professor Ernest Moniz, Director of MIT Energy Studies in the Laboratory for Energy and the Environment, and former Undersecretary of Energy in the Clinton Administration. They were joined this time by Arnold Kanter, Senior Fellow at the Washington, DC-based Forum for International Policy and former Special Assistant to the President for National Security Affairs and Undersecretary of State for Political Affairs (in the G.H.W. Bush Administration), and Daniel Poneman, a former staff member of the National Security Council (in the G.H.W. Bush and Clinton Administrations).

An immediate point of interest about the new plan was that it had been presented in the winter 2004-2005 issue of *Survival*, a publication of the International Institute for Strategic Studies, a London-based entity concerning itself with studies of political and military conflict. In other words, the most appropriate high-level forum for discussing the future of nuclear energy was seen as a nuclear weapons risk management context.

This observation is no criticism of the authors of the new plan, who were simply, and with constructive intent, responding to what they saw as one of the key aspects of nuclear energy that they believed the public (and politicians) regarded as most important: that is, the danger that nuclear power plants would be diverted to the making of nuclear weapons.

The ANSFI plan calls for countries who already have nuclear fuel preparation and disposal technologies to use these to service countries that don't. This way, countries not already possessing these technologies will be able to benefit from nuclear energy without having the means to create nuclear weapons.

This plan *sounds* reasonable. Whether it's consistent with human nature, and with natural tendencies to resent someone else who holds the keys to power, is another question. More important, perhaps, is that it emphasizes a social solution to the problem of nuclear proliferation rather than a technological solution. A social solution is one that calls for people to solve a problem by agreeing to stop doing whatever is causing the problem. A research solution looks for a technology to help solve the problem. To illustrate this point, consider the following hypothetical example. Imagine two communities living on either side of a valley. These communities are more or less equal in size and resources. For as long as the people in either community can remember, the land they've occupied has belonged to them, but the valley has been disputed, with neither community being able to prove ownership of it.

However, the valley happens to be the only agriculturally fertile area known to the two communities. Thus, farmers from each community maintain farms for their respective peoples in the valley. It's at the best of times an uneasy coexistence. War periodically breaks out, and even in peacetime there are skirmishes.

Now, a social solution to this problem is obviously to bring the leaders of the two communities together to reach an accord. And in any conceivable circumstances this would be a wise and mutually beneficial thing to do. But there's also another potential solution, which is technological. If the scientists of either community is able to develop a technology that greatly increases the agricultural yield of that community's share of the valley, to the extent that a large surplus of agricultural produce results, this could have a number of positive outcomes. One would be to enhance the potential for a solution similar to that which the ANSFI plan proposes. That is, the technologically superior community might be able to contract to its technologically inferior neighbor, in order to cultivate its "share" of the valley on terms that could include a lasting peace.

But there are other potential outcomes, too. The technologically superior community might share its technology outright with its neighbor, thus creating a fund of goodwill that will bring about a new era of good relations. On a less benign but nevertheless conceivable note, the technology empowered community might create such economic prosperity for itself that its economic growth and technological expertise enable it to make its portion of the valley militarily secure to the point where its neighbor ceases to be an issue. It might even take the entire valley by force, or enforce a treaty designed to suit it.

But even those possibilities do not exhaust the range of possible solutions that are imaginable if we pursue the premise that a technological solution is to be sought. The new technology could be so powerful that it enables enough food to be produced within the home territory to make the valley irrelevant. Yet another possibility is that, as often happens with new technology, one technology leads to others, and the community that's devoted itself to research finds that its technological empowerment allows it to make contact with previously inaccessible communities and trade with them, or even to discover uninhabited and hospitable lands which it can add to its territories.

We must re-engage nuclear technology with a sense of urgency

In all these ways, a technology-based solution can open new and previously unimagined doors of economic and cultural development that can vastly improve the lives of not only the people within the empowered community but also their neighbors. It's scarcely conceivable that such a transformation for the better in the fortunes of a close neighbor wouldn't be of great interest to the second community, and encourage it to nurture a new era of diplomatic and economic relations.

This story is illustrative and hypothetical, and such narratives shouldn't be pursued beyond a point or they can become strained. But it does indicate how research and the development of new technologies can open up a wider range of potential solutions than are offered by the quest for social solutions alone, no matter how undeniably valuable and indeed essential the social solutions may be.

Patrick Moore returned to this subject in an interview in *Newsweek* (*The Future Of Energy: A Renegade Against Greenpeace*, By Fareed Zakaria (April 21, 2008)[9]. He told the magazine that because he and his old associates at Greenpeace "were so focused on the destructive aspect of nuclear technology and nuclear war, we made the mistake of lumping nuclear energy in with nuclear weapons, as if all things nuclear were evil. And indeed today, Greenpeace still uses the word 'evil' to describe nuclear energy. I think that's as big a mistake as if you lumped nuclear medicine in with nuclear weapons. Nuclear medicine uses radioactive isotopes to successfully treat millions of people every year, and those isotopes are all produced in nuclear reactors."

Asked about the risk of proliferation, Moore replied: "You do not need a nuclear reactor to make a nuclear weapon. With centrifuge technology, it is far easier, quicker and cheaper to make a nuclear weapon by enriching uranium directly. No nuclear reactor was involved in making the Hiroshima bomb. You'll never change the fact that there are evil people in the world. The most deaths in combat in the last 20 years have not been caused by nuclear weapons or car bombs or rifles or land mines or any of the usual suspects, but the machete. And yet the machete is the most important tool for farmers in the developing world. Hundreds of millions of people use it to clear their land, to cut their firewood and harvest their crops. Banning the machete is not an option."

As to nuclear waste, he commented: "As is now planned, I'd establish a recycling industry for nuclear fuel, which reduces the amount of waste to less than 10 percent of what it would be without recycling. How many Americans know that 50 percent of the nuclear energy being produced in the U.S. is now coming from dismantled Russian nuclear warheads? The environmental movement is going on about how terrible it will be if someone does something destructive with these materials. Well, actually the opposite is occurring: all over the world, people are using former nuclear-weapons material for peaceful purposes – swords into plowshares. This constant propaganda about the cost of nuclear energy –that's just activists looking for the right buttons to push, and one of the key buttons to push is to make consumers afraid that their electricity prices will go up if nuclear energy is built. In fact, it's natural gas that is causing prices to go up."

It's now widely accepted that it is in the geopolitical and economic interests of the U.S. to diversify its national energy resources.

There's also wide support, both scientifically and politically, for the adoption of a national energy policy that would minimize global impacts on the physical environment. From both these perspectives it's desirable to expand the U.S.'s use of nuclear technology, in the forms of nuclear power stations and techniques for the storage of nuclear waste. These objectives will be met only if public perceptions of nuclear technology are considerably improved. It's highly advisable for government to make a major commitment to achieve such an improvement. It can do this by committing itself financially and politically to a new era of nuclear implementation, a new era of nuclear research and development, and a new era of public education about nuclear technology.

The need for these commitments by government is very urgent. (Referring to the Kyoto Protocol, an international treaty aimed at regulating the impacts of industry on global climate, science writer Jerry Pournelle has commented that "if all the nuclear plants on order at the time of Three Mile Island had actually been built, the United States would be in compliance with Kyoto or very nearly so." He adds: "I do not believe I have ever heard Al Gore or any of his supporters, or any of the Kyoto supporters, mention this." [10]

There are risks attached to nuclear technology, yes. But for all practical purposes, one way or the other, nuclear knowledge is going to spread, and it will be applied. The best way to control knowledge that any of us believe has dangerous potential is not to try to prevent it from spreading, but to generate new knowledge to help us deal with those risks. For all these reasons we very urgently need a new era of nuclear research, and of implementation of the nuclear knowledge that we already have. Harvesting the atom properly, with a national commitment that's long overdue, can bring America abundant electricity, a cleaner environment, better health, and the door to more new scientific discoveries that we can imagine. This is highly likely to include much economically potent new knowledge that America can share with the world. It will result in gratitude and good will, encouraging the social solutions that must necessarily be part of our vision. We need the fruits of the atom now. For all our sakes.

NOTES

1. http://web.mit.edu/nuclearppwer/
2. http://www.rmi.org/images/PDFs/Energy/E04-22_FutureNucPwr.pdf.
3. http://www.washingtonpost.com/wp-dyn/content/article/2006/04/14/AR2006041401209.html
4. *Physics Education* (Vol. 36, No.1, 2001)

5. *Nuclear Physics News* (Vol. 15, No.2, 2005),

6 http://upload.wikimedia.org/wikipedia/en/b/b2/Edward_Teller_Washington_Post_Ad.jpg

7. http://www.nytimes.com/2007/09/16/magazine/16wwln-freakonomics-t.html

8. http://www.sciencedaily.com/releases/2005/05/050509170546.html

9. http://www.newsweek.com/id/131753?GT1=43002

10. *The View From Chaos Manor* (Oct.1, 2008), http://www.jerrypournelle.com/view/2008/Q3/view538.html

CHAPTER 7

THE BIOTECHNOLOGY REVOLUTION

The 21st century will be a time of great technological choices. We won't only have to choose the technologies on which we stake our future; we must also choose, quite urgently, whether we're prepared to regain our technological nerve. Are we prepared to commit genuinely to a vigorous, sustained program of scientific and technological innovation, instead of just liking to think of ourselves as scientific and high-tech?

We've argued that we've let science and technology down by betraying their promise. We've become a civilization that likes to fantasize about state-of-the art technology but in fact shies away from bold scientific initiatives and from the commitment that these demand. Instead we've built an economy of paper, an automobile industry consisting of bloated bureaucracies which have perpetuated archaic technology, and a culture saturated with propaganda against science and technology.

We pretend we're a society of cutting-edge science and technology when in fact we evade the aggressive pursuit of major technological advance and confuse the superficial marketing of masses of stylish but trivial gadgetry with real technological advance. Our automobile and aircraft technology, financial systems technology, computer technology and much of our other technology is legacy intellectual material dating back decades.

The U.S. closed the 19th century and entered the 20th on a wave of scientific and technological momentum, much of it originated in the Old World. It rode this wave into the mid-20th century. Since then it' largely coasted on legacy intellectual assets.

Yet, paradoxically, the very extent of America's creatively attenuated use of legacy technology shows it's capable of more. Technologically, the U.S. is like a student who spends his days partying and never cracks a book, yet, at examination time, manages to pass, and even turn in some remarkable grades. So we wonder: what would he be capable of if he *really* applied himself? Contemporary American society has been built on a talent for getting as much as possible out of technologies, wringing them dry as long as possible without renewing them. It's a kind of perverse efficiency.

But there comes a time when every well runs dry. America has reached that point now with the technologies that formed its infrastructural foundations throughout the bulk of the 20th century.

We've argued that a major element of America's technological failure has been philosophical opposition to technology from both the political Left and Right. Leftists have chanted that technology is a manipulative tool of evil capitalists and destroyers of the environment. Conservatives have decried the inconveniently challenging changes that technology inevitably brings – changes not only in the make-up of financial fiefdoms but also in the aesthetic appearance, customs and very pace of the world, and in our interpretation of cherished values and philosophical interpretations.

Yet, the changes we have yet to bring about with advanced technology contain the keys to all that's most promising in our future. An example is biotechnology.

Like most if not all contemporary technologies, biotechnology has very old origins in both theory and practice. All methods of preserving and cooking food, including techniques going back to prehistory, are forms of biotechnology. We've always manipulated food to make it last longer, taste better and/or nourish us more effectively. Gardeners and farmers developed biotechnology since the earliest agriculture and horticulture: the hybridizing of plants, and the development of ways to cultivate them in ways better suited to human needs, involve "tweaking" organic nature in the light of human knowledge: i.e., biotechnology. The same applies to animal husbandry. Breeders of cattle and other domesticated animals are part of the long history of human intervention in the processes of life we call biotechnology. And medical science from ancient times has been a story of constant efforts by physicians to invent tools to cure illness and extend life.

Since the mapping of the DNA molecule, biotechnology has risen to new sophistication. Enormous positive possibilities have been opened up by modern genetics and nanotechnology. If pursued vigorously, this more advanced biotechnology can contribute immensely to the length and quality of human life. But it's important to realize that biotechnology in the 21st century is engaging the same spectrum of tasks as biologists did in previous centuries. Modern biotechnological techniques are only the latest form of as ancient quest.

Understanding this continuity between new biological aims and those of previous generations is essential. To build an optimal culture of scientific and technological innovation in the 21st century we must overcome the idea that modern science and technology are somehow alien to our nature. We must appreciate that they flow from long traditions and are deeply human enterprises that form the latest chapter in an age-old drama of the human spirit. An informed sense of how we got, scientifically and technology, to where we are today can help us re-invigorate our scientific and technological culture.

We've seen how our search for knowledge of the atom and the finer fabric of matter led to nuclear science and technology, only to give way to a cultural paralysis and inability or unwillingness to engage nuclear technology further. The promise of the 21st century depends in large measure on our will to overcome this paralysis. As we'll now see, a similar culture of technological reluctance affects genetic and molecular engineering. This is especially interesting because the story of biotechnology follows directly on from that of our pursuit of the atom.

Appreciating this linear line of intellectual descent not only helps us place biotechnology in a long saga of the human mind; it also shows how much of our creative scientific and technological progress is linked, so that if we obstruct development in one area we likely obstruct it in others. Conversely, cultivating one area of innovation often leads, as we've seen, to productive spin-offs in other areas. In this context, let's look at how biotechnology has developed.

The quest for the micro-world

By discovering the atom and gaining insight into its inner complexities, humankind unlocked the door to the world of the very small. While our curiosity about phenomena that are too small to be studied with the unaided eye go back a long way, it was a technological development in the 17th century that really began our adventure into the micro-world. This was the invention of the microscope, especially its refinement and use for pioneering scientific observations by two men with coincidentally similar names: Dutch draper, civil servant and amateur scientist Anton van Leeuwenhoek (1632–1723), and an English professional scientist, Robert Hooke (1635–1703), who served for over four decades as an important official of Britain's Royal Society.

Between them, Hooke and Van Leeuwenhoek laid the foundations of the science of microbiology. We're indebted to Hooke for, among other things, the term *cell*, and to Van Leeuwenhoek for the first observations of bacteria. The two men developed their own microscopes, and by the standards of the day Van Leeuwenhoek's was more powerful, although Hooke's was closer to later microscopic principles. (For many years Leeuwenhoek was popularly thought of as the first observer of microorganisms, but microbiologist and science historian Howard Gest has argued convincingly that Hooke's work, including an early description of a microfungus, entitles him to be recognized as the microbial world's first observer, and that Hooke and Van Leeuwenhoek should be regarded as co-discoverers of the microbial universe.[1])

Hooke and Van Leeuwenhoek were fascinating for many reasons, five of which relate directly to our understanding of contemporary technological innovation. The first is *the surprising slowness of the impact of their microscopic work*. Although its importance was quite widely recognized in their lifetimes, its effects were really felt only in the 19th century, when French chemist Louis Pasteur (1822–1895) confirmed the germ theory of disease. (It's sobering to realize Van Leeuwenhoek clearly grasped that an extensive biological environment – indeed, a whole world – existed all around us, and that life-forms teemed in a drop of water and on the surfaces of our teeth. However, he just didn't see the connection between disease and microbes.) This shows how the existence of a technology, and discoveries associated with it, doesn't mean practical effects automatically flow soon. Application tends to need nurturing and investment of time and money.

The second interesting point relates specifically to Van Leeuwenhoek's work. Like many innovations, his interest in developing the microscope was *a creative extension of existing technology which had very different purposes*. The drapery business, in which he'd been trained, used simple magnifying glasses to evaluate cloth. Van Leeuwenhoek saw that these could be developed for scientific uses. This illustrates the extent to which potential for innovations can be in plain sight yet need will, imagination and drive to make the leap from possibility to reality.

Thirdly, we see in the stories of both Hooke and Van Leeuwenhoek that *innovation usually has ancient roots*. It isn't so much the *ideas* that are new as are the social institutions, cultural incentives and intellectual support structures that make the emergence of a new technological era possible. Although the first microscopes appeared in Holland in the 16th century, magnifying lenses had been around a long time. The British Museum possesses a lens made of rock crystal from ancient Assyria, the Nimrud Lens, estimated to be some 3000 years old, which could have been used either as a visual aid (perhaps as part of a telescope) or to start fires, or both. Roman author and politician Lucius Seneca (about 4BC – about 65 AD) described the use of glass and water to assist reading. Chunks of polished glass called "reading stones" were used by 10th-century monks, and spectacles are dated to Italy in the 1200s.

Fourth, the work of both Hooke and Van Leeuwenhoek demonstrates *the resistance that new ideas often have to face* even when they've taken a long time to arrive and even when their results are quite apparent. Hooke's 1665 book *Micrographia* attracted great attention of the kind that our society today accords to television footage of Mars, or of strange creatures at the bottom of the sea. Hooke was a gifted artist and he not only described but visually portrayed cellular structures, the intricate architecture of feathers and the anatomy of the mite and the flea. The book helped inspire Van Leeuwenhoek's studies. Astonishingly, though, Hooke was also mocked for devoting such attention to apparently trivial phenomena, as if his investigations were no more than an eccentricity. And when Van Leeuwenhoek described seeing tiny animals invisible to the naked eye – he called them "animalcules" – he encountered such skepticism that he set about getting various respected members of his community to write letters corroborating his findings.

Skepticism is, of course, a healthy part of the scientific process. But what we learn afresh from the stories of Hooke and Van Leeuwenhoek is that new ideas about the world, and the discoveries yielded by new technology, aren't subject only to the kinds of impartial critical evaluation we associate with court cases. They're also subjected to the full range of human emotions, prejudices and foibles. Van Leeuwenhoek faced obstacles not only because he offered insights that contradicted prevailing beliefs -- he showed, for instance, that weevils didn't emerge spontaneously from food but were the result of microscopic eggs -- but also because he was of humble social station and had no university education in science or languages other than his native Dutch. Hooke didn't even deign to answer a letter written to him on Van Leeuwenhoek's behalf by a diplomat (although he later had little option but to recognize Van Leeuwenhoek's work).

In fact, the personalities of both these great scientific figures starkly illustrate the importance of not only cultural but also emotional and psychological idiosyncrasies in the institutions and processes of innovation. Van Leeuwenhoek actively publicized and disseminated much of his work yet was strangely secretive about other parts of it, contrary to the spirit of the scientific sharing of knowledge. For his part, Hooke seems to have been consumed by petty professional jealousies astonishing in a man so gifted: one would have thought he'd feel far too secure for such sentiments. He was involved, for example, in an ugly feud with Isaac Newton about who'd come up first with important ideas about motion and gravitation. It doesn't reflect well on either man and shows that far from being just a tale of rational and collegial amassing of knowledge in the interests of humanity, scientific and technological innovation also revolves around politics, social considerations and personal ambitions.

The fifth point about the work of both Hooke and Van Leeuwenhoek is that it's part of *the same investigation of the very small that led to the coming of the atomic era*. It's important to appreciate this if we're to understand a fact that's highly relevant to the technological prospects of the 21st century: the link between research on matter and research on life.

The twin domains of matter and life

At first glance, matter and life seem to represent two very different lines of scientific inquiry. Matter looks dead and inert; life appears animated by forces so mysterious that we intuitively suppose they must be qualitatively different from the forces governing non-living substances. However, much of our progress in charting the architecture of matter has shown us that the dividing-line between life and non-living material isn't clear-cut at all.

At the same time, our understanding of the processes of life seems increasingly dependent on what we learn about matter. We see foreshadowings of these connections in early science. Many pioneers of physical science were also important in the life sciences, and vice versa. Hooke, for example, not only founded cell biology and developed an early form of the theory of evolution, but was a physicist of great originality, establishing the principle of elasticity known as Hooke's Law and doing masterful work on gravitation which created the dispute over credit and priority between him and Isaac Newton.

In earlier pages we've seen how chemistry and physics came together in the early 20th century to create a new vision of the universe in which matter and energy were intertwined in ways that differed dramatically from assumptions that had previously prevailed, which regarded them as quite separate. As the 20th century advanced, a similar breakdown of hard-and-fast boundaries occurred between our study of matter and our understanding of life.

As with all of the innovations we're discussing, this conceptual change was a process, not a single event. We've seen how one of Einstein's most celebrated papers was on Brownian motion, a physical phenomenon relating to the movement of particles in a gas or liquid, but named after a botanist who'd introduced it into science as a result of observing spores and pollen in water. This use of *analogy* between living and non-living matter was turned into a *material connection* in the work of German-American molecular biologist and biophysicist Max Delbrück (1906–1981).

Delbrück's career provides us with a direct line between the early 20th-century's changes in the physical universe and the equally massive advance in our understanding of life that took place in later decades. Born in Berlin, Delbrück studied at Göttingen University, in Germany, where some of the seminal work of the new physics was done, especially during the 1920s, when the focus was on quantum mechanics – the physics of the subatomic. During those years at Göttingen the brilliant German physicist Max Born (1882–1970), who went on to win a Nobel Prize in 1954, presided over a glittering ensemble of thinkers whose names read like a Who's Who of the leading physical research of the age. Studying under Born, Delbrück earned a PhD in physics in 1930 for a thesis on the mathematics of the lithium molecule. (Lithium is a chemical element with many practical uses, from medicines to batteries to rocket fuel.)

He first tried a thesis on stars but gave it up, partly because he couldn't yet read English, in which most of the relevant works had been published. This linguistic deficiency was soon rectified; after receiving his doctorate, Delbrück went to work in England as well as in Switzerland and in Copenhagen, Denmark, where he studied with physicist Niels Bohr (1885-1962), who, with Rutherford, developed the "solar system" model of the atom, with electrons orbiting the nucleus the way planets orbit a sun. While Delbrück was in Copenhagen, Bohr initiated a discussion with him that changed Delbrück's life, launching him from physics into a career that would turn him into one of the great figures of 20th-century biology.

Bohr had originated an idea called *complementarity*, whereby light was sometimes treated as a wave and sometimes as a particle, with these two interpretations not contradicting but complementing each other. Bohr wondered if it might be useful to think of life in a similarly dualistic way, i.e. sometimes as an organically organized whole and sometimes as a set of mechanically explained molecular interactions. Bohr published this train of thought[2,] which fascinated Delbrück. In 1932 Delbrück landed a position in Berlin in 1932, assisting a co-discoverer of nuclear fission, Austrian-born physicist Lise Meitner (1878–1968. He organized a private discussion group of physicists and life scientists, including Russian geneticist Nikolay Timofeeff-Ressovsky (1900-1981) and German radiation scientist Karl G. Zimmer (1911–1988).

In 1935, Timofeeff-Ressovsky, Zimmer and Delbrück published a paper, *On the Nature of Gene Mutation and Gene Structure.* In the late 1920s it had been demonstrated that X-rays could cause hereditary genetic changes (mutations). Delbrück and his co-authors now put forward a model to explain this on a molecular level, using the language of quantum physics. The details of their explanation didn't become a lasting part of genetics, but what's more important is that up to then, *the gene had been a theoretical construct, as the atom had once been.* This paper established the gene as a *physical* entity, as real and mathematically approachable as the atom. Although the paper appeared in an obscure German journal, *Nachrichten der Gelehrten Gesellschaft der Wissenschaften,* it later achieved renown when famous Austrian physicist Erwin Schrödinger (1887 –1961) referenced it prominently in his 1945 book *What is Life?* (Schrödinger was a pioneer of quantum mechanics who shared a 1933 Nobel Prize with British physicist Paul Dirac (1902–1984).)

Delbrück relocated to America in 1937. Here a number of scientists who shared his interests began to gravitate around him. They came to be known as the Phage Group, *phage* being an abbreviation of bacteriophage, a type of virus that attacks bacteria. Delbrück not only conducted research on phage biology; he also interested other researchers to work on this subject, championed the use by biologists of the tools of physics and mathematics, and encouraged greater co-ordination of phase investigations. Two of his co-workers were American geneticist Alfred D. Hershey (1908–1997) and Italian-American microbiologist Salvador E. Luria (1912–1991).

In 1943 Luria and Delbrück showed that bacteria pass down traits from generation to generation in a way consistent with the Darwinian principles of evolution. Hershey discovered that two different types of phage could trade genetic information by infecting the same bacteria. He also conducted a famous experiment in 1952 with American geneticist Martha Cowles Chase (1927–2003), demonstrating that the molecule of Deoxyribonucleic acid (DNA) carries and transmits genetic content.

In 1969 Delbrück, Hershey and Luria shared a Nobel Prize for their joint work on the genetics of viruses. But the real testimony to what they had achieved came in the form of their impact on a generation of subsequent research. Hershey and Chase described their experiment in a paper, and this stimulated a fertile train of

thought in the mind of one of Luria's former students.
His name was James D. Watson.

Cracking the genetic code

Watson (1928-), an American, is now forever linked with the name of a British scientist, Francis H. Crick (1916–2004)and a New Zealander, Maurice H. Wilkins (1916–2004). These three molecular biologists jointly discovered the structure of the DNA molecule, in recognition of which they received a Nobel Prize in 1962. Just as Delbrück's story provides a conceptual and historical bridge between physics and biology, so the careers of Watson, Crick and Wilkins link the scientific triumphs of the first half of the 20th century with the technological challenges and potential of its second half. Understanding these challenges, and the continuities between them, is crucial to launching a new technological era in the 21st century.

Born in Chicago, Watson was inspired to study genetics by Schrödinger's book, *What Is Life?*, in which the great physicist speculated about the connections between physics and the life sciences, devoting a chapter to Delbrück's work. Watson did his doctoral research under Delbrück's research partner, Luria. By that time an important experiment had suggested that DNA could be the carrier of the genetic material of bacteria. This experiment was conducted by two Canadian-American researchers, Oswald T. Avery (1877-1955) and Colin M. MacLeod (1909-1972), and an American, Maclyn McCarty (1911-2005). In the light of this work, Watson set out to determine the make-up of DNA. He was aided in this by the success of Linus C. Pauling (1901–1994) in using X-rays to study the structures of molecules. (Pauling exemplified the cross-disciplinary nature of the scientific breakthroughs of the first half of the 20th century. He worked with both Bohr and Schrödinger.) In 1951 Watson began working at the physics laboratory of Cambridge University, England, where he met Crick, and eventually Wilkins.

At this stage of the tale we encounter one of those episodes that remind us how human a process scientific advance is, in the sense of being shaped by personalities, career interests, institutional politics and relationships between individuals. The importance of unraveling the structure of DNA was very much "in the air" at the time and there was a fierce sense of competition about who'd achieve it first. English physical chemist Rosalind E. Franklin (1920-1958) was at that time doing pivotal X-ray research on the molecular structure of DNA with English physicist Raymond Gosling (1926-). The work done by Franklin and Gosling appears to have been instrumental in the progress made by Watson and his other colleagues, but this didn't come to light until many years had passed, and troubling questions remain as to whether the credit for discovering the structure of DNA (and thus the Nobel Prize) should have been shared by more people, such as Franklin and her supervisor, Sir John Randall (see below). The exact circumstances may never be known as the events recede further into history. What matters for us here is that as a result of all this combined effort from many dedicated researchers, it was finally realized that the DNA molecule had a spiral shape of the kind known as a helix. In fact, it was a double helix.

In reviewing the chain of research that culminated in the discovery of the DNA helix, it's useful to notice how, again and again, the boundaries between the new physics and the new (molecular) biology blur, and how key individuals straddle both the physical sciences and the life sciences. We'll return to this point later when we discuss specialization and interdisciplinary research in the strategies that are needed to put 21st-century research on an optimal path. In passing, it's worthwhile to note the cross-disciplinary interests of people like Schrödinger and Pauling. This is echoed by Watson's partner Crick. Born in Weston Favell, England, he obtained a degree in physics and worked at Cambridge University's physics laboratory. He was fascinated by the relationship between the organic and the inorganic. Like Watson, he was inspired by Schrödinger. Like Schrödinger, he was intrigued by the borders between disciplines and the philosophically and scientifically interesting questions and answers that arise when these borders are crossed. (This led him in later years to forsake molecular biology for the investigation of how the structure of the brain relates to the phenomenon of consciousness.)

Crick's cross-disciplinary range of interests, and his desire to export the tools and concepts of the physical sciences from one discipline to another, was part of the intellectual atmosphere of science in his milieu. In his immediate environment it was powerfully represented by British physicist John T. Randall (1905-1984), a key figure in the development of radar during World War 2. Randall's work is also fundamental to today's microwave ovens. During the quest for DNA's molecular structure Randall was responsible for the work done at King's College, London, by researchers like Wilkins, Gosling and Franklin. He was, among other things, an expert on the electron microscope, a device which had carried magnification far beyond anything imagined by Hooke and Van Leeuwenhoek. Pioneered in the early thirties by two German researchers, physicist Ernst A. Ruska (1906–1988) and engineer Max Knoll (1897–1969), the electron microscope uses a beam of electrons, with a much shorter wavelength than light, to enlarge images to an order of (as of 2008) some two million. (The highly interlinked nature of 20ᵗʰ-century science and technology, and our dependence today on the scientific breakthroughs of the first half of the 20ᵗʰ century, is illustrated by the fact that the electron microscope design originated by Ruska and Knoll is an essential part of the manufacture of semiconductor components, on which the computer industry is based.)

Randall was thus another example of a generation of early-20ᵗʰ-century polymathic scientists who saw in the new concepts and technologies of the physical sciences a tremendously fertile set of vocabularies and tools that could be productively transplanted into a variety of disciplines. Quite apart from the intellectual content of their work, scientists like Randall were exciting role models for younger researchers and theoreticians who would go on to create the scientific framework of the second half of the 20ᵗʰ century.

Let's look at how that second half shaped up.

The philosophy of scientific entitlement

We've seen above how science and technology worked hand in hand to reveal the micro-world of bacteria, viruses and genes. The exploration of this domain has been, in one sense, separate from the pursuit of the atom, yet on another level closely intertwined with it. Step by step, the fine texture of organic existence yielded its secrets to an intensive application of techniques and knowledge that had been developed by physical scientists probing the atom, the molecule and various forms of radiation.

By the mid 20ᵗʰ century it seemed we were on the brink of a golden age.

Now, the intuition of an approaching golden age isn't new. It's arisen at other times in history and it will arise again, and each time it takes on nuances peculiar to its time. Understanding these nuances is important. In fact, if we're to succeed in navigating the challenges and opportunities of the 21ˢᵗ century, it's essential for us to understand the golden age assumptions of the mid-20ᵗʰ century, because these assumptions have shaped a good deal of late 20ᵗʰ-century and early 21ˢᵗ-century policy.

As far as popular perceptions of science and technology were concerned, the spirit of the middle of the 20ᵗʰ century was caught very well by the 1968 science fiction film *2001: A Space Odyssey*, which entranced moviegoers with its vision of the future of humanity. It was co-written by a revered British futurist and visionary of both real-life technology and science fiction, Sir Arthur C. Clarke

(1917–2008). In the 1940s Clarke conceived of communication satellites orbiting the Earth, which later became a reality of our global telecommunications. But the impact of 2001 didn't stem from literal scientific prediction. It wasn't that kind of film: it was rather an *allegorical* work that captured the idea that humanity had reached a moment of special transformation in its evolution. Space travel and artificial intelligence were metaphors for this change.

There was an interesting contradiction in the use of these metaphors, because the 1960s were notable for, among other things, a strong current of anti-technological sentiment. In its eagerness and excitement to make the world a better place socially, the counterculture movement of the sixties tended to associate science and technology with militarism, weapons, environmental despoliation and objectionable commercialism, and it identified wisdom with lifestyles that rejected these features of society.

Why, then, would a film using space travel and artificial intelligence as metaphors for transformation appeal to these counterculture constituencies as effectively as 2001 did? The answer lies in the kind of change that was envisaged. The change that was memorialized in the songs and other popular media products of the sixties was characterized by two important features. The first, which is implied by the use of space and travel and robotics as metaphors rather than literal predictions, is that it was primarily *social* change that was yearned for. The mood of the time wasn't concerned with *really* ushering humankind into a technologically advanced future; if anything, it was inclined to romanticize simpler lifestyles and rural settings as part of the desired social revolution. The transformation in human life that was desired was seen as a metamorphosis of attitudes, relationships, values and social customs, rather than involving technological innovation.

The second feature of this desired transformation was that change was not only *desired* but confidently *expected*, as an inevitability. The socially improved new world, it was felt by many, would emerge from the older one by virtue of the rightness of the time for such a transformation, combined with the accumulated pressures of history and the will of a large number of people.

The net effect of the above combination of attitudes – a professed disdain for technology and a belief in inevitable change for the better as a result of historical and social pressures – was a philosophy that didn't place a premium on *proactive scientific and technological effort*. It rather saw the fruits of scientific and technological effort as a given, a kind of faucet which had been turned on and would in future produce a stream of products which could be picked and chosen from, accepted, rejected or otherwise channeled according to changing social and cultural taste.

Ironically, this philosophy, which failed to appreciate the extraordinarily rare nature of the scientific advances that had taken place in the first half of the 20th century, was itself a product of the very successes of those advances. It was as if the appearance of the scientific and technological genius of that time meant the human race had somehow turned a corner in its development, so that innovation of a high order was now no more than what was due to any sufficiently complicated society. It was a philosophy of *scientific entitlement*.

Another way of expressing this philosophy is to call it *the fallacy of the released genie*.[3] In this figure of speech, scientific discovery and technological invention are like a genie (a magical being capable of granting wishes) which, once released, can't be returned to the bottle or lamp in which it had previously been confined. It's widely assumed that science and technology are irreversible, so that you can't "un-know" knowledge once it's been achieved, as though attained knowledge has a kind of immortality or perpetual motion. But the fallacy here is that although the genie may not be able to go back in the bottle, it can become ill and die. Science and technology can indeed run out of steam if the social and cultural supports they need aren't provided. This happened, as we've seen, to nuclear technology. Something similar happened, as we'll presently see, to biotechnology.

The philosophy of scientific entitlement had several intellectual roots, of which the impressive scope of scientific advance in the first half of the 20th century was one. Another was the self-satisfaction of America after World War II. The 1950s, in which the young people of the 1960s had grown up, were notable for great prosperity confidence among many Americans. The U.S. had defeated Hitler and his cohorts and established itself as the great democratic superpower, with apparently inexhaustible economic, intellectual and technological momentum.

If it seems odd that the 1960s counterculture ethos was empowered by the very lifestyles against which this ethos rebelled, it appears even stranger (because much of the 1960s counterculture ethos was nominally anti-capitalist) that this philosophy of scientific entitlement was shared by much of the capitalist thinking of the time. Yet, when you come to think of it, this isn't really as peculiar as it seems. If the young protestors of the 1960s were complacent toward the cornucopia of innovation and productivity with which America seemed awash by mid-century, is it that surprising that businesspeople felt similarly? After all, they had long embraced an economic philosophy that saw such innovation and productivity as an automatic offshoot of a business culture of rational self-interest.

Accordingly, as businesspeople learned of the mapping of the gene, many saw this as the advent of a rich new landscape of commercial biotechnology waiting for investors to come in and shake the fruit from the tree.

As it turned out, it wasn't that simple.

Science and technology as big business

Watson, Crick and Wilkins received their Nobel Prize for jointly discovering the structure of DNA in 1962. Fast forward now to a little over a quarter of a century later: October 29, 1989. On that day, *The New York Times* gave some 1500 words of space to an article headlined *Book & Business; The Selling Of DNA*, by science writer Natalie Angier. Its subject was a book just been published by Robert Teitelman, a financial journalist and writer for *Oncology Times*, a cancer research periodical. The book -- *Gene Dreams: Wall Street, Academia, and the Rise of Biotechnology* -- and the attention given to it by the *Times*, delivered a sobering evaluation of the progress of genetic technology up to that point, with the focus on the way Wall Street had turned genetic research from a scientific and technological enterprise adventure into a disappointing commercial adventure.

"From cold fusion to high-temperature superconductivity, from robotics to neural networks, many of the recent 'revolutions' in science and technology seem to have the half-life of an average teenage crush," Angier wrote. "Each one strides onto center stage to the boom of the media's timpani, promising to revitalize our sluggish economy, trounce our competitors, light up our homes, levitate our trains and otherwise make life easier, cheaper and more entertaining for all Americans. And almost inevitably, the 'miracle breakthroughs' prove disappointing: the science behind them is either wrong or too difficult to meet the demand for instant results. Perhaps the biggest letdown in recent history has been the business of biotechnology, which involves the manufacture of vast quantities of genetic material by isolating the DNA from the cells of one species (usually human) and splicing it into the cells of another (usually bacteria)."

Angier commented that biotechnology had seemed not only to guarantee America's resurgence on the world market but also to promise "amazing new therapeutics to thwart cancer, heart disease, diabetes and infectious diseases." Teitelman's book, she reported, documented persuasively how "the promise of biotechnology whipped Wall Street into an unprecedented state of near-religious febrility" as investors "who knew as little about DNA and RNA as they did about muons and quarks poured tens of millions of dollars into a passel of aggressive biotechnology ventures, among them Genentech, Cetus and Biogen. More astonishing still, the investments were made despite one niggling detail: all the biotech companies went public long before they had generated a single marketable or effective product." Despite the best efforts of scores of young scientists, Angier added, "some biological problems were just too complicated, too messy, for the corporate balance sheet." The hoped-for cure for cancer had not arrived, for example, and although Angier noted that Teitelman also recognized "some genuine successes in biotechnology, most notably Genentech's development of tissue-plasminogen activator, which dissolves clots in clogged arteries", she reported that "Mr. Teitelman believes that nature is profoundly complicated, and that the battle against cancer might well be 'not a sweeping victory' of 'powerfully elegant simplicity,' but a 'long, difficult war one tumor type, one disease, at a time.' No stock prospectus can make it otherwise."

The *Times* printed some quotes from the book, including that "Biotechnology sold itself on the belief that it could remedy the most profound economic and medical ills of the age, and please Wall Street as well"; that "Talk of medical breakthroughs became pretexts to raise more money; capital accumulation was confused with speculation; rhetoric was mistaken for reality"; and a portrayal of the biotechnology marketing pageant as a kind of circus encompassing "advisory boards, mice, consultants, forecasts, and laboratory miracles", in which "Substance or technique begin to matter less than ideas and style."

In March 1992 an interesting review of *Gene Dreams* appeared in the New York-based *Journal of General Internal Medicine*, written by a physician with a Master of Business Administration degree, James P. Patton.[5] This echoed elements of the *Times* article by beginning with the incongruity of mixing the stereotypical picture of the scientist with the slick carnival-barker atmosphere of Wall Street. "Images of white-coated scientists in gleaming laboratories juxtaposed with cocktail party tales of stock market speculation ("I bought Immunoviragenex when it was $1.50, now it is up to $88 -- how 'bout you?"). In many ways, this combination of science-fiction-come-true and sophisticated roulette is symbolic of our times, and Robert Teitelman's book should find a ready audience." But while Patton saw Teitelman's book as a good journalistic read about the beginnings of the biotechnology industry, providing the reader with entertaining gossip about entrepreneurs as well as some clear explanations of relevant science, he declared that it failed as an analysis of the shortcomings of biotechnology.

"*Gene Dreams* holds that biotechnology has failed in its revolutionary aspirations," he wrote, "although it is not clear what qualifies as a revolution, or even why this is important. Does revolution require building 'the next IBM,' or the initiation of a 'Schumpeterian' cycle of innovation, or a 'Kuhnian' paradigm shift, or something else?" Czech economist Joseph A. Schumpeter (1883–1950) had theorized about the nature of innovation and entrepreneurship; American philosopher of science Thomas S. Kuhn (1922–1996) had written about the nature of scientific revolutions. Patton's point was that Teitelman's book raised large philosophical questions about innovation, and its relationship to economic and social processes, but didn't follow through on them.

He also criticized Teitelman for unfairly portraying the business side of biotechnology, stating that the book "builds the case that biotechnology was overhyped from the start. Greed, science, and ready capital formed a seductive combination that overlooked mundane issues such as marketing and the FDA process. From this perspective, 'revolution' was just a concept for raising money and generating copy. Unfortunately Teitelman relies upon innuendo and anecdote to demonstrate the pernicious motivations of these small companies." Patton also noted that Teitelman was "suspicious of the fact that securities analysts (and everyone else) have so much trouble predicting future results for and assessing the value of biotechnology companies. It can't be real if it is so hard to project, or so the argument goes. This picture of the evils of finance would be more compelling if Teitelman proffered some alternative. Should inventors and entrepreneurs be expected to fully fund their enterprises with their own cash? Teitelman's disdain for the financial and operating side of biotechnology is overdramatized and under-reasoned."

Patton's annoyance with Teitelman's attack on the commercialization of biotechnology is understandable. The dissemination of knowledge into the marketplace needs money, and Wall Street has its ways of raising money which, like it or not, generally have to be put up with by anyone who wants to benefit from the things that American big business does well when all goes according to plan. (As of 2008, Patton was listed as a director of a New Jersey-based company called Advaxis, Inc., whose web site described itself as "Pioneering the next generation of immunotherapies", and as using "a modified infectious microorganism to activate the immune system to treat cancer, infectious disease or allergic syndromes.") On the other hand, it's difficult to read *Gene Dreams* without being convinced that the companies Teitelman describes represented a culture of marketing hyperbole that compared jarringly with the scientific spirit of the first half of the 20th century. It's hard to imagine people like Delbrück or Einstein functioning in the smooth-talking, jet-setting, investor-courting world that Teitelman's book describes. The impression one gets from the pages of *Gene Dreams* is that the scientific vocabularies are all very much still there but that they've become a footnote to the financial objectives, and that the science suffered as a result.

How can we assess this situation fairly? Some thought-provoking clues are provided from two sources. One happens to be the very same issue of the *Journal of General Internal Medicine* that published Patton's review. Patton's piece was immediately followed by a review of a book by Peter W. Huber called *Galileo's Revenge: Junk Science in the Courtroom* (1991). The relevance of Huber's book is that it highlights the attention given in the last years of the 20th century to the relationship between science and society, and to social pressures on scientists to conduct their professions in ways that may not always be in the best interests of scientific results. *Galileo's Revenge* is an exposé of what might be called the legal prostitution of science – that is, its use by lawyers to fight court cases about large sums of money with the aid of so-called expert witnesses. These often have seemingly impressive scientific credentials and tailor their explanation of science to suit the objectives of the lawyers who hire them.

The juxtaposition of Huber's book with Teitelman's is telling. It illustrates a turn-of-the-century philosophical unease with the relationship between science and society. Similarly, a review of *Gene Dreams* in *Science*, the journal of the American Association for the Advancement of Science, appeared alongside a review of a book which told the story of the development of the Hubble Space Telescope (HST), and in telling this tale also presented a window on the complicated links between science, government and private industry. The book was *The Space Telescope: A Study of NASA, Science, Technology, and Politics* (1989), by Robert W. Smith and others.

Science's reviewer, Bruce R. Wheaton, commented on Smith's study: "Here is a stark portrayal of what big science has become in the post-war period. As the author frequently points out, what may appear from the outside to be a straightforward technical accomplishment is actually the end-product of a frightening mixture of political, financial, technical, social, industrial, scientific, and ethical concerns that mesh in a sometimes violently confrontational manner." Wheaton noted that the National Aeronautics and Space Administration staff presence at the premises of a major commercial subcontractor was too small, and NASA "lost control over both budget and schedule for the seventy-million-dollar optical system. To correct this without seriously impairing the scientific capability of the HST required NASA to go back to Congress for additional money from a House committee whose chair had strongly opposed the telescope in the first place."

The story of the Hubble Space Telescope, like Huber's tale of science (or spurious science) becoming a tool in mercenary court cases, is relevant to our consideration of the promise of genetic research because it illustrates a growing awareness that if we're to enable science and technology to deliver the immense results of which they're capable, we must re-examine the relations between science, the private sector, government and academia. The Hubble project illustrates the issues with particular clarity. These issues include the difficulties scientists have in persuading government policymakers to support long-term research, and the debasement and sidetracking of science that can occur when scientists must turn themselves into something resembling entertainers to seek funds for projects aimed at serving the whole of society. The existence of Hubble is greatly in the interests of both the U.S. and the rest of the world, but its monetary, marketing and political obstacles were so vast that its completion seems miraculous.

The second of our two clues to evaluating the promise of genetic engineering lies in the first paragraph of the *New York Times* article quoted above: "From cold fusion to high-temperature superconductivity, from robotics to neural networks, many of the recent 'revolutions' in science and technology seem to have the half-life of an average teen-age crush. Each one strides onto center stage to the boom of the media's timpani, promising to revitalize our sluggish economy, trounce our competitors, light up our homes, levitate our trains and otherwise make life easier, cheaper and more entertaining for all Americans. And almost inevitably, the 'miracle breakthroughs' prove disappointing: the science behind them is either wrong or too difficult to meet the demand for instant results."

The promise of proteomics

This statement reflects a sweeping negativity, and even cynicism, about the transformative potential of science and technology, not just in one or two fields but across the board. This is especially evident when we discern the close connections that exist between biological science, nanotechnology, energy studies and computerization. An example of this connectivity is the development of the field called proteomics, which revolves around the study and manipulation of proteins – organic compounds which contain amino acids and are often called the building blocks of life.

Proteomics promises to help us understand and combat cancer, diabetes, heart disease and other illnesses. It intersects with nanotechnology because of the tiny scale of its research and technologies; it intersects with energy studies because we need to develop new fuels; and it intersects with computerization for two reasons. First, because the amount of data that proteomics research needs to store and interpret is so vast that new computer products are required to handle it; second, because what we're learning about the architecture of proteins contains principles applicable to the design of new data storage and information processing systems. (Remember how some nanotechnologists are looking to create tiny artifacts that replicate the information processing capabilities of DNA.)

Working in a field that's been in development since the mid 1990s, Japanese scientists at Osaka University recently published a paper describing how proteins isolated from certain bacteria might be used to store data on a level of efficiency far above the maximum potential of the data storage equipment computer companies presently use. The bacterial protein can be etched on glass, and in this form the data they hold can be read and manipulated. Computer memory circuits currently use metal superimposed on silicon, a process requiring very high temperatures that preclude the incorporation of thin materials like glass and plastic. The use of protein structures as memory devices could free computer designers from the constraints of high-temperature manufacturing. Such storage mechanisms might also be immune to magnetic interference.[7] Another fertile area of convergence between protein research and computerization is the design of personalized medications based on the idiosyncrasies of the patient's individual body chemistry, and the development of drugs that combat the HIV virus by depriving it of an essential enzyme. (An enzyme is a substance, usually a protein, that facilitates a chemical process.)

Proteomics also has an increasingly important application to the design of new diagnostic techniques. Historically, diagnosis has tended to be limited to that stage of an illness in which its effects are severe enough to be visible on a macro-level, by which time it is often late enough in the illness's progress to make treatment subject to numerous obstacles. But as we learn to "read" what is happening in living tissue at a molecular level, physicians become able to detect an individual's susceptibility to a specific illness earlier and earlier, thus helping to treat it before it reaches an advanced stage. An example of the many disorders to which protein research is relevant is Alzheimer's disease, a type of dementia that occurs most commonly past the age of 65 with symptoms that include memory degradation.

Alzheimer's is now known to be associated with anomalies in the arrangement ("folding") of proteins, which affects the healthy growth of neurons, the information processing and transmitting cells in our brains and nervous systems. And researchers have recently found evidence that the protein adiponectin could play important roles in heart disease, obesity and diabetes, in which case a better understanding of this protein's properties could provide us with more effective tools to diagnose, prevent and treat these conditions.

Yet another emerging area of interdisciplinary biological research is synthetic biology, which aligns engineering and mathematics with biological research with an eye to devising and manufacturing entirely new biological systems. Leading-edge work in this field is being done in the Synthetic Biology Department (established only in 2003, which indicates the relative novelty of this field of research) in the Physical Biosciences Division of the Lawrence Berkeley National Laboratory, a facility of the U.S. Department of Energy situated at the University of California at Berkeley. This laboratory and its current work on synthetic biology excellently illustrate points we've made in this book about (a) the historical role of government in scientific and technological research; (b) the interdisciplinary nature of modern technological development, and (c) the potential and importance of universities in a large-scale innovation. The Lawrence Berkeley National Laboratory started out as the Radiation Laboratory of the University of California in 1931. Its founding research was related to the cyclotron, a device for accelerating the velocity of subatomic particles, developed by American nuclear physicist Ernest O. Lawrence (1901-1958), after whom the laboratory is named. (Lawrence was awarded the 1939 Nobel Prize for Physics in recognition of his invention.) During World War II Lawrence helped develop the atom bomb.

An interesting reflection of the wide applicability of his research is the fact that he collaborated with his brother, physician John H. Lawrence (1904–1991), a founder of nuclear medicine who pioneered therapy for leukemia. In keeping with this interdisciplinary scope, the laboratory today embraces research in fields ranging from astrophysics to genetics, medicine and computer science. Lawrence's work at Berkeley formed part of the rise of 20th-century "big science" in America – scientific research and technological development projects conducted on a massive scale with government backing. Two other institutions that loomed large in this process were Johns Hopkins University, whose Applied Physics Laboratory was instrumental in developing the proximity fuse, which was of vast importance to the Allied victory in World War II (the fuse made it possible to explode a bomb only when it was close enough to its target for maximum military effect) and the radiation Laboratory at the Massachusetts Institute of Technology, played a key role in the emergence of radar.

From an interdisciplinary point of view it's significant that the Physical Biosciences Division of the Lawrence laboratory has stated: "Biology in the 21st century will be a quantitative and predictive science. We are now poised to return to the origins of scientific inquiry - natural philosophy - as the tools and concepts of physical science become applicable to the central concerns of biology. The mission of the Physical Biosciences Division is to provide the multidisciplinary intellectual backdrop and the physical resources to build the programs and tools that will make this vision a reality."[8]

The institution's synthetic biology program, it says, is aimed at, among other goals, engineering "environmentally friendly organisms to manufacture medicine and produce energy." One of its current projects is to produce an anti-malarial drug that "affordable, even to the world's poorest people."[9]

Synthetic biology holds out the promise of building new organisms capable of generating the components of powerful new medicines (which could, for example, repair damaged human cells and kill cancer growths more effectively than anything now existing). It could also help us destroy pollution, produce environmentally friendly, inexpensive substances which will be suitable for use as fuel, and even microscopic, living computers. Such bioengineering can involve modifying existing organisms, like, to equip them to carry out functions useful to human well-being. It might also entail the design and creation of new organisms for such purposes. Again, there are risks. But the potential for universal benefit is astronomical.

NOTES

1. Gest, Howard, *Fresh Views of 17th-Century Discoveries by Hooke and Van Leeuwenhoek, MICROBE MAGAZINE / American Society for Microbiology

(Vol.2, No.10, 2007) http://www.asm.org/ASM/files/ccLibraryFiles/Filename/000000003340/znw01007000483.pdf

2. *Light and Life*, NATURE (Vol.131, Issue 3308, pp. 421-423, 1933)

3. Slabbert, N.J., *The Fallacy Of The Released Genie: The Reversibility Of Scientific Progress* (Sept. 2005), TRUMAN LIBRARY REPORTS

4. (http://query.nytimes.com/gst/fullpage.html?res=950DE3DD113FF93AA15753C1A9 6F948260).

5. *Journal of General Internal Medicine* (Vol.7, No.2 http://www.springerlink.com/content/42w40564r5227495/),

6. *Science* (Mar.1990, Vol. 247, No.4947) http://www.sciencemag.org/cgi/pdf_extract/247/4947/1241.)

7. Nakayama,K, Tachikawa,T, Majima,T,*Protein Recording Material: Photorecord/Erasable Protein Array Using a UV-Eliminative Linker, Langmuir* (Vol.24, No.5, Jan.23,2008) http://pubs.acs.org/doi/pdfplus/10.1021/la703354c.)

8. http://pbd.lbl.gov/default.html

9. http://www.lbl.gov/Publications/Currents/Archive/Dec-17-2004.html#head0

CHAPTER 8

THE COMING TOGETHER OF ALL SCIENCES

Two key points arise from our discussion so far:

First, current research in the life sciences stems directly from the work done in the first half of the 20th century in the physical sciences.

Secondly, this *linearity* of intellectual descent is also the basis of an explosion of *laterality*, i.e. the interdisciplinary "spillage" of information from one field into another — a chain reaction of innovation across a wide disciplinary spectrum.

We've seen how nanotechnology, computer science and even energy research is intertwined with medicine and with physical research into the subatomic and molecular architecture of matter. This exciting sense of disciplinary convergence is the subject of a recently published book by American science essayist and editor Stanley A. Schmidt (1944+), *The Coming Convergence: The Surprising Ways Diverse Technologies Interact to Shape Our World and Change the Future* (2008).

Schmidt writes about interdisciplinary and multidisciplinary technologies and technology impacts which sound like science fiction but which are existing or emergent science fact, such as direct interactions between computers and the human brain, the lengthening of life, the reduction of our present environmental strain and the availability of increasing amounts of inexpensive food and technologically engineered fuel. He portrays the current state of innovation as a melting-pot in which biotechnology, information technology, nanotechnology and other fields are approaching a common boiling-point to merge and produce a new landscape.

Schmidt has an informed historical sense of how many of our most important existing technologies came about because of combinations or convergences of disciplines. Linking this historical insight with the state of interdisciplinary ferment that we see in innovation today has left him with a sense of the impressive momentum of cross-fertilizations now taking shape. He presents an impression of our being caught up in a headlong rush toward increasing convergence, so that we're facing an interdisciplinary Big Bang which could trigger innovations in so many directions that it will appear as if the world is being remade. And like many current writers on technological innovation, he warns of possible dire consequences if new technologies get out of hand, if they fall into evil hands, or if they turn out to have unintended consequences which it may prove difficult to reverse or control.

Schmidt's book is interesting for several reasons, three of which need concern us here. One is that its author isn't only a highly experienced science journalist and commentator with a Ph.D in physics from Case Western Reserve University, but he's also a member of the Foresight Institute, which we have previously mentioned in the context of nanotechnology. In 1997 Schmidt published an editorial[1] in the magazine *Analog Science Fiction and Fact*, criticizing a report about a Foresight Institute nanotechnology conference which had appeared in the magazine *Scientific American*. Schmidt accused the *Scientific American* report as being biased so as to emphasize doubts about the realism of the extrapolations of nanotechnology pioneer Eric Drexler. The report, by Gary Stix, was called *Waiting for Breakthroughs (Scientific American*, April 1996), and read as if it might have been written as a prelude to *Nano-Hype*, by David Berube, a book we discussed earlier.

Stix, Schmidt said, seemed "to be trying his best to make Drexler look like a wild visionary whose 'fanciful scenarios' far exceed anything that will actually happen, and strongly (but without supporting data) suggests that more reputable scientists and technologists agree with him than with Drexler. Heavily stressing the difficulties of detail being encountered by experimentalists, he largely ignores the significance of the fact that many of them thought enough of the subject to do the work and to go to this conference." He went on: "I seriously doubt that many early American frontiersmen and women were thinking about anything resembling modern American civilization, with its interstates, internet, and jet airplanes. They were much too busy trying to survive in a wilderness. But each generation made a little advance here and a little advance there, and since each could build on the gains of its predecessors, the process moved faster and faster. So, hard as our great-great-grandparents might have found it to imagine, we did get where we are now—and we haven't stopped.

"Scientific research is not exactly like settling a physical frontier, of course, any more than settling one frontier is exactly like settling any other. But there are similarities. The people who made the first vacuum tubes, early in this century, had plenty of trouble just getting them to work in quite simple circuits, and felt justifiable pride whenever they found a way to make them work a little better. At each stage, an experimenter with an idea might see one improvement he could reasonably aspire to making with the time and resources he had available. If you had described to him the tiny, powerful, ubiquitous computers of the late twentieth century, or the huge, sophisticated communications networks of the same period, he probably would have found it hard to believe you were serious. If you were his boss and told him he had to build one of those computers, he would have had little choice but to give up in despair. He would have had no idea how to do it, and no reasonable chance of learning. But he could take small steps on which others could build, and still others could build on those, and in mere decades those computers and networks were not only real, but taken for granted by millions of people.

"Similarly, I doubt that the Wright brothers or many of their contemporaries imagined just how far their pioneering steps in aviation might lead. If you had described the Concorde supersonic transport and told Orville and Wilbur to build one, they probably would have told you it was impossible. It was — for them. But it was — eventually —quite reasonable for the industry that grew from the seed they planted.

"And such things grow much faster now than they used to, because of the number of people working in fields that can help each other synergistically, and because of the enormously increased ease and speed with which those people can now talk to each other." And he concluded: "History is full of highly regarded scientists either saying that such things as airplanes, spaceships, telephones, and home computers either were impossible, or that they would have no commercial importance.

"Surely that's something to bear in mind in listening to debates about how far nanotechnology can go. Let's just hope that everybody doesn't get so discouraged by the immediate difficulties at each early step that they give up on the ultimate goal.

"And let's hope that the Foresight Institute keeps trying to look ahead at what this stuff can do for and to us —

and what we can do about it. We just may need that knowledge a lot sooner than some of us think."

This essay shows again the controversiality of nanotechnology, despite the fact that it's today so significant that even its critics are building careers out of it. More importantly for us here, the essay reveals two conflicting intellectual impulses: one is a sense of cumulative historical momentum; the other is an awareness that the discouragement of scientific and technological research may lead to the absence of knowledge, perhaps just when we need it most. As we've seen, the struggle between these two currents of thought runs throughout recent technological history, and perhaps through all technological history. The idea of technological inevitability involves faith that innovations will appear by themselves. The idea that inaction on our part, or actions such as protests or the passage of laws, can impede technology gives at least some of us the satisfaction of feeling powerful. And the odd thing is that these two impulses can co-exist in our culture, giving us the worst of both worlds.

Schmidt's book *The Coming Convergence*, published more than a decade after his essay on nanotechnology, suggests that he's moved along in his thinking and adopted a stronger belief in the cumulative momentum of scientific and technological development – so much so that he feels confident enough to give his book a title that smacks of prediction. If this suggestion is correct, it shows how deeply entrenched is the tendency to see science and technology as forces that are now virtually unstoppable. We've argued throughout this book that no matter how benignly intended it is, this philosophical view is false and dangerous. For all the undeniable momentum that interdisciplinary convergence may presently have, it isn't unstoppable. It will continue to grow only if it's allowed to, and it will grow at the pace we urgently need only if we help it to.

The second reason why Schmidt's book is interesting to us here is that in addition to being a prominent science essayist, Schmidt is also a writer and editor of science fiction. The magazine he edits, *Analog*, grew out of *Astounding*, an iconic pulp science fiction magazine of the early 20th century whose editor, John W. Campbell, Jr. (1910-1971) was a towering influence on American science fiction. This point is relevant because in Schmidt we see illustrated anew the close relationship that exists – and which we've previously referenced – between America's ideas about emerging science fact and the fictional interpretations of science that manifest themselves in science fiction. This relationship forms an element of American popular attitudes to science and technology whose importance can scarcely be overestimated. In Schmidt we see a further illustration that to engage science and technology in America isn't only to engage laboratories and research budgets: it's also to engage the nation's hopes, dreams, fears and folklore.

Thus, while Schmidt's book is full of interesting historical facts and explanations about the rise of science and technology, and while he eloquently shares his thrill about the extraordinary possibilities now opening up, much of his conception of the possible 21st century-world is vague, not only in detail (where he can be forgiven, because it's possible for so much to happen very fast), but, more importantly, on a philosophical level. Philosophically, the creation of a culture of innovation is bedeviled not only by those who fear new technological innovations, but to at least an equal extent by promoters of science and technology who fail to address the fears that radical innovation generates. Not only science fiction but a good deal of extrapolative scientific writing, by excited and well-informed promoters of science, alienates much of the intelligent non-scientific public from innovation in this way.

This takes us to the third reason why Schmidt's book is of interest to us here: it provides a useful bridge from the subject of interdisciplinary convergence to one of the key areas of this convergence that Schmidt identifies—computer science. This is one of the most fertile of the interdisciplinary fields now active, yet it evokes even more philosophical fears than nanotechnology: not merely fears of technology going awry in ways that may cause new environmental crises or other emergencies, but, on a deeper level, fears that computer technologists may change the very nature of humanity. In this regard, it's instructive to look at the work of Ray Kurzweil and Marvin Minsky, both of whom we referenced briefly when we discussed nanotechnology.

The advent of the Digital Age

To discuss Kurzweil and Minsky it's necessary to begin by revisiting the way the digital age evolved out of the analog age. As we saw when we discussed the rise of new concepts in physics in the early 20th century, the radical increase in our knowledge of the finer texture of matter, together with our growing ability to manipulate both matter and information on a miniature scale, led to modern computerization as well as the laser. One of the links between mainstream physical research and computerization was the study of electromagnetic radiation by Faraday and Maxwell, which led to Hertz's invention of radio technology. This led in turn to radar, and eventually the vacuum tube (a device that amplified and managed electronic signals) and its successor, the transistor. The latter revolutionized electronic technologies by incorporating materials like silicon, called semiconductors because of the flexibility of their ability to conduct electricity.

The result was a medium to manage electronic signals that was highly effective, relatively cheap and much smaller than the old vacuum tubes, opening the way to miniaturization of electronic devices culminating in the integrated circuit, or microchip. The latter was, appropriately to its intellectual lineage, pioneered by British radar researcher Geoffrey Dummer before being developed as a commercial technology by Americans Jack Kilby and Robert Noyce.

This period of technological history is often referred to as the transition from the analog era to the digital era. As we've seen, analog technology works by creating a technological "copy" or "analogy" of changing conditions that we wish the technology to help us record, manipulate or calculate – like an analog watch that represents the hours of a day on a dial. Digital technology, by contrast, translates the pattern of the original into a set of numbers – information that can be stored, transmitted and reassembled or manipulated. Integrated circuits can compress a huge amount of such information in a tiny space. One of the technological forms into which such circuits can be assembled is a machine that mimics not only the calculative ability of the brain but also other features of thought.

Because digital technology enables us to manage information more quickly, flexibly and space-efficiently than analog technology, it has vast implications for the presentation and dissemination of all products and socio-economic infrastructures that depend on the handling of information. These implications are very wide, because in principle, every artifact has an information component: information is essential not only to the manufacture of products but also to their effective use. A wood-burning oven, for example, requires its user to possess, and be able to apply to various situations, information about building the fire in the oven, keeping it going safely, extinguishing it properly at the appropriate time, and relating varying temperatures to the requirements of different cooking tasks. The only reason we don't usually think of such an oven as being an information-related artifact is that the information isn't built into the oven but resides outside it, in the brain of its user and in a user's manual.

But modern information technology allows us to incorporate information management devices *into* the ovens we now use, so an appliance like a microwave oven can be programmed to carry out a range of operations geared to differing circumstances and objectives. Appliances can also be equipped with automated feedback systems so their operations can vary according to changes in the environment, or in other information systems with which they interact. The number of appliances in which we're now able to install advanced information-processing mechanisms has now grown very large, so information processing plays an increasingly wide role across our whole spectrum of manufactured goods.

But it would be a mistake to think of the analog-to-digital revolution as an historical event that's over. It's in fact an ongoing process, because not only specific analog technologies but also the *habits of thought associated with analog technologies* are not easily put behind us. Our attachment to analog technology and culture remains great, and the problems besetting the transition from analog to digital in specific areas of technology can be considerable. This is part of the phenomenon of *technological lag* which requires an effort from us to overcome. The fact that converting to a new technology can be demonstrated to be in our interests doesn't necessarily mean it will be embraced. Some will object to it because they don't like some aesthetic or other aspect of it, others will reject it because it's strange and unfamiliar. Still others will dislike it because transitioning to it will be inconvenient and upset the habits associated with older technology. An example is the change from analog to digital broadcast television (DTV).

Because of its superiority to analogy technology in transmitting great amounts of information, DTV allows broadcasters greatly to enhance the sound and picture quality of their transmissions, to present television viewers with a much larger variety of programming, to provide viewers with tools to interact with the programming system, and (because the broadcast spectrum available to all our current broadcast technology is limited) to concentrate entertainment and news broadcasts more tightly so as to leave more capacity open, including for police and other public service broadcasts.

The U.S. Congress approved the transition to DTV in 1996 by authorizing assignment of an extra broadcast channel to each broadcast television station so they could phase in digital broadcasting alongside their analog service. It was subsequently decided that all full-power broadcast stations in the U.S. would stop all analog broadcasting on February 17, 2009, thereafter switching exclusively to digital. This meant everyone who wanted to continue receiving free, non-cable television broadcasts would either have to buy a digital television set by that date or, if they wished to keep their analog television set, buy a digital-to-analog converter box to attach to their analog set, so the box could translate the digital signals into a form usable by the analog system.

The analog-to-DTV transition illustrates several of the points we've addressed in this book: the federal government's role in the development of new technological infrastructures, technological lag (the fact that a better technology won't necessarily be quickly or easily embraced) and the responsibility of government to take action to smooth and expedite the transition to a new widely-used technology. The transition to DTV hasn't been as smooth as it might have been. Buying new digital television sets or converter boxes costs money, and it was felt the public shouldn't have to shoulder the whole cost of a transition to a new technology just because the government thought it wise. While some might argue that television is chiefly an entertainment medium and a luxury that households could reasonably be expected to do without if they couldn't afford it, this isn't so: television is also a medium through which people receive news. In emergency situations television, with radio, may be vital to survival. And just on an ordinary day-to-day basis, television is a unifying cultural force that creates a sense of community and reinforces civic order.

So a government fund was established to issue every household that applied with a coupon for funds that could be used toward the cost of transition. But the fund ran out of money. As the deadline of February 17 approached, polls showed in early January that 6.2 percent of television-watching households were "completely unready," according to Nielsen Media Services, with this percentage being higher in some communities than in others. It was estimated that as much as 11.5 percent of America's Hispanic population wasn't prepared for DTV. Moreover, compelling the nation to switch to DTV while so many households were unready would not only cut these households off from the world of television but would also financially penalize the stations serving their areas, since by losing viewership they would lose advertising.

In response to all this, the then President-elect, Barack Obama, called for the transition date to be delayed so steps could be taken to ensure that more people were ready for the change. But Kevin Martin, the outgoing Bush administration's chairman of the U.S. Federal Communication Commission, the agency controlling broadcasting and supervising the transition, disagreed, saying: "We spent a lot of time making sure everyone knows about February 17. What kind of message will that send if we are telling people that is the date and then we don't do it?" He pointed out that broadcaster companies had invested money in preparing for the anticipated date, and for the new allocations of broadcast spectrum. It was eventually decided to postpone compulsory national conversion to digital TV to June 12, 2009.

Regardless of what you think of the arguments for and against DTV, this issue illustrates how uncertain and divided America remains in its entry into the digital age. This uncertainty and divisiveness are even more evident when you look at the profound philosophical issues surrounding the movement toward radical innovations in computerization – an area which, like many fields of contemporary innovation, relates, yet again, to nanotechnology.

Artificial intelligence, robotics and nanotechnology

The concept of machines that mimic human intellectual functions is quite old: the modern computer has many ancestors. Calculating devices like the abacus (which is still used today) go back thousands of years before Christ. During the 17th century, calculating machines were designed and built by German linguist, astronomer and cartographer Wilhelm Schickard (1592–1635), French philosopher, mathematician and physicist Blaise Pascal (1623–1662), German philosopher, mathematician and physicist Gottfried W. Leibniz (1646–1716), who anticipated many concepts used by modern-day computer theory. Punched card technology, which became identified with mid-20th century computers, were in fact used in textile looms in the 18th and 19th centuries. A British philosopher and mathematician George Boole (1815–1864), invented Boolean algebra, a language of logical symbols used in the design of digital computers. British philosopher, mathematician and engineer Charles Babbage (1791–1871) conceived and designed an "analytical engine" that was programmable in the sense that we today think of computer operations. Programming for it was written by poet Lord Byron's daughter Augusta Ada King, the Countess of Lovelace (1815–1852).

The development of programming and information theory was no less essential to the evolution of computers than was the design of hardware. A pivotal figure in information theory history is American mathematician and engineer Claude E. Shannon (1916–2001), whose master's thesis at the Massachusetts Institute of Technology showed how Boolean algebra could be applied to the building of systems of switches that later came to underlie the information theory governing complex electronic devices. Joining the symbolic language of logic to the design of electronic circuits in this way opened the door to a new, reciprocal relationship between electronic circuitry and the language of logic.

On one hand this helped make it possible to build electronic circuits with a greater logical sophistication than had previously been possible; on the other hand it enabled such circuits to be used to solve problems that could be stated in logical symbols. From this *synthesis of logic and electronics* came the digital computer. When this work was in turn combined with the increasing trend toward miniaturization that progress in physics and chemistry were making possible, the foundations of modern computerization were in place. Appropriately, Shannon had degrees in both mathematics and electronics and his interests were highly interdisciplinary.

This leads us to Marvin Minsky.

Minsky (1927+) is an American scientist and philosopher known for his work in artificial intelligence and robotics. *Robotics* refers to the science and technology of designing and building robots – machines that carry out specific tasks assigned by their human creators. The word robot, derived from a Czech word meaning "work", or types of work, first appeared in a play called *R.U.R.* (1921), by Czech writer Karelapek (1890–1938). *Artificial intelligence*, called AI for short, involves attempts to develop computers that mimic limited aspects of human intelligence (like mathematical calculation), as well as ones that might be able to duplicate human cognition in an overall sense: in other words, machines capable of thinking on the same level of complexity, spontaneity, independence and variety of thought that we associate with the human brain.

The creation of an intelligent machine in this sense could be called the Holy Grail of computer science. The relationship between artificial intelligence theory and the rest of computer science provides an interesting example of the importance of vision and motive in innovation. If you look through the literature of computerization you see immediately that the idea of an intelligent machine is a passionately pursued ambition of computer theorists. As of the publication of this book we appear far from realizing this dream. Yet it's been a fertile dream because it has powerfully motivated much creative thought about the analogies between computer systems and human cognitive processes.

And this thought hasn't been only theoretical. Artificial intelligence research has been a driving force of applied computer science and a fertile source of some of its most important developments, including ones that have made the practical emergence of contemporary computerization possible. Minsky, whose doctorate is in mathematics, co-founded the AI Laboratory at the Massachusetts Institute of Technology, where at the time of writing this he's professor of electrical engineering, computer science and media arts and sciences.

Understanding at least some of Minsky's thinking is essential for anyone wanting to understand what computer science is really about and where it's headed. Without understanding Minsky, you might easily think that computerization is only about companies launching one new music storage device after another and one new hand-held executive communications tool after another – an endless source of gadget-entertainment and status symbols for teenagers and businesspeople with an image to consider.

Computerization of course produces such gadgets, but as it's also much more: it's a philosophical and intellectual adventure, and arguably a crucial gateway to our future.

To appreciate Minsky's importance it's useful to take a detour and compare his work to the development of rocketry and space exploration. As we'll see, there are important connections between the emergence of computerization, as conceived by cyber-philosophers like Minsky, and the rise and potential of space travel.

The long journey of the space travel visionaries

When American rocket pioneer Robert H. Goddard (1882–1945) launched the first liquid-fueled rocket in 1926, rockets were widely considered to fall into three categories: fireworks, military instruments of limited use, and imaginary artifacts about which fantasy writers concocted preposterous stories for pulp science fiction magazines. But Goddard took rockets very seriously. Excited by the visions of science fiction writers like Herbert G. ("H.G.") Wells, (1866–946), he believed powerful rockets capable of precisely controlled flight across vast distances could and would be built. And he believed they'd take human beings into space. While many people think of H.G. Wells as an inventor of fantastic fictions, he was in fact a prolific non-fiction writer who saw modern science and technology as a major turning-point in the evolution of the human species.

But this interplanetary vision, and its associated ideas about a new direction for human evolution, continued to be overshadowed by politics. While ideas of space exploration and even terrestrial aircraft were relegated by mainstream culture to the pages of science fiction, the young Robert Goddard's mind was filled with ideas of how technology could dramatically change the infrastructures of America and the world. In 1904 he read his class an essay he had written describing a magnetic levitation (maglev) train. (The essay was written in response to a class assignment to write about transportation in 1950. As we've seen, we're still struggling with maglev technology over a century later.) Goddard later wrote a story describing how people could use this technology to travel from Boston New York in ten minutes.

But Goddard was just beginning to learn how resistant people could be to innovation. His classmates found his concept unrealistic. Both *Scientific American* and *Popular Astronomy* magazine rejected as impractical an article by him on the possibility of investigating interplanetary space, but in 1907 his article *The Use of the Gyroscope in the Balancing and Steering of Airplanes* appeared in the *Scientific American Supplement*, and in early 1909 he published work on the design of a liquid-fueled rocket. (At that time rockets were designed for propulsion by solid fuels; the introduction of liquid hydrogen and liquid oxygen was aimed at producing a rocket with significantly greater fuel efficiency.)

In 1909 *Scientific American* published an article based on his class essay—*The Limit of Rapid Transit*. Because his research made it necessary for him to investigate aspects of radio waves (remember our outline earlier of how so much of 20th century innovation stemmed from radiation research?), Goddard devised an electronic oscillator circuit using a vacuum tube, for which he was awarded a patent in 1915. Vacuum tubes, devices which manage electronic signals, including amplifying them, were basic to the birth of the electronic age. Goddard earned a Ph.D at Clark University in Massachusetts before becoming a research fellow at Princeton University, New Jersey.

Advocating space travel: A career risk

As his work advanced, Goddard learned increasingly that space flight was something that it was perilous to discuss seriously if one wished to build a career in the academia. Still less was he encouraged to publicize his ideas about sending spacecraft to other star systems, space crews placed in suspended animation to survive long journeys, and solar-powered spacecraft. In 1920, he produced a report on his rocket research, *A method of reaching extreme altitude*, which he submitted to the Smithsonian Institution. In it he discussed the prospect of sending a rocket to the Moon. He also explained the concept of using unmanned spacecraft for extraterrestrial photography.

A copy of his report came into the hands of *The New York Times*, that same pillar of American media respectability that had dismissed heavier-than-air flight. The *Times* ridiculed and insulted Goddard, intimating that he didn't know as much fundamental physics as a schoolchild. This public attack laid the foundation for a chain of similar scorn that greeted reports of Goddard's subsequent rocket tests over the years, causing him to retreat from public view and conduct his research as privately as possible. Then, in 1929 he was approached by American aviator Charles A. Lindbergh (1902–1974), who was deeply interested in Goddard's work and tried to find financial backers for it. He was turned down by all except American businessman Daniel Guggenheim (1856–1930), whose family made important contributions to Goddard's research budget for years.

But it wasn't only Goddard's ideas about space travel that were too weird for minds wedded to conventional thought. Even his concepts for more immediate innovations were too hard to digest. Although he developed the principles of the bazooka, a portable rocket-launcher, for the U.S. military in the last days of World War I, his description to the U.S. military of long-range guided missiles, in 1940, was dismissed by military experts. They considered Goddard's ideas irrelevant to the kinds of warfare they anticipated in Europe.

However, if Goddard's ideas were too bold for the U.S., they weren't too bold for Germany. Between the world wars German scientists eagerly studied Goddard's work. After World War II Major-General Dr. Walter R. Dornberger (1895– 1980), one of the leaders of Hitler's rocket program, said he and his colleagues couldn't fathom why a man of Goddard's genius wasn't supported by his government in time to enable the Allies to use rockets to end the war. (The German Army initiated a rocket development program in 1931.) In the opinion of American science editor and Westinghouse Electric Corporation executive George E. Pendray (1901-1987), "If his own countrymen had listened to Dr. Goddard, the United States would be far ahead of its present position in the international space race. There might, in fact, have been no race."

As a result of the ridicule directed at him for his interest in space, Goddard withdrew into himself and became wary of forming alliances with others, for he'd learned that to do so exposed him to mockery. This concern was especially burdensome during years when illness afflicted him.

Early rocketry thus received more serious government attention in Germany than in America, a country that liked to think of itself as the world's hub of entrepreneurial invention. The philosophical vision that fed German rocket science was no less ambitious than Goddard's. This is evident from the careers of two of Germany's greatest rocket pioneers, physicist Hermann J. Oberth (1894–1989) and physicist-engineer Wernher M. M. von Braun (1912–1977). Like Goddard, Oberth found his imagination fired and formed by science fiction: in this case, it was the space stories of French novelist Jules G. Verne that mesmerized him. As a child Oberth built primitive rockets and worked out, on his own, the idea of rockets with several stages that would be jettisoned after their work was done

- a principle later incorporated into manned space flight.

After serving in World War I he studied physics, but his doctoral thesis on rocketry was rejected: it wasn't only interdisciplinary, which posed problems for the highly structured landscape of German universities, but it combined disciplines that weren't even recognized yet as academic fields of study – space medicine and space engineering. (Oberth had made a foray into medical studies before being drafted into World War I: his thesis not only addressed the physics and engineering of rocketry but also drew on his medical knowledge to explore the possible effects of space travel on the human body.) Oberth published a version of the thesis as a book, *Rockets to the Planets in Space* (1923), a later incarnation of which, *The Way to Spaceship Travel* (1929), won lasting fame as a groundbreaking text and received a prize from the French Astronomical Society.

At first Oberth earned his living as a high school math and science teacher, but space remained his passion. He attracted a circle of fans that formed a space club and advised Austrian filmmaker Friedrich C. ("Fritz") Lang (1890–1976) on production of the pioneering space film *Woman in the Moon* (1929), which became a beloved part of the culture of Germany's emerging community of rocket scientists. Oberth became a university teacher (his students included Wernher von Braun) and finally wound up at Peenemünde, Germany's rocketry development center from which came the V-2 rockets that Hitler would eventually launch against Britain. After the war he published ideas about the exploration of the Moon, space suits, space station design and the placement of a telescope in space, all of which have since become reality. He was also interested in the search for extraterrestrial life.

The career of Oberth's student, Von Braun, is one of the most extraordinary of the 20th century or any century. He went from being one of Hitler's top rocket scientists to attaining iconic status as the presiding genius of America's space program. It was a career rich in irony. Von Braun and his colleagues not only followed a research path parallel to Robert Goddard's, but studied Goddard's work avidly. Whereas Goddard was ridiculed in the American media and spurned by the U.S. military, Von Braun was later brought to America by the U.S. Government, for whom he helped develop intercontinental ballistic missiles. He eventually becoming the driving figure in designing the rocket used in the Apollo lunar mission. Yet, even after World War II in which Hitler's missiles had demonstrated the effectiveness of long-range rocketry as a weapon of war, it was far from plain sailing for Von Braun in America.

You see, despite his digressions into military rocket projects in Germany and America, it was the larger vision of space exploration that was Von Braun's deeper passion, just as it had been for Goddard and Oberth. In fact, it was Oberth's writings about humanity's future in space that confirmed the young Von Braun in his determination to devote himself to developing the incipient science of rocketry. As a young man he joined Germany's Spaceflight Society (Verein für Raumschiffahrt) and helped Oberth in his rocket research. One of his fellow members of the Spaceflight Society was German science writer Willy Ley (1906-1969), who went on to become a widely read popularizer of space travel concepts and technologies in America, via books and articles in science fiction magazines. (Von Braun and Ley later teamed up to promote space travel in America.) But the idea of space travel as a realistic undertaking that deserved the serious attention of the U.S. Government took a long time to develop in an America that had grown accustomed to associating space travel exclusively with science fiction. The fact that space advocates like Ley were strongly associated with science fiction magazines may have been a mixed blessing.

The Soviet space pioneers and the Space Race

An interesting aspect of Von Braun's early career is the light it casts on the difference between American and German attitudes to rocketry in the thirties. While Goddard failed to impress the U.S. military with the importance of rocketry in those years, Von Braun's 1934 Ph.D thesis on rocket design engineering was taken so seriously by the German military that they classified part of it as a state secret. And the situation in Russia was so significantly different from American attitudes to space that it had historic repercussions.

We mentioned above H.G. Wells's sense that humanity was on the brink of a great leap forward – a defining moment in history and perhaps in human evolution. This mood was shared by many late 19th-century and early 20th-century thinkers. But it tended to be eclipsed in the popular imagination, and in the minds of many intellectuals, by the political changes taking place at that time, such as the Russian Revolution and the rise of communism, whose brightest minds emphasized sociopolitical rather than technological change. Where such political intellectuals wrote about technological change, they treated it less as a fundamental shaper of a new era than as an adjunct of political change, with its main importance lying in the development of industries for commissars to direct. Speculation about massive technological change per se, on a scale huge enough to affect not only social relations but the very nature of human existence on Earth, was, for some social revolutionaries, an undesirable distraction from their political struggle, just as abstract art and non-political fiction and poetry were.

Nevertheless, serious thought about the transformation of human life by space travel and other technological development couldn't be stopped, and work on rocketry formed part of it. This work was explicitly linked to an earnest ambition to launch humanity into an era of interplanetary exploration. Russian mathematics teacher Konstantin E. Tsiolkovsky (1857-1935) argued that rockets capable of propelling human pilots and passengers into space were technically achievable. He also conceived the idea of the space elevator – a structure that would extend from the surface of the Earth up to orbital level, making it possible for spacecraft to be launched without rockets. He took inspiration from the writings of Russian philosopher Fyodorovich Fyodorov (1827-1903), who had declared that science was capable of taking humanity into space, extending civilization to the ocean beds and prolonging human life perhaps indefinitely.

Thus, even in the midst of an early 20th-century Russian culture that was focused on the political and economic practicalities of the communist revolution, a space movement arose. On one hand it was a drastic deviation from the obsessive emphasis of communism on the here and now of industrial efficiency and Soviet reconstruction; on the other hand it was peculiarly consistent with those impulses in Russia's upheaval that yearned to be part of a gigantic change in the condition of human life on Earth.

Out of this Russian ferment of ideology and philosophy came a leader of the Soviet Union's rocket and space programs, engineer Friedrich Zander (1887-1933). At high school Zander's imagination was fired by Tsiolkovsky's ideas about space travel and he soon became an ardent advocate of the exploration of the planet Mars. He was barely out of his teens when he published a discussion of manned space travel including thoughts on how human beings could sustain themselves on space journeys, through, for example, on-ship horticulture. The depth of his feelings about space research is reflected in the fact that he named his son Mercury and his little girl Astra.

Eventually he managed to get an opportunity to discuss his space work with the leader of the Russian state, Vladimir I. Ulyanov, better known as V.I. Lenin (1870-1924), at a conference of inventors. In the twenties he was influenced by the writings of Oberth and Goddard. He, Tsiolkovsky and space travel pioneer Oleksandr Gnatovich Shargei, also known as Yuri Vasilievich Kondratyuk (1897-1942), launched a society to promote space flight. In addition to this general fostering of the concept of space travel as a serious undertaking worthy of government backing, Zander made noteworthy technical suggestions to overcome the practical problems of space flight, including a patented rocket design and solar sailing (propelling a space vehicle by the pressure of light).

Zander's fellow space enthusiast Kondratyuk envisioned a mathematically detailed lunar exploration plan whereby a spacecraft would remain in orbit around the Moon while a shuttle craft descended to the surface – the method eventually used by America's Apollo team. Kondratyuk couldn't find a publisher for his book on rocket design, so he published it himself. He fell foul of the Soviet Government for reasons unrelated to his space work and was banished to Siberia.

Kondratyuk later worked on a wind power project and met Sergei Korolev (1907-1966), the engineer who ultimately directed the Soviet Union's space race with America. Korolev and Friedrich Zander together helped found the Soviet Union's government-controlled Jet Propulsion Research Group (GIRD), which Korolev headed. This entity evolved into a larger one group among whose members was engineer Valentin P. Glushko (1908-1989), who published articles about space flight and Moon exploration in the early twenties. The Stalin era was, however, marked by persecution of anyone who was even slightly suspected of disloyalty to the communist regime. Professional peers frequently used this situation as a career-enhancing tool, by casting political aspersions on their rivals, who might then be arrested and sent to a forced labor camp or worse. Korolev was convicted of such charges and underwent an ordeal of imprisonment and ill-treatment.

This kind of paranoia robbed Stalin's Soviet Union of much of its intellectual leadership. But Korolev was eventually allowed to return to work on the state's rocket development program. While he worked on military missiles for Moscow he promoted the idea of a Soviet space program and it was he who suggested sending a dog into space, which was later done. At first this work on space exploration was received coldly by military and political officials but Korolev was finally able to use the force of international political competitiveness in his favor, by arguing that it would be good for the Soviet Union's global public image to beat the U.S. into space. This led to the successful launch of Sputnik 1, the Earth's first man-made satellite, in 1957.

Korolev's team worked hard to follow this success up by sending unmanned spacecraft to the Moon. One struck the Moon and another took pictures of its far side. These events had tremendous cultural and psychological impact. The U.S. was stunned by the implication that the Soviet Union was its superior in the advanced technology of space exploration, which was seen as not only an indicator of the Soviet Union's level of sophistication in military rocketry but also as a general reflection of the communist state's position in cutting-edge technological innovation.

Since the prestige of America's intellectual firepower now seemed to be at stake, the U.S. hastily moved forward with its own space effort and in 1961 President Kennedy announced his desire that America should land a man on the Moon. But Korolev, who had ideas for sending spacecraft to Venus and Mars, had developed a momentum that was hard to beat, and his group once again scored a first against the U.S. by launching cosmonaut Yuri A. Gagarin (1934-1968) into space in an orbital spacecraft in 1961.

The space objectives that had once been so indifferently regarded by military leaders and politicians in both the U.S. and the Soviet Union now became a subject of eagerly pursued "firsts" in a serious competition between them. One of these competitive aims was to see who could achieve the first space walk, and this race too was won by the Soviets when, in 1965, Alexei A. Leonov (1934-) temporarily exited his spacecraft as it was orbiting. The next big prize, of course, was getting a manned mission to the Moon. This was achieved in 1969 by the US's Apollo crew – Moonwalkers Neil A. Armstrong (1930-) and Edwin E. "Buzz" Aldrin, Jr.(1930-) and pilot and Moon orbiter Michael Collins (1930-).

Space exploration, artificial intelligence and the philosophy of technological motivation

You may now be wondering why, despite its fascinating sidelights on technological history, we have chosen to discuss this mini-history of the space era here, as our prelude to a discussion of Marvin Minsky and artificial intelligence. The answer to this good question is both simple and important. It's this: perhaps more than any other narrative in scientific and technological history, the rise of the space era vividly demonstrates the importance of large philosophical and political motives in bringing about a massive new phase of technological growth.

Philosophical and political motivations are two different but overlapping things, and the coming of the space era is a story of both of them. The development of rocketry is about engineering and the solving of highly technical problems. Many people wouldn't readily associate it with abstract philosophical ideas. Yet, from its inception and throughout its various phases of development in the 20th century, rocketry was driven by a grand philosophical vision – the ambition to launch the human species into space and initiate an age of interplanetary, if not interstellar, space exploration. The story of rocketry is a drama of people who were consumed by a passion to accomplish this ambition. Thoughts about space travel were regarded by "practical" policymakers in government and the military as an incidental and even frivolous digression from more pressing, socially relevant uses of time and resources. But space visionaries like Goddard, Zander and Von Braun took exactly the opposite view, seeing space exploration as the real goal, with military pursuits being the digressions – although ones which they were willing to use, if necessary, as stepping-stones to get humanity into space.

If we examine the lives and personalities of the scientists and engineers who made space travel a reality, we see clear similarities among them. They weren't technicians alone, but dreamers who dreamed in the realm of technology, and the visions they dreamed were about human evolution and the advance to a new and different level of existence. The emergence of rocketry can scarcely be understood without taking this immense philosophical impetus into account.

The ambition to reach space wasn't only a unifying force that gave intellectual cohesion and purpose to the myriad of technical investigations that the design of workable rockets and space vehicles required. It was also a source of psychological force and determination that crossed international boundaries and energized a remarkable group of people who were pursuing parallel courses in separate countries. It compelled them to persist. It enabled them to endure ridicule, survive political persecution and navigate their way through regimes of draconian oppression. The drive to get humanity into space was a philosophical dream of immense power indeed.

We said above that philosophical and political motivations are two overlapping but different impulses. This too is illustrated by the development of rocketry and the advent of the space era. The Space Race between the Soviet Union and the U.S. was a political race. It could also be argued as having been to some extent a military one as well, because the development of space technology had practical implications including military ones. You could argue that the U.S. and the Soviet Union were trying to intimidate each other militarily by displays of cutting-edge astronautical sophistication. Nevertheless, the Space Race that took place in the late fifties and early sixties is most accurately describable as less a military than a political competition. It was about two political orders vying for prestige in the eyes of the world. It is also interesting to note that the space programs of both states were government enterprises, so it was really about two governments competing, from a morale-boosting point of view, for the good estimation of their own peoples.

The space program promoters in both political realms took full advantage of this political competitiveness to advance their objectives. Moreover, even the political side of the competition wasn't devoid of a strong philosophical dimension, since the Cold War between the Soviet Union and the U.S., of which the space race was part, was at heart an ideological and philosophical rivalry between two economic and government systems – communism and democracy.

The advent of the space age is thus an excellent example of the potency of philosophical ideas and large philosophical ambition and vision in the landscape of technological motivation. Numerous technical solutions of rocketry problems flowed in a more or less linear way from the evolution of physics and engineering, but the pace and integration of these was greatly accelerated by the sheer determination of the community of space exploration advocates. The passion of these enthusiasts brought momentum, energy and focus to rocketry development. Certainly the drive that the space lobby brought to rocketry doesn't appear to have been equaled by any other motivational force in the field of rocket development; attitudes to such research outside the space lobby seem rather to have varied from inertia and indifference to hostility and ridicule.

When the space lobby pushed rocketry to the point at which its military missile applications were so obvious that they could no longer be ignored, these applications were then taken up, but still with negligible interest in pursuing the vision of space exploration. A further round of lobbying was necessary to achieve space programs in the Soviet Union and the U.S., and for this effort it was again necessary to mobilize philosophical factors in the form of competitive ideological (and nationalistic) pride.

This at last brings us back to computerization and Minsky. The story of how we entered the space era provides us with useful insight into the rise of computerization in several ways. One relates to the role played by philosophical vision in technological advance. Computerization has been similarly fueled by a philosophical vision

— the creation of artificial intelligence.

Another parallel between space exploration and computerization has been the sense of the long term that has infused both fields; their respective enthusiasts have wanted to see their dreams turned into reality as quickly as possible, yet many have shown a clear awareness that they were involved in long-term enterprises that involved not just the immediate fates of specific projects but the larger evolution of their civilization, and even of humanity. There's been an interesting balance, in these trailblazing minds, between relentless urgency and the acceptance of long-term deliverables.

Yet another parallel is our old friend, interdisciplinary fertility, which we meet again as we turn now to Minsky's work.

NOTES

1. http://www.foresight.org/sciamdebate/Analog.html#anchor598868

CHAPTER 9

THINKING MACHINES, TELETECHNOLOGY AND THE KNOWLEDGE ECONOMY

We've seen how thinkers including Pascal, Leibniz and Babbage worked on techniques and artifacts to mimic human thought. They were, in effect, concerned with artificial intelligence ("AI") research – the quest to duplicate advanced intelligence as we understand it, which is currently human intelligence. Analogously to the role of rocketry by the vision of space exploration, the quest for AI is deeply rooted in the computer industry, not only as a center of philosophical ambition but as a practically important source of technical agendas for applied research. It's hard now to imagine any advanced computer innovation being done outside the framework of AI. The vocabulary of thinking-process mimicry is ingrained in the very language that computer researchers speak.

Like the idea of space travel, AI has deep roots in mythology, folklore and literature. Since ancient times, speculative tales have imagined the creation of artificial people and the problems this might cause. By the mid-20th century, the prospects for designing machines that would duplicate or exceed human intellectual skills seemed enormously exciting. But as with rocketry, investors, politicians and government officials have been wary of backing AI's philosophical vision. They've rather been concerned with marketable products in the short term. Funding AI research has been a rocky road.

Against this background, Marvin Minsky has emerged as a pioneering intellectual force in AI. As a student in the 1950s he built a learning device inspired by organic nervous systems. He invented a new kind of high-resolution microscope that's in wide use. He's devised robot instruments that impressively mimic human tactile, optical and manual functions. He's used his research on machine intelligence to make original contributions to the broader field of cognitive psychology -- the study of how minds process information, solve problems and make decisions. He has degrees in mathematics from Harvard and Princeton. A paper he published in 1961, *Steps Towards Artificial Intelligence*, placed AI research on a new level of sophistication as an independent discipline. His book *The Society of Mind* (1985) fascinatingly interprets intelligence as a diversity of many interacting mechanisms, as opposed to the more conventional concept of mind as governed by a few basic structures or processes. His other works include *Robotics* (1986) and *The Emotion Machine* (2006).

The passion Minsky evidently feels toward AI as a source of new insight in many fields is as powerful as that felt about space exploration by any of rocketry's most vigorous proponents, and as far-reaching. But unlike rocket pioneers like Robert Goddard, who learned to keep their space enthusiasm private for fear for attracting ridicule, Minsky seems to have no qualms about promoting his ideas in areas that draw controversy. For example, he sees AI as a more fertile guide to the nature of thought than the research of neuroscientists who study organic brains. Biological concepts of consciousness, he believes, are simplistic. In his opinion, the trains of thought that AI researchers have developed can produce results capable of enabling us to create creative intelligences superior to human intelligence. This is necessary, Minsky argues, to solve problems that are necessary to our future well-being and even to our survival but which may be beyond human intelligence.

If he's right, the only way to solve these problems in time is to build *machines that are more intelligent than we are.*

This ambition has enormous implications. It opens up the theoretical possibility of producing a generation of machines with the intellectual power to solve, perhaps within a generation or even a few years, problems of medical science, food production, energy and climate management which human intelligences may need centuries to solve if we're capable of solving them at all. But this vision faces several problems – or rather, whole areas of problems.

One is philosophical. For religious or other philosophical reasons, many people don't like the concept of building machines that are smarter than people. Another is funding. To achieve the potential of AI, Minsky argues, funding must enable new avenues in basic science to be opened up without short-term constraints. Funding, that is, with long-term vision. "There is no respect for basic science," Minsky complained in 2007. "In the 1960s General Electric had a great research laboratory; Bell Telephone's lab was legendary. I worked there one summer, and they said they wouldn't work on anything that would take less than 40 years to execute. CBS Laboratories, Stanford Research Lab—there were many great laboratories in the country, and there are none now."[1]

Funding has long been a bone of contention in the AI community, in which it's become customary to use the term "AI winter" to designate a period in which the outlook for financial support of AI research becomes particularly bleak. The attitude of AI critics in this regard strongly parallels the situation of nanotechnology, where the ambitions of some nanotechnologists are rejected as unlikely to deliver usable products in the immediate term. There's also a peculiarly schizoid posture toward funding on the part of some AI researchers as well as nanotechnologists.

It's illustrated by the controversy over a possible role that Minsky himself might have played in the substantial reduction of commercial interest in AI funding in the second half of the 1980s. In 1984 he cautioned investors against expecting unrealistic product deliverables from the state of AI research then prevailing. Within a few years of his warning, market interest did indeed crumble. Whether or not his warning played a role in this, it shows how many AI researchers tend to vacillate between emphasizing their lack of funding and indicating that there is, in fact, strong investor interest in AI research. The former is motivated by hunger for funding; the latter by the recognition among even the most market-ignorant researchers that if you want to attract backing, the last thing you should do is suggest nobody has faith in your product. So, many AI researchers consider it to be in their field's interest to identify it as a healthy attractor of funding rather than as a poverty-stricken research domain, even while they beg for funding. These two positions, adopted alternately or even simultaneously, can be confusing.

Much of this is semantics. If you stretch words in the right way, you can show that for at least a decade or more an enormous amount of money has been poured into "computer research". You could also show that AI interests and vocabularies have framed much if not most of the computer industry's research and development agendas. If you want to present a strong argument that AI is well funded, you could also help your case by extending your definition of both AI and computerization to include everything that's touched by computer technology, which these days is just about everything in our economy. But you'd really be playing games with words and numbers, because the fact is that AI research in the sense that's motivated the visions of Minsky and people like him is far from massively funded. It's highly debatable whether we're committing anything like the amount we could and should to the support of basic AI research. That is, the kind that will help us build a machine that's as independently intelligent as, or in a general sense more intelligent than, the human mind.

The record rather shows that for the past half century or more, budgets for advanced AI research have been driven by relatively short attention spans and impatience with the inability of AI research to meet short-term product delivery dates for marketable or governmentally usable end results. This history isn't quite identical with that of space research and rocketry, but there are enough parallels between the two to cast a thought-provoking light on how tight-fisted we are, as a civilization, about visionary research.

For example, in the 1950s and 1960s the U.S. Government was very keen to develop computers that would be able to translate Soviet texts quickly for intelligence analysis. After spending an amount which was claimed at the time to be around $20 million on machine translation research (but which has subsequently been estimated as being closer to $13 million) the government's Automatic Language Processing Advisory Committee (ALPAC) issued a report in 1966 expressing great skepticism about the research. And funding ended.[2]

Then, in 1969, the U.S. Government's Advanced Research Projects Agency (ARPA), which had been backing basic AI research by scientists including Minsky, decided to change its policy and started funding only those projects which showed a strong ability to deliver useful applications in the short term.

This agency, ARPA (later renamed DARPA, with the word *Defense* added in front) has an interesting history: its support made possible the development of the Internet, powerfully illustrating the importance of government support for large innovation enterprises. The first version of the Internet was called the Arpanet, short for Advanced Research Projects Agency Network. It arose from research showing information could be transmitted in "packets" enabling separate bundles of information to be communicated along the same routes simultaneously. This made possible groups of computers engaged in a constant exchange of information. It was a turning-point that ushered in the Internet landscape, which is now so ingrained in our lives that many people, especially those born into it, can scarcely imagine a non-Internet civilization.

We owe a great debt of gratitude to those who drove this work – a remarkably small number of people. A key figure among them was American scientist Joseph C. R. Licklider (1915–1990). His intellectual background illustrated the interdisciplinary nature of emergent information science. For his Bachelor's degree he majored in physics and mathematics as well as psychology, in which he obtained a doctorate for research on the psychology of sound perception. At the Massachusetts Institute of Technology he taught psychology to engineers, encouraging an understanding of the parallels between the neurological processing of information and the management of signals in electrical circuitry.

In 1962 Licklider became director of ARPA's Information Processing Techniques Office. He saw the vast potential of networks of computers and played a major role in funding the research that made such networks, and the personal computer, possible. His 1960 paper *Man-Computer Symbiosis*[3] stated that "for effective man-computer interaction, it will be necessary for the man and the computer to draw graphs and pictures and to write notes and equations to each other on the same display surface. The man should be able to present a function to the computer, in a rough but rapid fashion, by drawing a graph. The computer should read the man's writing, perhaps on the condition that it be in clear block capitals, and it should immediately post, at the location of each hand-drawn symbol, the corresponding character as interpreted and put into precise type-face.

"With such an input-output device, the operator would quickly learn to write or print in a manner legible to the machine. He could compose instructions and subroutines, set them into proper format, and check them over before introducing them finally into the computer's main memory ... He could correct the computer's data, instruct the machine via flow diagrams, and in general interact with it very much as he would with another engineer, except that the 'other engineer' would be a precise draftsman, a lightning calculator, a mnemonic wizard, and many other valuable partners all in one."

In this and other astonishing documents, like his *The Computer as a Communication Device* (1968) and *Memorandum For Members and Affiliates of the Intergalactic Computer Network* (1963) Licklider anticipated the development of the Internet and the digitization of our information infrastructures in pretty much the forms in which we know them now, including computer communities whose members are widely dispersed.

Exciting as this story is, it has a depressing side. For one thing, it shows that *the technology on which our current Internet-and-computer infrastructure is based dates from the 1960s, with the formative conceptual work having been done in the early years of that decade.* Rather than painting a picture of a high-technology civilization, it sadly evokes the technology-lagging society we've been describing in this book. This laggardliness is illustrated by the fact that when ARPA invited 140 organizations to bid for the task of building the Arpanet, *only a dozen bothered to reply, the rest apparently considering the job too far-fetched to take seriously.*

To add to the gloom, ARPA's ability to fund basic AI research was shut down by an amendment to the Military Authorization Act introduced in 1969 by Senator Michael J. Mansfield (1903–2001), a Democrat from Montana and Majority Leader of the U.S. Senate from 1961 to 1977. The amendment forbade the U.S. Department of Defense to fund "any research project or study unless such project or study has a direct and apparent relationship to a specific military function."

This had a withering effect on AI research finance in America. Nor was the axe against AI wielded by America alone. In 1973, a damning paper on AI research, dismissing the field's ability to produce deliverables, appeared under the title *Artificial Intelligence: A General Survey.* It was written by British mathematician Sir Michael James Lighthill(1924–1998) for Britain's Science Research Council. The British Government responded by terminating funds for most AI research in Britain, triggering an international mood of skepticism toward AI.

But it would be inaccurate to see the financial history of AI research as a single process of ups and downs, like a wave. Enthusiasm for it has waxed and waned over decades, but along with this we've seen changes in interpretations of AI and expectations of it, so it's arguable that the AI that's attracted fresh attention at one point may not really have been the same subject that turned investors off at another stage. In the early 1980's, for instance, AI experienced a resurgence when the Japanese Government decided to team up with their country's private sector to pump money temporarily into a computer race with the U.S. via an initiative called the Fifth Generation Project, which was expected to achieve a quantum leap into a new computer era. The project, and funding for it, eventually fizzled out and historians continue to debate the worth of the fragmented results it produced. But what's clear is that it didn't produce thinking machines of the kind Minsky considers possible. The reasons have yet to be fully explored and probably range from unique features of Japan's culture to a budget which, though seemingly large, wasn't really enough to get the job done.

One fact, though, immediately jumps out from the history of the Fifth Generation Project to tie in with all that we've been discussing in this book about the importance of philosophical motivation in technological development. This is that the project appears, ironically, to have reflected an attitude that's diametrically opposed to the spirit underlying much fundamental innovation, namely the passionate desire to achieve a philosophic goal. The Japanese project wasn't driven by a determination to bring about a new chapter in human existence, or even to prove the superiority of an ideology or philosophical worldview, as was the case in the U.S.-Soviet space race or the imperialism of Victorian Britain. It seems to have been an economic enterprise pure and simple, intended to achieve near-term commercial advantage against the U.S. And we've argued that economic motivation, while important, is insufficient on its own to bring about a major spurt in scientific and technological fundamentals, being too focused on short-term product deliverables. There must be a broader philosophical commitment and vision as well.

Minsky's work embodies such a vision. He's an authentic example of the blend of scientific sophistication, imaginative technological ambition and pure philosophical vision on which great innovations depend. What he's after is not a few interesting new consumer gadgets but a transformation of the conditions of human life. He AI as closely related, in this respect, to nanotechnology. In his 1992 paper *Virtual Molecular Reality*, for example, he wrote of the desire to overcome the problem of death itself, expressing annoyance that "we have to live only a hundred years just because of a few evolutionary mistakes, such as the way that our hearts are fed. Why must we submit to those quadruple bypass operations? Simply because a half billion years ago, the prevertebrate heart was small enough to take fuel and oxygen by diffusion from the blood passing through it. When that got more difficult, our ancestors chose a simple, quick fix: just extend a little branch from that nearby artery into the myocardium. It might have required a few more genes to do this in parallel at many sites inside the pericardium. That is not what happened, because evolution had no plan for what would happen later, and this mistake led to premature death for many of us. Evolution has no direct way to remedy architectural errors made eons ago." But when we design new mechanically-enhanced forms of life for ourselves, Minsky declared, we will direct our own evolution.[4]

In his essay *Will Robots Inherit the Earth?*, first published in *Scientific American* in 1994, he wrote: "Eventually we will entirely replace our brains -- using nanotechnology. Once delivered from the limitations of biology, we will be able to decide the length of our lives--with the option of immortality-- and choose among other, unimagined capabilities as well. In such a future, attaining wealth will not be a problem; the trouble will be in controlling it. Obviously, such changes are difficult to envision, and many thinkers still argue that these advances are impossible--particularly in the domain of artificial intelligence. But the sciences needed to enact this transition are already in the making, and it is time to consider what this new world will be like." He added: "In the end, we will find ways to replace every part of the body and brain--and thus repair all the defects and flaws that make our lives so brief. Needless to say, in doing so, we'll be making ourselves into machines. Does this mean that machines will replace us? I don't feel that it makes much sense to think in terms of 'us' and 'them'. I much prefer the attitude of Hans Moravec of Carnegie-Mellon University, who suggests that we think of those future intelligent machines as our own 'mind-children'. In the past, we have tended to see ourselves as a final product of evolution -- but our evolution has not ceased. Indeed, we are now evolving more rapidly--although not in the familiar, slow Darwinian way."

In a section of this paper headed *The Future of Intelligence*, Minsky asserted: "Many thinkers firmly maintain that machines will never have thoughts like ours, because no matter how we build them, they'll always lack some vital ingredient. They call this essence by various names--like sentience, consciousness, spirit, or soul. Philosophers write entire books to prove that, because of this deficiency, machines can never feel or understand the sorts of things that people do. However, every proof in each of those books is flawed by assuming, in one way or another, the thing that it purports to prove--the existence of some magical spark that has no detectable properties. I have no patience with such arguments. We should not be searching for any single missing part. Human thought has many ingredients, and every machine that we have ever built is missing dozens or hundreds of them!"

In the above paper Minsky challenged ethicists who oppose the quest to transform human life in these mechanically enhanced ways, and took issue with our cultural biases against such radical improvements. In a section headed *The Failures of Ethics*, he wrote: "When I decided to write this article, I tried these ideas out on several groups and had them respond to informal polls. I was amazed to find that at least three quarters of the audience seemed to feel that our life spans were already too long. 'Why would anyone want to live for five hundred years? Wouldn't it be boring? What if you outlived all your friends? What would you do with all that time?' they asked. It seemed as though they secretly feared that they did not deserve to live so long. I find it rather worrisome that so many people are resigned to die. Might not such people be dangerous, who feel that they do not have much to lose?"

These remarks make it clear that Minsky's campaign is far more than a drive to add a few more economically useful consumer conveniences to our society's inventory of merchandise. He's engaged in a philosophical quest that involves a profound shift in our ideas of human evolution. The value he places on the creation of a new era in our history parallels the desire of the early 20th century's space travel advocates to place human growth on a new road. Yet, Minsky has criticized the U.S.'s National Aeronautics and Space Administration (NASA) for putting us on the wrong technological track. Referring to NASA's emphasis on manned spacecraft instead of sending robots into space, he protested in a 1998 interview published in *The New York Times*: "It's not that they waste money. It's that they waste ALL the money... I would have a space station, but it would be unmanned. And we would throw some robots up there that are not intelligent, but just controlled through tele-operators and you could sort of feel what's doing. Then, we could build telescopes and all sorts of things and perhaps explore the moon and Mars by remote control... NASA's people are basically oriented toward keeping themselves alive. They are a big organization. And the biggest part of it is Houston and that has to be fed, and what Houston is good at is putting men in space. The Jet Propulsion Lab is much smaller and has a smaller staff and is good at doing everything else. So, I think, in order to support that, they get into this vicious circle where you have to convince yourself that's what the public wants. Now, I think, the public is more excited by *Sojourner* than by astronauts."[5]

Sojourner was a remotely controlled exploration vehicle activated on Mars in 1996 by NASA, in a project run by the Jet Propulsion Laboratory at the California Institute of Technology.

Minsky's characteristic combination of outspoken criticism, joy in interdisciplinary range, maverick personality, intellectual exuberance, technological ambition, enthusiastic commitment to innovation and philosophical passion is reminiscent of early 20th-century technological visionary Richard Buckminster Fuller (1895–1983). Like Fuller, he expresses himself in his own style and occupies a unique point in our landscape. His imagination is widely and justly revered as brilliant and prophetic. Yet many people find it hard to determine exactly how he fits into either the mundane aspects of everyday scientific life or the grand philosophical scenarios that are the stock in trade of the now growing industry of futurists. To get a firmer handle on Minsky's philosophical position it's helpful to see him in relation to not only AI but also the emergence of the knowledge economy.

The rise of the Knowledge Economy

The phrase "knowledge economy" was made fashionable by prolific Austrian-American management writer Peter F. Drucker (1909-2005). The senses in which he used it included a basic differentiation between manual laborers and workers whose skills required specialized theoretical knowledge. This meaning is open to the criticism of triviality, in that it embodies a truth which has always been widely known, namely that there are people who just *do* work, without necessarily even knowing what it's for, and those who *manage* work according to a larger plan which is known only to the class of managers, and even then perhaps only to some of them. The age-old practices of the military offer an example.

The term as used by Drucker is also arguably misleading (not to mention somewhat insulting to manual workers) because much manual work requires considerable theoretical knowledge which is just of a different kind from that of non-manual workers. From both these critical viewpoints it's possible to interpret Drucker's concept of the knowledge economy, at least in some of the contexts in which it's been used, as a piece of management-guru gobbledygook, a profitable consulting and publishing industry of which emerged in the 20th century. But for our discussion here what's more important is that whatever the origins of the term were, it's come to have an important meaning for the 21st century, although one that's yet to be clearly formulated and explored. *This meaning is inherently tied up with computer, Internet and information age issues that didn't exist when Drucker's use of the term started circulating in the 1960s and 1970s.* It can be summed up in the following 12 points:

1. *Civil society* – that whole complex apparatus of institutions and organized behavior that happens outside government – is now, for all practical purposes, Internet society,[6] and *is evolving globally into a community of broadband networks*. This is so not because of the extent to which the Internet forms the basis of civil society interactions (it's in fact far from an optimal extent), but because of the power it's demonstrated to serve as an efficient tool for these. This power is derived from the Internet's ability to circulate knowledge and, by doing so, to help generate new knowledge. Through infrastructures like broadband telecommunications and fiberoptic cable, the Internet can allow enormous volumes of data for a wide variety of purposes to be shared long-distance quickly, simultaneous-

ly and efficiently. The U.S. is lagging badly in its provision of broadband services, however. In a May 22, 2008 article headed *The Sad State of U.S. Broadband*, the magazine *Business Week* reported: "Although the Internet was started here, the U.S. can't seem to catch up with other developed nations when it comes to giving citizens access to high-speed connections. For the second year running, the U.S. ranked 15th among the 30 members of the Organization for Economic Cooperation & Development in terms of broadband availability. Denmark ranked first again in the annual OECD survey, followed by a host of European and Asian nations. Indeed, while the number of Americans with access to broadband service rose 20% last year, to nearly 70 million people, the most in the OECD, that amounted to just 23 of every 100 residents. By contrast, the top five countries in the OECD ranking all sport per-capita penetration rates of better than 30%...

"The U.S. has good reason to figure out some way to gain on the other OECD countries. A broadband connection is increasingly necessary to take advantage of the Web's interactive and rich media features, and is instrumental for e-commerce. 'Broadband not only plays a critical role in the workings of the economy, it connects consumers, businesses, governments, and facilitates interaction,' wrote OECD report authors Taylor Reynolds and Sacha Wunsch-Vincent."[7]

2. To unlock the knowledge-circulating power of telecommunications technology fully, America must implement the most sophisticated broadband telecommunications grid it can, nationally, and make this cheaply available to everyone everywhere in the country. This step will expedite the evolution of the Internet into a *knowledge grid*.

3. The knowledge grid will work optimally only if an integral part of it is the nation's *education system* at all levels. Schools, universities and other research and education establishments must become virtual as well as physical dispensers of knowledge. Educational telecommunications allow the best teachers to share their expertise with the widest possible audience, with distance posing no obstacle and without knowledge being shared outside the time limits of conventional classroom hours.

4. *Work patterns* must be redesigned to take full advantage of the knowledge grid. This means, among other things, aban-

doning high concentrations of personnel in favor of dispersed worker populations into *telecommunities*. Telecommunities are different from telecommuting, as commonly conceived. The latter means allowing workers to work from home periodically. A telecommunity is a community of people who, for example, may work electronically in New York City but live near each other in, say, Connecticut or New Jersey, or even farther afield. They can meet each other personally when necessary, but without going into their corporate center in the metropolis, although serving that center daily and being linked to it twenty-four hours a day by Internet and regular video conversation (which isn't quite the same as videoconferencing).

These knowledge grid circumstances make it possible to use urban space, transportation and other resources more efficiently, taking advantage of the fact that many people are already geographically dispersed (partly as an unintended consequence of the automobile and the highway system). This has profound implications for urban development. Pressure on cities and their transportation and other resource systems can be relieved. It's important to realize that this electronic organization of workers into telecommunities, in areas where *most or many of them already live*, isn't the same thing as urban sprawl. It's in fact the opposite of urban sprawl, since it encourages the development of outlying but densely cohesive communities. Many people still have difficulty in understanding this, though, since the general tendency is to confuse any kind of worker dispersal with sprawl.

5. The telecommunity component of the knowledge grid has huge potential to *revitalize small towns*, which will cease being bedroom communities of commuters who vacate their neighborhoods by day. Instead such towns will become live twenty-four-hour-a-day places, with distinctive characters of their own. They'll regain the self-contained economic vigor that small towns had in the past before they become nocturnal suburban bases for commuters who spent their days in a city or in vehicles crawling along congested highways. This renewed understanding of the importance of *place*, and of how telecommunication can promote rather than diminish it, is at odds with much current misperception of the Internet society. Community life and social lifestyle will be enhanced accordingly, with less time being wasted on long, unproductive commutes.

These changes also affect architecture, doing away with the need for massive buildings designed to accommodate huge concentrations of on-site workers. The conventional urban worker image of crowds working in enormous office buildings, many in cubicles, beside large windowless spaces for files and libraries, will recede into history. The paradigm of cramming large populations of workers into single buildings will become as obsolete as the idea of a paper-based society in which workers store and transmit information manually, with pens and pencils. The corporate headquarters in our New York City example will need less space and can devote its resources to management and symbolic representation of the corporation.

6. Because a telecommunity-structured knowledge grid implemented across America will have an immense impact on road traffic by reducing commuter traffic, *environmental pollution* will be reduced.

7. *National security* will be served by dispersing worker populations electronically in this way, since government and private entities providing essential services will be protected against disruption by natural or man-made disasters. Their dispersed workers will be able to function even if the corporate headquarters is put out of commission. This will include, as we've explained, many who are *already* dispersed and will just be empowered by this electronic infrastructure to perform their work more efficiently and securely.

8. By becoming the world's most advanced knowledge grid, the U.S. will position itself as *the world's foremost knowledge exporter.* It will be in the interests of the U.S. to supplement its *commercial* export of knowledge with the *goodwill* export of knowledge via government agencies such as a substantially re-budgeted, expanded and teletechnologically empowered Peace Corps.[8]

9. The knowledge grid must be implemented so as to enable a significant number of its users to appreciate the types and processes of knowledge, and to become aware of *knowledge exchange and production as a cardinal social activity.* This will include a wider understanding of the close, reciprocally reinforcing relationship between *basic research* and *applied research.*

10. The telecommunity component of the knowledge grid, by

revitalizing the sense of local community, will encourage the rise of a *new regionalism* and variety among communities, intellectually and culturally. Thus, the effect of the grid will not be culturally and socially uniforming and homogenizing but will rather foster group *diversity, localism, eccentricity and geographically-based distinctiveness of character.*

11. This diversity must extend to *diversity of media.* A vital paradox of the knowledge grid is that *a successful knowledge grid must always transcend its own underlying technology.* Thus, just as telecommunity implementation will necessarily encourage localism rather than a national or global uniformity in which the local community becomes irrelevant or marginalized, so will a knowledge grid empowered by computer technology and fiberoptic telecommunications (if effectively implemented) encourage the survival and prospering of print media, in the form, for example, of *small local newspapers* which will reflect community character and diversity of community opinion. (To fail in this aspect of the knowledge grid will be to imperil a vital element of democracy.)

12. An effective knowledge grid must *extend throughout the fabric of government.* It must be used by government to exchange information among government agencies, to abolish the counterproductive insularity of government fiefdoms and bureaucracies, to encourage government transparency, to promote government efficiency and to foster government-academe-private sector partnerships. This entails breaking with some long-standing habits of governmental thought – a mission which, with the best will in the world, will be difficult, as the example below illustrates. Yet it must be done if the U.S. is to become a knowledge-grid society.

Minsky's work may seem at first glance to be quite remote from these knowledge economy principles, but they're highly convergent with it. The conceptual overlaps between them include the highly *transformative* nature of the computerization of society (of which current telecommunications innovation is part), the *breadth* of this transformation and its positive implications not only for commerce but for *the quality of human life and experience* across a broad canvass. These overlaps are usefully illustrated on a practical level by the urban development thought of Jay Hellman.[9]

Minsky and Hellman (1947-) approach the theme of computerization and its effects from contrasting directions. Minsky, a consummate technologist with impressive patents to his credit, is an academic thinker whose distinguished career has unfolded in academe. His ideas are set out in an impressive body of publications. Hellman is an entrepreneur. He and Minsky are both applied thinkers, but in different ways. Hellman has spent decades in the private sector. Instead of looking to express his ideas primarily in published form, he has sought to embody them in commercial projects, as a designer and developer of technologically-based real estate projects.

The question of what the intensely practical business of real estate development has to do with complex issues of computerization is the story of Hellman's life. It's a tale that shows how hard it is for America to adjust its conventional thinking in business and public policy to the larger implications of a computerized society.

Unlike the careers of academics, who live largely in landscapes of ideas, the lives of entrepreneurs and other businesspeople are often best understood by looking at the practical projects from which they make money, or hope to. But though he has many significant commercial projects successfully behind him, Hellman can't be understood in any depth without looking at the ideas that drive him and inform his projects. Like Minsky, he's a visionary, motivated by a passion for ideas and social idealism as much as by any purely business consideration. He sees real business success as being impossible if these other forces are absent.

At the time of publication of this book, Hellman is based in Washington D.C., where, since the mid-1970s, he's run his own real estate development and research firm. He's well known to business and political figures on both sides of the Beltway as a tireless promoter of the idea that computers and telecommunication technologies aren't changing only the externals of our infrastructures but also some of the most fundamental aspects of our civilization -- including how we work, what we do with our leisure, how we build towns and cities and how we learn. His technology-driven ideas about regional and national infrastructure development and urban design are strongly based in a knowledge-economy context. He maintains telecommunications technology will change our world physically and culturally in the 21st century, at least as much as the tractor and railroads changed it in the 19th century and automobiles, airplanes, telephones and television changed it in the 20th. He trademarked the term *virtual adjacency*® to describe the work patterns, social structures and living conditions of an Internet-centered society. Unusually for a real estate entrepreneur, he's conceived and pursued real estate projects as applied examples of his theoretical ideas.

Hellman has championed his ideas in lectures on university campuses, at professional conferences, in the mass media and by personally buttonholing members of Congress, other government leaders, scholars and businesspeople of all kinds. In fact, anyone who will listen, if only for a while. It's impossible to be with him for longer than a few minutes without realizing that unlike most other successful entrepreneurs, he's at least as passionate about ideas as he is about making money. His work has found its way into publications ranging from reports of the National Academy of Sciences to National Public Radio. The *Washington Business Journal* has labeled him a genius. The present Majority Leader in the House of Representatives, Congressman Steny Hoyer (Md) sent a file on Hellman's work to Vice President Al Gore in 1996 urging that it be used to guide the process of "reinventing government". His many interesting comments on knowledge-economy aspects of infrastructure development include the declaration that we can't possibly have enough bandwidth (i.e., technological ability to distribute volume and diversity of information).

Hellman's career, though financially successful, tells a sobering story of the uphill struggle involved in efforts to introduce knowledge-economy thinking. He foresaw the personal computer and began researching its effects on real estate before it was invented. His perception of the connection between computerization, telecommunications, social structure, government policy and private sector development options go back to the seventies. He anticipated the rise of the personal computer as a force in economic and social life before it was invented, and in 1970 the RAND Corporation published a far-sighted paper that he wrote on the implications of data-gathering technology for privacy. He has five degrees from the Massachusetts Institute of Technology, including a doctorate in systems analysis, the study of how mathematics can be applied to the study of how complex systems work.

As a student he was inspired by the ideas of one of America's pioneering computer scientists, Jay Forrester, who applied engineering principles to the analysis of social organizations. Hellman similarly developed a holistic, multidisciplinary approach to real estate research and development based on the study of evolving computer and telecommunications technologies, focusing on how these changes affect the nature of work, the physical character of buildings and patterns of land use. On leaving MIT he worked for large real estate development and finance companies before setting up his own firm, whose projects including the research that led the National Association of Realtors, the US's biggest real estate trade organization, to build its new $45 million flagship Washington D.C. offices at 500 New Jersey Avenue, in 2004, a short distance from the grounds of the US Capitol. For years skeptics had dismissed this site in the heart of the metropolis, as undevelopable due to its small size and narrow, unusual shape. Hellman's research indicated otherwise, since it convinced him that teletechnology would in future make office buildings in cities shift to a largely communications function, making for smaller-footprinted buildings on prime real estate, occupied by far fewer people than in a pre-teletechnology era. He's similarly injected his technology ideas into numerous other successful development projects.

There are several reasons for Hellman's ability to leave an unforgettable impression. One is his sense of mission, the sincerity of which impresses even people who aren't usually attracted to abstract ideas. Another is the fact that even his most theoretical ideas are usually connected to events of great practical importance to society. In particular, Hellman's take on computerization and communication seems helpfully to shed some light on what a knowledge economy really entails. For him, the knowledge economy is where computerization and telecommunications impact the functioning of our everyday life.

An example: the Department of Homeland Security

An example is a prototype telecommunity project for the town of La Plata, Md.,which illustrates both telecommunity principles and the prevailing resistance to them. Hellman's project grew out of a long process of thought in which he envisaged the replacement of a road-centered work culture by a teletechnology-centered one. Its premise is to use teletechnology as the basis of a new Washington, D.C., headquarters for the Department of Homeland Security (DHS).

American public administration historically favors iconic buildings whose massiveness symbolizes institutional power. The Pentagon, for example, has three times the floor space of the Empire State Building. The Department of Defense proudly proclaims that the Pentagon is "virtually a city in itself." Some 23 000 military and civilian workers converge on it daily in over 8 700 cars requiring 16 parking lots, and by rail and bus. It has offices for around 3 000 more support personnel, and 17.5 miles of corridors. "This," Hellman comments, "is the epitome of the paper-based manual paradigm of work."

The Pentagon was conceived over a single weekend in the early 1940s, at a time when gigantic structures were made appropriate by America's seeming domestic impregnability. Computers and fiberoptic telecommunications weren't available, nor was there the massively documented understanding of environmental pollution (a product of road traffic, among other sources) and energy waste that exists today. And few recognized that giant buildings on U.S. soil aren't only citadels but also targets. We've learned otherwise since September 11, 2001. Nevertheless, DHS is, as of this writing, planning an enormous $3,5+ billion headquarters in Anacostia, Washington, D.C. - a Homeland Security Pentagon. (This budget reflects construction cost only, excluding the environmental and social costs of a commuter work force.)

The project's basic thinking is open to serious challenge. It shows the great difficulty government planners have in understanding telecommunity and the knowledge grid or, if they do understand it, in taking it seriously.

The DHS plan represents outdated thinking inappropriate to an era of high U.S. vulnerability to terrorist attack. It rests on obsolete assumptions about huge, fortress-like buildings and the reliability of roads to transport vital personnel. Ironically, President Dwight Eisenhower created the highway system in the 1950s with rapid transport in mind, hence its being called the Defense Highway System. But this infrastructure is now so congested it *impedes* strategic mobility and communication. A technologically driven, dispersal-based alternative to DHS' current Anacostia plan based on Hellman's work was proposed in 2004 by Hellman and Alan Feinberg (1944-), an architect, professional planner and former Department of Defense planning expert.(Feinberg, who's also interested in using knowledge economy principles to devise a new approach to small town revitalization, is currently working to develop another prototype 21st-century community next to Frederick, Maryland.) The Hellman-Feinberg plan envisages distributing DHS' National Capital Region workplaces throughout Maryland, Virginia and elsewhere. These would enable staff to work close to home full-time, connected to headquarters 24 hours a day by secure fiberoptic Internet. This nationally implementable plan offers DHS security, efficiency, budget, environmental, transportation and staff working condition benefits.

In 2005, Admiral William Owens, former vice chairman of the Joint Chiefs of Staff assigned to modernize the Department of Defense, described Hellman's telecommunity plan as "a fine example of the direction in which we should be heading," adding that government must "work with the private sector imaginatively on pioneering projects of this kind if we are to maintain our world leadership in terms of prosperity and security." In 2008 David Silverberg, editor of the homeland security affairs magazine *HSToday*, commented that the telecommunity plan for DHS had merit and " would keep DHS robust and functioning in the event of a disaster or attack." He also made the point that DHS needed flexibility to site its headquarters closer to the political center of the national capital. The telecommunity would allow this by enabling the headquarters to be physically much smaller.

The Hellman plan envisions DHS's headquarters as a small, high-security "front office," not a huge complex dependent on a horde of daily commuters. DHS employees would staff regional workplaces full time, linked to headquarters around the clock by the internet. The town of La Plata was studied as a prototype teleworking hub. Many of La Plata's 8,400-plus residents work in Washington and drive 30 miles twice a day on congested roads. But four intersecting fiber-optic networks make a La Plata broadband grid possible immediately. In principle the Hellman plan has a wide array of potential benefits of national scope far beyond Washington, D.C. But as of this writing DHS seems wedded to the obsolete big-building concept, encouraged by D.C. politicians who hope that the siting of a major new government complex within D.C. will bring economic benefits to locals. (A report on the present DHS plan by the independent Brookings Institution has offered reasons why it will in fact be bad for the city, including a warning of unrealistic local economic expectations. "All in all," the Brookings report has said, "the economic impact on neighborhood commercial establishments nearby could well be next to nothing.")

This example illustrates the great difficulty experienced by government planners in thinking within a knowledge economy / telecommunity framework. This difficulty is obviously not due to any shortage of intellectual power in government. It's caused rather by long-standing habits of thought and federal government culture coupled with a desperate desire of local government leaders to grasp at any straw in the hope of encouraging local economic development. These factors, combined with the unfamiliarity of telecommunity concepts, create a wall against new kinds of thinking.

An intriguing illustration of both the practical benefits and the social context of a digitized knowledge economy is the experience of Grantham University, an accredited online educational institution whose courses are used by serving and former members of the U.S. military. Grantham's Slidell, Louisiana, campus was destroyed by Hurricane Katrina in 2005. However, following Hurricane Ivan two years earlier, Grantham CEO Thomas Macon had arranged for the university's data to be digitized and stored on a secure server in Reston, Virginia. With all essential data thus protected, Grantham quickly converted a prior plan for a satellite campus in Kansas City, Missouri, into an emergency relocation plan. The Kansas City site was adopted as Grantham's new home. Some employees left Louisiana to staff the Missouri campus with newly hired locals. The institution re-established itself with remarkable speed, demonstrating how digital technology can enable organizations to survive physical catastrophes which might have been fatal in a pre-digital age.

However, the physical storm that destroyed Grantham's Louisiana campus was followed by a social and psychological one. Grantham's physically successful relocation triggered a barrage of negative Internet comment by former staff who'd lost their jobs to the move, as well by some students who were angry about disruptions caused by the upheaval. Most interesting from a digital economy point of view is that this wave of criticism seems to have been caused at least partly, if not wholly, by Grantham's adroitness in using technology to survive a disaster. It's debatable whether the school would have been bombarded by criticism if its digitization hadn't enabled it to survive Katrina. It's as if it were being penalized for its technological expertise. If Grantham hadn't been digitized, and as a result had been completely obliterated as an institution, presumably it would have received universal sympathy. But its use of technology to avoid obliteration exposed it to the anger of people who'd been impacted by the hurricane's devastation.

There's nothing new in the understandable rage felt by catastrophe victims toward fellow victims who survived the same catastrophe or came out of it seemingly better than many others. What's new in the Grantham case, and interesting for students of American attitudes to advanced technology in general and digitization in particular, is two points. First, the school's critics seem not to have seen its technology-empowered survival as in any way exceptional. They seemed rather to view it as a normal or expected response which the school should have managed better, so that more people derived benefit. This point illustrates again the tendency, which we've noted earlier, for Americans to see advanced technology not as something extraordinary but as a given which we're all entitled to regard as readily available to enable us to deal with any contingency. Secondly, the Grantham experience illustrates vividly the fact that moving into a digital economy isn't just a matter of technological implementation; it's also a profoundly human issue. It's unlikely that Grantham ever expected its successful use of digitization to expose it to criticism. But every implementation of advanced digital or other technology brings new human implications. Building a knowledge economy thus calls not only for technological change per se but also for a major philosophical, social and cultural reorientation. Without this, organizations may become victims of their own technological expertise, as appears to have happened to Grantham.[10]

The convergence of all our current telecommunications infrastructures into a unified knowledge economy with far-reaching human implications has been well expressed by David A. Irwin, Director of the Institute for Communications Law Studies at The Catholic University of America's Columbus School of Law, in Washington, D.C.

"Telecommunication is transforming the world politically, socially and individually," he says. "Breaking news from virtually anywhere on the planet is instantly available. We can live history as it happens. As print journalism, traditional wireline telephone networks, broadcasting and other legacy media decline, FaceBook, YouTube, Twitter, e-mail and instant messaging give new meaning to 'keeping in touch'.

"In the past, industry and the U.S. government have promoted universal access to wireline telephone service as a social goal. Telephone 'universal service' was an engine of U.S. economic growth in the 19th and 20th centuries. In the 21st century public policy should similarly promote universal broadband access. This can help re-energize the economy.

"The growing ubiquity of fiberoptic connections to our offices and homes, augmented by broadband wireless, offers us immediate access to movies, video, images and all manner of voice and data services. Infusing Internet telecommunications into the generation and use of electric power will produce an economically powerful smart grid.

"Additionally, wireless technologies hold much promise. The machines that provide CAT scans and MRIs will become untethered, coming to us instead of our being transported to them. Managed radio spectrum offers an interface between industrial and commercial audio-video and our home theaters. Orbital satellites working into terrestrial telecommunications enables technology like NASA's SERVIR, a global system that allows communities around the world to share massive geospatial data banks concerning natural disasters, climate change and public health management.[11]

"These technological developments mesh closely with human issues, reflected in social policy and law. As information is circulated in new ways, the creators or owners of intellectual property need new forms of protection for their rights and legitimate profits. Government and the institutions of law must champion the privacy and security of personal information. Yet these interests of individuals and special groups must be balanced against the need of the public to share fully in this information bonanza. We must, for example, ensure universal access to broadband lest we create a class of 'technopeasants' – people denied ready access to the flood of information enjoyed by the rest of the world."[12]

Irwin's summary resonates strongly with Hellman's vision of telecommunity -- in which telecommunications technology is used not to homogenize the world but to enrich geographically distinctive social experience and cultural diversity - will, he believes, soon reshape all corners of our cultural life.

Hellman's ideas, for example, form the basis of a new Los Angeles-based start-up, *SoundTrak Station®*, or STS, which has begun creating destination communities that will enable musicians and music lovers from around the world to interact in cyberspace and face to face, in physical STS locales around the world. Each physical STS location will reflect the character of that city, town, or neighborhood. Thus, the Nashville and Los Angeles communities will be very different from each other and from their counterparts in Stockholm and Amsterdam.

Hellman's dream is to see both government and the private sector adopt the telecommunity model as a standard approach. "It will transform America for the better," he says, "creating a cleaner, less congested society with a more efficient use of material sources and time, including leisure time. Computerization and telecommunications technology together have the power to liberate us if we let them."[13]

NOTES

1. http://discovermagazine.com/2007/jan/interview-minsky.

2. Hutchins, John, ALPAC: *the (in)famous report*, in MT NEWS INTERNATIONAL 14 (June 1996), reprinted in READINGS IN MACHINE TRANSLATION, ed. Nirenburg,S., Somers,H., Wilks, Y (2003) http://www.hutchinsweb.me.uk/ALPAC-1996.pdf

3. *IRE Transactions on Human Factors in Electronics* (Vol.HFE-1) http://groups.csail.mit.edu/medg/people/psz/Licklider.html

4. http://web.media.mit.edu/~minsky/papers/VirtualMolecularReality.html

5. http://query.nytimes.com/gst/fullpage.html?res=9806EED81F39F93BA15754C0A9 6E958260

6. Slabbert, N.J., *The Technologies of Peace*, HARVARD INTERNATIONAL REVIEW (May 2, 2007), http://www.harvardir.org/index.php?page=article&id=1336&p=;and *Civil Society As Internet Society: A Philosophical Redefinition* (Oct.2005), TRUMAN LIBRARY REPORTS

7. Holahan, Catherine, *The Sad State of U.S. Broadband*, BUSINESS WEEK (May 22, 2008) http://www.businessweek.com/print/technology/content/may2008/tc20080522_340989.htm

8. Slabbert, N.J., ibid

9. There is a most pressing need to apply knowledge economy principles and aggressive technological innovation to the reconstruction of America's cities. The economic, infrastructural, environmental and social impacts of such a mission would be enormously positive. See e.g. Ouroussoff, Nicolai,*Reinventing America's Cities: The Time Is Now*, THE NEW YORK TIMES (Mar.25, 2009) http://www.nytimes.com/2009/03/29/arts/design/29ouro.html?emc=eta1&pagewanted=print

10.Numerous personal contacts with Grantham sourced this section.

11. www.nasa.gov/mission_pages/servir/index.html

12. Personal communication with David irwin

13. Numerous personal interviews with Jay Hellman 2002-2009 sourced this section.

CHAPTER 10

CHOOSING A FUTURE

We've seen how the knowledge economy evolved not only around computerization and computer-driven telecommunications but via a wider convergence of disciplines.

We've also seen the importance of a philosophical sense of transformation, represented by thinkers like Minsky. And we've discussed the difficulties innovators have in "selling" their programs to the rest of society, whether to seek funding or just general cultural acceptance. An obstacle to innovation, financially and culturally (the two are usually intertwined), is that people who aren't innovators need to have innovation explained to them in terms that relate clearly to their familiar experience.

So far we've focused on the problems society creates for innovators. But innovators also bring problems on themselves by poor communication and salesmanship.

Even the most worthwhile ideas won't get far if they're communicated badly or if their promoters fail to understand how their concepts threaten traditional belief-systems.

Sometimes, of course, a new idea is just incompatible with an older one, and society must choose. There's not much ground for accommodation between an acceptance of slavery and abhorrence of it. But new scientific truths and the technologies that result from them aren't generally like that. The valuable moral insights of a religion, and indeed many of its articles of faith, can co-exist with scientific truths even when at first they seem in conflict. For this to happen, some sensitive philosophical interpretation is usually necessary on both sides.

Similarly, technology that at first appears destructive to cultural values can later serve those very same values. An example is the relationship between scientific knowledge and the environment. In the 19th and 20th centuries industrial technologies harmed the physical environment, so many people demonized the innovations that made those technologies possible. But it's now increasingly realized (although not widely enough or fast enough) that similar innovation and research can help reduce the harm and perhaps even reverse it.

Much therefore depends on how innovation is interpreted, explained and used. The innovators themselves have a heavy responsibility in this regard. Of course, there are limits to what they can do. A benignly intended piece of scientific knowledge might be used to devise a weapon, or some other harmful device, without the approval or even the knowledge of the researcher who originated it. In that case the best the researcher can do is speak out when the information comes to light. But there are other areas in which innovators can influence public perception and use of their work more or less from the start. This can offer great opportunity to encourage public acceptance of the work. This isn't always easy for innovators, though, since often the very aspects of the innovation that excites them most are those which other people dislike. So, with what can seem to be a kind of perversity, they can insist on alienating traditional society with intimations of the drastic changes that their innovation is likely to cause. They may even take an odd joy in shocking traditionalists, even when doing so doesn't do their ideas much good.

This brings us to American inventor Ray Kurzweil. Like Minsky, Kurzweil is a theorist with a vision for the future, but Kurzweil can better be described as a futurist or *futurologist*. To discuss him, we must take a moment to consider what this term means.

The future as an industry

Futurology is open to many definitions, one of which is an attempt to anticipate the economic, cultural, technological and other tendencies and problems that society is likely to exhibit in future. It takes many forms, including some we don't usually think of as examples of futurology. For instance, the Bible and other scriptures which map out a prophetic path for the life of the human race, can be seen, at least in part, as early exercises in futurology.

Intuitive prophecy, using astrology and the interpretation of omens as sources of knowledge of the future, is of great antiquity, making it clear that the need to orient ourselves to the future has deep roots in human nature. This explains why the prophecies of the French seer Michel Nostradamus (1503–1566) retain a perennial fascination. But futurology is also a long-established part of the history of rational inquiry. The imagining of ideal societies – utopias –

is an intellectual tool of this tradition. Writers using this genre have formulated visions of societies which, even when they've been hypothetical ("what if") rather than predictive ("what will be"), have clearly been intended to help humanity achieve a better future. An example is the great Greek philosopher Plato, who is believed to have lived in the fifth and fourth centuries BC. His book *The Republic*, dating from around the turn of those two centuries, described what he thought was an ideal political system. To the extent that he believed this ideal achievable, it could be regarded as a vision of a future society that would evolve if people behaved according to the principles Plato thought sensible. This technique of blending the hypothetical and the desired (or anticipated) became a literary and philosophical genre.

The word *Utopia* was invented by English scholar-statesman Sir Thomas More (1478–1535) as the name of an imaginary society which he described in a book by that name in 1516. His countryman Francis Bacon (1561–1626), a jurist-philosopher who was concerned with the potential to improve the society of his time, described his conception of a knowledge-governed civilization in an imaginative narrative called *The New Atlantis* (1627). English political economist Thomas R. Malthus (1766–1834) was a very different kind of futurologist: he used statistics to project, and thus theorize and warn about, the hazards of a growing population relative to available resources. His book *An Essay on the Principle of Population* (1798) is a milestone of pessimistic future-gazing but its statistical approach also introduced a scientific element into our study of how things change over long periods of time. This was an important concept for Darwin and other students of evolution.

Malthus is especially interesting for anyone concerned with the history of innovation and the culture of pessimism that's evolved alongside it. His work forms an important point in the emergence of experts who offer guidance to help societies avoid catastrophic futures, or, when these are perceived as inevitable, to survive them or otherwise deal with their advent. Malthus's intellectual descendents include The Club of Rome, an international group that came to prominence when it published the controversial book *The Limits to Growth* in 1972. The book sought to use statistical projections of factors like population growth and imitated natural resources to project a likely future. Its conclusions were grim. Its weaknesses, though, included the difficulty of predicting the emergence of new knowledge and new technologies.

The Club of Rome forms part of an industry of futurology that has grown up around the fear of the future. Very different from the

Club, but nonetheless its peer in the marketing of doom expertise, was German philosopher Oswald Spengler (1880–1936), one of the first 20th-century authors to create a stir by predicting the collapse of Western civilization, in his two-volume book *The Decline of the West*, published from 1918 to 1923. Spengler made no effort to give his work a scientific appearance of the kind presented by the Club of Rome's charts and graphs, but he did package his writing in a quasi-scientific way by purporting to have insight into the evolution of sciences, including mathematics.

Interestingly, optimistic writers about the future have on the whole been less successful than the doomsayers. H.G. Wells was a tireless promoter of the idea that science and technology could remake the world for the better, but he achieved his greatest fame less for these writings than for his science fiction disaster stories like *The Time Machine* (1895), depicting the deterioration of the human race and ultimately the end of the world, and *The War of the Worlds* (1898), portraying the near-obliteration of civilization by the superior technology of Martian invaders. It's significant that Wells is a good illustration of the psychological difficulty of some innovation promoters that we referenced above: he wanted to promote a new age, but he had no conception of a gentle or humane continuity between his desired new age and the older ways that it would replace. The images of mass destruction in *The War of the Worlds* seemed to embody his anxious desire to sever all connection with past traditions. For this reason he found it hard to get taken seriously as a prophet, especially in his later life.

The sense of disconnection between the past and the future that hampered Wells was turned into a successful commercial commodity by later futurists like the American writer Alvin Toffler (1928-), whose popular books like *Future Shock* (1970), *The Third Wave* (1980) and *Powershift: Knowledge, Wealth and Violence at the Edge of the 21st Century* (1990) emphasized the disconnection and were aimed at readers perplexed, disoriented and disturbed by it. Toffler's writing is an example of the tendency to invest personal speculation with a scientific or quasi-scientific aura; he pursues this by offering the reader many imaginatively improvised words and phrases that combine a sense of the learned with the crispness and memorability of good advertising copy.

Which brings us back to Kurzweil.

The future as a lifestyle choice

Kurzweil (1948-) represents both the exciting promise and the handicaps of the innovative imagination in 21st-century America.

His work brings together much of the positive momentum of fields such as AI and nanotechnology, yet seems to delight in portraying a vision of the future so disconnected from familiar human values that he doesn't care how many people dislike it. He is Wellsian. In one sense this is a great compliment; on the other hand, given what we've explained about Wells, it makes some aspects of his work a liability to the promotion of radical innovation rather than a help to it. His greatest value may be that both his strengths and his weaknesses show how our attitude to the future isn't just a choice about budgets: it's a *values* choice, a *philosophical* choice, a *lifestyle* choice.

Like others we've mentioned, Kurzweil grew up reading science fiction. He's an excellent example of interdisciplinary convergence. In his teens he developed sophisticated computer programs including one that wrote music in the manner of famous composers. This feat got him on national television. Even the Columbian Exposition reached out from the 19th century to touch him with its shadow when, in 1965, he reached the finals of the Westinghouse Corporation's national science talent contest. As a student at MIT later (where he graduated in computer studies and literature), he launched a computerized business that helped students find the right university; he later sold it for a handsome price. He quickly went on to devise a computer program that could read an unprecedented variety of typefaces. He became a national celebrity when, extending this work, he invented a machine that could read books to the blind. This technology was profitably applied elsewhere. Later he successfully reversed the process, developing a computer system capable of recording the human voice and transcribing it into text.

He also continued his teenage foray into the computerized analysis and synthesis of musical patterns by designing music synthesizers, bringing this technology an unprecedented accuracy in its duplication of the sounds of musical instruments. And he's created other products that apply computerization to commercial, educational and professional purposes.

Thus, Kurzweil is an impressive technological innovator. Moreover, he's thought deeply about the nature, possibilities and future of innovation and other aspects of life, and has expressed his opinions in several books, including *The Age of Intelligent Machines*(1990), *The 10% Solution for a Healthy Life* (1993), *The Age of Spiritual Machines* (1998), *Fantastic Voyage: Live Long Enough to Live Forever* (2004, written with Terry Grossman), and *The Singularity is Near* (2009) release. Kurzweil's authorship of books on health flows from his interest in prolonging human life. He also has a company that sells nutritional supplements. These biological concerns tie into his inventive ones. He's a buoyant technological optimist who sees the immediate prospect for the human race as a narrative of astounding technological advance and improvement through innovation.

The problem is that his criteria for optimism aren't universally shared. In fact, much of the future prospect that so excites him fills many people with horror. He subscribes to a philosophy called *transhumanism*, which predicts, and joyfully anticipates, the coming of the day when fully intelligent, sentient machines are devised and when human beings will exist who are more machine than human. This technological obsolescence of humanity is an unsettling notion for many. It recalls Wells's seeming wish to distance himself from the entire conventional concept of humanity, with all the values associates with it, both good and ill.

That this wish to transcend and perhaps abolish humanity coincides with an interest in prolonging human life and ending disease doesn't seem contradictory to Kurzweil. Rather, he mischievously appears to like annoying people who are concerned with such a things as contradiction. And so, while he's won many honors and is widely and justly revered as an inventor, his work as a philosopher of technology, though arousing tremendous interest, has also caused him to be seen simultaneously by many as a lovable crackpot. (Buckminster Fuller was regarded in much the same way.)

Kurzweil's perceived crackpottery isn't limited to his transhumanism. He's also written that it's possible to predict the growth and direction of technology, including its pace. He evidently believes this growth is more or less inevitable. (The authors of the present book believe it's possible to formulate realistic technological *scenarios* based on present knowledge, but that technological *predictions* are dangerous since they hinge on human *choices* and other contingent circumstances, and that belief in innovation outside such choices and circumstances tends toward superstition.) The overall impression that these ideas of Kurzweil's create was well captured in an article published by *The Boston Globe* on September 25, 2005: *The Age of Ray Kurzweil*, by Drake Bennett.[1]

"By any measure," Bennett wrote, "Kurzweil has had an exceptional career. Now, however, he has a new project: to be a god. And not just because he thinks he can live forever. Within decades, he predicts, he will be billions of times more intelligent than he is today, able to read minds, assume different forms, and reshape his physical environment at will. So will everyone. Today's human beings, mere quintessences of dust, will be as outmoded as Homo Erectus... Kurzweil offers a vision of technology as destiny, of transformative change that has slipped the bonds of politics, culture, and -- for many — credulity.

"...To his many critics, however, Kurzweil is simply spinning fairy tales, preaching transcendence but propagating ignorance.

"... Every day, Kurzweil takes hundreds of nutritional supplement pills, and once a week he takes several others intravenously... He is, as he puts it, 'reprogramming my biochemistry' and claims in so doing to have conquered his Type 2 diabetes. More importantly, he insists, he is stretching his natural lifespan until either genetic therapies, microscopic 'nanobots' (hypothetical robots on the scale of single atoms and molecules that Kurzweil believes will be able, among many other things, to take over some of the vital functions of the human body), or simply the ability to download one's mind onto a computer make immortality a reality.

"... Kurzweil's predictions have the ring of eschatology, of half-cocked end-times rapture. For him, though, it's surreal to hear people talk about the size of the Social Security shortfall in 2042-- by then, he believes, advances in nanotechnology will allow us to ward off disease and senescence and to manufacture all the goods we want for a pittance. By then, in other words, aging and poverty may hardly exist and people may not retire or even work in a way that's recognizable to us."

Referring to "the many thinkers who find Kurzweil's case less than compelling", Bennett added: "Since his theories take in the whole history of the universe, there is no shortage of points at which to contest them. Some skeptics dispute Kurzweil's computer science. They argue that even computers billions of times more powerful than today's wouldn't necessarily be meaningfully intelligent, much less spiritual. Any one of a number of hurdles--from the complexity of neural networks to the difficulty of recreating the brain's analog processing with a computer's digital circuitry to our continued inability to begin to articulate the essence of consciousness--might stand immovably in the way of human-level artificial intelligence."

Bennett quoted computer scientist Jaron Z. Lanier (1960-), popularizer of the term "virtual reality", as commenting to him: "Ray has incorporated in his little system of thought all of the elements of a religion that are selfish but none of the ones that are generous. His thing is purely, 'Here's how to live forever, here's how to be uploaded into the machine.' There's no concern for other people since it's assumed that everyone will be infinitely rich and happy in his future."

Bennett wrote that Kurzweil's critics see his "individualistic, mechanistic ethos" as hampering his ability to forecast, "because it ignores all the ways in which technologies are bounded by social forces."

What should we make of all this?

Well, at least a few of points seem fairly clear. One is that for all his obvious brilliance, Kurzweil's ideas about virtually saying goodbye to the human race in favor of a better evolutionary model probably don't do the cause of innovation much good. Kurzweil is a valuable example of a certain kind of innovator who doesn't care very much about packaging his ideas in forms that connect with familiar human experience so as to go down comfortably with the greatest possible mass of people. Yet, this kind of bridge-building between past and present is extremely important to the political progress of technology, as Daniel Burnham rightly sensed back in the day of the Columbian Exposition. Mere flag-waving on behalf of innovation isn't enough.

Kurzweil's enthusiasm is commendable, but his messianic personality is a turn-off to more people than he might suppose, which does his genuinely intriguing ideas (and those of other bold technological thinkers) more of a disservice than he may realize. If we want to promote innovation boldly in the 21st century, including some of Kurzweil's own stimulating ideas, a message of the *trans-human* is likely to be less productive than learning to speak more thoughtfully and skillfully about how technology might be made *more* human and more humane, and how it might be better integrated into our humanity rather than supplanting it.

This isn't a weakness of Kurzweil's alone but of futurology as it currently exists, of which he is but one eminent example. We need a philosophical vision that as many people as possible would truly *wish* to choose, rather than one that appalls or frightens them. Articulating such a vision is part of the philosophical task that awaits us urgently in the 21st century.

An element of this task must be a greater modesty of prediction that Kurzweil considers appropriate. His faith in his ability to see the future at times makes that of metaphysicians like Karl Marx and Oswald Spengler seem restrained. We've spoken in earlier pages of the hazards of overconfidence in an automatic stream of invention. In this regard, Bennett quoted Harvard cognitive scientist Steven A. Pinker (1954-) as commenting that "the track record of technological predictions is laughable. I remember a prediction in my childhood that by now we'd be living in domed cities and commuting by jet pack and eating protein pills instead of meals. On the other hand a lot of revolutions are predicted by no one. My favorite is that in the movie '2001,' you had space travel and human-level artificial intelligence, but people were still writing on clipboards. Arthur C. Clarke hadn't predicted the laptop."

The Law of Accelerating Returns

Yet, with all these vulnerabilities to criticism, Kurzweil is also an immensely stimulating and positive figure. As with nanotechnologist Drexler (and, for that matter, Minsky), if only a fraction of Kurzweil's vision comes true, we'll be vastly enriched, not by any inevitability of the kind in which Kurzweil believes, but by the *choices* we'll be empowered to make. If this range of choices is drawn from even a modest part of the array of technological capabilities that Kurzweil expects, then we can reasonably aspire to much, even if we have to work very hard to make these things happen (as the authors of this book believe will be the case).

So, if much of Kurzweil's pure philosophical vision is found wanting, that part of it that deals with genuine technological possibility must be listened to with respect, if only because he's already shown his mettle so effectively as a gifted inventor himself. In these respects he can be regarded as a welcome antidote to the reigning skepticism and pessimism about technology.

Kurzweil likes to speak of the momentum of technology in terms of what he calls the *Law of Accelerating Returns*, a principle opposed to the *Law of Diminishing Returns*. The latter is an economic postulate that once a production system passes an optimal point in its relationship with its environment, you'll start getting less and less out of it even if you put more and more in. (Malthus used this principle in his *Essay on Population*.) Kurzweil, by contrast, sees technological evolution as being now on a path that will give us exponentially increasing returns from less and less resources.

He therefore believes our energy problems will disappear as technology advances. (In an interview with Natasha Lomas of silicon.com published on November 20, 2008, Kurzweil said nanotechnology's improved energy capture capability would enable global energy needs to be "completely met by renewable sources such as solar as soon as 2028, doing away with the world's dependency on fossil fuels."[2])

It's interesting to go through the testimony that Kurzweil presented on April 9, 2003 to the Committee on Science of the U.S. House of Representatives Hearing to Examine the Societal Implications of Nanotechnology. Here are some excerpts:

"Our rapidly growing ability to manipulate matter and energy at ever smaller scales promises to transform virtually every sector of society, including health and medicine, manufacturing, electronics and computers, energy, travel, and defense. There will be increasing overlap between nanotechnology and other technologies of increasing influence, such as biotechnology and artificial intelligence...

"The golden age of nanotechnology is, therefore, a couple of decades away. This era will bring us the ability to essentially convert software, i.e., information, directly into physical products. We will be able to produce virtually any product for pennies per pound. Computers will have greater computational capacity than the human brain, and we will be completing the reverse engineering of the human brain to reveal the software design of human intelligence. We are already placing devices with narrow intelligence in our bodies for diagnostic and therapeutic purposes. With the advent of nanotechnology, we will be able to keep our bodies and brains in a healthy, optimal state indefinitely. We will have technologies to reverse environmental pollution.

"Nanotechnology and related advanced technologies of the 2020s will bring us the opportunity to overcome age-old problems, including pollution, poverty, disease, and aging... Human life expectancy was 37 years in 1800. Most humans at that time lived lives dominated by poverty, intense labor, disease, and misfortune. We are immeasurably better off as a result of technology, but there is still a lot of suffering in the world to overcome. We have a moral imperative, therefore, to continue the pursuit of knowledge and of advanced technologies that can continue to overcome human affliction...

"... the twenty-first century will see about a thousand times greater technological change than its predecessor."[3]

Building a culture of scientific and technological innovation: A task of ideas

Kurzweil's visions, expectations and personality all project important parts of the challenge of ideas that we face today in choosing a future.

Throughout this book we've encountered ideas which are complex and abstract, yet have powerful impacts on public attitudes and national policy concerning technology. What happens to America and the world in the 21st century will be shaped – not exclusively, but substantially -- in *battles about these ideas.*

We've entered the age of techno-ideology.

Because our evolving debates about technology relate to some of our deepest beliefs about human nature, it's impossible to discuss them intelligently without contextualizing them against a broad cultural background that many people don't associate with technology decisions. Ideas, including literary, religious, cultural and philosophical ones, are at the heart of our technology debates, just as much as budgets and technical problem-solving.

Let's look over some of the key issues we've discussed so far.

The myth of technological inevitability

Perpetuated by both Right and Left, this is the idea that technological innovation doesn't really have to be nurtured by the careful creation of the right conditions, but just happens, more or less unbidden. This philosophy of technological entitlement assumes we reached a point where we're entitled to technological innovation to make our lives more comfortable, whether or not we do anything to bring it about.

The strangeness of new technologies

This strangeness has a somewhat peculiar relationship with the literary and mass entertainment industry of science fiction, which has become both a big business and an influential part of American culture in the past half century or so – so influential that it's hardly realistic to try to understand America's attitudes to technology without considering science fiction's role in both expressing and shaping those attitudes.

The role of science fiction in retarding new technologies is paradoxical. You'd have thought the science fiction boom would help make us more comfortable with the future. Yet much of it's had the opposite effect. In the first half of the 20th century, science fiction in America was largely confined to pulp magazines that mainstream publishers considered rather disreputable. In the second half of the century it became an accepted literary form and the mainstay of highly profitable franchises in the once despised medium of comic books and in Hollywood. Computer graphics techniques have now made it possible to translate science fiction into special effects on the screen that were difficult if not impossible to obtain until quite recently.

However, by presenting the visions of science fiction in the grotesque, sensationalistic and preposterously menacing shapes and images that moviemakers often see as their best path to profits, this kind of science fiction hasn't shortened the gap between mundane technological reality and exciting technological possibility. On the contrary, it's lengthened the gap by branding all forms of visionary technological extrapolation as far-fetched entertainment. It's not at all true that we've become accustomed to radical technological change to the point where we see no real distinction between science fiction and our everyday reality. What we've really become accustomed to, and therefore expect, is seeing an ongoing stream of naturally occurring and essentially trivial enhancements of consumer gadgetry.

As far as our receptivity toward radical technological change is concerned, we relegate this to the world of fantasy -- usually filmic. So, bizarrely, science fiction has helped paralyze our appreciation of the possible by encouraging a credibility gap between existing technologies and radical improvements on them. ("Oh, that's just science fiction.") This effect is exacerbated by the repeated fictional presentation of high technology as a destructive, anti-human force.

An example is American novelist and film producer Michael Crichton (1942–2008), whose fictions about the catastrophic results of technological developments include *The Terminal Man* (1972) and *Jurassic Park* (1990), both adapted to the screen, and the film *Westworld* (1973), which he directed. His novel *Prey* (2002) presented a story of horrors unleashed by nanotechnology. In a review of *Prey* on the web site of the New York-based Center for Responsible Nanotechnology in January 2003, headlined *Don't let Crichton's Prey scare you--the science isn't real*, American nanotechnologist Chris Phoenix (1970-), the institute's director of research, wrote: "Imagine a horror story about baseball, in which the batter keeps hitting the ball hard enough to kill the fans. The story might be entertaining, but it's obviously unrealistic... Suppose further that at one point in the story, the author writes about someone walking back to the dugout after three 'fouls'. Does the author not know the difference between a foul and a strike, or was he simply in too much of a hurry to bother getting the words right? Either way, no one could learn the rules of baseball from that story. Even if it was mostly right, a few wrong facts make all the difference--especially if the reader does not know which facts are wrong. *Prey* contains comparable exaggerations and mistakes in science."[4]

Phoenix detailed numerous scientific mistakes in Crichton's sensationalistic account of yet another technology rising up to threaten an unsuspecting world, and added: "In Crichton's stories, the scientists are mad -- all but one who moans about how 'nature will find a way' and 'we should not play with things we don't understand'."

Stories like Crichton's contribute to public disorientation toward technological innovation in two ways: by perpetuating the idea of a rash, irresponsible, often incompetent and often unscrupulous scientific community rushing to threaten the world with sinister technologies, and by dressing up false presentations of science in terms that seem to be the lay reader to be authoritative and knowledgeable.

Everyone likes to be entertained by stories, but it's a pity there aren't more science fiction stories that present science and technology both accurately and positively. That would help educate the public, rather than confuse them by presenting research issues so preposterously that the science gets lost in a blaze of theatrics. The theatrics are entertaining, but the trouble is we've seen so much of it that readers and filmgoers can hardly be blamed for learning to associate any presentations of major technological innovation as just another dose of Hollywood moonshine.

We've seen a practical example of this imaginative obstacle in the perception of maglev trains as a fantastic idea rather than a reality which, though practical, won't be built until America believes in it.

The fear of losing the past

Another way in which science fiction has paradoxically helped impede innovation is by reinforcing the fear that it will make us lose the past, depriving us of the best of our heritage. This attitude to technology is related to, but different from, the credibility gap.

Much if not most science fiction, at least in recent decades, has tended to be highly pessimistic about technological innovation not just because of technology-specific threats but because innovation is generally seen as a culture-destroying phenomenon.

Science fiction that promotes this pessimism is an imaginative and allegorical expression of the Luddite tradition. Intertwined with this tradition is, here again, the marketing consideration that pessimistic science fiction makes for good stories. This is especially so for anyone writing for the contemporary film industry, which derives so much of its income from films that rejoice in presenting explosions, horrifying transformations, conspiracies by evil government agencies supported by corporate technologists, doomsday scenarios, and endless stories of The Terrible Things That Happen When Science Goes Wrong.

It's important not to lump all science fiction together in this respect. There's a valuable role for science fiction that thoughtfully warns of dangers that could lurk in emerging technologies. But this kind of science-fiction-as-warning product would be more helpful as part of a body of thought that points out with equal attention and eloquence the positive potential of possible technological changes. An example of this mixed approach is American writer Ray Bradbury (1920-), who has combined vigorous support of manned space exploration with equally passionate antipathy toward the Internet and its technological universe. This latter state of mind finds its fullest form in his famous novel *Fahrenheit 451* (1953), which is the closest any American author has come to writing a dystopian literary classic on the level of the 20th century's two iconic dystopian novels by British authors: *Nineteen Eighty-Four* (1949) by George Orwell (1903-1950), and *Brave New World* (1932) by Orwell's former teacher, Aldous Huxley (1894-1963).

These three future-fearing works are very different but all three share a dread of a tomorrow which they have imagined as bringing technological gateways to the decline of intelligence, freedom and the human spirit. Bradbury has said that his novel wasn't intended to predict a future but to prevent one.[5]

Aspects of the technological world that Bradbury envisioned in *Fahrenheit 451* effectively if superficially connect with aspects of real-life 21st-century Internet society, at least as this society is seen through jaundiced eyes. (He conceived a literatureless, culturally starved, imaginatively numbed society of couch potatoes who sacrifice every vestige of independent thought for a comfortable enslavement to mindless, interactive and electronically delivered mass entertainment.)

But the core of the book and the key to its popularity is its central plot device, which postulates that, in the future society of which Bradbury wrote, books themselves would be outlawed because of their ability to admit readers to alternative intellectual worlds from which they would be able to criticize the prevailing social order of their day.

In this hypothetical future society there exist, therefore, firemen whose job it is not to extinguish fires but to extinguish thought by seeking out books and burning them. This strand in the book is best understood by reading *Fahrenheit 451* alongside Bradbury's many other books, which together evoke the nostalgia he feels for an idealized rural and small-town America that now seems lost to the ages. This nostalgia for a golden past which technology has allegedly eroded powerfully permeates much science fiction of this sort even where its readers have little or no knowledge of the vanished golden age. (Their failure of memory may not necessarily mean memories have been destroyed by an evil technology; it may rather mean that times change regardless of technology ... or that cherished aspects of the purported golden age never existed.)

A more hopeful picture of the human technological future appears in Bradbury's book *The Martian Chronicles* (1950), which offers a poetic vision of humanity moving into space and taking with it not only its weaknesses but also its strengths and its optimistic hope that new worlds could bring opportunities for renewal. Bradbury paints a picture of space travel as a new frontier for pioneers fleeing from an exhausted Earth, but he sees as us taking into space all those cultural goods with which we have historically defined our that humanity, ranging from the trivial artifacts of popular culture to religion.

Bradbury's occasional optimism about the potential of human technological ingenuity (and his insight into the importance to innovation of motivation and commitment) are especially evident in his short story *The Toynbee Convector*, published in a 1988 book of the same name. An inventor convinces the world that he has devised a way to visit the future, using a procedure so complex that it will offer only a single opportunity to penetrate the veil of years. He embarks on this journey through time to determine whether tomorrow is going to be as dreadful as present environmental and political crises suggest. The world eagerly awaits his report. He returns with good news: in the future, the leaders of nations will come to their senses and work together with scientists, technologists, and philosophers to create a planetary civilization that is clean, humane, secure, and beautiful. At the end of the tale, we learn that his report was accurate inasmuch as the events he described do indeed come to pass. But it is also revealed that he lied about traveling through time. He made no such excursion. He fabricated the whole story because he was convinced that humanity could and would solve its problems only if it could be convinced of its power to choose its own future.

The logic of the story could well be disputed, not least because it could be argued that an impression of inevitable progress might tend to encourage complacency rather than determination to succeed.

But although *The Martian Chronicles* is a widely revered book which has entered into America's pantheon of great works of literary imagination, it stands alone. Nobody has been able to imitate Bradbury's idiosyncratic style successfully and while his positive vision of America has millions of admirers, it can't really be said to have influenced American culture or even reflected it much. The negative side of his vision, on the other hand, is highly representative of a future-distrusting element in American culture that has become pervasive. So the need for positive science fiction in literary, filmic and other media products is strong, given the importance of science fiction as a powerful influence on popular culture.

The culture of negativism

We've seen that while the history of American technological achievement, is to a significant extent a history of self-confidence and inventive determination, technological negativism has been well represented in it, including a long history of antipathy toward the city in favor of rural culture.

We've seen, too, that there's a difference between scientific skepticism, imbued with positive tenets that enables science to progress, and the negative attitude that adopts an exaggerated disbelief in the possibilities and purposes of science and technology.

Healthy skepticism is a cornerstone of a rational attitude to the universe and to the quest to develop theories that are testable, falsifiable and based on evidence rather than unsubstantiated assertion. This kind of scientific skepticism is deeply ingrained in the origins of American culture. It's informed by a democratic spirit because it sees the growth of knowledge as depending on healthy criticism and free exchanges of ideas. It's not negative in spirit, but positive and constructive. It's balanced by a number of affirmative convictions, such as the principle that knowledge has a value in and of itself, and the principle that the universe has an order which intelligence can reasonably hope to fathom, and the principle that there are such things as objective truths which are not human inventions.

Negativism toward science and technology, on the other hand, may seem to resemble scientific skepticism but is really quite different from it. It has little to do with the growth of knowledge and is rather derived from the desire to further social objectives, such as the retention of a kind of society which is deemed to be aesthetically, theologically or for other reasons threatened by scientific and technological innovation.

Negativism toward science and technology may be driven by convictions which are diametrically opposed to those on which the advancement of science and technology depends. These may include:

1.The principle that knowledge has no value in and of itself, but is worth while only if it serves a religious dogma or political agenda.

2.The principle that the universe either has no order or that it has one which is beyond penetration by human intelligence.

3.The principle that there are no such things as objective truths which are not human inventions.

Negativism may combine or vary these principles in various subtle and complex ways. This, together with the fact that negativism is often dressed up in the language of science and technology, can make it very hard, at times, to distinguish between genuine scientific skepticism and negativism which seeks to obstruct scientific and technological development.

Negativism may even pay lip service to the principles that underlie genuine scientific skepticism, and purport to be in favor of scientific and technological development, while in practice seeking to stall scientific and technological development in a science-policy equivalent of what politicians call filibustering: that is, by insisting that a scientific of technological development program is subjected to so much legalistic (rather than scientific) review that in practice such development is indefinitely obstructed.

Then there's the negativism that arises within science itself, from scientists who oppose new scientific theories or technological advances not for scientific reasons but because they threaten theoretical positions or established technologies on which established careers rely. All these and other considerations are among the many that underlie the culture of negativism toward science and technology.

Disbelief in the non-social realities of science and technology

We've seen that science and technology require constant collective review, but that review alone cannot determine what is scientifically and technologically feasible, because scientific truth cannot be decided by vote. Only research can determine this, and even then it's necessary for research to be conducted with a high sense of motivation and interest in the subject, for only in this way will adequate resource of money and energy be brought to bear.

Accepting this means accepting that science and technology are rooted in a non-social reality as well as in a social reality. It is clear that science and technology are social activities and most certainly require social support in the forms of community motivation, funding, institutional support and in other ways. It's equally clear that there are important senses in which science and technology are not social, but require and depend on our proactive interaction with non-human reality.

The problem of technological momentum

We've noted, in discussing Kurzweil and others, that some of the most important fields of contemporary technology now appear to have so much momentum that aspects of their innovation seem virtually unstoppable. If there is any truth in these perceptions, how do we reconcile them with our claim that technological innovation is not inevitable, and that we not only can but must take proactive steps to shape its progress?

The answer lies in the difference between technological *evolution*, technological *impact* and technological *navigation*.

Technological evolution is analogous to natural (that is, spontaneously occurring, as opposed to genetically engineered) biological evolution. It will take place whether we like it or not and in ways that we cannot foresee, unless by "foresee" we mean guesswork.

Now, we can make guesses about biological evolution. For example, by gathering statistics about human height over a long period we may be able to see a trend whereby people are getting taller, and this may lead us to guess how tall people will be in future. But this still remains guesswork, because it's unlikely that we'll be able to know all the factors that are contributing to the height gains and how these factors may change in future. The best we can say is that it looks as if human height will in future be X assuming everything currently affecting our statistics stays the same. Since it's unlikely that everything will stay the same and almost certain that new environmental and other factors will enter the picture in future, this may not be saying very much. All we can really be sure of is that since biological evolution is a function of interactions between organisms and environmental conditions, and since environmental conditions change, there will be biological evolution.

Similar considerations apply to spontaneous technological evolution -- that is, evolution that happens as a result of the historical momentum of what has gone before. It's extremely hard if not impossible to predict the course of spontaneous technological evolution. Just about the only thing that history seems to teach us about this is that it's very risky to say that a technology that we can think of, however dimly, definitely won't happen.

Just as with biological evolution, however, we can be fairly sure that technological evolution will occur as long as there is intelligent life to manufacture technologies. But as with biological evolution, we can't predict how technology will evolve if left to develop without any concerted effort to steer innovation along a particular path. We can make extrapolations based on existing science and technology, but we've seen from the example of the learned astronomer Simon Newcomb how reliable that can be.

So, it's safe to say that some degree of evolution will occur as long as a civilization exists to sustain it, and to that extent technological evolution is inevitable, but what shapes and directions it will take we do not know. George Orwell remarked in an essay in 1946 on how little change had occurred over thousands of years in basic household artifacts like pots, pans and the comb. A Discover magazine article we quoted earlier remarked on how surprisingly little change had occurred in the late 20th   century in things that we are accustomed to thinking of as indicators of radical technological development, like aircraft, automobiles and computers.

Technological evolution may take the form of superficial or trivial changes rather than radical innovations in basic design. It may even, as we have seen with legacy technology like fossil fuel energy systems, take the form of an entrenchment of old technology to an extent that discourages the development of alternative technology. This is analogous to a weed that is successful in evolutionary terms in that it evolves and adapts to an increasingly large environment but in doing so kills of other growth.

This brings us to *technology impact*, which is sometimes confused with technological evolution but is different from it and can even be hostile to it. It seems safe to say that all technologies that are put into wide use will have some impact, either social or physical, if not both. If television technology is used by the media industry to create a culture of mindless programming content whose sole purpose is to persuade the public to buy merchandise that no one really needs, the evolution of this technologically supported culture may be complex and very interesting, but it will not represent technological innovation. It represents cultural choices and social forces that have nothing to do with technological innovation, since the technology that enables it may be frozen in one form for a long period for all the programmers and merchandisers care, and for economic reasons they may perhaps even prefer it to stay unchanged permanently. So here we have change which is related to technology and which may seem to represent technology but which is not at all necessarily linked to a process of technological innovation.

So we can see from the above that what looks like inevitable technological innovation isn't. It's rather technological change and technological impact, neither of which need be linked to innovation at all but could even discourage it.

We then come to *technological navigation*. By this we mean the taking of active steps not only to encourage technological innovation but also to anticipate the potential impacts of innovations to the extent possible, and to devise ways to deal pre-emptively with those impacts. The aim is to steer technology in a socially beneficial direction that will have the least possible disruptive effects on society, the innovative process and the physical environment.

Technological navigation is an interesting and challenging concept. We've chosen the term "navigation" to identify it because we specifically want, among other things, to differentiate it from the ideas of (a) regulation and control and (b) technological management.

Let's talk about regulation and control first. The computer development and artificial intelligence fields, and studies related to them like systems theory, have come to carry connotations of control that go back to the Greek root of the word cybernetics. *Cyber* is now widely used as a prefix to indicate anything to do with computer systems and culture, such as cyberspace and cyberlaw. Now, *cyber is* an ancient Greek word meaning *pilot* or *helmsman* (he who steers or who guides a ship). But even in ancient times it was also associated with government and governing. The Greek philosopher Plato used it in this sense, which has come down to us through the ages.

Computer technology was popularly and lastingly identified as a science of control by American mathematician Norbert Wiener (1894–1964) in his book *The Human Use of Human Beings: Cybernetics and Society* (1950). While the influence of one word and its origins shouldn't be overestimated, it's nevertheless a fact that the idea of control has not been a happy one for computerization and technology generally, in terms of its interpretation by our general culture. Critics of technology have seen the use of technology to control people (or to control the physical environment, in an exploitative sense) as one of its most damning features. Obviously technology is an array of tools whereby we control our environment (or try to) our physical circumstances. But why emphasize this aspect of technology any further, when it's become so emotionally charged? So let's get away from identifying technology with control. It's more accurate to think of it as a way of achieving optimal symbiosis with our environments.

A need to re-think the concept of technological management

The phrase *technological management*, on the other hand, is also problematical, for two reasons. The less important reason is that it, too, implies control. But many managers and experts on management will argue that if management is a form of control, it is surely at its best a form of benign control, aimed at bringing order and efficiency into an enterprise, and that no enterprise can flourish without good management in these senses. The more important reason that technological management is problematical, however, is far more politically sensitive and controversial , and may ruffle managerial feathers somewhat more. In brief, it is this.

The discipline of management -- a very valuable and indeed essential discipline -- is not really a single discipline but a spectrum of disciplines that ranges from accounting practices and the efficient organization of work schedules to the motivation of staff, the effective formation of teams, workplace morale, negotiation with unions and government agencies, and the effective marketing of the enterprise's products to customers.

While it is unquestionable that excellent theoretical and applied work has been done on management, it is also the case that a great deal of popular management literature -- popular among the general public as well as among management professors and consultants -- has the flimsiest bearing on the development of technology in laboratory and workroom. A good deal of management theory has, in fact, been based on the attitude toward technology that we have criticized in this book: the idea that technology occurs, and that the role of management is to preside over its occurrence sophisticatedly and to bring order to the chaos of the inventive mind. By no means all books on management, but many, appear to have their strongest point in the creative invention of jargon that's calculated to capitalize on the fashionable concepts and vocabularies of the day. Many an inventive mind smiles wryly at this sort of lofty managerial expertise, the pompous reality of which is familiar to anyone who has ever worked in a large organization, and which is so ably satirized in the comic strip *Dilbert*.

As an alternative to both the notion of technological control and the notion of technological management, therefore, we suggest the concept of technological navigation to indicate the way in which technology may be fruitfully and realistically guided. This idea restores that part of the original, ancient Greek meaning of the word *cyber* which has been allowed to recede: the idea not of a governor but of a guide and steersman.

Consider the function of the navigator. His role is not the same as that of the captain, but it is essential to the captain's effective execution of his duties of governing the ship and serving its welfare. In order to serve his captain and the ship for which his captain was responsible, the navigator in ancient seafaring nations, like his successors today, had to have a healthy respect for the non-human forces and laws of nature. He had to steer the ship in such a way that it followed the desired direction of the captain within the limits of what such non-human factors as ocean currents and winds would permit. He had to find his way by the stars. But he did not slavishly put his vessel at the beck and call of natural circumstances; if that happened his ship would quickly end up on the rocks or at the bottom of the sea. He developed and applied a navigational skill that allowed him to put what he had learned of nature to use in carrying out the captain's will, to the best extent that sensitivity to natural laws and forces would allow. The navigator was thus not a political or socially managerial functionary. He was a kind of intermediary between the policies of his captain and the laws of nature. The navigator had to know science, in the forms of astronomy and oceanography, and he had to know technology, in the form of his ship and whatever implements the technology of the day gave him to help him plot course and steer -- purposefully, rationally and decisively.

This vision of the navigator is much in tune with the strongest ideas that the intellectual traditions of ancient Greece have bequeathed to us. Socrates was, after all, not a politician, emperor, dictator or even a senator. He was a guide to students who wished to navigate the pitfalls and labyrinths of philosophy. He helped his students make rational choices and, through patient and systematic inquiry, to assemble information that would make such choices possible. And though Socrates was neither a scientist nor a technologist, in the modern senses, his critical, patient spirit, and his confidence in human intelligence (which was shared by other great Greek philosophers like Aristotle) was in important ways the cradle of the modern scientific spirit and continues to inform it. It is relative to this spirit that technological navigation, as distinct from technological evolution and technological impact, is an area in which human choice can and must be exercised. And it is vital to our prosperity and survival in the 21st century that we become technological navigators in this sense.

What must we do in order to become effective technological navigators? At least two things: we must build a culture of scientific and technological motivation, and we must build an economy devoted to scientific and technological innovation.

For guidance on these tasks we can look to Britain's Great Exhibition of 1851 and America's Chicago Exposition of 1893. The fact that these events took place in the 19th century does not at all mean that they cannot teach us valuable lessons that we can apply in the 21st. The task of building a culture of scientific and technological motivation, like all cultural tasks, can only benefit from historical knowledge. The fact that we neither can nor should try to replicate the 19th century doesn't mean we can't learn from it. If we couldn't, we might as well convince ourselves that the principles of the Founding Fathers of the American Republic aren't relevant to the conduct of American life today. Building a scientific and technological society is a human undertaking, and should in no way impede our recognition of the fact that science and technology depend on our acquiring knowledge of non-human facts.

We have considered the adventures of Aaron Burr. We have seen how London's Great Exhibition demonstrated, focused and energized the British people's national sense of purpose as a world leader in new technologies, and how the event was politically and symbolically driven by the British government and the monarchy. We have seen how this branded the event as not just an industrial project but a national enterprise intended to characterize not only Britain's development path but its very identity, both at home and in the community of nations. We saw how Prince Albert, a passionate promoter of science and technology, battled the naysayers about the Exhibition, and we noted the enormous success it achieved.

Against the background of the Exhibition's vision of British technological advancement we saw how the railroads emerged in Britain as a product of national pride, technological resourcefulness, entrepreneurial motivation and government encouragement, and a 19th-century British culture of technological expansion created a platform for the accomplishments of innovators like Isambard Kingdom Brunel. And we saw the difficulty of disentangling this complex of motivational impulses from Britain's self-image as an empire. Understandably, this connection embarrasses some in a post-imperial era. Nevertheless, it tells us something important about the value of a sense of national purpose.

We then saw how America's Columbian Exposition of 1893 played a similar role in the US. It illuminated six key aspects of 19th-century America's philosophy of technological development: (a) enthusiasm for interdisciplinary research and management; (b) a determined commitment to innovation as a cornerstone of progress; (c) a sense of necessary social continuity between the nation's past and its future; (d) a willingness to think on a large, even sweeping scale; (e) a sense of the great importance of effective mass communication as a tool for bringing the public into the innovation process; and (f) the role of government as partner of private invention.

One of the things we learn from these American experiences is the importance of the laterality of American political and economic development.

By laterality we mean (a) the historical fact that American technological innovation and development have progressed as a function of partnerships and alliances among a wide variety of groups, including the federal government, the private sector, state governments and other groups, and (b) the fact that in order for this tendency toward laterality to be effectively extended into our current society we need to include in it all groups possessing intellectual assets of importance to the public welfare.

The former is a major feature of America's emergence as a great political, economic and technological power, and to the extent that we regard the U.S. as having accomplished successes in these areas we must acknowledge this laterality as a substantive factor in these successes. The latter references groups which may include universities where cutting-edge research is done, and independent think tanks.

It is a mistake to assign an undue weight to any one of these groups. To do so would be to ignore laterality. An economy controlled by government is not lateral; it is a planned economy built not on alliances and partnerships but on bureaucratic edict, and a recipe for disasters of the kind that ended the Soviet Union.

By the same token, an economy based on exaggerated faith in a free market of private enterprise is similarly non-lateral and ignores the vital role that history has demonstrated for government in great programs of scientific and technological research since the days of Francis Bacon. Nor is the commonly perceived idea of a "mixed economy" an adequate reflection of the importance of laterality, since mixed-economy scenarios have tended to focus on alliances between government officers and commercial managers, whereas we know that universities and think tanks today contain much of our society's research assets.

America is today sorely in need of an intellectual revolution in the role that universities and other educational institutions play in U.S. society. And not only the role of universities, for a revolution is needed in all cooperations between the great institutions of American society. The goal of this revolution must be to launch a new era of innovation, indeed a new American civilization based on a profound new commitment to scientific and technological advance.

Hungarian-British engineer Dennis Gabor (1900 - 1979), who won the 1971 Nobel Prize for Physics for his invention of holography, wrote: "The future cannot be predicted, but futures can be invented." America must now invent its own 21st-century future, and the world's. Let's look at what must be done to accomplish this.

NOTES

1. Bennett, Drake, The Age of Ray Kurzweil, THE BOSTON GLOBE (Sept.25, 2005) http://www.boston.com/news/globe/ideas/articles/2005/09/25/the_age_of_ray_kurzweil/

2. Nanotech to solve global warming by 2028, http://www.silicon.com/research/specialreports/agenda-setters-2008/nanotech-to-solve-global-warming-by-2028-39345604.htmL

3. http://www.kurzweilai.net/meme/frame.html?main=/articles/art0556.html

4. http://www.nanotech-now.com/Chris-Phoenix/prey-critique.html

5. http://www.wired.com/wired/archive/6.10/bradburypr.html

CHAPTER 11

WHAT MUST BE DONE: TEN POINTS TO RETURN AMERICA TO THE TECHNOLOGY STANDARD

In the light of the observations and facts presented in this book, we offer ten propositions as the basis of a new technological culture in America. These should, we argue, be adopted by the federal government as high-priority steps for implementation as quickly as is feasible.

1. Restore the U.S.'s global intellectual leadership.

The U.S. must restore its place as world leader in scientific and technological innovation. This statement will almost certainly attract two immediate objections. The first involves skepticism about whether the U.S. was *ever* really the world's leader in scientific and technological advance. Secondly, the idea that America should be the world's leader in cutting-edge knowledge will displease those who see the U.S. as a global bully concerned only with the interests of a relatively small number of huge corporations. Both objections can be credibly countered.

Regarding the first, it could well be argued that this very book challenges the claim that the U.S. has ever "led" global technological innovation. We've noted that America has lagged technologically in recent decades, that its culture has contained a strong anti-technological element and that much American know-how has in fact stemmed from innovative momentum imported from other countries.

But these circumstances must be balanced by other considerations which are at least as important, if not more. Despite its disturbing technological lag, America hasn't (yet, anyway) been massively excelled by any other nation as an all-round center of scientific and technological progress. Other countries have moved

faster in specific areas, but like chipmunks darting ahead of a lum-
bering elephant. The chipmunks have impressive nervous energy
for small spurts, but who has the greater power? As a matter of
historical fact, the concentration of the world's most advanced scientific and technological ingenuity in America in the first half of
the 20th century is arguably the most decisive technological fact of
the past hundred years or more of global history. The closest any
society over this period has come to equaling America's critical
mass in technological resources has been the Soviet Union, and
even that approximation turns out, when you look at it closely, to
be largely an illusion.

If the U.S.'s temporary infatuation with its space program in
the 1960s was mainly a knee-jerk political reaction to the loss of
face following the Soviets' Sputnik, manned-launch and spacewalk
victories, Moscow's motives for its space effort were at least as
superficial. While a strong philosophical and visionary fervor drove
some of the U.S.S.R's space scientists, the desire of commissars to
beat America into space was political, not scientific. Moreover, it
was achieved at great human cost by a government that chose
to invest in political and military competition at the expense of
maintaining a free, economically healthy and humane society. The
oppression and inefficiencies within the Soviet Union eventually
caused its collapse. Its temporary show of scooting past America
in the space race can hardly be held up as evidence of cultural or
governmental excellence.

Furthermore, although it's not widely remembered today,
America contributed crucially to Russia's industrial, economic and
military fortunes in the 20th century, including aid from the American Relief Administration in the 1920s, substantial support from
U.S. companies and engineers in the 1930s, and material valued in
the billions of dollars during World War II. While no one can say
how history would have turned out if not for this American aid to
Moscow, it's reasonable to suppose it at least played an important
role, perhaps even a critical one, in enabling the Soviet Union to
develop sufficiently to wage the Cold War. And if we discount the
Soviet Union as a rival, we're left to recognize the U.S. as the most
powerful engine of technological innovation in the 20th century,
regardless of its more recent performance.

As for the anti-technological aspects of American culture and
the fact that U.S. innovation has been spurred by intellectual momentum from other countries, these two considerations are linked.
Yes, American culture has a very strong anti-technological streak.
Yes, many of America's finest minds have been immigrants, and

vital parts of U.S. culture have been imports. But America hasn't imported only the strengths of other countries; it's also imported their weaknesses, which have understandably contributed to American faults and foibles. Yet, if this mixture of multinational weakness and strength has built an America that's far from perfect, it's also created an America which, in the first half of the 20th century, became the largest, most dynamic environment of innovation in the world, and today, with all its shortcomings, retains the greatest potential to generate the innovations on which 21st-century global prosperity depends.

Yes, the U.S. has lapsed into technological complacency. Yes, it's bruised by recent and current economic, military and geopolitical developments. But no other country is equipped, economically or culturally, to take its place or shoulder its responsibility. The burden of that responsibility at present requires of the U.S. nothing less than to embrace with renewed commitment the position of the world's scientific and technological leader.

To do this, America must vigorously pursue the ten propositions here listed, beginning with this first one: *the country must commit wholeheartedly to a doctrine of global scientific and technological intellectual leadership.* This doctrine holds that history has delivered to America a moral responsibility to provide the world with such leadership.

It's important to be clear about what this leadership means. As used here, the word has *no military or imperial connotations.* It signifies the ability and will to inspire and guide by moral example, persuasion and the force and dignity of reason. It inescapably carries the implication of teaching. There are those outside the U.S. and within it who will recoil from the notion that the U.S. has a responsibility to teach, holding that this smacks of arrogance. But the fact is that even in its present, unfulfilled and still embryonic scientific and technological condition, America has vast knowledge assets to share with the world and will have even vaster ones if it chooses to unlock its full potential. Its greatest treasures are its assets of knowledge – those it has gathered from all corners of the world, and those it has produced itself and can continue to produce in ever-increasing ratio if it resolves to do so.

There can be no finer or more humane cause than to produce and share this knowledge. For too long we've tended to think of leaders as commanders in battle. Brave, devoted and able military commanders deserve our gratitude and respect, but they don't represent the only kind of leader. The sharing of knowledge is also leadership, and perhaps the best kind.

If the phrase "knowledge economy" is to have any worthwhile meaning, it must be made to mean *the global economy that America helps build in the 21ˢᵗ century by sharing knowledge with the world*. The creation of this global knowledge economy on a foundation of American intellectual leadership is the premise and goal of the propositions that follow. If America takes this goal seriously it should communicate this by *making global knowledge economy leadership the responsibility of a secretaryship within the Cabinet*.

The pursuit of knowledge, the creation of new knowledge and technological innovation, the sharing of knowledge globally, and the development and implementation of strategies and institutions to facilitate these aims, are essential to all the responsibilities of the U.S. Government, no less than the protection of the security of the state, for without successful knowledge production the state cannot endure. But while there are dedicated government agencies devoted to national security, no dedicated government agency is devoted to the aims listed above. So whether we call it a Secretary of Knowledge Creation and Distribution, a Secretary of Technological Innovation, or some similar title, such a secretaryship should be created, thereby signaling to America and the world that the President of the United States regards the creation, distribution and application of new knowledge, and technological innovation, as a primary priority of the U.S. Government.

2. Create a new era of innovation-based economic partnerships between government and non-governmental entities.

If the U.S. seriously commits itself to global intellectual leadership, it must demonstrate this with a new approach to economic development. The traditional, partisan approach of a pendulum that swings periodically between big government and minimal government is simplistic and no longer fits our needs, if it ever did. In our brief outline earlier of the growth of U.S. infrastructures, we saw how a characteristically American economic style stemmed not only from the undeniable richness of America in energetic, visionary individuals but also, and equally importantly, from the ingenuity of such individuals in crafting fertile partnerships with government. We've argued that government has been instrumental to innovation – not by imposing controls on the private sector as in autocratic societies, but encouraging the private sector in the form of fruitful alliances, something that's happened repeatedly in the most fertile moments of American economic history. It's essential for the U.S. Government in the 21ˢᵗ century to re-energize this role in leading, encouraging and working with private industry. Where it's apparent that the interests of the country would be served by innovations whose development requires resources and timeframes inconsistent with the conventional demands of short-term private investment, *government must serve as midwife in birthing these innovations.*

This implies a new era of government-initiated partnerships between the private sector and government agencies. One of the authors of this book worked for over thirty years in one of the U.S.'s leading technology innovation corporations, Westinghouse, where numerous alliances with government entities led to highly productive and in some cases historic results. This protracted body of on-the-ground experience yielded two vital lessons: (a) that such alliances are capable of enormous fertility, amply repaying the investment made by government in the form of benefits to the public; and (b) that we today have nothing like the number, size and quality of these alliances that we need.

One of the areas in which more such cooperations are needed is the realm of military partnerships with civilian organizations.[1] *It is time for the U.S. to accept the economic and technological implications of the fact that the largest, most highly organized research-oriented entity in not only the U.S. but the world is none other than the U.S. Department of Defense.* This agency possesses planning and administrative structures and budget oversight capabilities that dwarf most if not all government agencies in the U.S. and anywhere else in the world. Moreover, the research and development needs of the Department of Defense are so diverse that with a wholly achievable amount of creative consideration, the department's research agendas can be made to incorporate many research programs that relate to the production of non-military knowledge assets. Military research is a potential gold mine of civilian technology innovation.

The U.S. military establishment is potentially the most fertile research and development institution in history. It has a vast organizational capability to coordinate both basic and applied research and to partner with private sector and academic organizations. These qualities have interesting historical predecessors but are unique to the U.S. in their present forms.

The U.S. Department of Defense has economy-of-scale assets which are particularly well suited to the pursuit of extremely large and imaginative research undertakings. Moreover, the military's mission of protecting the national interest and well-being of the public, in the short, medium and long terms, is wholly appropriate to the sense of urgency needed to drive technological innovation in the 21st century.

The idea of the military as a driver of technological innovation and as a generator of knowledge products for civilian as well as military benefit will be counterintuitive to many military and civilian leaders, since it is at odds with several stereotypes of the military role. But when it is closely examined, this idea suggests a conceptual refinement of the military mission that is greatly in tune with 21st-century needs and conditions.[2]

We've long been prevented from reaping the benefits of this fortunate circumstance by several factors, including remarks made by U.S. President Dwight D. Eisenhower when he ended his tenure, warning against the threat posed to civilian government and society by the growth of a "military-industrial complex". It's high time to put behind us the mythology that's evolved around this concept. By doing so, we stand to:

* Enrich the intellectual and practical product inventories of government agencies;

* Increase the payback to government and taxpayer from every dollar that the Department of Defense and other agencies commit to research;

* Bring enormously increased resources to the solution of technological problems of national and global significance;

* Refresh the creative energies and budgets of civilian and private sector innovation research programs.

This one step, in fact, has by itself the potential to re-energize a Wall Street battered by the failures of enterprises that rest on non-technological trading activities. It offers an entirely fresh and more prosperous outlook for a new age of 21st-century American enterprise. A newly empowered set of research and development alliances between the military establishment, private corporations and civilian public institutions across the board will also powerfully motivate and valuably redefine the U.S. Department of Defense in a post-Iraq environment. This will help greatly to restore the morale and renew the sense of purpose of a valiant organization whose members have endured much in recent years.

3. Invest more money in research and development.

On January 30, 2008, the U.S. Department of Energy's Under Secretary for Science, Dr Raymond L. Orbach, told the Council of Presidents of the Universities Research Association in Washington, DC: "Though you have heard this phrase before, we are now at a perilous moment in the history of funding for science in the United

States."

Orbach, who said he believed his views were shared by other leaders of federal agencies that supported science, was talking about "the consequences for the funding for science" of two legislative items, the Fiscal Year 2008 Omnibus Bill and the preceding Fiscal Year 2007 Continuing Resolution. Both, he said, "failed to provide adequate funding for the physical sciences in the United States and for many other fields of science", despite a call by President George W. Bush for Congress to double federal support for critical basic research in the physical sciences. Orbach warned that unless action was taken quickly to ensure a substantial new allocation of funds for research, "the future of the physical sciences will be in jeopardy. Opportunities will be lost forever: for science, and our country."

This is an extraordinarily disturbing statement to come from a senior officer of the U.S. Government. It's so startling in its implications that it bears repetition:

> Without more money, "the future of the physical sciences will be in jeopardy. Opportunities will be lost forever: for science, and our country."

Consider: this is no third-world country we're discussing. This is the United States of America. The land of Thomas Jefferson, Ben Franklin, Thomas Edison, Buckminster Fuller and, by adoption, Albert Einstein.

This is a national embarrassment and disgrace to all who value the U.S.'s traditional image as a world center of enterprise, excellence of achievement, education, industrial innovation, humane culture and scientific learning. These things are all closely connected. A flourishing community of basic scientific research is essential to them all. The physical sciences, in particular, have in many ways been the central font of new insights across a wide spectrum of scientific disciplines and humane enlightenment.

Orbach's statement is also cause for very real alarm for all who are concerned about the well-being of America in any sense – economically, militarily, educationally or otherwise. A vigorous cultivation of the physical sciences are fundamental for civic health in numerous core areas of a great nation's life.

Orbach quoted an op-ed article published in the January 20, 2008 edition of the *San Francisco Chronicle*, headlined *Flagging Economy Needs Science Investment*, by Craig Barrett, Chairman of Intel Corporation, the world's biggest manufacturer of the semiconductor, a basic tool of the modern electronics industry, including computers. Orbach cited this passage: "Two years ago, the National

Academies published the seminal study on U.S. competitiveness entitled 'Rising Above the Gathering Storm.' The study identified major shortcomings in U.S. investment in basic scientific research as well as in math and science education for our youngsters. The suggestions contained in this study were immediately picked up by the Democratic House Leadership as their competitiveness strategy and later by President Bush in his State of the Union message under his American Competitiveness Initiative. Legislation in the form of the America COMPETES Act was passed in the House and Senate in 2007, and it appeared the United States was finally going to move forward after years of neglect to increase investment in math, science and basic research. All parties agreed that our competitiveness in the 21st century was at stake and we needed to act."

However, Orbach pointed out, the Fiscal Year 2008 Omnibus Bill "at best ignored" the president's request for the American Competitiveness Initiative, which would have doubled the budgets of the National Science Foundation, the Department of Energy Office of Science and the National Institute of Standards and Technology. He quoted Barrett's article further:

"The United States stands at a pivotal point in our history. Competition is heating up around the world with millions of industrious, highly educated workers who are willing to compete at salaries far below those paid here. The only way we can hope to compete is with brains and ideas that set us above the competition – and that only comes from investments in education and R&D. Practically everyone who has traveled outside the United States in the last decade has seen this dynamic at work...It may already be too late; but I genuinely think the citizenry of this country wants the United States to compete."

Orbach noted that for the Office of Science, "the budget without earmarks was reduced by $500 million from the President's request, and is only 2.6% above FY 07, which itself was down by $300 million from the President's FY 07 request. The loss of more than three quarters of a billion dollars for the physical sciences for the Office of Science will never be recovered. Worse, specific areas of science within the physical sciences were marked for major reductions from the President's request. I speak of High Energy Physics for which the enacted FY 08 budget was $63.5 million less than enacted in FY 07, and by $94 million from the President's request for FY 08. Fusion Energy Sciences was reduced by $32.4 million from FY 07, and by $141 million from the President's request for FY 08, zeroing our Nation's contribution to ITER construction. Nuclear Physics was slightly increased by $10 million from FY 07, but cut by $38.6

million from the President's request for FY 08. Finally, the budget for Basic Energy Sciences was increased by $19.7 million from FY 07, but cut by $229 million from the President's request, eliminating funding for basic research energy initiatives such as solar and electrical energy storage."

Orbach acknowledged that the budgets for biological and environmental research and advanced scientific computing research had been augmented above the president's request, but he added: "Nevertheless, the consequences of the FY 2008 Omnibus Bill for the U.S. scientific workforce are substantial. Office of Science funding for Ph.Ds, graduate students, and others was decreased from the President's Request by over 4,300. This at a time when other nations around the world are increasing their scientific workforce. "

Soberingly, and indeed chillingly, Orbach observed that these budget decisions weren't the result of hasty last-minute actions. *They represent the will of the people, as expressed through their elected representatives."*

This last statement, which we've italicized, tragically confirms the bizarre but documentable fact that American culture is dangerously handicapped by a negative attitude toward scientific and technological research. It's a stance that incorporates a spectrum of moods and attitudes, including indifference, a resentment of any basic research that's not clearly linked to quick-fix, short-term, commercially marketable products, a stubborn belief in the myth that scientific and technological innovation will happen by themselves without any great shared effort on our part, and hostility toward the changes and choices that new technologies and scientific discoveries bring. (This hostility can comfortably if illogically co-exist with a willingness, and even eagerness, to enjoy the fruits of scientific and technological research, in the forms of new jobs and convenient gadgets.)

Orbach elaborated: "The American public, through its duly elected Congress, has made its priorities clear: short-term applied research wins over the full spectrum of long-term basic research." It was the job of the scientific community, he said, "to make clear to the American people that our country will 'run out of gas' if the latter is not supported. In the absence of breakthroughs in fundamental science, current technologies will simply not be able to meet the energy and environmental challenges that loom ahead for our Nation. Progress in basic science is essential to America's continued prosperity and strength in the twenty-first century."

It's not clear whether Orbach meant inattention to basic science would make America run out of gas literally or figuratively, but the warning is true in both senses. In an energy sense, we're running out of gasoline and don't have anything of appropriate quality or magnitude waiting to replace it. In a larger and metaphorical but even more important sense, America *will certainly run out of gas as a country if it keeps underfunding scientific and technological research,* because the products of this research underpin the entire economy. Orbach called on scientists "to actively make the case for the support of long-term basic research across those fields that have historically represented U.S. world leadership." U.S. citizens, he said, "must understand that these investments in basic research have held the key to America's prosperity and strength in modern times. As Vannevar Bush wrote to President Truman more than half a century ago: '...without scientific progress no amount of achievement in other directions can insure our health, prosperity, and security as a nation in the modern world.' " (American engineer Vannevar Bush [1890–1974] was a prominent advisor to the U.S. Government on science policy during World War II and after.)

The *really* troubling thing about Orbach's comments is that even *with* the budget increases that President Bush recommended, the U.S. would still be far behind what it should be doing in basic research – not only in physics but across the board. The lag in innovation doesn't apply to just a couple of years of Congressional budgets. It's been going on so long – half a century or more – that it's going to take a gigantic effort to restore it.

This poses interesting questions. One is: how much money are we talking about? Another is: where is this money going to come from?

Now, when a critic of any funding proposal for a large, complicated set of projects seeks to pin you down on exactly how much money you're talking about, it's often just a stalling device, because everybody knows that motivating exact figures for something on this scale takes time, and you can quibble about the decimal points forever. But it's also a legitimate question that can't be dodged. Fortunately there's a reasonable way to provide a short answer which, as it happens, has the added advantage of answering the second question as well, about where the money is supposed to come from.

The short answer to the question of *How Much?* is that scientific and research funding provided by the federal government – including basic research – should be at least as much as that provided for other key areas of government activity. Figures for other such areas are readily available, so we have lots of detailed information to go by. Some of it's very thought-provoking. A March 19, 2008

New York Times article headlined *Estimates of Iraq War Cost Were Not Close to Ballpark,* by David M. Herszenhorn, reported:

"At the outset of the Iraq war, the Bush administration pre- dicted that it would cost $50 billion to $60 billion to oust Saddam Hussein, restore order and install a new government. Getting at the true cost of the war is difficult. Expenses like a troop increase were paid from the base defense budget, not war bills. Five years in, the Pentagon tags the cost of the Iraq war at roughly $600 billion and counting. Joseph E. Stiglitz, a Nobel Prize-winning economist and critic of the war, pegs the long-term cost at more than $4 trillion."[3]

Compare this with the proposed 2009 budget for the National Science Foundation (NSF) -- *$6.85 billion.* (The National Science Foun- dation is a federal agency whose job is to "promote the progress of science; to advance the national health, prosperity, and welfare; to secure the national defense."[4]

Then again, compare the NSF budget with the numbers for the government bailout of financial institutions. A headline that puts these figures into perspective is *Bailout Is As Big as Budget for Penta- gon,* which introduced an article by Alejandro Lazo and Lori Mont- gomery in the Washington Post on September 20, 2008. The piece reported: "The $500 billion that the U.S. government estimates that it will cost to buy the risky investments of financial institutions in coming months approaches what it costs to run the Pentagon for a year. That estimate of the economic rescue plan that Treasury Secretary Henry M. Paulson Jr. announced yesterday is on top of the nearly $200 billion he said earlier this month that he is willing to spend on the government's rescue of Fannie Mae and Freddie Mac.

"The Pentagon budget last year was about $600 billion. Over time, Congress has appropriated a total of about $650 billion for the war in Iraq, plus $200 billion for Afghanistan."[5]

Or compare the NSF budget with the numbers discussed to bail out automobile companies which, arguably, should have updated their technology long ago but failed to do so, ending up asking the taxpayer for relief. On December 20, 2008, a New York Times article headed *Bush Aids Detroit, but Hard Choices Wait for Obama,* by David E. Sanger, David M. Herszenhorn and Bill Vlasic, reported that the emergency bailout of General Motors and Chrysler announced by President Bush would pour $13.4 billion into the troubled compa- nies by mid-January, drawing on the fund that Congress authorized to rescue the financial industry. "In February, another $4 billion will be available for G.M. if the rest of the $700 billion bailout package has been released."[6] Washington's amazing bailouts of huge, failed corporations has, of course, continued into the Obama era, where it is an ongoing saga causing great public anguish and bewilderment.

These examples answer the two questions we posed above. They answer the first question of *How Much?* by showing the levels of government funding that should, by any stretch of reasonable and realistic insight into the needs of the U.S., be allocated to scientific and technological research -- including and emphasizing basic research, from which proceeds knowledge of the most valuable sort: the unexpected kind. And these examples answer the second question, *Where is the money supposed to come from?* as well. *The money is already there.* If we can find the money for foreign wars as costly as the Iraq war, and to bail out poorly managed insurance companies, banks and automobile concerns whose well-paid executives have made poor management decisions or chosen to adhere to obsolete technologies, then we can find the money to obtain new scientific knowledge and innovative, life-saving, job-creating new technologies that will bring *genuine* value to America and the world, instead of subsidizing corporate expense accounts, fancy offices and piles of corporate paper.

To claim otherwise is casuistry -- a position that has no credibility whatsoever.

On the subject of the National Science Foundation's budget, incidentally, it's relevant to point out that the work of this foundation is among the most important being undertaken in America by any institution. We've argued that as the U.S. navigates its way through the 21st century, it will be essential for it to develop a renewed and expanded national commitment to science on every level. Philosophically, the NSF pre-eminently represents the idea that the scientific attitude is deeply rooted in all that is best in America, despite the fact that public appreciation of the meaning of science is far less than it should be.

If we are prepared recognize anew, constantly remind ourselves, that science is infinitely more than a body of facts and instruments, and that it's a cultural force which, if we are to succeed in this century, must pervade all areas of America's national life, we must give the highest possible support to the NSF. If we sincerely accept that science stands for impartial intelligence, for the dignity as well as the authority of the rational intellect, and yes, for a sense of openness and community, then every American must share a national commitment to the NSF's mission.

This mission shows science as resonating with the subtlest and strongest national traits that make America culturally unique and yet, in its very uniqueness, representative of the intellectual treasures of all nations and all peoples. The work of the NSF shows that science represents power over our physical circumstances, as Bacon saw all those centuries ago, but that this is only part of its story. The power it unlocks is at best a hollow one if it is not accompanied by the joy of discovery for the sake of knowing and for fulfilling the age-old human impulse of curiosity: the yearning to learn how the universe works, and, through that knowledge, to draw closer to its mystery and wonder.

These ambitions and assets of the mind are served by many American institutions; they belong to no one fiefdom. Yet, the National Science Foundation is in many ways America's central custodian of them, and if one national entity has a special place in the renewal of reverence for scientific knowledge, innovation and discovery that is America's key to greatness in the 21st century, it is the NSF. Let this foundation be given an increasing voice, not only in government, industry and academe but in the mass media and all the conversations that make up the public spirit in this century of transition.

4. Service the global marketplace.

Globalization has become what is called a "buzz word": a fashionable term that finds its way into speeches, books, articles and pitches by consultants principally because it's fashionable and to refrain from using it would stamp a speaker or writer as out of touch with the latest trends. But what does *globalization* really mean? Does it mean nations are becoming more cooperative? Anyone who reads the news regularly will raise eyebrows at such a claim. Does it mean countries are becoming more alike? It's hard to see how this could be said to be happening in any but the most superficial sense. Does it mean the Internet is now dominating the world's economic and political structures? If so, how, exactly? And how does this relate to the vast amount of economic and political activity that takes place *outside* the arguably narrow circles in which Internet writers and servicers tend to exist?

These questions, and many more like them, indicate the foggy nature of the term "globalization", which seems to represent the current stage of world history less as a photograph represents reality than as a cartoon does. And cartoons often tell us more about those who drew and bought them than about the realities they purport to describe.

Thus, the real value of the word "globalization" may reside less in what it tells us about what's happening in the world today than about what we like to *think* is happening, or what we *want* (or fear) to see happening. In this spirit, what does the great popularity of globalization talk in America today tell us, not about the world, but about America?

One answer is that globalization is so widespread a reference in current American discourse because American leaders of thought, industry, culture and public policy have been sensing increasingly in recent years the truth to which our Proposition One, above, is a response: that America's leadership role in the world has receded (if not crumbled) and deserves to be restored.

This interpretation runs counter to much popular discourse. In the prevailing wisdom, globalization seems often to be regarded as a mystical force of history of the kind that 19th-century German philosophers like Hegel and Marx believed shaped human destiny. However, for better or worse, the world is really far from unification, economically or in any other sense, although the need for global perspectives in policymaking is great. This means there's a need for global leadership in the sense that we described in Proposition one above.

Since knowledge leadership translates into economic effects, this means America must think economically in terms of servicing the global economy. All that the U.S. does economically on a national scale must be geared to this requirement. It's insufficient for U.S. government agencies, companies and other institutions to look inward and content themselves with servicing a domestic market. Even the principle of global competitiveness needs to be revised, because competition implies a level playing field, whereas America's technological history, coupled with the current state of technological development worldwide, means that *America's international role (regardless of how effectively it has been fulfilling it) is that of Global Technological Engine.*

If we accept America's role as the world's primary exporter of innovative knowledge in the 21st century, and if also accept a need to enter into new kinds of partnership, it follows that America must look to a new era of international business partnerships. Not just trade treaties as we've seen them in the past, and not only the encouragement by government of international business deals concluded by the private sector, but truly international projects launched by government, with the involvement of the U.S. Government, foreign corporations and U.S. corporations. Such projects must be aimed at generating two kinds of product: physical products suitable for international consumption, and knowledge products in the form of research and development outputs and expertise provided by the U.S. to international partners. Only in this way will America be able to assume a genuine role as a builder of a global economy. And only in this way can the nation develop a global community in a way which will be truly consistent with American interests.

These interests will be served in at least five key ways. First, by crafting cross-border enterprises in which America is the source of critical expertise, including mentoring, American companies will secure equity in international projects and accrue income that will flow into America from foreign sources.

Second, by having the U.S. Government occupy the role of orchestrator and primary investor in such enterprises, government will be in a position to stipulate that a healthy proportion of all revenue flowing back to the U.S. from such enterprises must be invested in the creation and maintenance of jobs on U.S. soil occupied by U.S. nationals.

Third, by servicing the global economy in a way that builds economic structures throughout the world, America will avoid the mistake once perpetrated by colonial powers, whereby a mother country enriched itself at the expense of colonies which were forbidden to acquire and exercise expertise. America will rather be empowering workers throughout the world while at the same enhancing the standard of living of citizens of other countries by providing a broad range of goods tailored to local needs. These actions will make for a stable and healthy community of nations, which is much in America's interest, especially if the U.S.'s global leadership role is accepted as a reality for the foreseeable future.

Fourth, the goodwill that these actions can reasonably be expected to generate will be of incalculable value to America, geopolitically, economically and in other ways.

Fifth, these initiatives will greatly enrich America's intellectual capital, since a natural result of the export of American intellectual, financial, technological, professional and management expertise is likely to be the recruitment of the best and brightest minds in other countries, to help run these partnership enterprises in both their native countries and in their American offices. So the export of American knowledge will result in a vigorous exchange of intellectual assets, and in the infusion into American industry and culture of the most dynamic perspectives and intellectual energies of other nations. Of such infusions have the best American accomplishments of previous generations been made, so in this process a long tradition of American strength will be renewed.

This notion of globalization requires a substantial change in America's current approach to the world order. It also means changes of attitude and policy within the American Government itself. No such dispensation as is outlined above will be attainable unless the Department of State is involved, since what we're suggesting is a concerted American diplomatic effort. This won't entail diplomacy as normally conceived but in a manner that is reconceived to achieve business partnerships of vast scope. Indeed, a new era in cooperation between several government agencies involved in economic development is implied. Additionally, these objectives will not be achievable unless American immigration policy is effectively overhauled, allowing the unimpeded flow of honest contributors to American well-being into the United States. This will not be a price to pay, but a dividend for America to reap.

5. Improve U.S. education and respect for basic science – and start by convincing the public why this must be done.

In 2005 the National Academies Press, based in Washington, DC, published a report called

Rising Above the Gathering Storm: Energizing and Employing America for a Brighter Economic Future.

It called for the U.S. to

(a) vastly improve mathematics and science education from kindergarten through high school,

(b) strengthen the nation's commitment to long-term basic research,

(c) develop, recruit, and retain top students, scientists, and engineers from the U.S. and abroad, and

(d) ensure that U.S. world leadership in innovation.

The report was updated in 2007 and 2008. The July 2008 revisions stated:

* that fewer than a third of U.S. 8th-graders were proficient in math,

* *that about a fifth of U.S. 4th graders and a third of 8th graders knew even basic math,*

* that in 1999, 69% of U.S. 5th-8th-graders had math teachers lacking a degree or certification in math,

* that in 2000, 93% of 5th–8th-graders had physical science teachers lacking a major or certification in the physical sciences,

* *that in 2003 U.S. 15-year-olds ranked 27th out of 39 countries*

participating in the Program for International Student Assessment (PISA) examination, which assessed students' ability to apply math to real-world problems,

* that the proportion of bachelor's degrees in physics to total degrees awarded in 2004 *was half that of 1956 (the year before Sputnik),* which was considered a time of dangerous educational neglect,

* that in 2001, *U.S. industry spent more on tort litigation than on research,* that federal funding of research in the physical sciences, as a percentage of gross domestic product (GDP), was 45% less in fiscal year 2004 than in fiscal year 1976, and

* that the amount invested annually by the U.S. federal government in research in the physical sciences, mathematics, and engineering combined *equals the annual increase in U.S. health-care costs incurred every six weeks.*

These statistics should alarm anyone who cares about America's future, economic or otherwise. The concept of American companies spending more on lawsuits than on research is a frightening commentary on American society. Accordingly, it's not unreasonable to suppose that this report would, on its first release, have brought about major changes in American policy, becoming the country's Number One talking point in the mass media, dominating radio talk shows and newspaper and television headlines.

But it didn't.

The message preached by *Rising Above the Gathering Storm* received a respectful reception from its own choir of technology wonks, among whose circles it continues to be deferentially referenced as a landmark statement of its kind. But not even its most worshipful admirers can credibly hold that it has revolutionized American culture or national American attitudes to the funding of scientific research and education, or that it has even made a dent in national awareness of these subjects. A Google search for "RISING ABOVE THE GATHERING STORM" on February 4, 2009, yielded 36 800 references, whereas a search for "PARIS HILTON" yielded 79 600 000. It seems reasonable, and not unduly disrespectful, to wonder how many people outside a fairly specialized policy elite have even heard of the report.

In fairness, the man and woman in the street don't read technical medical papers either. But presumably a technical medical report announcing a cure for cancer would trigger sufficient media attention to ensure that a broad mass of the population became aware of it. So who is to blame for the fact that *Rising Above The Gathering Storm* isn't being discussed in bars, diners and talk shows across the nation?

The answer to this is that blame is hardly an appropriately diagnostic tool for something so pervasive. History shows that when fundamental aspects of a culture need overhauling, one of the least productive things you can do is look for a scapegoat – some professional, commercial or other group who is painted as the villain. *The fact is that all Americans currently old enough and intellectually competent to vote are complicit in the shocking state of scientific and technological innovation and their respective support structures in research and education.* To the extent that there is responsibility for leading the country in a new direction, therefore (and it's more constructive to talk about this that about culpability), it falls, in a democracy, on the people's chosen government to take at least a central leadership or orchestrative role.

To do this, more is going to be necessary than to issue weighty reports in judicial language whose press releases say things like: "In a world where advanced knowledge is widespread and low-cost labor is readily available, U.S. advantages in the marketplace and in science and technology have begun to erode. A comprehensive and coordinated federal effort is urgently needed to bolster U.S. competitiveness and pre-eminence in these areas." If the U.S. Government seriously wishes to embark on a new era in the funding of scientific research and education, it's necessary to sell this objective to the American people. *The cultural alteration that's called for is seismic.*

Because of this, it's misleading and misguided to over-use the Manhattan Project model, as some have fashionably begun to do.[7] The "Manhattan Project model" invokes World War II's Manhattan Project, which developed the atomic bomb, as an example of the kind of massively financed, highly organized, top-priority government project that we need to solve 21st-century problems like climate change and alternative energy sourcing. However, while the Manhattan Project may illustrate the kind of resources we need to bring to bear, there's a big difference between that project and our current scientific and technological objectives.

The Manhattan Project was conducted in secret. Its management, including the vast resources that the U.S. Government poured into it (which included the construction of entire towns in out-of-the way areas), was kept a closely-guarded secret until the end of the war. *This is the exact opposite of what we need to achieve now.*

Neither distinguished reports circulated among the elect nor secret government projects are suited to either the goals or the political and cultural conditions that prevail today.

The Manhattan Project was launched as a subsidiary of a public communications enterprise that the U.S. Government had already successful waged, namely U.S. entry into World War II and the total commitment of the U.S. to the defeat of Hitler and his cohorts. Thus, the *reasons* for the Manhattan project were largely understood and accepted by the public. Today we have no such bloc of public belief. Public appreciation of the reasons to raise our scientific and technological capabilities seems negligible. This fact is reflected in the budgets allocated to science and technology by Congress.

What is needed, therefore, is for the Executive Branch of the U.S. Government to *communicate a sense of urgency to the nation* – to voters and their elected representatives – that is equivalent to the sense of urgency inherent in a state of war.

The Executive Branch must communicate to the people of the United States that the national scientific and technological agenda *is, indeed, a war.*

It's a different kind of war from that waged in Iraq and Vietnam and against Hitler. But it's a war nevertheless: a war on our scientific, educational and technological shortcomings and weaknesses, and on the current effects of our technological and public policy mistakes of the past. This war shares at least some key characteristics of other wars. It's about *survival* – not only America's, but the world's. It has a *moral motivation*, since it seeks a victory that will benefit all peoples. It has an *insidious enemy* who operates invisibly among us: *ignorance.*

One of the forms this enterprise must take is the conduct of the biggest publicity campaign in U.S. history. Its aim must be to persuade the American people that:

* High standards in scientific education and research are *not* alien to the U.S. but are *integral to its values and to its interests, fulfillment and survival as a nation.*

* *Basic* research, like education, is essential to applied research, and long-term scientific projects, pure scientific curiosity, and the pursuit of knowledge for its own sake, are the surest path to practically usable technological deliverables. These provide the stem capabilities from which flows all applied technological innovation.

* The university and the school must regain their positions as the centers of our culture as both custodians and generators

of knowledge, and government and industry alike must look afresh upon universities as knowledge factories from which all of the real wealth of America proceeds.

6. Focus on building a new American infrastructure, rather than on just rebuilding the old one.

In May 2008 the magazine *Popular Mechanics* published a report titled *Rebuilding America Special Report: How to Fix U.S. Infrastructure* (by Erik Sofge and The Editors of *Popular Mechanics*[8].

Its opening paragraph proclaimed that "American infrastructure is in trouble, from collapsed bridges to leaking dams," adding that to fix it the country needed "fresh ideas, smart engineering and new technology".

Like *Rising Above The Gathering Storm, Rebuilding America* made disturbing reading. "Americans," it declared, "need to face the sobering reality that the country's infrastructure is in trouble. Most of it was built in the 20th century, during the greatest age of construction the world has seen. The continent was wired for electricity and phone service, and colossal projects, including the Hoover Dam, the Golden Gate Bridge and the interstate highway system, were completed—along with thousands of smaller bridges, water tunnels and more. We are living off an inheritance of steel-and-concrete wonders, grander than anything built by Rome, constructed by everyday giants bearing trowels, welding torches and rivet guns."

According to the report, the American Society of Civil Engineers had estimated that fixing the nation's infrastructure – "from dilapidated levees to congested roadways and ports" – would cost $1.6 trillion over five years, or $120 billion per year. The amount sounds astronomical until you read that the U.S. Government's February 2008 economic stimulus package provided $168 billion to individuals to spend, as *Popular Mechanics* put it, "in a best-case scenario, on new TVs and restaurant meals."

The report noted that "New information technology, fresh engineering and advanced materials can help us not just restore, but improve our infrastructure in the coming century. Planned and managed properly, next-gen projects can be smarter and more resilient than what came before." But perhaps the most important point in the report are these sentences:

* "Engineers and construction workers know how to get the job done. But first, *we must gather the national will.*"

* "While more funds are needed, *how they're spent is equally important.*"

In both the above points the italics are ours.

While the need to rebuild America physically must surely be obvious to anyone who looks at the state and age of the country's increasing obsolete infrastructure, it's essential to rebuild with the right goals. This includes a need to act on appropriate lessons of history. As we've seen, an often-quoted example cited in discussions of enormous, government-backed technology projects is the Manhattan Project, which is indeed a valuable case study to take account – provided one contextualizes it properly and doesn't overlook, for instance, that it was essentially a secret project, which limits its applicability to the kinds of public project we need today. Similarly, two historical examples that loom large in our imaginations when we consider great infrastructural projects are the Apollo Space Program, which put Americans on the Moon, and the New Deal public works agenda of President Franklin Delano Roosevelt.

Of course, the Apollo Program wasn't an infrastructure-building enterprise. If anything, it could be seen as the opposite of that, taking funds away from infrastructure-building (although whether those funds would have been used for infrastructural innovation if they hadn't been used for the space effort is highly debatable). But the Apollo Program is relevant to infrastructure-building for two reasons, one positive and two negative.

On the positive side it showed that the federal government can marshal great financial and morale resources in a superbly organized way, and to do so in a way that captures the public imagination, when the political leadership of the country makes up its mind to do so. This is highly relevant today because it is precisely what the U.S. needs to do now in committing itself to a new era of scientific and technological growth. It is also what the U.S. now needs to do in order to rebuild the country's infrastructure. Apollo represents the kind of political will that *Popular Mechanics* correctly referred to in its report as a prerequisite for infrastructural renewal.

A negative reason for Apollo's current relevance, on the other hand, is that although America's space effort has persisted beyond Apollo, it can hardly be said to have continued at anything like the level of governmental or national enthusiasm that attended the first Moon landing. Space science has rather had to wage a constant struggle to retain its funding, which has been at best grudgingly allocated. So we can find in Apollo a cautionary lesson about political stamina and the need for long-term versus short-term vision and national commitment. Despite the rhetoric that accompanied it, Apollo was to a significant extent, as we've seen, a stunt undertaken less for the long-term sake of science than for short-term political objectives related to the Cold War.

But the infrastructural mission on which America needs to embark can't be seen as a short-term project. It would be very dangerous to do so. We can't afford to see this mission as something which will be self-contained and done within a span of a few years. The relatively short claim that Apollo really had on America's national attention span thus teaches us what we should avoid rather than emulate when we think about ushering in a new era of technology that will include infrastructural renewal.

This aspect of the Apollo program is connected with yet another of the many apparent paradoxes of technology. On the one hand, the dynamics of our marketing culture have accustomed us to value projects which are completed *fast*, giving marketers a frequent turnover of new products. We naturally tend to impose this same value on technological projects, even when the research needs that go with them can only be met by longer-term efforts and budgets.

On the other hand, cultural history has accustomed us to value projects that *last*, like the buildings of ancient Rome and Greece that still survive today, and the pyramids of Egypt. These values pull us in opposing directions, and this may be healthy, since the opposition encourages us to find a middle path between *durability* and *transience* in our cultural artifacts. It also encourages us to find ways to tell the difference between contexts in which each of these two values has its legitimate place.

As far as technological innovation in the 21st century is concerned, this polarization seems paradoxical not only because it contains an apparent contradiction but because our contemporary need for innovation demands values over and above these. To yield the kinds of technological solution we need in the 21st century, our innovation must indeed take immediate pressures into account, *but it's unrealistic to see it as a short-term mission.* We've reached a stage in our technological history at which we can't expect to introduce a range of new technologies in a short span of time, such as in a five-year or ten-year plan, and expect these to see us through for decades to come. *In the 21st century there will be no final technological destinations*, and perhaps not even any long-term ones, taking "long-term" to mean results that will last a generation or more, as the technological bounty of the early 20th century encouraged us to expect. Quick fixes are out of the question, and still less can we expect to create technological monuments that will last for the ages.

In entering the 21st- century era of infrastructural renewal we must accept that *it is not only our artifacts that we have to renew but our attitude to those artifacts.* We have to create a new culture of ongoing technological renewal that is committed to painstaking and perennial innovation. Innovation must become a way of American life that is not predicated only on short-term market needs nor on the expectation that any technological output will ever be done once and for all. *We must become innovators for the long, long haul.*

The other negative reason why Apollo is relevant to our infrastructural condition is related to the above considerations but are subtly separate from them. As a national technological enterprise, Apollo was flawed because its short-term political goal eclipsed not only technological effectiveness but the real long-term motives that are necessary to all true scientific advance, which underpins and conditions technological progress. As one commentator on Kennedy's decision has put it, the space race "was not about science. It was about who would create the future, and JFK decided that ownership of the future was worth just about any risk."[9]

But while this statement accurately notes that the space race wasn't about science, it's not quite true that it was about the future. It's more accurate to say it was about the *present* as Kennedy saw it. But there's no meaningful sense in which a short-term political objective can be realistically regarded as being about the future in the same way that pure science is about the future, and it's highly questionable whether Kennedy was concerned with pure science. This is not to disrespect his legacy, since the fact that he backed the space program at all, for whatever motive, is a fine tribute to his memory for which the world will always owe him a debt of gratitude. But it's important in the 21st century to accept that *neither America's interests nor the world's will be served by any infrastructural program that does not support basic research and the development of pure science,* as part of a vision to keep America's infrastructure in a state of constant renewal.

Similar considerations apply to the New Deal public works agenda of President Franklin Delano Roosevelt, which, like the Apollo program, casts a long shadow over contemporary discussions of infrastructural renewal. Economic historians and commentators continue to debate the real effects of Roosevelt's actions, some seeing Roosevelt as a savior of the country and others regarding his program as a wasteful exercise that may not have helped America out of the Depression as much as some have claimed.

These debates will persist, because it's in the nature of both history and politics to encourage the regular revisiting of great historical events from ideological and other perspectives. But one thing that seems quite clear is that apart, perhaps, from its size and scope, the New Deal wasn't as good a model for 21st-century infra-structural renewal as it may at first glance seem to be.

Roosevelt's program wasn't geared to usher America into a new technological era but rather to extend the existing infrastructure. It's also questionable whether Roosevelt gave any substantial impetus to scientific advance other than the Manhattan Project. So here again, it's important to ensure that when we seek to learn from the past, we learn the right lessons.

Infrastructural renewal cannot be productively undertaken in response to 21st-century challenges unless it goes hand in hand with efforts to reverse the erosion of science in the U.S.

This erosion was summarized afresh in a report headed *U.S. Experts Bemoan Nation's Loss of Stature in the World of Science*, by Keith B. Richburg, in *The Washington Post* of May 29, 2008. It began: "Some of the nation's leading scientists, including Secretary of State Condoleezza Rice's top science adviser, today sharply criticized the diminished role of science in the United States and the shortage of federal funding for research, even as science becomes increasingly important to combating problems such as climate change and the global food shortage. Speaking at a science summit that opens this week's first World Science Festival, the expert panel of scientists, and audience members, agreed that the United States is losing stature because of a perceived high-level disdain for science."

The report quoted biologist and Nobel Prizewinner David Baltimore, board chairman of the American Association for the Advancement of Science, as stating: "I think there's a loss of American power and prestige that came about as a result of our anti-science policies ... What we need is leadership that respects science."

According to the *Post*, the panelists expressed concern about the absence of science funding from presidential campaigning in 2008, while molecular biologist Nina Fedoroff, Rice's science and technology adviser, said science in the U.S. "has really kind of died over a quarter of a century, even as the importance of science has grown."[10]

It's an overstatement to say science has died in the U.S. But as a figure of speech conveying the gravity of America's situation, it's apt, and directly relevant to the decisions that must be made about rebuilding America's infrastructure. For if infrastructural renewal isn't conceived and implemented side by side with the re-energizing of scientific innovation, America's ability to generate new technologies may well die. That will be catastrophic, for such technologies are critically needed not only to breathe new life into the U.S.'s infrastructure but to ensure that its health is sustained in a rapidly changing world.

7. Introduce a national smart grid.

As our Proposition Number Six we've proposed that the U.S. should focus on building a new American infrastructure, rather than on just rebuilding the old one. This is a policy recommendation that relates to the *spirit* in which the country should go about infrastructure renewal. Since we've argued that the effectiveness of technology is critically shaped by philosophical motivation, it follows that we see the spirit in which infrastructure renewal is undertaken as being extremely important. This is why we've made it a proposition in its own right, separate from any particular infrastructural priority. But the *chief infrastructural tasks* that America prioritizes will of course be no less important. Rather, these priorities will not only translate the philosophy into action but will illustrate implications for other needed tasks. Thus, our Propositions Seven through Nine are specific infrastructural missions.

If the U.S. commits itself to these key goals of infrastructural renewal, it will be well on the way to creating a new technological era, since these tasks don't involve merely extending existing or obsolete technologies: if achieved, they will usher in a *genuinely renewed infrastructure,* incorporating technologies which are not only innovative but will also signal a new age of national innovation commitment. The order in which these tasks are listed here don't indicate their respective importance – each is immensely important to the U.S.

We begin with the need to introduce a national smart grid. We've spoken in earlier pages of the change from analog to digital technology, of how this change grew out of some of the most fundamental scientific and technological advances of the 20th century, and of the sweeping implications of our need to introduce digital technologies and digital thinking throughout our society. One of the most important areas in which this must be done is America's electrical power grid. It's sobering to consider that the U.S. has entered the 21st century with a national electrical management system whose origins lie in the 19th century, with the so-called Battle of the Currents between Thomas Edison and Nikola Tesla at the Columbian Exposition.

Changing the country's power grid is long overdue, and is necessary for many reasons including economic, environmental and even symbolic considerations. Since electricity is the lifeblood of the economy, it's essential to America's national well-being in the 21st century for this commodity, perhaps above all others, to be delivered, distributed and managed via the most advanced techno-logical systems that are achievable. In our time, this means digital systems. Moreover, it's a cultural anomaly for the national electri-cal grid, the hub of the country's economic, governmental and civil life, to be managed in any way less than state-of-the-art, if America seriously wants to be perceived as the world's technological leader. Symbolically, there can be few more effective ways to signal de-termination to lead the world technologically than to introduce a national smart grid.

The basic idea of a smart grid is to use computerization to in-crease the efficiency of electrical distribution. A simple illustration is the introduction of monitoring devices that would enable a pow-er provider to know more quickly and accurately when and where outages occur, instead of waiting for customers to call it in. A fully implemented smart grid would enable not only the power com-pany but also its customers to know how much electricity they're using, when and for what, adjusting their consumption according to their needs and preferences.

Think about it. If you buy gasoline periodically, looking at the changing price at the gas station, it's hard *not* to be aware of how much you're spending on gas. Even the least financially organized of us can hardly fail to be aware of those price signs as we drive up, and of the amount of our hard-earned cash we pay each time we fill up. Similarly with supermarkets. Anyone who shops regularly for their own groceries gets a feel for how much they're spend-ing (or overspending) on various product categories. Similarly with clothing. You have a budget and when you go out to supplement your wardrobe you know how much you want to spend on shoes and how much on pants and you make your decisions based on the price tags you see.

But electricity just comes into your home. How much electric-ity did you buy today? In the morning? In the afternoon? How much power did your computer use? Who knows? The bills just come and we pay them, if we can. But imagine you were keeping an alert eye on how much the price of electricity varied through-out the day (as it does) or from one part of the year to another (as it does), or even from room to room and even from appliance to appliance in your house. The odds are you'd not only become as aware of power prices as you are of gas prices but would also be able to translate this awareness into cost savings through informed choices. Or perhaps you'd be glad to instruct the power company to monitor your power consumption and manage it for you so as to get you the most efficient possible usage, thus cutting your bills.

The technology to implement such cost-cutting measures, through the use of computerized monitoring and management of power consumption, is available. A *CNET News* item published on January 9, 2008, headed *GridWise trial finds 'smart grids' cut electricity bills*, by Martin LaMonica, reported: "Results from a year-long study on high-tech electricity meters found smart grid technology performed as intended, saving consumers about 10 percent on their bills while easing strain on the power grid.

"The Department of Energy's Pacific Northwest Laboratory on Wednesday released the findings from its GridWise project, which tested the use of Internet-connected thermostats and other controls in 112 homes in the Seattle area. Consumers also tried out appliances, like water heaters and dryers, that were able to automatically change their settings according to signals sent by the utility over the power grid. The trial showed that consumers are willing to have utilities remotely dial down the appliances to lessen the load on the power grid and reduce their consumption, said Rob Pratt, program manager at Pacific Northwest National Lab."

These changes, according to the report, might be as seemingly negligible as having the dryer's heat automatically switched off while it continues to tumble for a few minutes. But the cost implications of such apparently small measures mount up. The *CNET* story quotes Pratt as stating: "We could save $70 billion in investments in the next 20 years by offsetting construction of new infrastructure that would otherwise be needed to meet load growth."

The study found smart grid technology would also provide more reliability to the power grid, allowing utilities to identify and locate problems more easily. Clean power sources like wind and solar, which need special technological handling because they don't generate power evenly, can be integrated into the nation's electricity grid more effectively with smart grid equipment.

As of the researching of this book (2008), high-level political and governmental support for smart grid implementation *seems* significant. But we know from the history of both politics and technology that supportive statements from government agencies and politicians don't necessarily turn into supportive actions. Campaign rhetoric often proves to be just that and no more. Promising-sounding statements by government agency leaders often turn out to be just publicity material issued for short-term strategic objectives. Even the most sincere government statements of intent have a way of vanishing into the mists of bureaucracy and/or the labyrinths of horse-trading in Congress. Then there are the utility companies, who have profits, losses, investment risks and government subsidies to consider, all of which, understandably, affect their decisions about how cooperative to be with initiatives that may be good for the country at the expense of inconveniencing them or exposing them to what they may regard as unacceptable risk. For all change, no matter how clearly benign in intent and likely result, brings inconvenience and at least some risk to at least some people.

Nevertheless, it's vital for the White House, preferably with the full support of Congress, to take the lead in motivating and guiding both the utility companies and their consumers in making a swift and unimpeded transition from the present antiquated and unaffordable national grid to a smart grid suited to the 21st century. The country is ready to this and urgently needs to do it, using computer technologies that are now available and others that can be developed if the political will to do so is decisively exerted.

8. Go nuclear while simultaneously launching a determined national effort to create a new alternative energy industry.

Our previous proposition, Number Seven, calls for implementation of a highly computerized national system to manage our *distribution* of electricity. Introducing such a grid will undoubtedly strengthen the U.S.'s national position as an energy consumer and manager. But to work optimally, it will have to go hand in hand with a much more effective energy *production* policy. Otherwise America will be like a merchandiser who designs and builds the best possible shopping mall to sell his wares without bothering about where those goods are going to come from. Effective energy management is only one side of the coin. The other is effective energy production.

What do we mean by effective energy production? Against the background of the U.S.'s energy experiences in recent years, this means an energy policy that meets several important requirements. One is *environmental acceptability.* That is, we must produce power that doesn't damage the complex ecology of the planet more than we've already damaged it. In fact, we don't just have to stop damaging the planet: we must do everything we can to *reverse* the damage already done.

Another requirement is that we must produce *affordable* energy, since it's hardly going to be productive to introduce an energy source that's environmentally clean but unaffordable by householders or businesses.

Thirdly, the U.S. needs energy resources that can be *controlled from within the country,* or, if they're international, are at least not subject to hostile control by cartels that might choose to hold the country to ransom by manipulating prices, or by interests which might, for political reasons, decide to make it difficult or impossible for the U.S. to gain access to energy resources on any legitimate market basis.

To achieve the above objectives the U.S. must adopt an energy policy that encompasses several simultaneous steps, each pursued with powerful national determination. These steps can be simply summarized: America must (a) introduce *nuclear power* on a wide scale across the nation while simultaneously (b) launching a determined, government-led effort to create a vigorous *alternative energy* industry, and (c) taking prudent action to release *the last commercially viable reserves of petroleum* on which much of our present economy is dependent.

Like all simple statements recommended to governments, this summary's simplicity is deceptive. As anyone with any knowledge of American politics must know, it implies a labyrinth of commercial and political nuances and negotiations between the private sector and the various institutions of government. But it would be equally deceptive to hide behind these complexities. To invoke them to pretend that there are no fertile truths that can be simply stated, or that the red tape and conflicts between different interest groups are so difficult that to all intents and purposes the proposition we've stated here is impracticable, would be playing with words.

Much of our message in this book has been that it will always be possible to find many reasons why great undertakings are too complicated to be undertaken. Yet, experience has shown that where there's sufficient will, the simplicity of a great objective can override a vast number of complications raised by nay-sayers. While the Apollo Program isn't a perfect model for the tasks now confronting the U.S., it certainly did and does illustrate this point. The director of President Kennedy's own Science Advisory Committee, Jerome B. Wiesner, advised him to cancel Project Mercury, the beginning of the manned space program, for a variety of reasons. But Kennedy countered all these reasons with a simple statement of political will. *"We choose,"* he said, *"to go to the Moon."*

Similar choices of political will, stated with simplicity and conviction, have brought about great changes in civil rights in the face of arguments from nay-sayers who maintained that such changes were unthinkable because of their complexity. America must now bring to its energy needs the same ability to express national political will in response to simply stated national requirements, regardless of the complexity of the tools needed to get the job done.

Implementing the above tasks will make real technological and national policy sense *if and only if they are accepted as inherently interrelated.* In our previous proposition we noted that the introduction of a national smart grid will, among other things, help integrate some alternative energy sources into the grid. Similarly, it's necessary to accept that each of the above energy tasks isn't a separate enterprise but an interlocking part of a single mission to make the U.S. both energy-independent and energy-efficient. Weakness in any one of the tasks weakens the overall mission; effectiveness in any one of the tasks strengthens the mission, but only to the extent that each task is seen as part of an integrated whole.

An example of this integration is the connection between hydrogen power and nuclear power. Supported by appropriate research and development, nuclear technology has the capability to produce hydrogen cost-effectively as an environmentally clean byproduct in sufficient quantity to make hydrogen use a mainstay of the U.S. economy. The production of hydrogen on a wide, efficient scale via nuclear technology has enormous industrial implications. Hydrogen is used to refine crude oil into economically viable fuel and to manufacture thousands of consumer products. Perhaps most importantly, it offers great potential as a direct source of transportation power in the form of hydrogen combustion engines and hydrogen fuel cells to power automobiles with zero pollutants. This automotive technology will be vastly superior to both the hybrid cars that are now available and the plug-in electrically-powered vehicles now in development.

Hydrogen is a tantalizing component of our energy landscape. Unlike petroleum, which has to be sought out in special environments, it's everywhere around us, being a fundamental building-block of matter, including water. But chemically releasing hydrogen from naturally available sources with current technologies tends to be expensive and/or to produce greenhouse gases, which we don't want since they contribute to our environmental problems. Nuclear technology, on the other hand, has potential to mass-produce hydrogen without releasing greenhouse gases. But to achieve this a determined research and development effort is necessary. It's essential that this is adequately funded and pursued with a top-priority commitment.

While nuclear power has the potential to facilitate the birth of a hydrogen economy if we apply a sufficiently strong research and development effort to it, it's also a direct energy source capable of contributing crucially to U.S. energy self-reliance. This can't happen overnight. It will take several decades to build enough nuclear power stations across the U.S. to meet national needs. During this time research must be done to create new ways to treat spent nuclear fuel. *But the weaker the U.S.'s commitment to roll these actions out, and the more it shies away from funding them, the longer it will take.* There must be a *massive* commitment to make the U.S. nuclear, now.

If there are any areas at all in which a wartime sense of urgency must prevail, this is one. While no method of producing and distributing energy in great quantity is without challenges, nuclear power is remarkably safe, secure, readily available, environmentally clean and cost-efficient relative to other energy options. America must end its political and public relations vendetta against nuclear power. It's costing the country heavily to allow it to endure.

Alongside a drive to build new nuclear power stations across the nation, the U.S. must launch a vigorous research campaign to develop new energy sources, not only in such widely discussed areas as solar and wind power but also in categories like the search for new hydrocarbon fuels which we'll be able to use for their energy value without burning them, perhaps applying this same technology to existing petroleum stocks. Then there's oil shale extraction, a process that produces synthetic crude oil out of rock. The rock, oil shale, is a chemical cousin of the crude oil that's more familiar to us, but it has to be converted into usable liquid form technologically. This technology exists and is being used in several countries, including the U.S., but it needs research and development work to come up with a production process that's both more cost-effective and more environmentally acceptable than what we presently have.

Finally, the U.S. must deal more effectively with the petroleum reserves already available to it in its adjacent oceans and Alaska. This doesn't mean charging in thoughtlessly and drilling in ways that will damage the oceanic environment and ruin one of the most valuable wildernesses left to the U.S. and the world. It would be a policy disaster, a global environmental error of staggering proportions and a national tragedy for the U.S. if the country were to define its role in the 21st century by exacerbating the extensive damage already done to the ocean by pollutants and by ruining even a significant part of one of the world's most important remaining wildlife habitats. Instead, the U.S. must look at the remaining reserves of Alaskan and seabed oil as not just a commercial opportunity but a technological challenge to which America's intellectual resources must rise. The country that put humankind on the Moon must surely be capable of harnessing sufficient research resources to find ways to extract these remaining petroleum reserves without unacceptable environmental damage.

This is a mission that the U.S. must undertake and successfully complete if it is to demonstrate energy independence while at the same time maintaining the high moral ground as a protector and not despoiler of the environment. Here, as with all the challenges we've enumerated, technological ingenuity is the key. To unlock ingenuity it's necessary first to deploy political will and a research budget adequate to the task.

9. Commit to a radically new national mass transit system.

We've spoken of the need to integrate all parts of the national energy and infrastructure-renewal mission. A new national mass transit system must take shape at the heart of this program. It must not only be new, but, as the above headline suggests, *radically* new. Few things will differentiate an infrastructurally renewed 21st-century America from 20th-century America as powerfully as a mass transit system characterized by the efficiency, speed, convenience, technological sophistication and aesthetic of a new age.

The nation's mission to redefine its energy use will be incomplete without also redefining the transportation systems that consume so much of our energy output. To do this meaningfully, America must leave behind it, as an image to be associated forever with the 20th century, its dependence on a national highway system designed for long-distance automotive travel in slow, expensive and environmentally destructive vehicles. It must also relegate to the history books the age of congested airports serviced by ponderous aircraft which are, in effect, flying automobiles. These cumbersome behemoths, which transfer the environmental, time-management, cost and other inefficiencies of the automobile to the sky, don't belong in 21st-century America as a means of transcontinental mass transit. Nor do the rumbling railroads of yesteryear, which served America well from their inception in the 19th century but which must now be consigned to the museums where they belong.

To replace the era of these creaking giants of road, air and rail, America must create a new skyline. The country must be crisscrossed from coast to coast by a magnetic levitation rail system that will be one of the wonders of the 21st-century world and a model for other nations. Comfortable, environmentally clean and rapid beyond the reach of any conventional 20th-century mass conveyance, *maglev will liberate the population of the U.S.* geographically, recreationally and in terms of livelihood and lifestyle options. This new era of cheap countrywide mobility will have massively positive effects on the economy. It will be like having the economic benefits that flowed from the invention of the automobile all over again, but offering much greater speed and comfort at far less cost and without the pollution. The socio-economically unifying and energizing effect on the country will be of a magnitude not seen in America since the introduction of the transcontinental railroad system in the 19th century.

This effect will be compounded by the provision of broadband telecommunications service to every community. While national access to sophisticated broadband will be profoundly important, maglev will unite the country physically in a way with which virtual unification can't really compete. But the two forms of unification will complement each other powerfully.

Psychologically, these gains will have a price tag, since the sense of vast distance that has historically been an intrinsic part of U.S. identity will disappear. But in its place will come scope to offer all Americans the opportunity to identify themselves with not just one or two parts of the country's physical and cultural landscapes but with the total nation. For many Americans, most of their own country is still today, and has long been, as remote as a foreign land. Maglev will end that. Traveling across the country will change from being a rare occurrence, limited to career changes and long-planned vacations, to a common experience. Tourism and all its support activities will boom. As maglev and broadband increase the range of employment options open to U.S. workers, the real estate industry will flourish anew as it becomes possible for employers in highly populated metropolitan areas to take on staff in locales which had previously been outside the employability perimeter because of long commuting times. One result will be a new ruralism, since Americans will be able to live in places previously undeveloped because of their remoteness.

Doubtless some will see this as an undesirable further encroachment on wilderness. But there's no reason why it shouldn't be an excellent thing environmentally. Maglev and telecommunications will bring about a great redistribution of America's population, relieving environmental and infrastructural pressures on overcrowded metropolitan regions. It will make practicable, for the first time, a regional approach to community planning of an unprecedentedly thoughtful and environmentally sensitive kind advocated in the 20th century by environmentalists like Lewis Mumford, but impeded by the limited, highly centralized industrial and lifestyle options afforded by 20th-century infrastructural technologies.

Despite the great difference in size between the populations of the 21ˢᵗ, 20ᵗʰ and 19ᵗʰ centuries, America will experience a sense of space and breathing room unknown for generations. Small towns, with their charm, lore leisurely pace and distinctive qualities of life, will become a feature of America again as physical and cultural entities distinct from cities and bedroom-community suburbs. Cities themselves will be reconceptualized and take on different functions, becoming centers of symbolic, touristic and management activities rather than conglomerations of congested, inhospitable living accommodations and mass workplaces. New opportunities will arise to make them things of beauty rather than frenzy and dehumanization.

Managing this transformation will be a gigantic undertaking. Not unachievable – just huge. Like the nuclear power station roll-out, it will be a work of decades. Like nuclear roll-out, it will start showing results the sooner America starts, so *it needs to get under way now, with a sense of national determination and urgency.* It will be economically beneficial from the outset. Producing and assembling the components of a national maglev system will create a new manufacturing and maintenance industry in itself, as the railroads once did, generating a wide array of types of work for Americans throughout the country. This bonanza of work could not come at a better time than now.

The present configuration of American landscapes, settlement areas and economic corridors will make it sensible to launch a national maglev grid with at least three main lines linking the east and west coasts at different latitudes. In addition there'll be lines linking north and south, on the coasts and probably down the heartland. From these principal maglev bands subsidiary routes will spin off to put the system eventually within easy reach of everyone everywhere within the country's continental borders.

Then there should be an extension of the system outside the U.S. This will require international agreements and project partnerships, but as the objectives will be beneficial to everyone involved, there's no substantial reason why these shouldn't be quickly achievable. It will be in the interests of both Canada and the U.S. for the American maglev grid to be extended into a Canadian counterpart, not only for the sake of integrating Alaska into the U.S. grid, but to enable Canada to benefit from a maglev grid and its own maglev industry. A similar extension into South America promises enormous economic benefits to all participating countries and an opportunity to develop the two American continents into an integrated economic powerhouse.

It can be a time of plenty for all, if we will it to be so and are prepared to act to make the will reality.

10. Create a government-led new national culture of technological innovation.

All the propositions we've listed so far share one overarching feature: to be adopted effectively, or in some cases even at all, the task that each proposition describes must be seen not as an isolated act but as part of a larger transformation. This mission is nothing less than *the renewal of American culture*. We've argued that there's a direct, potent link between culture and technological innovation. Fertile cultural conditions encourage innovation and can bring about spurts in technological progress: cultural opposition to technological innovation, or indifference to it, can retard it or even make it impracticable.

It's a political and cultural folly to suppose any government can impose on a society characteristics that are culturally alien or highly repugnant to it. History is littered with the graves of dictators who've tried this. But we also know that leaders who perceptively tap into existing cultural impulses and channel them creatively can motivate and guide their societies to astonishing achievements in the face of pessimism and cynical detractors. Winston Churchill's leadership of Britain against tremendous odds in World War II may be the most vivid illustration of this phenomenon in recent history, but there are others too, perhaps less dramatic but no less valuable as examples of what the right national leadership at the right time can accomplish.

We've seen how Prince Albert played an instrumental role in the Great Exhibition that helped launch 19th-century Britain into a new age of technological innovation. We've seen that while Abraham Lincoln's career tends to be identified almost solely with the healing of a Republic torn apart by a terrible war, he was also crucial in guiding his country toward the transcontinental unification made possible by the railroads. The importance of the right leadership at the right time is a real and potent factor in the balance of history. *America needs the right leadership now if it's to develop the culture of innovation on which its national success in the 21st century depends.*

The development of this culture of innovation depends on encouraging those aspects of the American national character that fit well with innovative drive: curiosity, love of learning and self-improvement, pleasure in the exercise of mastery and skill, a can-do outlook, self-reliance, independence, self-confidence, an ability to improvise, a sense of limitless possibilities, faith in the ability of democracy to correct its own mistakes, and, too, patriotism, which in its best sense means not shallow sloganeering but pride in a great cultural heritage and a desire to share its gifts.

But the development of a culture of innovation depends equally on discouraging those traits that work against the unlocking of America's vast potential: cynicism and negativity (which aren't the same as healthy skepticism), complacency, the feeling of entitlement, an inability to tell the difference between constrictive rules and high standards, and rejection of the most valuable discipline of all, namely self-discipline.

Who can and should encourage the positive traits we've just listed and discourage the negative ones? Many people. Parents. Teachers at all levels of the educational system. Community leaders of every kind, including the many celebrities who, because of the positions in society that they have derived from wealth, talent or just plain fame, wield vast power to act as role models -- good and inspiring ones, or shameful ones who squander their opportunities to influence American lives, especially young ones, for the better. In this landscape of figures who can influence American culture, the leaders of government occupy a special place. And among the leaders of government, few wield a power comparable to that of the President of the United States.

Though this office has been tarnished by some who have occupied it, it remains a remarkable and indeed unique one. It is among other things, as President Theodore Roosevelt called it, a pulpit unlike any other. It is rich with the resonance of history – not, admittedly, the history of ancient kingdoms and long-forgotten civilizations which the governments of older lands can invoke, but with the no less magical history of modern democracy in its most vital form, which the American presidency personifies with a power and credibility that no other officer of government in the world can rival. If the President of the United States places the full moral, symbolic and political authority of this iconic office behind an idea that is well-conceived, worthy of his or her support and in touch with the best that is in the extraordinary national character of the American people, wonders can be performed.

It is essential to the needs of the United States and the world for this power to be deployed now to create a renewed culture of scientific and technological innovation. Such deployment can't be limited to a few words of public relations rhetoric in occasional press releases. It must be a campaign conducted with the concerted resources and political might of the presidency and with the sense of urgency that's warranted by both the national interest and the global interest. Upon Lincoln's shoulders fell the responsibility to preserve and unite the Union. Upon the shoulders of President Obama, and also on the shoulders of his successors, now falls the responsibility to lead the United States into a new era of technological innovation, and to rebuild the nation's culture in ways necessary to make a new era happen.

If he is to carry out this responsibility effectively, the President must identify it visibly as a top priority by creating a dedicated Cabinet position entrusted with the task of fostering innovation and a culture of innovation. This position, answerable directly to the President, can in no way be that of a Technology Czar. The worst way to seek to promote innovation is to try to control it from above and centralize the processes of its incubation. What's needed is not control but coordination, facilitation, encouragement and support. There are already excellent agencies of technological and scientific development in the federal structures of the U.S. Government. Dedicated, highly skilled people can be found in its ranks at all levels. This has been the case for decades. Such people don't have to be found. Complicated new agencies don't have to be created.

But what is sorely needed is the appointment of a Cabinet-level officer whose job it will be to ease the work of these agencies and their personnel, to help them obtain the funding they want, to place the political support of the President more readily behind their own efforts, and to emphasize and nurture the potential for innovation that lies within much federal effort but which all too often is obscured by the many administrative needs to which federal officers must cater. The President's Innovation Officer must, furthermore, be entrusted with the task of coordinating and encouraging a national communications effort to rekindle the American public's respect for innovation, and a national perception of the urgent need for the U.S. to reassert the role of scientific and technological advance in the nation's life.

While making no pretence to be a Czar or anything resembling it, the President's Innovation Officer must certainly be a diplomat, carrying the moral and political authority of the White House to all corners of the federal establishment in which innovation can be encouraged and nurtured, as well as to all corners of the private world. A primary task of this ambassador of innovation must not be criticism or supervision but the building of a *consensus of innovation and commitment,* and the creation of as many alliances as possible, within and among the many domains of the federal government, the private sector and the great institutions of learning and research that make up the community of American universities.

This latter community is populated by an immense number of extraordinary minds. There is every reason to expect that an easier movement of these minds between academe, the private sector and government will be to the country's advantage, helping to unlock intellectual assets more speedily and more fruitfully than is presently the case.

We've remarked on various paradoxes throughout this book and in regard to this function of the proposed Innovation Officer we find yet another: the fact that the very success of some American developments of the past century has created national disadvantages. The success of government in building agencies of administration dedicated to specific federal tasks has created structures which, in their focus and commitment, have become insulated from other agencies and from some of the private institutions with which they might most fruitfully interact. The success of universities has created an independence of university life which is on one hand healthy but on the other hand can constrain the flow of university assets into the body social.

This constraint is often hard to see precisely because universities have become so good at crafting certain kinds of bridge between academe and the rest of society that the absence of others is overlooked. If this were not the case there would not be a huge potential to increase the flow of university-based intellectual assets into American society, but such a huge potential clearly exists.

Then there's the success of Wall Street and the business community it represents, both financially and symbolically. It's presently unpopular to speak of the success of Wall Street and its world, because we've seen so much evidence recently of the collapse of the philosophies and methodologies for which that world stands. It's true that a great deal has occurred in America's business community that's cause for grave concern. Yet here too, it should be remembered that this same community has contributed much to the country's past prosperity and the world's. And here a paradox arises similar to those which we described above in relation to government and academe. The past successes of Wall Street were so great that they insulated the culture of parts of the business landscape -- certainly the financial community – from the very intellectual sources which had nourished that community in the past.

We speak here of the wellsprings of technological innovation that created much of America's past prosperity. While a good deal of that prosperity came from the accessing and processing of natural resources, much of the profitability of the accessing and processing came from technologies that were geared to make America supreme in the world in the efficient conduct of such work. Then, too, much of America's prosperity hasn't come primarily from natural sources but from minds of entrepreneurs and inventors. The full spectrum of the story of American economic prosperity is ineradicably a story of innovation and technological advance.

Sections of the American private sector have erred in separating themselves from that advance. They've come to suppose that prosperity can be reduced to the trading and processing of paper (using this word as a convenient shorthand to mean not just physical paper alone but business documentations and financial instruments of all kinds, including those recorded electronically). But paper is only paper: it represents empty abstractions if it doesn't represent substantive innovation and technological advance. In those periods and economies where the gold standard has been applied, the value of commercial paper has been determined by its correlation with a certain amount of gold. But over a considerable part of its history, the American economy has for practical purposes been governed by what might be called *the technology standard.*[1]

In this de facto system, the value of American wealth has been determined by the amount of technological innovation acting upon the U.S. economy at any given time. The depletion of this bedrock of the economy is more serious than the loss of any naturally occurring physical resource. By separating themselves from the engines of technological innovation, and from the duties of stoking the furnaces of these engines, the leaders of American finance have allowed the country's economy to be separated from its root sources of value and wealth.

This error must be corrected by creating a renewed culture of innovation. It must be a mission of the White House to work with the business community to re-ignite the fires of American invention. For ultimately, all the economic goods that have made America a great force in the world have been nothing beside the American spirit. America must refresh and release again those energies of mind and imagination that made possible all of its most durable achievements of the past. It will be the finest tribute to the accomplishments of former times if they can be transcended by the greatness that America achieves in the 21st century. This will come to pass if, as a nation, America chooses to make it so.

NOTES

1. Slabbert, N.J., *The Military-Industrial Complex Revisited: A Call To Use The Military's Strengths To Combat Climate Change And Re-Energize Wall Street* (April 2005), TRUMAN LIBRARY REPORTS

2. One of the best illustrations of this potential is the controversial Strategic Defense Initiative, which combined military objectives with a rich potential for space research funding, albeit in a politically contentious context.

3. http://www.nytimes.com/2008/03/19/washington/19cost.html

4. http://www.nsf.gov/about/glance.jsp 5.http://www.washingtonpost.com/wp-dyn/content/article/2008/09/19/AR2008091903406.html

6. http://www.nytimes.com/2008/12/20/business/20auto.html

7. Slabbert, N.J., *ibid*

8. http://www.popularmechanics.com/technology/transportation/4258053.html

9. Axelrod, Alan, *Profiles in Audacity* (2006), p114

10. http://www.washingtonpost.com/wp-dyn/content/article/2008/05/28/AR2008052802947.html?nav=rss_nation

11. Slabbert, N.J., *The Technology Standard In Economic History* (Aug. 2003), TRUMAN LIBRARY REPORTS

Printed in the United States
218338BV00002B/2/P

9 780982 373408